THE COMPLETE FILMS OF
VINCENT PRICE

London, 1935

The Complete Films of
VINCENT PRICE

Lucy Chase Williams

With an Introduction by
VINCENT PRICE

A CITADEL PRESS BOOK
Published by Carol Publishing Group

Tend the garden of my grave.
Plant it with life. Be brave.
And somehow let me know, oh do.
I have not died in you.

—V.L.P.

FOR BINK
with love—always

Carol Publishing Group Edition, 1998

Copyright © 1995 by Lucy Chase Williams
All rights reserved. No part of this book may be
reproduced in any form,except by a newspaper or
magazine reviewer who wishes to quote brief
passages in connection with a review.

A Citadel Press Book
Published by Carol Publishing Group
Citadel Press is a registered trademark of Carol
Communications, Inc.

Editorial, sales and distribution, rights and permis-
sions inquiries should be addressed to Carol
Publishing Group, 120 Enterprise Avenue,
Secaucus, N.J. 07094

In Canada: Canadian Manda Group,
One Atlantic Avenue, Suite 105,
Toronto, Ontario M6K 3E7

Carol Publishing Group books may be purchased
in bulk at special discounts for sales promotions,
fund-raising, or educational purposes.
Special editions can be created to specifications.
For details, contact
Special Sales Department, Carol Publishing Group,
120 Enterprise Avenue,
Secaucus, N.J. 07094

Designed by A. Christopher Simon

Manufactured in the United States of America
10 9 8 7 6 5 4 3 2

Library of CongressCataloging-in-Publication Data

Williams, Lucy Chase.
    The complete films of Vincent Price /
Lucy Chase Williams; introduction by
Vincent Price.
            p.   cm.
    "A Citadel Press book."
    ISBN 0-8065-1600-3 (pbk.)
    1. Price, Vincent, 1911–93. I. Title.
PN2287.P72W56 1995   95-19775
791.43'028'092—dc20   CIP

ACKNOWLEDGMENTS

This book was truly a labor of love. I'm enormously grateful to the many friends and colleagues whose help made it as accurate, as complete, and, I hope, as entertaining as possible.

Sincere thanks to those who actually made it happen: my family (who have supported me unconditionally throughout my life); Pat Broeske; Craig L. Byrd; and Laura Kells, archivist at the Library of Congress Manuscript Division (for her professional expertise and personal dedication, both VLP and I owe an enormous debt.) Also to Steve Schragis and Allan J. Wilson of Carol Publishing and my agent, Alice Martell.

Tom Weaver was my adviser extraordinaire, *the* horror source who provided "trivia" inexhaustibly, making innumerable spelling corrections without a single recrimination, a peerless scholar whose twisted humor fuels my fire.

Authoritative contributions were made by James Gavin, Preston Jones, Irv Letofsky, Lee Pfeiffer, Ken Roe (the London office of Chase Consulting); Robert Sokol; and Ted and Sally Thomas. A special thank you to V. B. Price and Victoria Price.

Other significant roles were played by: John Antosiewicz; Steve Barkett; Buddy Barnett/Cinema Collectors; Jerry Beck; Laurel Benton; Michael Brandman; Jim Broeske; Michael Schwartz/Camden House (for rare posters); Tim Campbell; Jeff Carrier; James V. D'Arc, curator, Arts & Communications Archives, BYU (for definitive background on *Brigham Young*); Barry Dennen & James McGachy; Wheeler Winston Dixon (for quotes from his phone interview with Vincent); my colleagues on the Tim Burton documentary: Angelo Corraro, Mark Freedman/Freedman-Lippert, Sam Hurwitz, Diane Minter; John Drennon; William K. Everson (for the loan of his print of *Rogues' Regiment*); Roger Fenton; Lawrence French; Dan Golden; Mike Hawks and Pete Bateman/Larry Edmunds Bookshop; Lilly Fonda; friends for Vinnie alerts of every description over the years; Harry Goldman (for quotes from his phone interview with Vincent regarding the Mercury Theatre); Carol Keis/Hanna-Barbera Productions, Inc.; Eric Caidin/Hollywood Book and Poster; Amy Krell; Christina Lee; the wonderful staff of the Manuscript Division of the Library of Congress:

A. Edwards, E. Emrich, F. Bauman, J. Flannery, M. Klein, K. McDonough, M. Wolfskill; staff of the Prints & Photographs Division of the Library of Congress; Tim Lucas (for arcane videos); Bob Madison; Lauria Meica; Anne Moore; staff at the Margaret Herrick Library of the Academy of Motion Picture Arts and Sciences; Jim Nemeth; Ted Okuda; Steve Pepper; Mark Pierson; John Peoples; Henrietta Kleinpell Randolph and Susan Rice & Mickey Fromkin (for providing roofs during research trips); Gary Smith; George Stover (for arcane videos); Jeff Matteson/TNT; Bonnie Vitti; Jerry Vermilye; Mike Wozniak; staff of the Yale University Sterling Memorial Library Manuscript Division; Doug Youngkin.

To Vincent's friends and colleagues who shared their personal and professional memories with this author, special gratitude: Samuel Z. Arkoff, Jeff Burr, Tim Burton, Antony Carbone, William Claxton, Allan Converse, Roger Corman, Hazel Court, Peggy Cummins, Douglas Fairbanks Jr., Sally Forrest, William Goldstein, Eric Harrison, Gordon Hessler, Charlton Heston, Louis M. Heyward, Joy Hodges, Dennis Hopper, Marsha Hunt, Phyllis Kirk, Alexander Knox, Angela Lansbury, Christopher Lee, Norman Lloyd, Robert Mitchum, Ricardo Montalban, Maureen O'Hara, Gregory Peck, Cassandra Peterson, Robert Quarry, Jane Russell, Thomas Silliman, Edmond G. (Ted) Thomas, Philip Waddilove.

Much respect is due the still and portrait photographers whose artistry illustrates these pages. Acknowledgment is made to companies which distributed or aired these films and television shows and to the following public research facilities: Academy of Motion Picture Arts and Sciences; Alive Films; Allied Artists; American International Pictures; Joseph Brenner Associates; Cannon Films; Cinema National Corp.; Columbia Pictures; Goldfarb Films; Hanna-Barbera Productions, Inc.; Library of Congress; Billy Rose Theatre Collection of the New York Public Library at Lincoln Center; Lippert Pictures, Inc.; Majestic Films and Television; MGM/United Artists; The Movie Store; New World Prods., Ltd.; Orion Pictures Corporation; Paramount Pictures; RKO; Republic; Sterling Memorial Library; TNT; Turner Pictures; 20th Century-Fox; Universal Pictures; Vestron; Walt Disney Productions; Warner Bros.

CONTENTS

Introduction: The Villain Still Pursues Me

VINCENT PRICE

The heroine teetered on the edge of an enormous tank. The camera moved into a close shot of an evil, round eye leering upward, then panned along the great slimy head and down the gigantic tentacles undulating and throbbing to receive her in a watery embrace of death. There was a splash—and it was plain to see that Pearl White had finally met her fate in the arms of the huge octopus.

Then suddenly the lights came on and with them the deliciously sickening realization that next week nothing could keep you from coming back to see the triumphant expression on the villain's face as the next episode began with Pearl in the throes of death. A trapdoor would open, of course, and she would be saved in the nick of time, but the damp excitement of that week-old moment of horror was still fresh in your mind. Though the hero was in command for the moment, what really mattered was that you could count on the villain, whose nimble mind had been working all week just to get those two terribly good people into another horrible predicament—one more "peril" for "Pauline. . . ."

The storybook witches and cruel stepmothers, the boy-eating giants living underneath the earth and above it, the forces of terror that jumped at one out of the thunderstorm and from dark corners and closets—they became tame and pale as the procession of horror and thrills paraded before you on the silver screen to whet your imagination and charge your adrenaline.

There's no question who's the more fascinating, Dr. Jekyll or Mr. Hyde. Dr. Jekyll, nice a man as he is in your mind, should always keep a slug of his fiendish fizz water close at hand. Your home chemical set unfortunately does not come equipped with instant Hyde-ro-chloric acid, but the bathroom mirror is witness to a juvenile transformation equal in every respect to John Barrymore's—even though the wonders of makeup have to be achieved with quill toothpicks for fangs and your mother's old "rats" glued on with library paste to your forehead to create a diabolically low brow. Sister's pretty lace pillow stuffed under one shoulder of your coat and you're properly deformed. A sagging eyelid, a trickle of drool out of your lasciviously limp lower lip, and the picture is complete. Even the cute cook whom you've been chasing in all kinds of disguises for years lets out a genuine yelp when the evil Mr. Hyde seeks her out to force his vile attentions upon her on the dark back staircase. Your mother's suggestion that it might be more rewarding to attempt John Barrymore's Dr. Jekyll face falls on deaf ears—anyone can look like John Barrymore. . . . Then, too, the indolence of the villain is very appealing. To be a wicked Roman emperor or a dissatisfied and sinister millionaire is much further from the truth of being a fourteen-year-old boy from St. Louis. And who wants to be fourteen in St. Louis? . . .

The cinematic world of adventure is taking over completely—an adventurous world known to the villain alone. The hero must live the humdrum life of everyone you know, content with his faithful wife, his half-paid-for home. While you, drawing the line at murder, of course, through your manifold manic manipulations, have access to a dozen exotic women, soot-eyed and soft; and emeralds and pearls enough to deck them all; with a properly unpretentious one for yourself in the most masculine setting on your second finger, a conceit dear to all successful ne'er-do-gooders. . . .

Another reason you prefer the evil ones is that the hero seldom causes anyone, least of all himself, to laugh. The villain, through his ability to make you and his fellow actors lose control of emotions, brings about all the fun, particularly in plays in which his identity is closely guarded to the last curtain. Nobody has any trouble figuring out who the hero is—there he is, every inch a dreamboat, grim-jawed, inevitably beloved by the one person the villain desires. Everybody rushes to the noble one for help, and he is usually an idiot who walks in where angels fear to tread. . . . A hero could not be a hero unless he had a villain to chase, to be tricked and finally to conquer. Drama is the conflict between good and evil, to quote Aristotle, Dr. Johnson, and Jack Warner. . . .

That the villain always got his comeuppance could easily be wiped out of one's mind by handy clichés like "Whom the gods love die young" and "A short, happy life." . . . Of course, one could get disastrously close to the real thing in one's determination to experience every whim of villainy. Trying to see how long you can breathe under water through a tube in your mouth held just slightly above the waterline while holding yourself at the bottom of the bathtub by propping your feet against the towel rack can be precarious, especially if your older sister catches you and puts a wad of toilet tissue in the end of the tube. Still, it had to be tried, for someday they might remake *The Phantom of the Opera*, and when you were grown up, they might beg you to play Lon Chaney's part. . . .

But youth is coming to an end, and many of your

pleasantest memories are having the daylights scared out of you. . . . To all the lascivious kings, noblemen, renegade knights of the round table, fiends, foreclosers of mortgages, sexy patent leather–haired pursuers of inviolate innocence, the mustache twirlers and eyebrow raisers—to all of them and their kind, you owe an undying debt of gratitude for white nights and black nightmares. . . .

Time: 1935. Place: London, England. Cut to close shot of budding young actor, Vincent Price. My first acting job was a surly cop in the London production of the American gangster play *Chicago*. I had one line and taught the English actresses who were valiantly trying to be gunmen's molls to chew gum without swallowing it. And if that was the moment I swallowed the bait of drama, I wanted to swallow it hook, line, and—if you'll pardon a pun—stinker. I wanted to start my career playing villains; ambitiously, I wanted to play Iago, Richard III. But my years and blond American-boy looks were against me, so my first big break was to be cast as one of the goodest men who ever lived, so good in fact that history has dubbed him "Albert the Good"—Queen Victoria's husband, father of the straightlaced, purveyor of the proper. . . .

Three years I was Albert the Good, and after that I apprenticed (at Helen Hayes's suggestion) in a dozen parts in stock, but nary a heavy. I was Parnell, the Earl of Essex, the Minister in *Romance*, even the Lord in *The Passing of the Third Floor Back*—all good, good, good men. A singularly unsuccessful stab at being a movie actor teamed me with Constance Bennett in a part they wanted Jimmy Stewart for—and they should have had him! Back on Broadway, I was cast as the sweet young minister in the all-star revival of *Outward Bound*, and I longed to play the drunk. Goodness—what to do? . . .

Then one night I saw a play called *Gaslight* at a little theater in Hollywood. I was intrigued by the character of the husband, Jack Manningham, who was trying to drive his wife mad and who turned out to be a thief and a murderer. The actor in the role was good, but somehow you never could understand why Bella Manningham put up with him. There had to be something more, and I thought I knew what it was—sex! Then I was asked to do what became *Angel Street* on Broadway, and I couldn't wait. Here was a chance to play one of the meanest men ever written, and a damned attractive one at that. After opening night, I was launched as a villain—a sadistic heavy, a suave killer, a wife beater, a sexy extrovert, a diabolical introvert—take your pick! . . .

Twentieth Century-Fox brought me back to Hollywood to do a succession of fairly unpleasant gentlemen. It seemed to be imperative at the time to play something besides the meany—I didn't want to have my cake and nothing else. Comedy came to my rescue with a variety of extravagantly slapstick film roles, and television guest shots gave me a chance to be ridiculously myself. I got even further away from my lugubrious roles through lectures on art. One film, however, seemed to identify me: Apparently everyone saw *House of Wax*, and almost everyone loved it, and once again I set out upon a life of crime. . . .

I suppose the one question I get asked by the public more than any other is why I like playing these parts. Well, in the first place, they're much more interesting than playing Vincent Price, who, in my opinion at least, is a rather prosaic man from Missouri; who has a good, soft, typically Missouri voice; who likes animals, art, fishing, and my family, my home, and my friends; and almost most of all, likes the public who like him in pictures that are a little wacky, very scary, and are in truth as far from the truth as possible.

And in the second place—BOO! It's as much fun to scare as to be scared.

The uncut text of this previously unpublished memoir, written around 1959, became the basis for a hugely popular lecture of the same name, which Vincent Price delivered to audiences across the country throughout the seventies and eighties.

THE MAN

A man who limits his interests, limits his life.

—Vincent Price

I think that art, and the appreciation of art, is curiosity about life and the capacity for wonder. This expression . . . really sums up my entire philosophy of life . . . the capacity for wonder.

—Vincent Price (*Vincent Price: Actor and Art Collector*, 1982)

I'm going to give the people what they want—sensation, horror, shock. Send them out in the streets to tell their friends how *wonderful* it is to be scared to death.

—Vincent Price as Prof. Henry Jarrod in *House of Wax* (1953)

In his youth, on Broadway, and then in Hollywood, Vincent Price demonstrated a brilliant acting ability. The talent he displayed in more mainstream movies carried over into the horror pictures but was demonstrated in many other avenues. The horror films I made with Vincent were among the finest films he made, but they must be remembered as only one portion of his career.

—Roger Corman (October 1994)

He's a perfectly wonderful, terrible man. Everybody adores him. He has the most marvelous sense of humor in the world. He seems so gra-a-and, and he's just a naughty boy!

—Jane Russell (American Cinémathèque tribute to Vincent Price, June 1990)

Vincent was so funny. I told him every time I saw him, "You missed your calling. You should have been a comedian. You are just the funniest man I ever met." He just cracked me up all the time.

—Cassandra Peterson, "Elvira, Mistress of the Dark" (September 1994)

I would like to be remembered by something I strongly believe in—that there is a great difference between earning a living and knowing how to live. I think an awful lot of people earn a living to put it in their bellies. It should be put in your head. When you get to old age, it is the experience of life that is really the only thing that sustains you. The thing that sustains me is what I've learned about how to live.

—Vincent Price (summer 1992)

Vincent Leonard Price holding Vincent Leonard Price Jr.

The Price children: Hat, Mortie, Lollie, and Vinnie

A formal portrait of Vincent L. Price Jr. in his teens

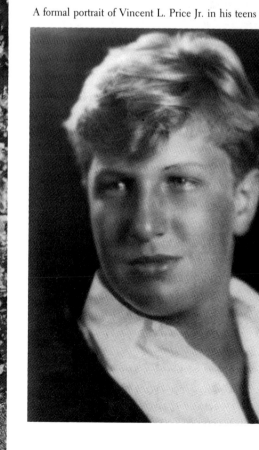

Young Vinnie

"Tour 22": The summer of 1928. VP and friends in Europe

New Haven, May 4, 1933. Ted Thomas's twenty-first birthday. VP (*left, on arm of couch*), "Pee Wee" Lee (VP's roommate senior year), Ted Thomas, three classmates.

In 1972, Vincent Price was the subject of the popular television series *This is Your Life*. Summing up the tribute, host Ralph Edwards commented with a smile, "This is your *life*, Vincent? No, these are your *lives*." The quintessential "Renaissance man," Vincent Price was an actor, art historian, eclectic private collector, gourmet author of cookbooks, lecturer, baseball fan, nationally syndicated columnist, unpublished poet, unheralded philanthropist, devoted father and devoted husband, and sappy dog lover.

In a career spanning nearly sixty years, the man who would become best known as "the Master of Menace" made one hundred feature films. They included dramas, comedies, costume pictures, animation, Westerns, musicals, and a couple of the best-loved motion-picture classics. And yes, about 30 percent were horror movies — some comedic and tongue-in-cheek; some grim and violent; some genuinely atmospheric and delightfully, deliciously scary.

Price flourished in a cobweb-draped nineteenth-century Gothic world, impeccably clad in frock coat and ruffled shirt, a swirling cape or a monogrammed dressing gown, thriving on madness, despair, doom, and death. He interred relatives alive and was himself entombed; he wrestled with hideous terrors of the imagination as well as a few decidedly corporeal monsters. A rich, expressive voice savored the most outlandishly rococo dialogue, ruminating on imaginative methods of torture or reciting poetry to a long-dead love. He perfected a genuine empathy for portraying good men betrayed; individuals beleaguered by fate, beset by tragedy or a great wrong. Innate intelligence and sensitivity brought sympathy to characters consumed by passion, driven by circumstances beyond their control. When he played an out-and-out contemporary villain, he was still well spoken, debonair, suave. But usually with a sense of humor. And the public responded, especially young people, who spotted the wicked twinkle in Price's eye which clued them in that the actor was having as much fun as the audience.

Vincent Price was a star, a true luminary of Hollywood's Golden Age who became a familiar media fixture, contemporary in every decade. A matinee idol in the thirties and a character actor in the forties, he found his career revitalized in the fifties. He was as groovy in the sixties as he was awesome in the eighties. But despite the larger-than-life star quality he radiated offscreen as well, Vinnie remained approachable, accessible, the type of guy who did his own grocery shopping. He could often be spotted in the neighborhood market, strolling up and down the aisles behind a shopping cart with a wonky wheel, greeting grinning fans with a cheerful "How *are* ya?"

A lean six feet four, blue-eyed and wavy-haired, with patrician features and a fine, mellifluous voice, Price started out playing good guys. In fact, he began his career at only twenty-four playing one of the "goodest" men in history and was heralded by the critics as a hunk who physically was "a child of the gods." But over the years, after he dipped young women in wax for his museum and gave more than one torture-chamber guided tour, audiences reacted most enthusiastically to Price's Gothic roles, and the multifaceted actor resigned himself with good grace to his horrific stereotype. That image, which he had no misgivings about cultivating and which he sent up at every opportunity, was in fact the greatest charade of his career. The least "horrible" of men, Vincent was erudite, exuberant, reflective, gracious, funny and generous, bursting with what Kipling called "'satiable curiosity." An authentic professional respected by peers and cherished by friends and fans, he truly enjoyed what he did, explaining happily: "I really feel that every day is an enormous surprise!"

The man regarded for most of his career as characteristically European, who many believed to be British, was as American as they come. Although the ancestry of the name Price is Welsh, Vincent Price was directly descended on his paternal grandmother's side from Peregrine White, the first child born on the *Mayflower* as the Pilgrims landed at Plymouth Rock. All his life Price remained inordinately down to earth: "If I were a dog, I'd like to be a mutt, and come to think of it, as a person I prefer being a mutt, too, not too closely identified with any race, which I'm not, being English, Welsh, French, and heaven knows what else. As a matter of fact, it's what I like about being an American. We have all the best mutt characteristics until we become grand or take ourselves too seriously."

Grandfather Vincent C. Price was a black-haired, black-mustached "black" Welshman, a medical doctor who graduated at twenty and grew a full beard because he looked too young to practice medicine. In addition to his private practice, he had an interest in chemistry; tinkering in the lab led to his inventing baking powder. He founded the Price Extract Company but made (and

would lose in the crash of 1892) a fortune with Dr. Price's Baking Powder. His son Vincent Leonard Price was born in Waukegan, Illinois. He went to school in Wisconsin and college in Connecticut and married Marguerite Willcox in October 1894. The couple lived to celebrate their golden anniversary; in one of his first press interviews, their youngest son would assert: "My mother and father fell in love when they were nine and never saw anyone else." After moving the family to St. Louis, Missouri, Price eventually became president of the National Candy Company, which made jelly beans and jawbreakers. Prominent in the National Confectioners Association, he was still remembered by colleagues twenty years after his death; in 1966 the honorary chairman of the annual convention dubbed Price "the most impressive industry figure" he could recall.

The Prices had three much older children: Harriet, "Hat"; James Mortimer, "Mort"; and Lauralouise, "Lollie." The third male Price in succession to bear the name of Vincent was born on May 27, 1911, and christened Vincent Leonard Price Jr. Members of the National Confectioners Association presented the proud papa with a medallion commemorating the event, inscribed with the full name of the child, the birth date, and a nickname which remained a family joke, "the Candy Kid."

"The Kid" was raised in a well-to-do midwestern ambience which encouraged artistic expression. (Price's own definition of "well-to-do" was "not rich enough to evoke envy and just successful enough to demand respect. It is the ultimate plateau in American life and is only reached by hard work, just enough ambition, and the guidance of a good woman.") Vincent described his mother as "French, Dutch, and English, but American through and through. . . . My mother was a truly delightful creature, and it is to her I owe so much of my love of the beautiful and also my desire to share it with other people." Price senior was civic-minded, a former vice president and director of the St. Louis Chamber of Commerce. When Mrs. Price, who taught on a nonpaying basis, became dissatisfied with local education, she and other neighborhood women founded the St. Louis Community School, which Vincent attended through fifth grade.

According to notes kept by a doting father, the new baby spoke his first word, "Daddy," on June 27, 1912. Some biographies list a kindergarten Christmas play, in which he played an angel and forgot his lines, as his first acting experience. Actually, Vincent Price made his theatrical debut when he was only four, in a scene-stealing appearance in a neighborhood "playlet" titled *Spring*, as a curly-headed blond "water sprite" wrapped in green chiffon. The first motion picture Vincent remembered seeing was *Der Golem*, an atmospheric Ger-

May 27, 1933

VP made a few prints of this original drawing by cartoonist James Thurber and mailed one to this author on May 11, 1993, inscribed: "Dear Lucy: Artist—James Thurber. Subject—Vincent Price, "Youth" age twenty-two. Occasion—Birthday! New Haven. Sender—Vincent Price, age eighty-two. Mystery—where did the sixty years go? Love V.P." Envelopes were always hand addressed.

Alistair Cooke (*left, later host of Masterpiece Theatre*) had been a Cambridge University exchange student at Yale. On his way to Hollywood in the summer of 1933, he stopped off in St. Louis to visit school friends VP (*right*) and Ted Thomas, who took the picture.

Earliest publicity portrait session, London, 1935

man silent about the legendary man-made creature. The man who would become best known for his own horrific cinematic portrayals was so frightened by the movie that he wet his pants!

To many fans, Vincent Price would equally be respected as a gourmet and author of cookbooks. Price described the home in which he grew up as a place in

Victoria Regina Broadway, 1935, as Prince Albert

had its foundations in a Boston bull terrier called Happy which the Prices owned from the time Vincent was six until he was sixteen. Music was also a large part of the household. His siblings all played piano, but Vincent claimed that his right hand "never seemed to figure out" what his left hand was doing. He submitted to lessons, anyway, but directed his own musical appreciation toward singing.

In 1920 the St. Louis Community School presented an adaptation of *The Pied Piper of Hamelin*; Vincent's third grade made up the contingents of cats, dogs, and all-important rats. He had a crush on classmate Barbara O'Neil, a beauty who would also make a career in acting and became best known as Scarlett O'Hara's mother in *Gone With the Wind*. As a young man, Price fell in love with the enigmatic O'Neil, and their romance continued on and off for the next two decades.

Because he was much younger than his siblings, Vincent spent a great deal of time alone, inspired by frequent visits to the highly regarded St. Louis Museum. In an illustrated history in his elder sister's library, he "found the world I knew I wanted to live in for the rest of my life—the world of man's creation—art." At age twelve, with money saved from selling magazines and newspapers, Vincent made his first acquisition: a small Rembrandt etching titled *Two Academical Nudes, One Standing*. He paid the princely sum of $37.50, putting five dollars down and vowing to pay something on account every week until the balance was paid. Five dollars down: "At twelve, that's all the world, and more," he remembered fondly as an adult. "It's future sweets, future trespasses on cigarettes, dates with girls, and movies sneaked on Sunday afternoons. But it was worth it, though it meant six long months of hoarding, work, and abstinences beyond the call of adolescent propriety." By the time he was fifteen, he had several entries in a small leather notebook, neatly inscribed "The Private Collection of Vincent L. Price, Jr. 1926."

While attending St. Louis Country Day School, a single-sex college prep, Vincent spent a summer with schoolmates on a dude ranch near the Mesa Verde National Park in southwestern Colorado. Digging in the ancient cliff dwellers' villages, he and a friend discovered an Indian burial ground that was later traced back to the Mesa Verde civilization. It was the beginning of a lifelong interest in Native Americans and their art; Price served many years on the U.S. Department of the Interior's Indian Arts and Crafts Board, and for the last three decades of his life he wore a handsome, Indian-made, bracelet-style watchband of sterling silver and turquoise.

Because of Mr. Price's business, Christmas in the 1920s inevitably brought pounds of sugary delights from professional colleagues, including Mr. Hershey. Wary

which "the greatest achievement was superb cooking. . . . My family were very adventurous in the kitchen." He displayed an early interest in that subject, sitting on a stool and watching the art of pancake making as executed by mother's helper Louise Ell, just twenty when Vincent was born. Each time she flipped a flapjack, the little boy would clap his hands and shout, "More, more!" Vincent's lifelong attachment to animals, and dogs in particular,

over excessive consumption (and probably especially that of her youngest son, who was growing by leaps and bounds), Mrs. Price confiscated most of the candy, occasionally permitting the children to share with friends. Vincent remembered trotting off with a box of chocolates under his arm to try to impress the young lady whose favor he was currently seeking. "More often than not, I got small favors at most. What else can you expect at fourteen?"

His passion for art had led him to wage a concerted and "unsubtle campaign to get to Europe." In the summer of 1928, he made it. Although it may sound surprising that the Prices permitted their youngest son to tackle Europe in a tourist group sans family, he was mature for his years and at age seventeen already stood six feet two and three quarter inches tall. He paid for the trip with his own money, a bequest from his grandmother and "some help from Dad" (his share of the sale of the family summer home in Canada, which Price senior had put aside for each of the children.) Vincent signed up for what he later described as five weeks of "Seven Capitals of Europe. . . . Where other tours included famous battlefields and natural phenomena, . . . Tour 22 was heavy on the churches and museums." His height allowed him to pass for older than he was, and he "had champagne all over Paris" in the company of fellow tourists and other young people they met.

Vincent was athletic in high school, playing soccer and running track. He also appeared in the annual school plays and drew for the senior yearbook; the success he had with his little sketches gave him the idea of becoming an artist. In that final year, he tried painting, sculpting, and woodcutting but learned "a fact that I wasn't about to admit for five years . . . I had no talent at all." In fact, Price was overly modest about his abilities; lifelong self-deprecation reflected high personal standards. He was no mean sketch artist and sculpted his own fireplace-wood carvings after his first marriage. The week after his eighteenth birthday, Vincent Leonard Price Jr. graduated from St. Louis Country Day School. His senior quote: "Isn't that the nerts?"

Vincent Price Sr. had graduated from Yale, earning a degree in engineering in 1894. Vincent's older brother, Mort, had done the same in 1921. A sister married a Yale man. So it's hardly surprising that in the summer of 1929 his father sent his vacationing younger son a cable: "You have been admitted to Yale with no pull exerted. Don't break any furniture in your excitement."

Freshman courses were practically a reprisal of the last years of prep school, and Vincent found motivation in only one class: the history of religion, which confirmed his belief that art and religion were inextricably tied together. Sophomore year, the students were able to se-

Victoria Regina Broadway, 1935, with Helen Hayes

lect their roommates, and Vincent teamed up with his best friend from St. Louis Country Day School, Edmond G. "Ted" Thomas. Leaving their Old Campus suite one day and horsing around on the stairs, Thomas tried to get a headlock on Price and accidentally smashed him in the face with his elbow. "I busted his nose; I could hear it go crunch. He took his three fingers and molded it all back, blood streaming. Later in the summer, he had to have surgery!" Needless to say, their friendship endured for seventy years. That semester, Vincent heeled for a campus literary publication, *The Record*. He joined a fraternity and was also invited to become a member of the prestigious Elizabethan Club, which was a literary association and not a dramatic society. Somehow he also managed to squeeze his final height of six feet four inches into a scull to row college crew. Prohibition was no deterrent to intrepid college boys, and according to Ted Thomas, Vincent "would never even stop when he had the most *terrible* hangovers. When he was rushed by the frat, they brought him back at two in the morning and propped him against our door. Through the smoky glass I could see there was a tall object out there, so I opened the door, and he fell right in. I had to drag him into the room and roll him into his bed. But he was up before I was the next day, dressed and showered, out walking, walking, walking, until he walked it off."

While a Yale undergrad, Vincent became close with author/cartoonist James Thurber. Price had a real admiration for the place of the cartoonist in culture; in fact, he himself submitted a sketch to a campus magazine. It was the art-history courses he took in junior year which changed his life. The young man kept his self-described "scheme" of becoming an actor to himself, and studies "clinched the deal" between himself and art. He fueled his passion by frequent trips into New York, and on more than one occasion he was lured from scholarly pursuits by debutante parties and visits to speakeasies with other Ivy Leaguers. Although Vincent reckoned he saw every movie, concert, and play that came to New Haven during his tenure, the Yale Drama School hadn't appealed to him despite his secret desires about becoming an actor (and despite the fact that Barbara O'Neil, his hometown sweetheart, spent a couple of years at the drama school herself). Being a "confirmed extrovert," Vincent found the solution in the glee club, which he joined as a second bass. In the summer of 1932, the sixty-five-member Yale Glee Club went on an extensive tour of Europe, but when the group sailed back to America, Vincent stayed on for another several weeks. In Vienna he met a young female nightclub singer who helped him get a job singing in her club and dancing with customers. He lived cheaply; bought lithos by Daumier. In Venice, he slept two days in a bathtub with a mattress for twenty-five cents a day.

Back in New Haven, Ted Thomas reluctantly moved out: "At the end of junior year, I thought, I'm having much too good a time. I've got to do some work, and I can't do any work when I'm around this guy! So I said, 'Vinnie, I don't think I'm giving my family their money's worth! I'm gonna have to go solo next year.' He was pretty upset about that, because that was not the way

he'd planned it. So senior year, he went in with another guy, and they had an uproarious time, and I spent *all* my time in *their* room!"

Vincent graduated from Yale in June 1933, and although he knew he wanted to make a career in the arts, he "hadn't the slightest inkling" how. He decided that it would help clarify his own thoughts if he tried to impart them to others, and he took a job at the Riverdale School on the Hudson in New York, teaching art appreciation, coaching amateur dramatics, and even driving a school bus. Although later he called it "wet-nursing some of the richest delinquents on the eastern seaboard," at the time he was more optimistic, informing his parents, "If I can only give these brats something of the great stuff which has been mine from you, I will be happy." In April 1934 the Riverdale Players presented three benefit performances of Gilbert and Sullivan's *H.M.S. Pinafore*; Vincent played the Captain. "I missed not having you out front to sing to," he wrote his parents. ". . . I do love the stage, and never before have I realized how much at home I am on it. I simply must try it some day and prove to myself that I can't do it or can do it. So don't be surprised if I join a stock company this summer if I get a chance." As if a presentiment, he added, "Save the clippings." His parents had already preserved much memorabilia from their youngest child's life and would proudly maintain enormous scrapbooks on his career until their deaths.

Although Price enjoyed the opportunity to educate, the experience led to self-discovery: "I found out how little I had learned at college, which I think an awful lot of us do. . . . Continued learning is the true key to all existence." With the check his father gave him as a graduation present, Vincent bought himself what was intended to be two years of further education—at the newly founded Courtauld Institute, a department of the University of London, which would become one of the most prestigious museums/art schools in the world. Arriving in London in September 1934, Vincent took as the subject for his projected M.A. "Dürer and the School of the Danube." Every one of his lecturers was a leader in his field, and Vincent was "superbly happy." That Christmas, he took off for Vienna to ski in the Austrian Alps. He visited museums in Germany and saw Dürers in their natural habitat, although he never attended Nuremberg University, which some biographies have asserted. For Price, the real fascination of that year lay in London itself. He fell in love with the theater, which wasn't difficult; tickets were inexpensive, and the greatest actors in the world could be seen on West End stages. In the fall of 1934, John Gielgud was the talk of the town as *Hamlet*; the following summer, *Romeo and Juliet* boasted not only Gielgud in the cast but also Laurence

The Shoemaker's Holiday The Mercury Theatre, 1939, with Alice Frost

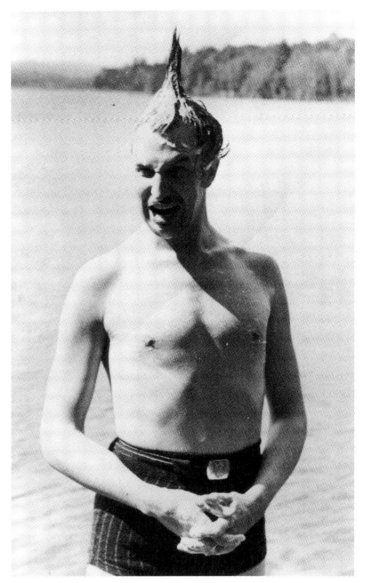

Cooling off during summer stock at Lakewood, Maine (girlfriend/ leading lady Edith Barrett was responsible for the shampoo)

Olivier, Peggy Ashcroft, and Edith Evans.

The first hint of things to come was discreetly buried in a letter Vincent wrote his parents in February 1935. He discussed his Courtauld courses and was already beginning to sound disenchanted. Then the young student nonchalantly worked in a reference to a new activity— *acting.* "My lectures are slowly becoming very dull as three of the best men are sick. So I have been museuming & gallerying a lot. . . . I have just gotten a small part in a play at the Gate Theatre, which is a very famous

17

Newlyweds Edith Barrett Price and VP at home

little theatre company here, and so you know (or don't you!) how happy I am—there is nothing in the world like the profession to me, but don't worry dearests I am not slacking my work. But please don't be angry as I can no more leave it alone than I can give up my love of life for it is so wonderful—Pray that I make a go of it." The play was called *Chicago*; Price always claimed that he got into the cast only because he could teach the English girls trying to be gunmen's molls how to chew gum without swallowing it. At the time, he wrote home: "I was just getting very English when this so American part came along, now I'm complete mid-west and ever so tough." As an afterthought, he insisted: "My studies are still great." *Chicago* opened on March 13, 1935, with Vincent Price in two roles: "Charles E. Murdock, police sergeant," and "the Judge."

Obviously, the young man was finding himself happier onstage than in the classroom, and his life was changed forever when he heard about the Gate's next production. Written by Laurence Housman, *Victoria Regina* recounted the queen's accession at age twenty-five and her romance with German cousin Prince Albert of Saxe-Coburg through sixty years of the reign which gave her name to the period. It was the first time that Queen Victoria would appear as the chief character in a full-length play in London, since British statutes, intent on preserving royal dignity, prohibited the depiction of monarchs onstage for three generations. However, since the Gate was not a West End theater but technically a private club, *Victoria Regina* wasn't subject to the restrictions. The neophyte actor who only a few weeks before had been "complete mid-west" snagged the showy costarring role of Prince Albert, a part for which he was ideally suited physically; with his long blond hair and slim height, he bore a remarkable resemblance to the German consort. With the exuberance of youth, Vincent translated the role into German and back into English to make it just slightly unfamiliar, because the real prince had never been entirely comfortable in English. So unknown was the young performer that a local paper described him as "an English actor who has played a great deal in Germany and is therefore able to simulate the German accent to perfection." But Vincent Price didn't remain anonymous for long.

Victoria Regina opened on May 1, 1935, less than four weeks before Price's twenty-fourth birthday, and reviews of the unusual production were very favorable. Price's natural grace and charm were immediately remarked upon; one critic wrote: "We should hear of him again." The part not only brought him theatrical kudos but made him a sought-after guest at posh soirees throughout the city. He was in his element on the stage: "Do you see your little boy is getting into these hearts," he wrote his parents two weeks later. "I pray every night that God will allow me to continue to give pleasure to people—it is a grand wish—a great desire—and a glorious mission." The young actor's celebrity garnered Price an offer to participate in the 1935 summer season of Shakespeare in the Open-Air Theatre in London's Regent's Park. "It may mean some of my Courtauld work will have to go," he informed the family, oh, so reluctantly. "I am seeing . . . [if] I can go on with the thesis or be just an occasional student. . . . But the impetus to work is lacking." As it happened, the British Labour Ministry refused to grant the foreigner a work permit for the legitimate theater, since his visa listed him as a student without employment privileges.

Meanwhile, noted American theatrical producer Gilbert Miller had been drawn to *Victoria Regina* as a vehicle for another reigning queen, Broadway's Helen Hayes, and he invited Price to re-create his Prince Albert in New York. Hayes apparently had nothing to say about it, but it seems possible that the thirty-five-year-old actress, who made her own Broadway debut two years before Vincent was born, would have had reservations about a leading man who was an inexperienced twenty-four-year-old and completely unknown in his own country. Vincent's parents expected him home mid-fall, but he was delayed by another stage role for a couple of weeks in October: "I have accepted a grand part in a play at the Gate, [Arthur] Schnitzler's *Anatole* . . . I do feel I need this part, as it is straight & comedy both of which I need badly and it will take my mind off Albert for a while." Less than a month later, Vincent Price left London, and his uncompleted master's degree in art history, behind him.

He returned to the United States on the S.S. *Aquitania* on November 5, 1935—in steerage, since he (and his half-Siamese cat, Albert the Good) were broke and Gilbert Miller had refused to advance any funds. Price asserted he arrived in New York "looking like an immigrant and smelling like a goat." The ship docked eight hours late due to bad weather; Price and Albert cleared customs and checked into a cheap hotel. The next day, when Vincent reported for rehearsal, Miller "blasted" the young man, accusing him of pulling a "Garbo" by not greeting the press invited to meet the ship. The media, of course, had gone to the first-class disembarkation for an introduction to Helen Hayes's new leading man, not realizing that a gawky Yale grad, cat in tow, had been traveling practically in the baggage department. The papers immediately began to herald the "young and handsome leading man who is making a rather spectacular leap from relative obscurity into the brightest Broadway limelight." Vincent's family was thrilled for him. "We are still pinching ourselves when we think of you being

Publicity portrait for Warner Bros. by George Hurrell, 1939

Service De Luxe With Constance Bennett

Tower of London With Basil Rathbone

Helen Hayes's leading man on Broadway. . . . Guess you pinch yourself once in a while also."

Victoria Regina previewed for a week in Baltimore and Washington (with First Lady Eleanor Roosevelt in the audience) before opening in New York on December 26, 1935. And Vincent Leonard Price Jr. was catapulted to stardom: "Suddenly, with absolutely no experience at all and right out of college, I was the leading man to the biggest star on Broadway in the greatest sort of success of her career." Reviews were glowing; audiences demanded numerous curtain calls nightly. *Victoria Regina* made the cover of *Time* magazine, and Vincent even appeared in print ads for Chiclets gum, declaring it was "royally delicious." A letter from Dad kept stardom in proportion. "Since you have become famous it has added greatly to your father's duties at home, at office and socially. . . . I spend much time interviewing individuals who desire to share your wealth—so far my list includes [in part]: 32 Life Insurance Agents; 62 Bond and Share

Pushers; 9 Book Agents, who have books which will land you in Hollywood or jail; 3 Winners of local beauty contests, who want you to further their ambitions; 9 Artists, who want to paint your portrait while you are still young and beautiful; 1 Yale Professor, who needed financial assistance and explained what a difficult time he had getting you through your exams." He concluded

19

with: "I trust my services are satisfactory and that you will reward them by writing often. Affectionately, Dad."

Soon after *Victoria Regina* opened, Price reportedly was offered a million-dollar contract to come to Hollywood, and on June 29, 1936, the "first matinee idol in years" flew west for a screen test. While in town, he was the guest of honor at a party at Joan Crawford's. One paper reported that David O. Selznick "immediately took an option on Price's services," and Selznick's son recently confirmed that Vincent was one of the masses who tested for the role of Ashley Wilkes in *Gone With the Wind*. He also made a color test for Selznick's picture *The Garden of Allah*, in which he looks very young, very handsome, and very nervous.

But Helen Hayes had counseled Vincent that he needed more acting experience, a fair comment from an established star to an overnight sensation: "It was Helen who taught me just how hard I had to work to learn the business after my beginner's luck." During the 1936 "summer recess" of *Victoria Regina*, Price followed her advice and elected to hone his craft in summer stock. He starred in two productions at the Westchester Playhouse in White Plains, New York, both opposite Mildred Natwick: J. M. Barrie's comedy *What Every Woman Knows* and Maxwell Anderson's *Elizabeth the Queen*, in which he played the Earl of Essex. He also appeared in *Parnell* at the County Theatre in Suffern, New York, opposite old schoolmate Barbara O'Neil, who continued to be an on-again, off-again romance and to whom he had given a ring in the spring. *Victoria Regina* reopened on August 31, 1936, and Price carried on as Albert until the next "recess," on May 29, 1937. That month, papers announced (erroneously) that Hal Roach had signed him to a seven-year contract and that his first film would be *Road Show*, a solo turn for Oliver Hardy.

During the 1937 summer season Price appeared in several plays at the Lakewood Theatre in Skowhegan, Maine, one of the oldest "straw hat" playhouses in the country. Founded in 1901, it had a tradition of "Broadway quality," producing plays with well-known personalities on a challenging weekly turnover. After Ibsen's *The Wild Duck*, he starred again in the title role of *Parnell*, the romantic story of the ill-fated nineteenth-century Irish leader; this time, his leading lady was a highly regarded actress named Edith Barrett. Born Edith Barrett Williams about thirty years earlier, she was the granddaughter of a colleague of the legendary Edwin Booth and already had a substantial stage career under her belt, having made her debut at age seventeen. Price played three more roles at Lakewood (and a second opposite Edith Barrett) and then moved back to the Westchester Playhouse for a couple of productions. Reviewers were in ecstasy: "Physically, he is a child of the gods. Exception-

ally tall, he is exceptionally handsome, exceptionally graceful for all his inches. He is one man who can be called beautiful in the sense that a thoroughbred of seventeen hands is beautiful . . ." The fall of 1937 took Helen Hayes and *Victoria Regina* on the road, but without their leading man: Vincent Price had matured far beyond Albert the Good.

He stayed on the Great White Way in *The Lady Has a Heart*, which a critic commented "lingered longer on Broadway than it should have, owing its box-office draw to the fact that Vincent Price is the leading matinee idol in the New York theatre." Although the New York *Variety* review was good, remarking, "Lad should make a grand catch for Hollywood, possessing as he does both looks and ability," most of the notices were lukewarm or unfavorable, placing undue emphasis on the young star's physical attractions. "Women make up eighty percent of the audience," wrote one reviewer. "The handsome, blond actor had a strong feminine appeal in *Victoria Regina*. It seems to be even stronger now." Vincent was genuinely distraught over the negative reviews, since they seemed more personally critical than was appropriate, and he was exasperated over the inevitable comparisons with the triumph of his Prince Albert. Interestingly, he never forgot the disappointment. In his 1978 autobiography for young readers, Price wrote: "When you are a big success in the beginning of your career, it is hard to swallow adverse criticism. All actors are criticized from time to time, of course. But we still resent it—we are hurt. . . . The problem is that it bothers you that someone didn't think you were as good as you thought you were. At other times you might think that you have not been very good, but the critic raves about you. That's often harder to take, because you want the critics to be honest."

Two days after the opening, Price "wandered down Sixth Avenue in that critically induced state of amnesia in which all actors forget themselves when connected with a failure." Finding himself in front of a pet store, he shook off his blues and bought a white English bulldog puppy he christened Johnny. He also found solace sending love to Barbara O'Neil in Hollywood and denouncing the reviews. ("Took expected pokes about Albert etc. so obvious!") *The Lady Has a Heart* ran for three months, during which time the gossip columnists made much of the long-distance romance: "Vincent Price [is] the new Romeo with Barbara O'Neil." The papers simply could not get enough of the new sensation, reporting one evening on the town in which "Tallulah Bankhead and her darling husband, John Emery, were poured out of the El Morocco club at five in the moaning [sic], aided and abetted by the Westport Playhouse heartbreaker, Vincent Price."

In December, Price was again on the West Coast,

testing for the romantic male lead in M-G-M's *Marie Antoinette*, which starred Norma Shearer. He told his parents he was offered the part but turned it down because he didn't want "to go in to the movies" until he was "sure of himself." Instead, he elected to stay in New York, where he found himself being wooed by *enfant terrible* Orson Welles to join the Mercury Theatre, the fledgling repertory company the twenty-two-year-old actor-director had founded with John Houseman. Their inaugural production, a modern-dress *Julius Caesar*, had been a smash, and Welles signed Price to a six-play contract with the prestigious new group, which was often being called the Old Vic of the USA. "I felt that Orson and the company really were what I wanted out of the theater," Price explained in the 1980s, "sort of a place to identify and to learn my business. . . . The Mercury was, at that time, really hotter than a pistol." So was Price. Norman Lloyd (later a celebrated actor/director/ producer) was an original member of the Mercury company and explains that "we were not big theater names with marquee value. So when Vincent arrived, it was an affirmation of the status of the Mercury, because here was a leading man who was *hot* on Broadway. I thought, What the hell, all the ladies are going to come and see him!" In the 1938 season, Price appeared in the Elizabethan comedy *The Shoemaker's Holiday*, which opened on New Year's Day (Joseph Cotten and Edith Barrett costarred). "We were really like an Elizabethan company," Norman Lloyd remembers, laughing. "We were wild and nutty and full of great theater energy and joy. Vincent was so elegant, and *right*, and we were so scruffy and dirty and awful." On April 25, Price was among the cast of the revival of Bernard Shaw's *Heartbreak House*.

Despite the fact that he was performing onstage nightly opposite the zany and enticing Edith Barrett, Price's love affair with Barbara O'Neil was still going strong. After a February visit from her, he wrote: "I do miss you, darling . . . unless you hurry back or I hurry out, I am going to become a confirmed bachelor . . ." He mentioned that some pieces from his art collection were on loan and garnering attention, and he expressed dissatisfaction with the Mercury, because it is "the private enterprise of one man. Orson is a genius, and a grand guy, but I fear that the Mercury is his, and that all others are disregarded, even the actors working with him. . . ." He was increasingly philosophical about his calling, as he sensed the continued professional success before him, but torn between films and the stage: "I wonder if there isn't something great for every man to do during his life, and that if we try hard enough and prepare ourselves well enough, if the genius will not one day enter us and demand to make itself heard. I have always had a feeling that there

was something for me to do, and I knew that I must give pleasure to people, and the theatre seemed the way to do that. . . . I will know the end of this week if or no I come to Hollywood this summer." And he still wanted a commitment from Barbara: ". . . anytime you are ready just let me know . . . I have searched everywhere for someone to take your place and found no one that can even approach you, and now I have given up and don't search anymore."

But O'Neil evidently continued to vacillate, leading Price to search very close to home, and sometime during *Shoemaker's Holiday*, he made things formal with costar Edith Barrett. Vincent and Edith were married on Saturday, April 23, 1938, at Manhattan's "fashionable" St. Thomas Protestant Episcopal Church, with two hundred guests and family in attendance (and his "scruffy" Mercury costars relegated to the rear of the house). *Shoemaker* had closed the night before, but Price was to open Monday in *Heartbreak House*. With less than forty-eight hours until the groom was due back at work, the couple's "honeymoon" was "a motor trip through eastern vacation spots." The papers attested that "Edith and Vincent make the most romantic couple in the theatrical world. . . . The nuptials are no surprise to the exclusive colony in Lakewood, Maine, who witnessed Price's lovemaking to Edith when they played *Parnell* there last summer." Perhaps the union was a surprise only to Vincent's family, who, of course, were well aware that their youngest son had been involved for years with hometown *amour* Barbara O'Neil. At least sister Lollie seemed taken aback by the news: "You certainly should have warned me a bit. All I can say is, darling, she must be a lamb or you wouldn't have chosen her. . . . Dearest baby brother I am so happy happy for you and for Edith."

When *Heartbreak House* closed, the young actor was anxious to give Hollywood a serious whirl. (The popular artist was announced for subsequent Mercury productions, including the title role in *Henry V*, but the young Welles, whom Price regarded as "a marvelous director, a real genius" but "terribly undisciplined," broke the contract. Vincent's association with the company ended after only two plays; in fact, the Mercury itself existed only one full season.) He sent his father a telegram: "Pappy, the birds go west for better pickings. May there be an early worm. Will peep upon arrival." Having been much courted by several studios, Price finally signed with Universal. Announced to the media in July 1938, his contract was an exceptional one for the film industry, allowing the actor six months a year to return to the legitimate stage. Previously, he had tested against Brian Aherne, the eventual choice, for the role of Maximilian in Warner Bros.' *Juarez* before his contract was signed with Universal. "Warner Brothers are very excited about my tests. . . . I will be allowed by Universal to do it, if they (W.B.) want me still." (He also mentioned that, as new Hollywood residents, he and his new wife were seeing "a lot of Barbara [O'Neil] and all is well—she and Edie get along well and we are all great friends! *Grace a Dieu!*") Films announced as Price's debut vehicle included *The Sun Never Sets*, *Rio* opposite Danielle Darrieux and *The Storm* (for a role which probably went to Preston Foster). He had time for a final summer-stock production in August before returning to Hollywood to finally start his first motion picture: *Service De Luxe*.

Service De Luxe was an undemanding screwball comedy which gave Vincent the opportunity to prove himself movie-leading-man material. He had the advantages of an established leading lady (Constance Bennett), a wonderful supporting cast (including the inimitable Charlie Ruggles), and a director in whom he had great confidence (Rowland V. Lee). From the beginning, Price seemed to be in his element, furthering his film technique by studying with Laura Elliot, a popular and prominent instructor who helped many stage-trained actors learn not to "mug" before the camera. The midwestern boy who had traveled Europe on his own, lived in London, and spent a couple of years in and out of New York City wrote his parents that he wasn't too sure what to make of the West Coast. "I am very enthusiastic about the possibilities of Calif. but it will take time and a great effort culturally to make it what it should be. Bad taste is more apparent here than in any other part of the country—they are years behind the times in architecture and what modern efforts they've made are too extreme. But O this climate has limitless advantages—it should make things so easy for culture to flourish." Working in Hollywood, however, meant that he and his wife of only six months were separated, since Edith remained for a time in New York. The young husband was confident about the success of his marriage: "I know Edith and I will be able to work this out—being apart I mean—it's part of our job . . ." He was still convinced that Edith needed—and wanted—only a stage success to be happy.

In 1938, various movie studios joined forces to produce a twenty-minute short called *The World Is Ours*, to promote why "motion pictures are your best entertainment." Forty stars of "the past, present and future" were showcased, including Price. Shown at first-run horses, *The World Is Ours* preceded *Service De Luxe* where the feature played; therefore, that little two-reeler would have been Vincent Price's first official film appearance. Reviews for both the comedy and the new star were enthusiastic across the boards, touting him as a leading man to be reckoned with. One newspaper reported: "This fellow, Vincent Price . . . needs and deserves a buildup. He's the newest threat to all the established heart crushers of Hollywood, and every time he looks around Bob Taylor and Tyrone Power and the rest of the boys have taken to running high temperatures." In later years, Price would be unkind about his film debut, declaiming himself as unsuited to be a straightforward "good guy." But if he truly was uncomfortable as a leading man, it didn't show before the cameras; perhaps some of his dissatisfaction stemmed from awareness that his acting technique was still in development. The explanation for why Universal didn't continue him in such parts is difficult to pinpoint. Despite his personal affability, Price's aristocratic good looks weren't those of the average Joe, and his height was certainly a factor when he lined up with leading ladies of the day—and most of the leading men. Price didn't appear in really *good* films at this time simply because Universal wasn't *making* the big-budget, star-studded classics remembered today.

After only one motion picture, Vincent returned to the New York stage in late December 1938 to appear in the popular fantasy *Outward Bound*, directed by Otto Preminger. During the run he came back to Hollywood for a weekend so that Universal could test him for a role opposite Irene Dunne in *A Modern Cinderella*, a film which was eventually titled *When Tomorrow Comes* and costarred Charles Boyer. When *Outward Bound* closed after 225 performances, Price was recalled by his studio and informed that for his second movie he was being loaned out to Warner Bros. to play a small part in *The Private Lives of Elizabeth and Essex*. While shooting *Service De Luxe*, Price had confided to his family that he hoped his next picture would provide him with "a serious character role—that's when acting is fun, when you must convince an audience and yourself that you're someone else." Vincent strutted through the perfunctory role of Sir Walter Raleigh in the Technicolor extravaganza which starred Bette Davis and Errol Flynn.

Vincent's next two features, both under his Universal contract, were roles as small as Sir Walter. In another costume picture he had his first exposure to horror in *Tower of London*; costars Basil Rathbone and Boris Karloff would still figure in his professional career nearly thirty years later. At the same time, on the same lot, he filmed *Green Hell*, a jungle epic which Price always regarded as "one of the corniest pictures ever made." Interestingly, after these two small parts, he was given the title role in his next film, Universal's first follow-up to its 1933 hit *The Invisible Man*. He played a new character with the same "problem" in *The Invisible Man Returns*, which had even more impressive special effects than the original, making for painstaking work for the actor—a ninety-eight-second scene in which Price borrows clothes from a scarecrow took all day to film. Next, in the screen adaptation of Nathaniel Hawthorne's *The*

House of the Seven Gables, Vincent was cast as the "good brother" framed for murder by "evil brother" George Sanders. It was to be Price's last picture under his inaugural movie contract; Universal elected not to renew, although the decision was probably a blessing in disguise for the actor, since the studio clearly was not in the forefront of quality filmmaking and had done little to further his career.

In 1940, Vincent signed a seven-year contract with 20th Century-Fox, a deal which again permitted him time off for stage commitments. Although he was beginning to make his mark as a character performer and not a standard male lead, he was still highly touted by fan magazines as a heartthrob. The hugely popular *Photoplay* printed an article titled "With or Without," encouraging readers to "Cast Your Moustache Vote Now!" as to whether they preferred certain stars hirsute or clean-shaven. In addition to Price, in the survey were a nineteen-year-old Robert Preston; Basil Rathbone; Robert Taylor, with whom Price was often compared; Clark Gable; and Errol Flynn.

Price's first picture for Fox, filmed in the spring of 1940, was yet another historical drama, *Brigham Young*. As Joseph Smith, founder of the Mormon religion, he was dispatched early on but still made an impression with his directness and sincerity. The next month, he returned to Maine and Lakewood Theatre summer stock for the first time since 1937. Now an accredited film star as well as a Broadway veteran, he was "hard at work" on a play he himself had written. He was alone and "lonesome," since Edith remained at their L.A. home, expecting their child in September. Reviews of *Poet's Corner* were good, in fact better for Price the author than for Price the actor (who played a supporting role), and the "hyphenate" was encouraged: ". . . at least I feel confident to go on and write"—which he had done since childhood and continued until the end of his life. After appearing in two more plays, he was off to Hollywood, anxious "to see my Edi . . . and to take a test for the best part I've ever been offered"—the male lead in what was then titled *Hudson Bay Company*. Within the week Price was back in Maine, once again playing Essex in Anderson's *Elizabeth the Queen*, but this time he was famous enough to merit solo billing over the title.

Vincent returned home just in time for the birth of Vincent Barrett, on August 30, 1940. The new father adored his son; in a few years, one of their favorite things to share was a visit to the amusement park. "Barrett and I both thought of Ocean Park as something sacred," he would poignantly recall years later. "We spent many a hectic happy evening there, vying with one another in games of skill and chance, and seeing who could find the raciest scene among those ridiculously stilted,

nightie-clad naughties on the flip card machines in the Penny Arcade. We let our handwritings be analyzed and our weights guessed and his chin and my moustache get gummed up by huge, pink clouds of cotton candy." When the young boy demurred at the daunting curves of what the midwestern Price called the "rollycoaster," the actor delightedly rode the track himself.

When *Hudson's Bay* finally went before the cameras, Paul Muni was in the lead; Price played King Charles II, England's Merry Monarch, another small role with only a couple of scenes. It was to be his last movie for three years. Playwright Patrick Hamilton's creepy Victorian stage thriller *Gaslight*, about a murderer who tries to drive his wife insane, had premiered in London's West End in 1938. Vincent Price was set to costar in the Broadway production opposite wife Edith Barrett, but when she became ill, the L.A. company's female lead, Canadian-born Judith Evelyn, re-created her role. Retitled *Angel Street*, the play opened at the Golden Theatre in New York on Friday, December 5, 1941—hardly an auspicious week for entertainment. In fact, producers expected the play to close immediately and only printed three days' worth of programs and tickets. But the show received raves and was one of the hits not only of the season but of the war years. As of 1980, it was forty-first on the list of New York productions running more than five hundred performances, surpassing *The King and I*, *The Odd Couple*, and *Oliver!* Price had succeeded in getting as far away from Albert the Good as possible, and he was loving it. "The whole audience hissed," he recalled with glee. "I had found my niche." Even as a child, Vincent had always considered villains more interesting characters than heroes and seemed to have a premonition that his professional success would lie in that direction, since he knew the key was *survival*. "Villains last—they go on, and on, and on. The minute the hero loses his hair and gets bags under his eyes and a double chin, he's through. But not the villain! The more crinkly and crevassed he gets, the better you like him!"

Some of his free afternoons during *Angel Street* were spent acting without billing in radio soap operas—"because they were such fun and you learned a whole area of acting that you were never trained to do." During those first months of the war, Vincent also did his bit for the Stage Door Canteen, making sandwiches and working as a busboy with Alfred Lunt. "We waited tables three nights a week. The servicemen came there free. The wonderful thing was that they never heard of Lunt and Fontanne or Helen Hayes. But let Betty Grable come in—Sex! Wow!"

In October 1942, Louella Parsons reported that Fox had decided to bring Vincent back to Hollywood, since they were "losing Power, Romero, Fonda and so many of their male stars" to the war effort. The actor had some trepidation about leaving the security of *Angel Street* for another assault on Hollywood: "I think it was most certainly the desire to be an American, and not a New Yorker (or even a Californian), that has always made me eager to get on with the delightful duty of knowing my country; and to this day [1959] I feel that the West, with the least to offer culturally, has the most to offer American-ly. . . . And so it was to California that I was bound to go, not only because I loved the West, but because, for all my love of the theatre, I was still a Missouri boy whose original theatrical contact was with Pearl White, Charlie Chaplin and those other fabled creatures of the 'Silver Screen.'"

Price stepped offstage on December 5, 1942, after exactly a year, but when he returned to the movies, the malevolent ambience of *Angel Street* still clung to him. In preparing for his role, Vincent had read Krafft-Ebing's classic *Psychopathia sexualis* and studied the psychology of evil. Although Jack Manningham had been an out-and-out "rotter," in Price's own words "one of the meanest men ever written," he was also "a damned attractive one at that." Vincent discovered the curious sensuality of wickedness and would begin to find professional success in roles founded on human weakness which still retained an irresistible air of suave gentility. George Sanders characterized his own screen persona: "I was beastly, but I was never coarse." The same description would apply to Vincent Price's screen bad guys, who, as Price always pointed out, were cultured, erudite gentlemen who never saw themselves as villains.

A sea yarn called *Star Over Scotland* was announced as the actor's "comeback" vehicle, and in early February 1943 he tested for *Jane Eyre*. (The role went to Henry Daniell; wife Edith landed the dramatic, showy part of the housekeeper, Mrs. Fairfax.) Ultimately, Vincent Price's first movie in three years was the ambitious *The Song of Bernadette*, which he filmed in the spring of 1943. As the skeptical imperial prosecutor who refuses to believe in the young girl's visions of the Virgin Mary, Price had the first really complex role of his film career. During the months of filming *Bernadette*, Vincent and colleague George Macready (who had played his brother on Broadway in *Victoria Regina*) opened The Little Gallery in Beverly Hills. "We rented a hole in the wall next door to Martindale's book shop and a very popular bar, figuring correctly that we'd catch a mixed clientele of erudites and inebriates." Price and Macready saw the gallery not only as an indulgence of their own interests but as a showcase for young artists and a way to expose the general public to art and art appreciation. The establishment merited photos and two full columns in *Newsweek* magazine, but rent increases forced The Little Gallery to close after two years. Price remembered Igor Stravinsky, Thomas Mann, and Sergei Rachmaninoff browsing through the gallery and then going to the nearby deli for lox and bagels.

At this time, Price began lecturing across the country on a regular basis; as far back as the fall of 1937, while appearing on Broadway in *The Lady Has a Heart*, he had spoken at Hunter College on the subject "Why I Don't Want to Be a Matinee Idol"! Price maintained the activity, particularly dear to his heart, for forty years. "I try to create in a lecture an exchange of ideas . . . so that I come to the audience as an 'answerer,' not a lecturer; as a listener, not a speaker." Vincent Price would be touted as the highest-paid lecturer in the country (after Mrs. Roosevelt, of course), and his talks on art and art history, American literature, and villainy, among others, established him as a legitimate influence on popular culture. Perhaps more important, it brought him one-on-one through the decades with young people, who would come to feel as much affection for him as he felt for them. At one period in the 1950s he hit fifty-three cities in sixty days. "Nothing I have ever done has been of more value," he would state feelingly. In the early seventies, at a time when he was particularly dissatisfied with recent film roles, he informed his agent: "The lectures . . . are my only . . . *rewarding work.*"

The screen adaptation of Maxwell Anderson's play *The Eve of St. Mark*, shot in the fall of 1943, gave Price one of the best roles of his career. He excelled as a poetry-spouting southern soldier in the war drama and garnered superior reviews. Incomprehensibly, after the meaty part in *St. Mark*, Fox put Price into *Wilson*, their sumptuous modern historical drama based on the life of the twenty-eighth president, in a role with only half a dozen lines. In his next assignment, *The Keys of the Kingdom*, he fared no better. Despite the fact that his character, a supercilious bishop, played a pivotal role in the life of leading man Gregory Peck, Vincent had only three scenes in a two-and-a-quarter-hour film. Fortunately for Price's dramatic muscles, his next movie for Fox offered him not only a wonderful role but would remain an all-time classic. Made in the spring of 1944, *Laura* was a glossy, delicious film noir which teamed Vincent with old friend Clifton Webb, Dana Andrews, Judith Anderson, and the gorgeous Gene Tierney. Ironically, the novel on which the film was based was written by Vera Caspary, who had penned the original story for *Service De Luxe*; the same author was responsible not only for Vincent's first movie but for one of his very best as well.

In *A Royal Scandal*, a farce about the loves of Catherine the Great of Russia, Price again had only a couple of scenes, both of which were with the one and only Tallulah Bankhead. His next picture, *Leave Her to*

Outward Bound Broadway, 1939, Morgan Farley, Louis Hector, Alexander Kirkland, Helen Chandler, Bramwell Fletcher, Florence Reed, VP, Laurette Taylor, Thomas Chalmers

"October 19, 1940, Future Screen Star! Vincent Barrett Price, aged seven weeks and photographed for the first time yesterday, says he can't miss! His mother, the former Edith Barrett, is a well-known stage actress, while his father, Vincent Price, is famous both on stage and screen. . . . So-o-o-o, that future career is practically in the bag. The baby is the fourth generation of Vincent Prices, having arrived in Southern California for his screen career on August 3rd, at the Good Samaritan Hospital." (AP/WWP)

Angel Street Broadway, 1941, with Judith Evelyn

25

The Song of Bernadette Off camera with wife, Edith Barrett, who had a small part in the picture

Laura With Dana Andrews, Gene Tierney, and Clifton Webb

Portrait of a 20th Century-Fox contract player

July 1945 Broadcasting "The Undecided Molecule" on CBS Radio. (*Left*) Chatting with costar Norman Lloyd; (*Right*) Groucho Marx at mike, VP, Sylvia Sidney, Norman Lloyd at second mike

Shock With Lynn Bari

Dragonwyck

Heaven, was a showcase for leading lady Gene Tierney, but Price's characterization of an unrelenting prosecuting attorney received special attention from critics. He was technically the male lead in the stylish *Dragonwyck,* which he made in the spring of 1945, although he received third billing behind Gene Tierney and Walter Huston, who played her father. His character, Nicholas Van Ryn, the haughty lord of the manor, was in many respects a precursor of the tormented antiheroes of the Edgar Allan Poe films of the 1960s with which he would later become so identified.

Vincent's career at 20th Century-Fox had included several successes in which he had been a slightly unsavory character. His first solo starring vehicle continued the trend. While not a horror picture, *Shock* is a psychological thriller, with Price exhorted by his Lady Macbeth *paramour* to cover up one murder with a second. Shot in the fall of 1945, it was conceived as a B movie, and although reviews were slightly mixed, it was elevated into the A houses. *Shock* proved that Price could carry a picture, and he began to establish himself as a villain, conveying complicated characters driven by circumstances beyond their control.

Vincent and Edith Price were frequently on opposite coasts physically, and in 1944 they had separated legally as well. When they reconciled in 1946, Louella Parsons's column noted that the two had "talked things over" and quoted the actor as stating that Edith was "giving up her career so that we need never be separated again. Don't think I don't know what that means with her talent and her love of the theatre. . . ." However, whereas Vincent was clearly headed for stardom, Edith's film roles were less notable. "I think she really got married to get out of the theatre," he would theorize much later. "Here I was,

27

goggle-eyed to be married to this actress, and it was a terrible blow to me. It didn't do our marriage any good, I'll tell you that."

That summer, Price was among the cast of Fox's Technicolor period romance *Forever Amber* when Darryl F. Zanuck became dissatisfied with the extensive footage already shot. Both the director and the female star, English actress Peggy Cummins, were replaced. By the time the dust settled, Price, too, was out; his costarring role of Lord Almsbury, the best friend of leading man Cornel Wilde, went to Richard Greene. (Many film books list Price playing Charles II. In fact, Reginald Denny was cast as the king in the Cummins version and was replaced for the final film by George Sanders.) It is interesting to speculate how the heroic, flashy part in the popular picture might have influenced Price's career. Instead, he went right into *The Long Night*, costarring as a manipulative Svengali with designs on Henry Fonda's girlfriend, played in her film debut by Barbara Bel Geddes. Ironically, the leading lady in Price's next picture was Peggy Cummins, who had lost the title role in *Forever Amber*. In the Victorian melodrama *Moss Rose*, she played a cockney girl involved with a suspected murderer; Price was the Columboesque inspector on the trail. Fox then allowed Price's contract to lapse when the actor balked at taking a role in *Captain From Castile*—"the most despicable character I'd ever read . . . [who] was cruel actually for no reason except to make Tyrone Power look good. I refused to do it, and so they let my option drop." On another occasion, Price explained leaving the studio: "I liked it for a time. But I felt that I would make the giant step into real star parts if I left Fox and become a freelance actor, free to choose only the roles I wanted and not be forced to go into picture after picture where I was part of the wallpaper!"

Price started off 1947 as a free agent, and other motion-picture studios were quick to pick him up, although his career pinballed without a set studio career plan. For several years there were no more out-and-out leads, although he worked steadily in supporting roles. *The Web* was a standard crime thriller, with Price playing the villain to Edmond O'Brien's uninteresting hero. In *Up in Central Park*, he appeared in a role drastically rewritten from the stage musical on which the film was based; female lead Deanna Durbin remained a friend until his death. It was probably while he was shooting *Central Park* that he recorded a voice-over for *Abbott and Costello Meet Frankenstein*, delivering the punch line as the Invisible Man. At the same time, he was also developing a reputation as a popular radio performer, starring in the title role of *The Saint*. Price considered the medium "a great teacher—some of the best drama ever done in America was produced during the heyday of radio." He

had made his debut back in June 1936 while he was on Broadway in *Victoria Regina*; the announcer for *Fleischmann's Yeast Hour* introduced the matinee idol as "Vincent Prince"! Price continued to work on radio right up through the 1970s, participating as a cohost when CBS began "an exciting new era of radio drama" with *Sears Radio Theatre*.

Unfortunately, Vincent and Edith were still unable to make their marriage work; in December 1947 the couple separated for a final time, and Vincent spent a despondent Christmas alone without his estranged wife and son. The day after the holiday, he wandered by a pet store and came home with his best friend of the next sixteen years, a mongrel mutt named Joe. Edith sued for divorce on grounds of mental cruelty in January 1948, but Vincent stayed busy, joining other Hollywood art lovers, including Edward G. Robinson, comedienne Fanny Brice, and Sam and Mildred Jaffe, to open The Modern Institute of Art. In two years they built a membership of five thousand and an annual attendance of forty thousand, but like The Little Gallery, it closed after only a couple of years due to lack of corporate support. Price was "disgusted" that all the love, devotion, and work lavished on the institute had been for nothing because of Los Angeles's disinterest and Los Angelenos's "apathy for culture." But he was also elected to the board of directors of the fledgling Los Angeles County Museum, a commitment he maintained throughout his life.

M-G-M's *Three Musketeers* was an enormous production made in early 1948, with Price again a natural in the period costuming he wore so well in the role of a suave, witty villain (Richelieu) with a sense of humor. He followed *Musketeers* with *Rogues' Regiment*, an inadequate Universal thriller, as a gunrunner helping out a Nazi in hiding and matching wits with Dick Powell. By June the Prices' divorce was final. Edith received large property and cash settlements and was granted custody of seven-year-old Barrett. During the ensuing months she made it difficult for Price to see his son; it was a lonely time, during which he also lost his father. (His mother had passed away in October 1946.)

His next film, *The Bribe*, could boast a superior cast, including Robert Taylor and Charles Laughton, and Vincent had the opportunity to work with the woman he regarded as the most glamorous sex symbol in the movies, Ava Gardner. In *Bagdad*, he was a blue-eyed Arab threatening torture of another gorgeous lady, Maureen O'Hara. In the fall of 1949, he made one of his favorite films, although, curiously, *Champagne for Caesar* didn't do well at the box office. In it, Price's idol, Ronald Colman, played an intellectual contestant out to take a popular quiz show for every dime. As the tycoon of the soap company sponsoring the program, Price had ample op-

Forever Amber Never-before-seen photos from the discarded version of the picture: VP taking advantage of Peggy Cummins as Amber

Forever Amber With Peggy Cummins and Cornel Wilde

Forever Amber With Peggy Cummins

Up in Central Park VP looks skeptical as the still photographer suggests he climb aboard the bicycle

portunity to indulge his gifts of comedy timing and delivery.

A few weeks after making *Champagne*, in October 1949, Vincent Price surprised the media when it was revealed he had been married for more than a month. His new wife, (Eleanor) Mary Grant, was born in South Wales, England, on February 20, 1918. Her British parents traveled a great deal, finally settling in Canada, and Mary began a career in New York as a commercial dressmaker and stage costume designer. She first met Vincent Price when she came to Hollywood to do costumes for *Up in Central Park*. In November 1947, *Holly-*

Publicity portrait

The Three Musketeers

wood Citizen News had run a feature on a "new look" Mary had designed for gentlemen, a cross between a zoot suit and mechanic's overalls. "'I showed it to Vincent Price, the actor,' Miss Grant said, 'and he went crazy about it.' We checked with Price and he backed her up. . . . Price has been a little self-conscious about his clothes ever since his first publicity break in a Hollywood column. 'Who,' sneered the gossip, 'is the person who wears Vincent Price's clothes around for two years before he turns them over to the actor?'" (Throughout his life Vincent Price always liked comfort, dressing very casually in his office, and once happily described his appearance as "unmade-bed-looking.") Supposedly, Price and Grant didn't meet again until the spring of 1949. Together with friend Perry Rathbone, the couple went to San Diego for an impromptu holiday and then elected to slip down to Mexico to tie the knot. The papers reported the date as August 25, although Vincent's diary entry is Saturday, August 27: "Married Mary Grant—P. Rathbone witness Tijuana." Afterward, Vincent had time to grow a beard before he made *The Baron of Arizona*, a remarkable true story about a man who concocted an incredible scheme to swindle the United States out of the territory of Arizona in the 1870s. It, too, was one of Price's favorite movies; again, a poor box-office showing.

Following their honeymoon in Peru, the enormously talented Mary set about decorating their house in Beverly Hills, the huge "Mediterranean kind of home which we chose more or less as a setting for Vincent's art collection." "It was just magnificent," remembers long-time friend Dennis Hopper. "Labor-intensive. It was the first time I ever saw contemporary things work with antiques. It was a wonderful place to be. Los Angeles is art-poor; basically, actors did not collect art and were not involved. But Vincent and Mary, they were on the cutting edge." Price had continued purchasing work since his teens and was amassing a wonderful, highly eclectic collection. "Mine is so personal. . . . It's filled with things that don't go together at all except that I like them." According to Dennis Hopper, "It's been said that a true collector is a person one who collects what he wishes he had made. Well, I think Vincent was very much in that school. He instilled the idea in you that a piece's *importance* wasn't the reason for acquiring art. It should be something *you* could live with, that *you* understood. And if it meant something to you, and you wished that you had made it, then it was something that should be valuable to you. And of course, if you had a really good track on things, it would be valuable to everybody." In addition to tribal art and classic paintings and drawings, Price always looked for work by young people or unheralded artists. During the fifties and sixties the Prices hosted frequent open houses for charity or museum fund-raisers and also

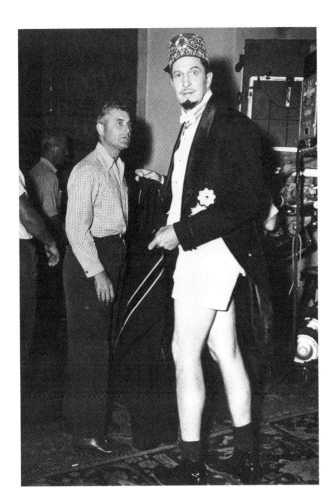

Bagdad "Vincent Price is caught by the cameraman while in the act of putting on his pants in order to go into a scene. Assistant director Ronnie Rondell is trying to hurry the actor along." (Academy of Motion Picture Arts and Sciences)

Champagne for Caesar With Barbara Britton, Ronald Colman, and Celeste Holm

donated works of art. (They gave a Fragonard valued at $45,000 to the UCLA art galleries.)

In February 1950, Price made *Curtain Call at Cactus Creek*, a comedy Western starring the versatile Donald O'Connor, which gave Vincent his first opportunity to play a ham actor. He followed it in May with a similar type of character in a completely different film: *His Kind of Woman* was an exciting action/adventure with well-placed humor supplied by Price in one of his best characterizations. The leading lady he lost to Bob Mitchum was the fabulous Jane Russell, glamorous, savvy, compassionate. "I fell in love with Vinnie," she admits. "He was my Gemini brother. He could charm the birds out of the trees. I could tell him anything." In August, Price and his wife went to France to make *Adventures of Captain Fabian*, a tired swashbuckler an equally tired Errol Flynn. The couple had several weeks at liberty in Paris on salary while they waited for Flynn to arrive and spent it "cruising" around the countryside, picking up *objets d'art* for their collection.

In January 1951 legal proceedings were occupying the Prices, as a member of the family found himself in Superior Court, the victim of a lawsuit—the family mutt,

The Baron of Arizona Press book advertisement

Joe. Back in August 1949 the animal had tangled with a crazed bicyclist who decided to sue Joe's master for over $13,000 in damages. After presenting his client's case in court, Joe's attorney won complete vindication; Joe's owner, who insisted he was only present to preserve Joe's honor, was satisfied. Even the postman on the jury voted to acquit. Sometime early in 1951, Vincent contributed to a unique kind of feature film, *Pictura—Adventure in Art*, which presented vignettes on great artists narrated by prominent actors, including Price, Gregory Peck, and Henry Fonda. *The Las Vegas Story* was Vincent's second teaming with Jane Russell, a more mundane story than their first picture, about gambling and jewel theft.

It was also during 1951 that Vincent first visited the campus of East Los Angeles College. Invited to lecture on "The Aesthetic Responsibilities of the Citizen," he arrived and found he was "speaking in a Quonset hut on a mud flat." Struck by the spirit of the students and the community's need for the opportunity to experience original art works firsthand, Vincent donated some ninety pieces to establish the first "teaching art collection" owned by a community college in the United States. Over the decades, Price and other patrons continued to contribute art with the goal of illustrating diverse periods, styles, mediums, and techniques; from Egyptian sculpture (circa 600 B.C.) to 1990s serigraphs. The Vincent Price Gallery would become one of his most enduring legacies.

The summer of 1952 found him at the La Jolla Playhouse in director Norman Lloyd's brilliant production of Christopher Fry's *Lady's Not for Burning*. Glamorous costar Marsha Hunt had read lines with him for his 1936 screen test. She described his appearance in Fry's Elizabethan comedy as "beautiful and bearded"; resplendent in period finery, he remarked humorously to her, "Gad, I'm virile!" The play went up to San Francisco, after which Price went on board the well-received theatrical tour of *Don Juan in Hell* with Sir Cedric Hardwicke, Agnes Moorehead, and Charles Boyer, taking over acting duties from director/costar Charles Laughton. At the end of the year, actor/director José Ferrer offered Vincent another stage role in an upcoming production of *My Three Angels* (the play on which the film *We're No Angels* would be based). It was a charming comedy, but Price turned it down. Instead, he took a gamble on an unusual movie he was offered at the same time, a gimmick picture for Warner Bros. That decision changed the course of his career—for better and worse.

House of Wax was a remake of Warners' own *Mystery of the Wax Museum* (1933) and was shot in 3-D in January 1953. The studio was counting on it to give an enormous shot in the arm both to the studio and to the motion-picture industry, which was suffering due to the growing popularity of television. Vincent often described his "specialty" as "playing men who have been hurt by life, men who have been betrayed. There was always a reason, no matter how demented, for why these characters behaved the way they did." *House of Wax*'s protagonist, Professor Jarrod, is a gentle sculptor whose greedy partner sets fire to the wax museum for the insurance money. Scarred in mind and body, Jarrod returns to wreak revenge, but despite his murders, he remains a tortured, tragic figure. In Jarrod, Price revealed a real gift for inspiring sympathy and terror in the same role. "The most interesting villains are the ones who have been *made* villains through circumstance," he would explain. " 'There but for the grace of God go I.' "

Price's next films were a far cry from the horror genre. In *Son of Sinbad*, a raucous romp chock-full of beautiful starlets, Price was a strong supporting buddy for hero Dale Robertson, supplying comic relief and common sense—such as there was. *Dangerous Mission* was a standard melodrama, for which the location (Glacier National Park) far outclassed the standard script. Around the same time, Price played a cameo for friend Bob Hope in the comedian's costume spoof *Casanova's Big Night*. In the fall, Price was back in a 3-D horror picture; in fact, he was almost back in the same horror picture, since *The Mad Magician* had an author, director, and several crew members in common with *House of Wax*. These screen scares were followed by one of the Bard's most chilling stage plays: on December 10, 1953, Price opened in *Richard III* at the New York City Center as the Duke of Buckingham opposite José Ferrer's "Crookback." Reviews were mixed for everyone, and the play closed within a month.

In 1954, Price didn't make a film. That spring, he appeared in two stage productions in his hometown of St. Louis: *The Lady's Not for Burning*, again with Marsha Hunt, and *Death Takes a Holiday*. In July, he toured for a few weeks with Terence Rattigan's brilliant legal drama *The Winslow Boy*, in the showy role of the cagey barrister. Notices were reminiscent of those first kudos for Prince Albert: ". . . Vincent Price of London, Broadway, Hollywood, and Missouri, all six feet four inches of him, steel blue eyes and suave mustache, [is] a bit overwhelming like one's first sight of the Rockies. Mr. Price possesses a kind of magnetic vigor that comes zinging over the footlights like a warrior's arrow to stab an audience into quivering awareness. Everyone adored him. . . ." His next play, a sex farce, was not so popular: *Black-Eyed Susan* was panned across the board during a brief Broadway run.

Sometime in March 1955, Price filmed his role in Cecil B. DeMille's biblical epic *The Ten Commandments* and then returned to the twentieth century as the head of a multimedia conglomerate in Fritz Lang's *While the City Sleeps*. In October he played the kind of suave, witty sophisticate he excelled at in *Serenade* with operatic singer Mario Lanza. It was probably early in 1956 that he recorded a brief voice-over narration for another version of the François Villon story, *The Vagabond King*.

Price had been appearing on television since 1949; in fact, he was one of a dozen performers on the very first coast-to-coast broadcast. He guested on the popular celebrity charades show *Pantomime Quiz* and in numerous respected dramatic playhouses, among them *Lux Video Theater*, *Climax*, and *Playhouse 90*. He even was part of a hilarious consequence on *Truth or Consequences*. Twice in 1956 he competed as a contestant on The *$64,000 Challenge* in the category of art and art history. Although the program was quite a time commitment, Price felt his appearances made a substantial contribution to wider public appreciation. Aline B. Saarinen was prompted to write in the *New York Times*: "At once urbane and appealing, [Price] communicated to millions an infectious enthusiasm and an adventuresomeness into modern art. His reactions seemed fresh and unhackneyed. When he said, 'You don't need $64,000 to be a collector or enjoy art—it doesn't even cost sixty-four cents to go to a museum,' he took art off its pedestal and showed it to be alive and pertinent." No review of his acting could have meant more to him.

Price finished the year acting again with Ronald Colman in Irwin Allen's star-studded film *The Story of Mankind*, an unsuccessful picture which nonetheless offered a wealth of amusing, if preposterous, cameos by some of Hollywood's most celebrated names. March 1957 brought Price one of the best-remembered films of his career, *The Fly*. In this classic horror story, he played the good-guy brother of the scientist who became "the monster created by atoms gone wild." In September the Prices experienced a real scare when a fire caused $10,000 worth of damage to their Beverly Glen home, destroying the garage apartment. Vincent was out of town, lecturing back East; when firemen arrived, they found Mary and seventeen-year-old Barrett training garden hoses on the flames.

In the fall of 1958, Price made the first of his two movies for showman extraordinaire producer William Castle. *House on Haunted Hill* was an entertaining "spook house" thriller, with the added attraction of "Emergo" at selected theatres—a skeleton flying through the air out into the audience! Price briefly got away from horror when he played the red herring in ringmaster's clothing for *The Big Circus*, but he buzzed right back for the inevitable sequel to Fox's hit *The Fly*. *Return of the Fly* was a pale (literally, since it was made in black and white) continuation of the first story, with Price again

the beleaguered good guy. In the spring of 1959, Price made *The Tingler*, a less credible but no less enjoyable William Castle production. When the bizarre title creature infiltrated a silent cinema in the story, Castle got his audiences where they lived by rigging theater seats to "tingle." A considerably less effective chiller followed for Price; *The Bat* was a creaky adaptation of a dated stage melodrama.

The two Castle films, coming so soon in his career after *The Fly*, indelibly stamped Vincent Price with the "horror film star" tag. He would continue to secure other kinds of roles, some quite good ones, but despite non-genre work (for example, a huge number of comedic television appearances) and his growing stature as an art authority, he would remain dogged by the horror image. His name alone was enough to sell one of the Gothic pictures, although it is surprising the small number of times he actually received sole star billing in a movie. Of all his "colleagues," including Boris Karloff, Bela Lugosi, Lon Chaney Jr., Peter Lorre, and latterly Peter Cushing and Christopher Lee, Price remained the most well rounded, with multiple personal interests and varied professional activities. For the rest of his career he would be questioned endlessly by reporters about the stereotype. "It's this thing of being typecast that makes you desirable,"—he would insist in his lecture "The Villains Still Pursue Me"—"that makes you employable in the movie business. And believe me, in my business, you had better be famous or you won't get another job. . . . I want to assure you that though I may play villains, in real life I'm kind of a pussycat. . . . And, of course, the thing I love most about playing villains is that they appeal to *women*! It's absolutely true. When you girls, you married girls, were going steady with your fellow or pinned or whatever, you didn't call your girlfriend up the next morning and say, 'Oh, I was out with Sam last night and he was so *nice*.' Noooo, that's not what you said. You said, "Oooooh, I was out with Sam last night and what he *did*! Oooooh. Man, just what I wanted him to.' Yup. And then you marry him and you reform him and that's the end of that!"

The year 1959 saw the publication of *I Like What I Know*, Price's self-styled "visual autobiography," which was less about his life and career than it was an exultation of art and art appreciation. It was well received; the prolific writer went on the publish several more books and, over the years, to pen in longhand hundreds of columns on a variety of subjects for newspapers in both the United States and England. He also continued a teenage passion for writing poetry—on the back of deli menus, customs receipts, and bank deposit slips, on hotel stationery from around the world, on movie call sheets, and on reams of lined notebook paper. Together with

Rehearsal read-through
for *His Kind of Woman*
With Jane Russell
and others

The drawing room in Mary and Vincent's home—an abstract painting by Richard Diebenkorn
hangs next to an early Mexican religious carving. Also displayed are bronzes, paintings by French
masters, and Pre-Columbian and African figures.

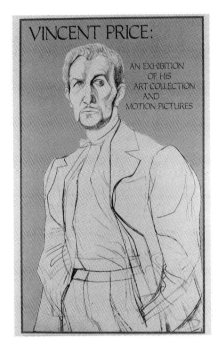

Exhibit poster for The Vincent Price Art Gallery: "Portrait of Vincent Price," pencil sketch by Rico Lubrun, circa 1950, a gift by the subject to the gallery

On stage in *The Lady's Not For Burning*, directed by Norman Lloyd—Lamont Johnson, Marsha Hunt as the accused witch, and VP as the world-weary soldier who falls in love with her

House of Wax

The Mad Magician With Director John Brahm

The Ten Commandments As Baka, the Pharaoh's master builder

Introducing Hollywood's greatest cowboys in a pilot for a 1960 TV series, *It Happened in Hollywood*. (The hat is the one he wore in *Baron of Arizona*.)

VP and his *$64,000 Challenge* adversary, jockey and fellow art expert Billy Pearson, at the 1956 premiere of *Lust for Life*, starring Kirk Douglas as artist Vincent Van Gogh.

Mansion Siniestra Spanish lobby card for *House on Haunted Hill* (note misspelling of Price's first name)

The Book of Joe

"May 4, 1962—Hollywood Newcomer—Actor Vincent Price and his wife, Mary Grant Price, show off their baby daughter May 4 as they leave St. John's Hospital in Santa Monica, Calif., where the baby was born by Caesarian section a week earlier. The baby, their first, weighed 7 pounds and 13 ounces and has been named Mary Victoria." (AP/WWP)

The Raven With Samuel Z. Arkoff holding trademark cigar, James H. Nicholson and Peter Lorre

The Bat

unpublished stories and memoirs, the introspective verses reflect the serious, philosophical side of his complex (Gemini) personality. That fall, Price was on a fifty-five-city lecture and book-signing tour, and the press, usually extremely Price-friendly, were full of questions about an extraordinary controversy which had arisen. Since the actor's appearance on *The $64,000 Challenge* three years earlier, many quiz shows had come under fire for coaching contestants, although Price categorically denied allegations and never was implicated in the scandal.

It was in January 1960 that the partnership began which would cement Price's place in the cinema history books. Young producer/director Roger Corman, who had been making successful low-budget black-and-white films for American International Pictures (AIP), sold AIP on the concept of making one color movie on twice the allotment. He chose as his subject an atmospheric tale by Edgar Allan Poe, an American icon in the classrooms but poorly represented on celluloid. *House of Usher* integrated all the elements which would make so successful the eight Price Poe pictures Corman eventually directed. The actor's intelligence, his aristocratic voice and bearing, combined with an ability to communicate larger-than-life sensitivity and angst, not only made the unbelievable believable but profitable as well. The films were shot in less than three weeks and often with dozens of setups each day. Price (who had always been a quick study) had no objection to the pace; in fact, he "much prefer[red] to do things on a short, quick schedule. . . . Basically you learned your lines and did it. Got on with it, you know? And then you'd do other pictures that would take nine months, and you'd feel like having the baby and getting *out* of there. Oh, boy!"

AIP's next vehicle for its new star, *Master of the World*, was an attempt to further exploit the science-fiction works of Jules Verne. (Disney had made *20,000 Leagues Under the Sea* in 1954, and Fox released *Journey to the Center of the Earth* in 1959.) But the limited budget, which didn't seem to cramp the style of the AIP Poe films set on *terra firma*, was all too obvious in a tale dominated by a giant airship, although Price excelled as the highly moral if highly monomaniacal inventor, Robur. (To some degree, the "limited budget" also applied to Price's salary. Although many sources have reported that the actor received upwards of $80,000 and even $100,000 per film, in fact, his fee for at least the first two American International movies was $35,000, paid in installments of $3,000 per month over the subsequent year.) The year 1961 began with the second in the Corman/AIP Poe series—*Pit and the Pendulum* was a highly atmospheric, beautifully lensed film, and in Nicholas Medina, Price created one of his most memorable characters, a tortured

man driven to torture by passion and deceit. That spring and summer, the actor spent several months in Italy filming *Rage of the Buccaneers* with Ricardo Montalban and *Queen of the Nile* with Jeanne Crain. Price made only a handful of foreign films which were dubbed into English; these two, both costume pictures, gave him little opportunity to act but every opportunity to discover what the museums and galleries of Europe had to offer.

In press interviews Price tended to simplify the reasons for his success in costume horror pictures by pointing to the trend in the fifties and sixties toward Method acting and "mumbling." Classically trained actors who spoke clearly and succinctly, perhaps less naturally, were a far cry from angry young rebels like Brando and Dean. "We make the unbelievable believable," Price once charged. "The Method actor makes the believable unbelievable. It's really true. Nobody is as real as those people Method actors play. The Method actor is doing as much make-believe as the actor who is playing the most flamboyant part in a horror picture. Brando is one of the most flamboyant, baroque actors who ever lived, but that's not real. I've never met anybody like that. . . . Those of us who were more classical were consigned to costume dramas. Even those so-called horror movies were costume dramas." Like many of his colleagues, Price disliked the term "horror movies," preferring the more accurate description "Gothic." Horror movies, as far as Price was concerned, were "the modern terror films featuring overdoses of gore and sadism and sex."

During his long career, Price frequently lent his voice (often without fee) to student projects and even industrial films. *Naked Terror* was a feature-length documentary depicting "the savage native Zulus of Africa." His next movie, *Convicts 4*, was the true saga of a convicted felon whose rehabilitation was brought about by the discovery of his artistic talent. It was the only time Price ever played an art expert on film, although the appearance was a cameo. *Confessions of an Opium Eater*, made in October, was a seedy exploitation picture which cast Price in his only action role. He went immediately into another Roger Corman Poe film, *Tales of Terror*, a trilogy of stories which gave him great latitude to strut his stuff. He excelled in all three segments, working with cohorts Basil Rathbone and Peter Lorre. Vicent was especially busy in 1961 in addition to his acting. He was invited to serve on the White House Art Committee, the only actor ever to do so, advising the new president's wife, Jackie Kennedy, on the restoration of paintings. "The place had been allowed to go to ruin," he confided. "Former Presidents had pillaged it. Jackie once found a magnificent head of Washington in the men's room in the basement." That year, Vincent also wrote *The Book of Joe*, an endearing little memoir about his love affair with animals, dogs in general, and one dog in particular. The hero of the story was Price's companion of fourteen years, the mongrel mutt he had purchased in the wake of his first divorce.

In January 1962, Price found himself making a highly unexpected disclosure to Deanna Durbin and her husband, whom he and his wife had visited during a recent trip to France. "My poor Mary, who if you remember was ailing that night and throughout our stay in Paris, came home to find that the cause of her complaint was proof that we aren't as old as we thought we were. She is presenting me with a Baby Price somewhere around the first of May. We are overjoyed at the prospect naturally and looking forward to being born again in it." Price's second child, Mary Victoria, was born on April 27, 1962—twenty-two years after his son, Barrett. Vincent was devoted to the little blond girl, proudly saving scribbles and annotating them with her full name and the date. He attended school activities and displayed an early example of her artistic abilities on Art Linkletter's television show. (In October, Mr. and Mrs. Barrett Price welcomed son Jody Barrett, and Vincent became a grandfather and a new father in the same year. Grandson Kier Christopher was born in 1963.) "I would love to have had six children," Price admitted in the eighties, "but none of my wives was interested. In fact, when I married Coral in 1974 [when he was sixty-three and she sixty-one], she said, 'It's too late, dear—thank God!'"

Right after the birth of his daughter, Price's career—and life—took on another challenge from an unlikely source. "For twenty-five years I had been carrying on the battle of bringing art to people in their daily living," he explained. "I have a kind of self-appointed mission to try and interest the public in American art." The ubiquitous Sears, Roebuck and Company approached Vincent in his capacity of art expert/enthusiast with a completely unique and irresistible idea: to put together a collection of fine art to be sold in Sears stores across the nation. The Vincent Price Collection (Price had enough faith in the project to permit his name to be attached to it) began with twenty-seven hundred items; over the next decade, the actor purchased some fifty-five thousand pieces. In general, the art was a tie-in with sales in the home-furnishing and furniture departments, based on the promotional theme that a work of art was the ultimate in home decoration. Price went to major markets throughout the United States and in Western Europe locating classical and contemporary artwork by Rembrandt, Dürer, Goya, and Chagall as well as a number of first-rate but unknown young people. Mary Price was also very involved in the project, designing the mats and frames for the paintings, lithographs, and etchings. While in New York City to promote his movie *Tales of Terror*,

Vincent "had a morning off" and went to a few galleries, "picking up" one-hundred Chagalls, thirteen Picassos, and eleven Miros. "We're bringing art, fine art, to the people," he explained proudly. ". . . What matters in art is the beauty, not the money."

Back on-screen, Price appeared in another version of the 1939 "historical" horror film which had first teamed him with Karloff and Rathbone. Roger Corman's *Tower of London* was as faithful to history as the first movie, which is to say, hardly at all, although Price improved his rank, playing King Richard III instead of princely brother the duke of Clarence. *Diary of a Madman*, made in July, explored the cinematic potential of French writer Guy de Maupassant, and the actor was convincing as a late-nineteenth-century magistrate possessed by an evil entity which causes him to kill. Price's old friend Boris Karloff was brought into the AIP fold in September for *The Raven*, joining Vincent and Peter Lorre in a comedy which included a young Jack Nicholson in the cast. *Twice-Told Tales* was a predominantly unsuccessful attempt to mine the horrific potential of the works of Nathaniel Hawthorne, spiffing up a segment rehashing *The House of the Seven Gables*, with the house gushing blood as it collapsed.

Vincent was back in Italy in January 1963 as *The Last Man on Earth*, based on an original novel by Poe film adaptor Richard Matheson. The black-and-white picture effectively created an atmosphere of a bleak, plague-ridden world, and the actor was understated as the weary, unique human being of the title, spending his days dispatching vampires created by a deadly disease. Price's spooky activities weren't confined to the movie screen. In May he participated in a wonderful stunt at the Movieland Wax Museum in Buena Park, California, replacing his own sculpted figure in their *House of Wax* exhibit. Motionless when customers entered the room, he "came to life" and squirted the crowd with a large hypodermic full of water. The escapade merited front-page coverage in the *Los Angeles Times*.

Perhaps the new lease on life supplied by his baby had rejuvenated Price. The actor had a delightfully groovy cameo in AIP's teen-oriented *Beach Party*, although he was back in the dungeon again for *The Haunted Palace*, playing the dual role of a warlock burned at the stake and the descendant whose body he uses to wreak revenge on the scions of the villagers who condemned him. *The Comedy of Terrors* teamed up four masters of the Gothic-suspense genre—Price, Karloff, Lorre, and Basil Rathbone—in a cheerfully silly farce. Next, Vincent was off to England—the beginning of a professional trend which would continue for two decades—for *The Masque of the Red Death*, which had a literate screenplay and photography by acclaimed cameraman Nicolas Roeg. The film

Twice-Told Tales VP shares a cigarette with a costar (another costar, Mari Blanchard, who had guarded the secret of Greek Fire in *Son of Sinbad*, looks on)

War-Gods of the Deep

Helping "harrassed workmen" hang paintings for a Sears show of The Vincent Price Collection at the Los Angeles Sports Arena, first week of October, 1964. "Shortly afterwards, he greeted guests, calm, quiet and collected in a tux. The beard is being grown for a movie Mr. Price will be starting in London mid-October (*War-Gods of the Deep*)." (*Herald Examiner* Collection, Los Angeles Public Library)

Batman As Special Guest Villain Egghead with "Chief" Edward Everett Horton

H.G. Wells's *2267 AD—When The Sleeper Awakes* Trade announcement for a film which was never made

Witchfinder General With Mary Grant Price and producer Philip Waddilove, between takes

"Cauliflower McPugg" gives VP a few pugilistic pointers on *The Red Skelton Show*

*Co*Star* Record album jacket

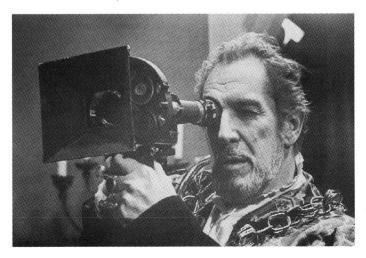

Scream and Scream Again On the set with a couple of young fans

Cry of the Banshee VP gets behind the camera

was highly regarded by critics and audiences alike. While in London, Vincent purchased some $30,000 worth of art to be shipped back to the States for Sears, reportedly rushing off one day during a break in filming while still in makeup. "So far this year I've bought works worth nearly three-quarters of a million dollars," he admitted. "I guess no one's been buying on this scale since the Medici."

At the 1964 Oscars, the winner of Best Two-Reel Documentary was a short subject called *Chagall*, for which Price had recorded the narration. On June 24, he flew to London and the very next day was having costume fittings for *The Tomb of Ligeia*, the last of Roger Corman's Poe films. A complex, psychologically driven screenplay about a love which survives beyond death made for an intriguing picture and a fine ending to a successful series. Price followed it in October with the unconvincing *War-Gods of the Deep* and then immediately went into rehearsals for a role he was surely born to play—"the swiniest swine in the world," Captain Hook, in an L.A. production of the immortal *Peter Pan* which ran over Christmas.

Seizing the opportunity to capitalize on a recent movie trend of "shockumentaries" (like *Mondo Cane*), AIP had purchased the domestic rights to an exploitation picture called *Taboos of the World* and in March 1965 had their contract star record a voice-over narration for the film's American distribution. He then headlined their extremely successful sci-fi/horror comedy *Dr. Goldfoot and the Bikini Machine*. That same year, Price was presented with the George Washington Carver Memorial Institute Award, bestowed annually for outstanding contribution to art, science, education, and the betterment of race relations.

In addition to his autobiography and buddy Joe's story, Vincent had edited two art books, one a collection of Delacroix and the other a Bible with plate illustrations of the works of Michelangelo. In 1965, Mr. and Mrs. Price collaborated on *A Treasury of Great Recipes*, a handsome, leather-tooled volume which included submissions from the greatest restaurants in Europe as well as the ultimate in haute cuisine, "L.A. Dodger Dogs," fresh from the stadium. ("There is nothing quite as good as a hot dog at the ballpark.") Friend Jane Russell remembers meals at the Price's Benedict Canyon home. "[Mary and Vincent] were wonderful together. They had the biggest kitchen in the whole world, and all these pots and pans hanging down, and they were going through recipes, and Vinnie was being uproarious, and Mary was trying to keep him on the straight and narrow, because she wasn't as nutty as Vinnie. We had a ball." *Treasury* remained in print for years and still has pride of place on many gourmet shelves; in 1994, one of its recipes

was printed in an issue of *Bon Appetit* magazine. Vincent, however, never liked the appellation "gourmet." "I'm *not* a gourmet chef," he insisted. "I'm a home cooker. Gourmet is a word I really despise. It just means you put a lot of sauce on something that isn't very good. No, I just study cooking. . . . I love to eat, and loving to eat, I love learning how to eat well. . . . I believe the history of cultures is bound very much with the history of cuisine." Vincent was always making notes for articles and doodling potential titles: "Gentleman in the Kitchen," "The Can, The Cook, and Creativity," and "How To Become A Born Cook."

He continued to be busy on the small screen, appearing on the popular *The Man From U.N.C.L.E.*, and of course the cult favorite *Batman* (filmed at his old studio, Fox), on which he was "Guest Villain" Egghead, a.k.a. "Eggy Baby." For 1966–67, American International Pictures announced a "big planned program of twenty feature productions," which included the return of *Dr. Goldfoot*, *The Trip* (Jack Nicholson's film), and the never-realized *2267 A.D.* . . *When the Sleeper Awakes.* (*Sleeper* was a pet project of Louis M. "Deke" Heyward's, which the producer describes as a futuristic story loosely based on H. G. Wells about a ruler kept in suspended animation for a thousand years, until he is reawakened to take over the government.) The promised sequel, *Dr. Goldfoot and the Girl Bombs*, filmed in Italy in March, was overwhelmed by a myriad of weaknesses, not the least of which was that it had a bad screenplay and later was equally badly dubbed. Price's next professional engagement couldn't have been more American: In September, he was a judge at the Miss America Pageant in Atlantic City. A couple of weeks later, he flew to South Africa to make *The Jackals*, a standard Western story in which he had a wonderful role as a grizzled, rum-swigging prospector.

In April 1967 he was once again out of costume for modern evildoings in *House of a Thousand Dolls*, indulging in white slavery under cover of a magician's cloak. *Witchfinder General* (U.S. title: *Conqueror Worm*) brought him back to London in November for a film which remains a highly regarded but heavy-handed example of absolute power corrupting absolutely. As the title character, Price managed to inject chilling touches of feeling into the proceedings, but the explicit sadism depicted was a far cry from the implied menace and atmosphere which hallmarked his earlier films. Perhaps it was more a sign of the times and the direction in which horror films, in fact, films in general, were heading. Price left England on the red-eye after the last night of filming of *Witchfinder* to go into rehearsals for the stage musical *Married Alive!* After out-of-town tryouts, the show became *Darling of the Day* for its Broadway opening. It was to be one of the major personal disappointments of his career, closing in less than four weeks; a series of production problems led to mixed critical reviews, although audiences enjoyed the story of a famous artist who embarks on a new life after faking his own death.

Price's next two films had him working in the Old West. In June 1968 he had a nice supporting role in *More Dead Than Alive*, in which big Clint Walker played a reformed gunfighter vainly attempting to escape his "killer" image. In the fall Price played a showy scene as a traveling road show lecturer in an Elvis Presley vehicle called *The Trouble With Girls*, although he didn't act opposite the King.

Throughout the years, an enormous number of Price's prolific television credits had been comedic. On shows opposite Danny Kaye, Milton Berle, George Gobel, Tennessee Ernie Ford, and Jack Benny, he enjoyed "making fun of the character who became known as 'Vincent Price.'" In 1968, he made one of several appearances on Red Skelton's show, co–guest starring with Boris Karloff. In 1989, Red wrote his old friend: "Vincent, you have always been my favorite person, and as an actor, if I had it my way, and I am sure the public too, you would have a room filled with Oscars, Emmys, Tonys, and whatever awards are given for talent, plus a special award for elegance and eloquence—and I say this at every press interview I give, for you are an inspiration." In November, Price went back to England for *The Oblong Box*, for which British horror king Christopher Lee was given special guest-star billing, although he and Vincent had only a single short scene together. Around that time, AIP had Price recite a voice-over poem for an arty foreign horror film it was distributing in America called *Spirits of the Dead*.

In the spring of 1969, Price starred in the contemporary sci-fi picture *Scream and Scream Again*. It was his first teaming with both Christopher Lee and *his* oft-costar Peter Cushing. Coincidentally, all three men shared the astrological sign of Gemini: Cushing was born on May 26; Price and Lee, on the same day, May 27. That was more than they had to do with each other in *Scream and Scream Again*, however; they would have to wait nearly fifteen years before all three made another movie together. In the fall Price recorded one of his more popular albums, *Witchcraft and Magic*, taping all 122 pages of text at a single sitting, a five-hour job. Over the decades Price made many diverse recordings, ranging from American poetry and art appreciation to the "rap" for the 1982 Michael Jackson megahit song "Thriller," which earned the actor both gold and platinum records.

The next month, Vincent returned to the United Kingdom for AIP's *Cry of the Banshee*, another standard costume horror. The film's press kit quoted Price as saying,

"I'm sure if I'd done other things in my career, I could be more distinguished. On the other hand, of course, I could be starving." That presupposes that he had a choice. Price's decade-long association with American International Pictures, at first a guarantee of steady employment, was now a double-edged sword. The AIP films had cemented his status as the Horror King, but the terms of his contract prohibited him from capitalizing on that reputation and making genre films for any other studio. Meanwhile, AIP kept stranding their star in unimaginative, unworthy vehicles. In a March 1970 letter to his agent, Price was clearly unhappy: "I'm sure when you made the original contract you never thought of the very serious consequences that all-exclusivity clause could cause. I hope you can make [Arkoff] see how it keeps me from doing anything for the next three years in that line. I like the English script 'The House That Dripped Blood.' . . . I'd like to do it. . . . It certainly can't hurt to be in a good film—it might even carry me over the next lousy one AIP might make me do."

Visiting Paris in 1961, Price had been "so happy and so lucky to be away from this inconsequential inferno called Hollywood." By the end of the decade, the actor who felt so much promise in his new hometown in 1938 was "completely disenchanted with California. I never thought it would happen. The smog, the city that became physically enormous but never grew with it. You don't feel safe there anymore. . . . I was in London when Sharon Tate and the others were murdered. . . . The ideal thing would be to live half the time in London. . . ." He found solace onstage and in a proliferation of TV appearances. During the 1970s, Price toured three times in another tailor-made role, playing Fagin in the musical *Oliver!* He continued to make dozens and dozens of guest stints on popular TV shows: *Mod Squad, Love, American Style, Laugh-In, Columbo, Rod Serling's Night Gallery, The Bionic Woman, The Love Boat*. He starred in an innovative, sixty-minute, one-man interpretation of *An Evening of Edgar Allan Poe* and was a favorite regular on *The Hollywood Squares* for over a decade. In November 1970 he was back in London for one of his most popular horror films. As *The Abominable Dr. Phibes*, he created a truly memorable character, one of the few he played in extensive effects makeup. Directed by Robert Fuest, the film had a handsome art deco production design in keeping with its 1920s setting. The witty script concocted nine diabolical murders by which the methodical Phibes dispatched the operating team he held responsible for the death of his beloved wife.

Price's speaking engagements weren't confined to the lectern. In April of their 1971 season, the Saint Louis Symphony Orchestra world-premiered conductor Leonard Slatkin's "The Raven." It was Slatkin's first composition for full orchestra and consisted of four Poe poems read to the music by a narrator. At the end of the final instrumental piece, the entire orchestra shouted, "Nevermore!" Price had been submitted the concept, and on agreement, the piece was written with him in mind.

On May 27, 1971, Vincent Price turned sixty. His career, covering every medium, had spanned more than thirty-five years. He would be ubiquitous over the next decade, achieving even greater popularity among baby boomers, who regarded him with both affection and respect. The early greats (Lugosi, Karloff, Rathbone, Lorre, Chaney Jr.) were gone; Brits Lee and Cushing failed to achieve international stardom; upcoming "slasher stars" were never in contention. Vincent Price gracefully took his place as the unrivaled Master of Menace, and fans would come to consider him a permanent fixture in their lives.

Before flying to London in December to begin the inevitable (and inferior) sequel *Dr. Phibes Rises Again*, Price served as master of ceremonies at the U.S. State Department's celebration party marking the twenty-sixth anniversary of the United Nations. In April 1972 the Missouri Repertory Theatre invited Vincent to join it for the upcoming summer season, offering the roles of James Tyrone in *Long Day's Journey Into Night* and Beckett in *Murder in the Cathedral*. Performance dates would have conflicted with the filming of his next movie; Price's notes on the correspondence include "Answered No *damn it*." Clearly it was the kind of work he would have liked to have done, and he was chafing at continual professional restrictions. "I have been on the road for almost ten years," he wrote his agent with uncharacteristic bitterness. "Obviously I have not been able to save enough to retire if I wanted to . . . but the question before me at 61 is not money but peace of mind—some family life—AND dignity in my profession. I have managed to *survive* all the crap of AIP, of Sears' destruction of my art image, but the wear and tear has me down at long last, and now I want to settle things before I find myself permanently unsettled by the dissonances of my life." Price's next project would be challenging enough to alleviate some professional upheaval, although one of his costars would have an enormous impact on personal "dissonances."

Theater of Blood was shot in London in July and August, with Price in a dream role as a fed-up Shakespearean actor who dispatches his unappreciative critics in murders straight out of the plays of the Immortal Bard. The concept was irresistible, the script one of the cleverest and most erudite ever for a so-called horror film. The all-star cast boasted a single female victim—Coral Browne a woman as well known for her salty sense of humor as for her gifts as an actress.

Edith Coral Brown (she added the *e*) was born on July 23, 1913, in Melbourne, Australia. Well educated, she studied painting before making acting her career and had appeared in twenty-eight plays before arriving in England at the age of twenty-one. Tall, with a statuesque bearing and a commanding voice, Coral amassed impressive credits in the West End. She was considered the prime exponent of drawing-room comedy in the 1930s and was equally well received in Shakespeare. Her film debut came in 1935, but American audiences knew her best for Rosalind Russell's *Auntie Mame* (1958). A marriage in 1950 to agent Philip Pearman had ended with his death in 1964. The *London Times* called Coral Browne "one of the wittiest actresses of her generation and an equally striking personality off it." She was renowned for a "robust" sense of humor, and stories about her bawdy remarks were legendary—and unprintable; writer Christopher Buckley described her as speaking "like a grand duchess who has spent some time in East End pubs." Although Price was a married man, he was immediately struck by the actress, whom he likened to "the Great Barrier Reef—beautiful, exotic, and dangerous. . . . I was like a bird dog." "I remember he electrocuted me on my birthday," Coral would later comment; "That was the scene where I killed her," Vincent agreed. "I said to Diana Rigg, 'I understand it's Miss Browne's birthday. What could I get her?' And Diana said, 'Well, I know what she wants. You!'" With his personal life in flux, Price's next movie wasn't until a year later. *Madhouse*, shot in May 1973, had an entertaining premise, a horror-film star caught up in a series of murders which appear to have been committed by his own fiendish film character. It could have scored on the strength of Price's popularity and his scenes with the equally classy Peter Cushing, but the poor script made for a disappointment.

That fall, Price was the subject of a *This Is Your Life* television tribute. Guests included lifelong friend Ted Thomas, AIP's Sam Arkoff, a representative from the U.S. Secretary of the Interior's Department of Indian Affairs, his wife, Mary, and children Barrett and Victoria. It was one of the family's last appearances together; Price and Coral Browne were deeply in love, and Mary sued for divorce in August 1973. The following February, 1974, Coral was in London rehearsing a play. The actress was miserable, the director was "utterly incapable," and worse, she was desperately missing Vincent. "Love you most terrible like and want to be with you SO SO SO SO much—frightfully low today & that makes my need even greater—WHY ARE WE APART—" she wrote furiously. From the beginning, many gossip items appeared in print about their liberated lifestyle, which Vincent explained: "Coral and I have formed the permissive society for the elderly."

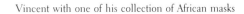
Vincent with one of his collection of African masks

Oliver! As Fagin

An Evening of Edgar Allan Poe (1970) "The Pit and the Pendulum" segment

Here's Lucy VP charms everybody's favorite redhead in 1970

Dr. Phibes Rises Again With Valli Kemp, Valerie Heyward, Robert Quarry, Fiona Lewis, Louis M. "Deke" Heyward

Letters between them and the frank recollections of friends reflect a relationship as physically passionate as it was emotionally fulfilling. As to why they hadn't made it official: "I just want it to be a love affair for a while," he said.

Perhaps ironically, Price's next film was a British sex farce called *Percy's Progress*. The American title, *It's Not the Size That Counts*, says it all. That year he also made his only Canadian picture, *Journey Into Fear*, a routine political thriller. Price didn't make another movie for four years. Activities in his other areas of interest kept him busy, beginning with his personal life. By the summer of 1974 the papers were referring to Vincent and Coral as "inseparable." After quietly taking out a license at the Santa Barbara County Courthouse on October 24, the couple married. The judge only came in on Saturdays, so they had to get an attorney whose secretary acted as witness. "Halfway through the ceremony," Coral described, "Vincent remembers there's no wedding ring. My fingers are jammed with rings, so I take one off and slip it on the appropriate finger. Then off we go to a Mexican restaurant for the reception, just the two of us. And there was no honeymoon. I had arranged to cook dinner for Maggie Smith the following night." Later, the new Mrs. Price wore a proper engagement ring, quite delicate, with two tiny diamonds set in it. "It's the smallest diamond in the world," Coral complained. "I don't want you to get secure" was her loving husband's rejoinder.

Back in 1935, Vincent's career had been launched in an English private club and not in a legitimate theater. So forty years later, when he and his bride costarred in Jean Anouilh's *Ardele*, the production marked the actor's official debut in London's illustrious West End. Other stage appearances during that time included return engagements as the Devil on summer tours in 1976 and 1978 in the hit stage musical *Damn Yankees* and *Charley's Aunt* with Coral and Roddy McDowall. (When Vincent played *Damn Yankees* in St. Louis, the producers asked the enthusiastic baseball fan if he wanted to throw out the first pitch in a Cardinals/Mets game.) On February 22, 1977, Edith Barrett died in Albuquerque, New Mexico. Rancor on both sides had dwindled; indeed, her notes during the sixties sent love to Mary, and when Vincent and Coral opened in *Ardele*, she wired a gracious congratulatory telegram.

In 1969, Price had mused: "Oh, one day I'll probably stop these [horror] films and sit back waiting for the right part to turn up. I've always felt that my greatest success would come at the end of my career." He was right, and it wasn't in a film. The theater had established Vincent Price's career, and it was on stages all over the world that he delivered what can be argued was his finest performance as an actor. During a strike by the Writers Guild of America, noted teleplaywright and dramatist John Gay had taken advantage of forced unemployment to create a remarkable one-man show based on the life and works of Oscar Wilde. *Diversions and Delights* was a tour de force; fiercely funny and poignantly moving, it would be the challenge of a career. Coral encouraged her husband, "Go stick your neck out," and Vincent devoted himself to careful research and months of grueling preparation for the role of the brilliant, tragic author. *Diversions* opened in San Francisco at the Marines' Memorial Theatre on July 11, 1977. Critics across the country raved: "Superlative," "Virtuoso," "One-man brilliance not to be missed." For the next five years, on and off, Price would tour with *Diversions and Delights*, giving eight hundred performances in three hundred cities. He played showcase amphitheaters and rural college campuses, taking the show as far as Hong Kong and Sydney. Sometimes it lasted ten minutes longer due to audience laughter and applause. *Diversions* had a very brief Broadway run in April 1978 but was better suited to smaller, more intimate houses in which Price's magnetism and Wilde's tragedy could touch audiences on a personal level. In many ways it was the performance of a lifetime. "I believe my role as Oscar Wilde was my . . . great achievement as an actor," Price reflected in 1992. "It was really extraordinary. It was the only time ever in my whole life when I really, completely, fell into the character. I was really able to escape into . . . the wit and brilliance of the man. A divine feeling." It was a feeling shared by audiences who were astounded by the depth and subtlety of an actor whose performances were sometimes criticized for being "over the top." Lamentably, plans to preserve the show on video never materialized.

In September 1977, Vincent was in Detroit and Chicago with *Diversions*. Coral was increasingly concerned about his health. "You are *not* as tough as you think—& you really must be *tougher* & refuse to do so much TV, etc. WHAT is the point of all this if the end is Forest Lawn—if you don't care about yourself you really must think of me—I simply couldn't cope with my life without you & we *should* have a few years left, with any luck so PLEASE see to it that we do. . . . PLEASE buy a book & stay in your room 24 hours one day a week. . . ." Throughout most of his career Price was seemingly *driven* to work. "Life has a funny way of sidetracking one," he once wrote his daughter-in-law, "of making too important things of the moment, but I've never learned—and I guess I never will—how to put work aside when it is too much and just have fun with the ones I love. It's the curse of the American male, but perhaps in time it is curable." For Vincent Price, apparently it never was. At least he occasionally had the opportunity to work with his wife: in the spring of 1979 they costarred in a short-lived weekly TV series called *Time Express*, guiding guests back in time in an effort to change their past and influence their future.

Price took off a few days from *Diversions* in April to play a cameo in the star-studded comedy *Scavenger Hunt*. In July he recorded the narration for the reality-based *Days of Fury*, a feature-length "up-to-the-minute account of disasters that have changed our world." He *didn't* make a picture which frequently turns up in Price filmographies—*Romance in a Jugular Vein*, an Australian project eventually produced under the title *Outback Vampires* and released on video as *The Wicked*. Other titles which sometimes erroneously appear in Price's feature film credits include *The Butterfly Ball* (a three-minute animated short), *Escapes* (a straight-to-video horror omnibus), and *Devil's Triangle* (a fifty-five-minute, nontheatrical maritime documentary.) In 1980, Vincent and Coral were joint emcees at the Eleventh Annual Los Angeles Drama Critics Awards (LADCA), which the *Los Angeles Times* called "the most stylish cornucopia of glitter and tribute in the LADCA's eleven year history." The two artists got a bit of their own back with a screening of the trailer for *Theater of Blood*. In May, Price went back to England to make *The Monster Club*, a horror anthology for which his contribution consisted of framing wraparounds with old friend John Carradine, with whom he had last worked in the fifties in *The Story of Mankind*.

Throughout his life Vincent was a talk-show host's dream—charming, witty, never without a story. Appearances on *Mike Douglas*, *Dinah Shore*, *John Davidson*, *Art Linkletter*, *Merv Griffin*, *Joan Rivers*, and on the *Tonight* show made him a familiar face in homes across the country. Earlier in 1980, PBS television had begun an anthology series called *Mystery!* which presented British thrillers, suspense stories, and detective dramas. The original host, film critic Gene Shalit, was dropped after a dispute with the producing station in Boston, WGBH. Vincent Price was announced as his replacement in November; it was a relationship the actor would maintain with the popular series for the next decade. For weekly audiences, Vincent became a familiar, elegantly clad fixture, seated in the wonderful Edward Goreyesque set. He himself was a longtime mystery buff: "While I was touring *Don Juan in Hell* with Charles Boyer, Sir Cedric Hardwicke, and Agnes Moorehead, Charles wouldn't fly, so we traveled by bus. We bought paper bags full of paperback mysteries and thrillers. We made a pact. If a girl hadn't been seduced or if there hadn't been a murder by page thirty, out it went. Cedric and Charles were men of great dignity, but they were seen throwing paperbacks out the windows of the bus. We must have gone through four or five hundred."

In May 1981, Vincent received a letter from an executive at Walt Disney Studios introducing "a very talented young [Disney] artist—Tim Burton. His style is entirely original . . . you are his idol. I thought you might enjoy the enclosed rough outline for a book which Tim put together one evening while watching a movie of yours on the late show. It is my hope to eventually put this story into animation—as a Disney cartoon short." That rough outline became *Vincent*, a six-minute, black-and-white, stop-motion animated short which cost about $60,000 to make. It was an "off the lot" project, meaning that Disney put up the funds, and the team of designer/director Burton, creative producer Rick Heinrich, animator Stephen Chiodo, and cameraman Victor Abdalov was responsible for production. Price recorded the poem which comprised the story line in December 1981: "Vincent Malloy is seven years old / He's always polite, and does what he's told. / For a boy his age, he's considerate and nice. / But he wants to be just like—Vincent Price." Instead of a T-shirt and shorts, the youngster envisions himself in a smoking jacket with a cigarette holder and sporting a tiny mustache. He imagines dipping his sister in wax and exhumes his "wife's body" from his mother's flower garden. At the end he collapses artistically in the "tower of doom" (when his mother banishes him to his room), quoting "The Raven." The project was unabashedly autobiographical for the twenty-four-year-old Burton, who had grown up on Price's Poe films. "I was hoping at best that Vincent would think [the poem] was just kind of a nice kind of fan letter," he admits with a laugh. "I realized as he read it that he completely understood what it was about; that made me feel special. I was very nervous about the whole situation, since it was the first thing I'd done, but Vincent set the tone for me. Obviously he didn't need my help [during the recording], but he was interested in what I thought. He always made *you* feel comfortable. That's the brilliance of a great and sensitive and confident person—it taught me to be confident enough about myself to hear other people and work with people. Because that's the fun of it; that's the energy. You're not alone." Production was completed by the summer of 1982, and *Vincent* won Best Short Subject at the Chicago Film Festival, although distribution was minimal.

Price's enormous influence on popular culture even manifested itself in *Penthouse* magazine. The July 1981 issue featured articles on Reagan's economy, the American hostages in Iran, and "the increasingly complex amatory misadventures of Ron Embleton and Bob Guccione's amazing heroine, Sweet Chastity." The six-page color comic began: "Multi-billionaire Howard Huge has agreed to finance Vincent, 13th Baron, Von Frankenstein's attempt to make the perfect woman." The Baron is a surprisingly faithful likeness of Price, who succeeds

Dr. Anton Phibes

The Brady Bunch Way-leid in Hawaii in 1972

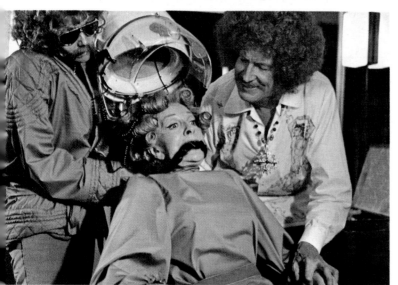

Theater of Blood Coral Browne gets her final shampoo, set, and pedicure

Diversions and Delights As Oscar Wilde (photo by Martha Swope)

The Monster Club VP suggests a drink from an unusual menu

The naked truth about salad dressings.

"People can get pretty tired of the usual bottled dressings," says Vincent Price. "But even the most ordinary dressings take on a fresh note with just a teaspoon of Angostura® aromatic bitters per pint. Or try this: a great new sour cream dressing. Blend 1 pint sour cream, 2 teaspoons salt, 2 teaspoons sugar, 2 tablespoons herb vinegar, 2 teaspoons Angostura. Fold in 5 tablespoons minced onion and chill. And what goes great with a cool salad? A frosty pink gin and tonic made with two dashes of Angostura. Refreshing. And that's the naked truth." For 82 other recipes, write to: FREE COOKBOOK, Box 123, Elmhurst, N.Y. 11373.

1971 *TV Guide* advertisement for cooking tips

The Butterfly Ball—a 1974 animated short based on a song and book of the same name, about a day when animals stop fighting among themselves and go into the forest for a fantastic feast

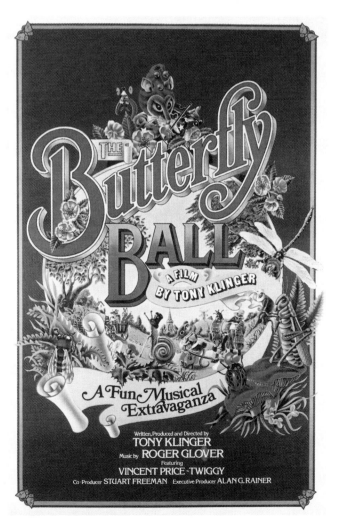

in creating an outrageously voluptuous naked heroine, with a mane of pink hair. Apropos of Reaganism, Price had been an outspoken critic of the president, not the least reason for which was that "When Reagan was a spokesman years ago for our actors' union in Los Angeles, he was in charge of negotiations about the showing of old movies on television. He didn't negotiate repeat fees for actors. Last year, thirty-five of my films were shown on television, and I didn't get a penny. I'm disappointed that Reagan didn't have the foresight to see that TV would have to live on old movies."

In December 1981, Vincent collaborated for the only time with writer son V. B. Price. Their book *Monsters* was an exhaustively researched, lavishly illustrated homage which included dinosaurs, Charles Manson, literary characters, and the Loch Ness Monster. Early in 1982 the actor returned to Gilbert and Sullivan for the first time since amateur days in 1934, singing and dancing in the spooky *Ruddigore*, an entry in an ambitious British television series of the famous operettas. In August he was back to England for his first movie in two years, *House of the Long Shadows*, which reunited him with Christopher Lee, Peter Cushing, and John Carradine. "It's not nasty or distasteful," he said at the time. "We just go all out to scare audiences. It's what's expected of us." Unfortunately, audiences also expected a sensible story, and the finished product did not make for an auspicious reunion.

In 1983, Coral Browne won the Best Actress Award from the British Academy of Film & Television Arts for her autobiographical role in *An Englishman Abroad*. Written by Alan Bennett and directed by John Schlesinger, the telefilm was based on an actual experience of the actress—meeting notorious British spy Guy Burgess while she was in Russia on a 1958 tour with the Royal Shakespeare Company. Apparently, Cher was also at the awards ceremony; Coral described the tall, slender singer as "dressed all in black. She looked like a burnt out twig from the stake of Joan of Arc." In that same year, the Prices faced a devastating crisis, and Vincent, who had always been "very religious," converted to Catholicism, his wife's faith. Just prior to *An Englishman Abroad*, Coral was diagnosed with breast cancer. She would undergo several surgeries, and though she railed against it, her slow decline would contribute to the subsequent infrequency of Vincent's film work. His only picture in 1983 was *Bloodbath at the House of Death*, a tasteless English horror/comedy.

The Yale Film Study Center sponsored a six-day Vincent Price retrospective for their famous grad in March 1984. A young campus writer for the *Yale Alumni Magazine* was "one of the few members of Price's entourage who managed to keep up with the actor during his whirl-wind University visit. . . . At 73, Price is vigorous, elegantly trim, warm, mannerly and witty. His energy seems boundless." He expended a lot of that energy in his next movie. Despite the fact that *The Great Mouse Detective* was an animated film, Price's "role" as Professor Ratigan, the evil nemesis of Basil, the Sherlock Holmes–like mouse, was one of his best and most full bodied performances. That fall, his voice also graced the small screen—on the popular Saturday morning cartoon series *The 13 Ghosts of Scooby-Doo*, as host "Vincent Van Ghoul."

In October the Hollywood Press Club presented Price with its Annual Life Achievement Award, and for the next year or so, he made a concerted effort to retire. "I almost lost my marbles," he complained. Gardening only took five hours a week; the microwave made cooking a snap. He looked for books "I couldn't put down—never found them." When an opportunity came to work, he grabbed at it. In April 1986, Price contributed the framing story to a contemporary, graphic horror film called *The Offspring*. "I believe in this kind of low-budget filmmaking," he said during production. "There is something very genuine about young people attempting something of quality on a low budget." His next project was exactly the type of film in which he deserved to have been involved more often. Shot in the fall on an island off the coast of Maine, *The Whales of August* was a gentle, character-driven vignette which teamed Price not with aging horror stars but cinema legends Lillian Gish, Bette Davis, and Ann Sothern. "You could barely get on the set for all the crutches and canes in the way," Vincent joked. "It looked like Lourdes." Price's role of a courteous Russian émigré wasn't a large one, but he was happy: "You don't have to carry the picture. You walk in, play your little scene, and walk out with people remembering you. I notice that most of the lines critics quote are mine, so I must have made some impression." *Whales* was produced by an independent company called Alive Films; the combined ages of the stars prompted Coral Browne to comment wryly that it should be titled *Just Barely*.

That same year, the Prices appeared together in a humorous TV ad for Citibank MasterCard, in which they used the bonus points awarded by the credit card to purchase "something *strictly* for Vincent's amusement"—an electronic bug zapper! Vincent adored making commercials, describing them as "a great challenge. Try to sit down and talk about a product for thirty seconds, what you do with it, how you do this and that with it, before they say 'cut.' Oh, boy! Believe me, it tests any skill you may have acquired." Over the years, Vincent's diverse TV pitches included peanut-butter-and-*no*-jelly candy bars, British Airways first-class travel, board games

The original *Vincent* storyboards Tim Burton created to interest VP in the project included portraits of "Vincent Malloy" and his alter-ego

Mystery!

Immortalized in cement in 1982 at the Movieland Starprint Plaza outside the Movieland Wax Museum in Buena Park, California

As a Red Herring Suspect on a Fall, 1985 Cunard "Mystery Cruise" in the Bermuda Triangle (victim is fellow passenger Bob Madison)

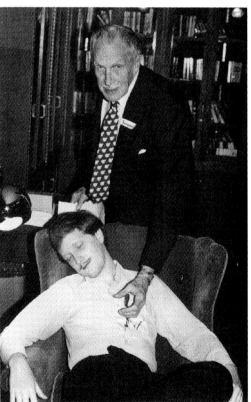

March 29, 1989—Coral and Vincent Price attending the 1989 Oscars

At a casual gathering of friends at the home of Eric Harrison

like "Hangman" and "Shrunken Head Apple Sculpture," wine coolers, the United Dairy Industry Association, Tilex cleaner (for removing nightmarish mildew stains), Easter Seals, Isuzu automobiles, and even public-service statements on behalf of the IRS.

Price made his final horror film in August 1987. A spoof starring Joe Piscopo and Treat Williams, *Dead Heat* was not well received, although in his small role Price was typically elegant and suave. The next spring, he had a cameo in old friend Dennis Hopper's directorial effort *Backtrack*, a violent mob thriller.

Family and friends were aware that Vincent had been diagnosed with Parkinson's disease, a devastating affliction of the central nervous system which would eventually slow his walk and inhibit his articulation, making work difficult. Nonetheless, in April 1990 he recorded the "Ghost Host" voice-over narration for the Phantom Manor attraction, a.k.a. the Haunted Mansion, for Disneyland Paris in both English and French. "I love it here at Disney," he said, "and the work I do today will be around for a long, long time." Since directing *Vincent* in 1982, its imaginative creator had gone on to make feature films, including *Beetlejuice* and the megahit *Batman*. Tim Burton's next movie was a semiautobiographical fantasy about an isolated boy-creature with scissors instead of hands. In June 1990, Vincent Price shot his footage for the brief but important role of the Inventor of *Edward Scissorhands*, appearing in the "persona" admiring fans had *really* come to expect of him—not a tormented movie character out of Poe but a lovable, favorite great-uncle from whom one wanted to hear a delightfully witty Grimms' fairy tale.

Old friends stayed in touch. There were letters from Deanna Durbin and her husband in France; postcards from Roddy McDowall; witty, ribald notes from boyhood friend Ted Thomas; birthday greetings from Peter Cushing or Christopher Lee. Cassandra Peterson and husband Mark Pierson sent a book on herbal medicines. Better known as Elvira, Mistress of the Dark, Cassandra was one of Vincent's biggest fans. "He was so witty, so funny, so quick and sharp. He'd remember details; things about you that other people would miss, he'd always notice. He would always ask about my husband. Even though Vincent was my idol, I wouldn't be afraid when I was working with him, because he'd make you feel so comfortable. And he'd make you look good, too." The actor also maintained weekly contact with the Vincent Price Gallery at East Los Angeles College. His passion for art was "especially important when I have one of my gloomy moods," he would explain. "After all, I'm Welsh, and the Celtic twilight sometimes descends at odd moments. I worry about pollution, our inner cities, the fate of our farmers or nuclear war—all those things that sometimes seem to make hell right here on earth. Still, looking at art will bring me through."

In July the American Cinémathèque paid a long-over-due tribute to "a distinctive artist and beloved star" with a weekend festival of Price's films. Colleagues who came to honor the actor included Jane Russell, Dennis Hopper, Tab Hunter, Andre de Toth, John Frankenheimer, and Charlton Heston. That fall, Vincent stepped down as the host of *Mystery!* after ten years, citing general ill health and because "I couldn't use my voice the way I wanted." He also preferred to spend more time with Coral, who was losing her battle with cancer. His successor as emcee was the equally elegant Diana Rigg; Price himself had suggested his *Theater of Blood* costar to the producers of *Mystery!* Although he was curtailing professional commitments, Vincent remained as media-friendly as always. He gave an interview at home where, "in between stirring the risotto and touring his house, Price [played] with his one-year-old dogs, a pair of Schipperkes. 'I get up early in the morning to be with them and take them out,' he says fondly, ruffling their hair. 'They sure can tow you. But they're wonderful. They're full of so much vitality, I wish I could bottle it.'"

In the spring of 1991, Tim Burton began an homage to the screen persona which had fascinated him in his youth, spending three days with Price at the East Los Angeles College gallery discussing his horror films. Film clips were incorporated into the black-and-white *A Visit With Vincent* to illustrate that aspect of the actor's career which had influenced the young filmmaker: the

haunted, reclusive characters from Poe, outsiders withdrawn from society. In recognition of Vincent's eightieth birthday in May, the *Washington Post* "Weekend Section" ran a surprisingly tough quiz about a career which had extended into its seventh decade with the release of *Edward Scissorhands*. (Only three out of ten questions related to horror films.) Despite his own health problems and Coral's decline, Vincent was still wickedly funny. Journalist Angela Fox Dunn was invited up to their house. "'You know what's good about being eighty?'" he asked rhetorically. "'You can say anything you damn please. You don't have to worry anymore about what people will think. I was driving down the street the other day when somebody cut in front of me. At the next stoplight, I found myself next to him, and I said out the

Shelley Duvall's *Fairie Tale Theatre: Snow White* As the Wicked Queen's Mirror

window, "What the hell do you think you were doing? And don't yell back at me—I'm eighty years old!" He just drove off laughing!'"

Finally, after suffering for years, Coral Price succumbed to cancer on May 29, 1991, at age seventy-seven, at home with her husband. Director John Schlesinger read a letter from Vincent at a memorial service in London. ". . . I've come to believe remembering someone is not the highest compliment—it is missing them. I find I miss every hour of Coral's life—I miss her morning cloudiness, noon mellowness, evening brightness. I miss her in every corner of our house, every crevice of my life. In missing her, I feel I'm missing much of life itself. . . . Many of you have shared more of her life than I have, but that very private and intense passion for her is mine alone." It might be tempting to infer that Vincent gave up after Coral died, but he found real strength in his steadfast faith and was a trouper to the last. He actually shot another day of interviews for the Tim Burton documentary right after his wife's death. In October he filmed a cameo in a final movie, the made-for-cable *The Heart of Justice*. The film noir–style thriller was broadcast on Showtime in February 1993. "Vincent loved to work," says Jane Russell. "He wanted to keep doing something all the time; it was 'Let's go lecture, let's do this, let's do that, I want to be active.' Being in bed was just driving him crazy." The actor's illnesses were as much a psychological blow as they were physical. "Somebody offered me a television show the other day called *Life Begins at Eighty*," he commented. "I said, 'You're out of your cotton-picking mind! What are you going to do, wheel in the contestants?' Boring . . . it's very boring to get old. Unless you have really robust health, which few people do, it's a trying time. To hell with the Golden Years!" British actress and costar Hazel Court remembers him joking to the end. "He never really moaned or groaned, but he *hated* being old, hated it, more perhaps than anyone I've ever known. He was a prisoner. But his *mind*! His zest for life was so intense."

During his life, Price received dozens of honors. He was a member of the Royal Society of the Arts and of the Whitney Museum Friends of American Art; important universities granted honorary degrees; the Hollywood Press Club presented him with its Annual Life Achievement Award. The Los Angeles Film Critics Association paid tribute with their own career-achievement salute in January 1992. "It was very exciting," Vincent admitted. "Everybody was there, and they gave me a standing ovation. It was very touching. It's pretty nice to be remembered when you're eighty years old!" He quipped that Coral would have commented, "Well, you old fart, I see they got you just in the nick of time!" But there was still a little time left; over the next eighteen months Vincent

continued to be in touch with production people on *A Visit With Vincent*, and friends frequently came by the house when it became difficult for him to get around.

It made international headlines when, on Monday, October 25, 1993, Parkinson's disease and lung cancer, among other complications, took the life of Vincent Price. Just a couple of weeks before, he had purchased a new abstract painting by a young, unheralded artist and sent his assistant to Tower Classical for the just-released boxed set of Vladimir Horowitz recordings. The funeral mass was at St. Victor's in West Hollywood; at his request, Vincent's ashes were scattered off the coast amid a spray of bouquets. The family was able to laugh as a young seal surfaced through the petals, nearly donning the actor's favorite straw hat which had also been cast into the water. On November 21 a private celebration of Vincent's life was held at East Los Angeles College. Brightly colored helium balloons led the way to the gallery, which featured a fitting tribute to its beloved patron, a selection of the pieces of art Vincent had donated over the decades. About one hundred people enjoyed hors d'oeuvres from The City, one of Vincent's favorite restaurants, and shared reminiscences and anecdotes. Daughter Toria spoke and then introduced the college president, who talked about Vincent's educational and spiritual legacy. Roddy McDowall delivered an emotional reminiscence which left most in tears, and pianist Michael Feinstein played.

The week of his death, Arts & Entertainment Network aired *Biography: Vincent Price*, which had been completed sometime before and was being held for broadcast at Halloween. Some friends felt that the retrospective placed undue emphasis on the horror films and relied on inappropriately dismissive commentary; a review in the *New York Daily News* called it "superficial." Only a month later, London's *Film Guide* described a BBC broadcast of *Tales of Terror* as "starring splendid Vincent Price, already greatly missed."

Over the years, creative studio publicists had promoted a couple of Price's films as his one hundredth movie. Ironically, he actually made ninety-nine—until the announcement in 1995 of the long-awaited release of Richard Williams's animated feature *Arabian Knight*. Vincent recorded the voice for the wicked Grand Vizier in this comedy/adventure back in 1973, and so a movie aimed at children of all ages, in which Price plays a characteristically, deliciously over the top villain, will at last be film number one hundred.

But other legacies remain as well. The Vincent Price Gallery, on the campus of East Los Angeles College, continues to present world-class art exhibitions which would otherwise be unavailable to most, let alone those living in L.A.'s East Side. There has seldom been much

The Offspring (photo by Dan Golden)

The Great Mouse Detective Celebrating his seventy-fifth birthday with "alter-ego" Prof. Ratigan

"Vinnie the P" with Elvira, Mistress of the Dark (Cassandra Peterson) (photo by Mark Pierson, © 1982 "Queen Bee" Productions)

Vincent's eightieth birthday on the set of Tim Burton's documentary. Coproducer Diane Minter, author LCW (*fourth from left*), co-producer Sam Hurwitz, VP Gallery director Thomas Silliman, Tim Burton (*far right*) (photo by Elizabeth Annas)

Vincent and Coral at home (photo by Dan Golden)

Wrap yourself in something special

EMBA MINK

One of eleven special shades from EMBA® Lunaraine® natural dark-brown American mink coat by Michael Forrest.

Print ad for Emba mink

VINCENT PRICE GALLERY

Students at the Vincent Price Gallery holding art objects from the gallery collection; at right, gallery director Thomas Silliman (photo courtesy of The Vincent Price Gallery/East Los Angeles College)

Lorenzo patronized more than just art...

He pursued all that intrigued him. Art, science, politics, women. And not necessarily in that order.

Lorenzo de' Medici was indeed the father of the Renaissance, protector of men of letters and patron to such as Michaelangelo and da Vinci. But he was also known for the magnificence of his table, where feasted the crème de la crème of the Golden Age.

"Lorenzo the Magnificent," he was called...a much deserved title, for he most assuredly had a flair for splendor. Legend has it, Lorenzo's guests were first to be favored by the gracious warmth of a golden spirit which was secretly formulated to enhance the grandeur of his hospitality.

Tuaca is the classic Italian liqueur of indescribable taste...straight, over ice, in coffee...or to impart flavorful flattery to foods and desserts.

Tuaca. Try it when you want to be really magnificent.

A self addressed stamped envelope will bring you a free booklet of Tuaca recipes expressing five centuries of good taste.
Write: Tuaca Recipes / P.O. Box 1626
F.D.R. Station / New York, N.Y. 10022

Tuaca
ITALIAN DEMI-SEC LIQUEUR

FOUR ROSES DISTILLERS COMPANY, NEW YORK, N.Y. • SOLE IMPORTERS FOR U.S.A. • 84 PROOF

crafts by whiting
M B MILTON BRADLEY COMPANY

A CRAFT FOR THE WHOLE FAMILY

"Create your own collection of delightful Shrunken Heads."
VINCENT PRICE

AGES 12 to ADULT

Shrunken Head
APPLE SCULPTURE

INCLUDES "THE SHRINKER" ATTACHES TO ANY STANDARD TABLE LAMP

Contains material to make 8 complete Shrunken Heads • APPLES NOT INCLUDED

The SHRINKER

UNASSEMBLED

Milton Bradley's "Shrunken Head Apple Sculpture" kit

Print ad for Tuaca Italian Demi-sec Liqueur

American Cinematheque Tribute, 1990 with friend and costar Jane Russell

press: "We just wanted it to serve the community," explained Vincent in 1991. "We didn't want to make publicity out of it, since everything actors do is suspect! We just shut up and let it grow." The superb collection, which contains approximately two thousand pieces and has been valued in excess of five million dollars, offers a unique, hands-on educational resource and inspiration to generations of students, several of whom have made successful careers in the art world. The Vincent Price Art Gallery Foundation (East Los Angeles College, 1301 Avenida Cesar Chavez, Monterey Park, California 91754) is a nonprofit organization providing the major funding for operation and administration. Mary Grant Price and daughter Victoria Price are on the board of directors. In 1986, Mary had expressed a desire to donate, and Vincent was delighted by his ex-wife's renewed interest. Shortly before Coral Browne Price's death, the actress "gave her blessing" for Mary to be invited to serve on the board. Director Thomas Silliman calls Vincent "the inspiration of my life. . . . It's amazing, with all the man had to do, all of his obligations, all of his other interests, this gallery was the top of the list with him. This is a little junior college out in the boonies. The most common question we're asked is 'Why East L.A. College? Why not the L.A. County Museum? Or the Museum of Modern Art?' Vincent's answer was 'Because this is where it's

needed.'" "'Of the hundreds of art projects that I have been involved with throughout my life," Price asserted, "the art gallery at East Los Angeles College has been the most rewarding of all."

Son V. B. Price is an anthropologist and poet who has also been a teacher at the Westinghouse Learning Institute. In an article in the early 1970s he wrote: "The heroes of 'Vincent Price movies' are good Aristotle—they inspire pity and cause catharsis. He never really plays a monster. No, sir. Not my dad. He's been severely wronged by fate and put into tragic circumstances for which he must pay tragically. And it breaks my heart. And I'm proud as punch."

Price was a frequent contributor of both time and money to charities and fund-raisers for a wide variety of causes, from cancer research to the preservation of local theaters. In 1970 he was approached by the Library of Congress in Washington with a signal honor—an invitation to donate his private papers to their Manuscript Division. The collection documents all aspects of American history and culture and includes some of the nation's greatest manuscript treasures. Private papers include those of artists and writers, scientists and inventors, and "other prominent Americans whose lives reflect our country's evolution." The archive now preserves 60,000 items relating to Vincent Price's life and work.

Throughout his career Price couldn't be tempted into seriously disparaging the films that made him famous— not in public, anyway. "I was furious," he once remarked, "when I read a book called the hundred worst pictures ever made, to see that several of mine weren't in it! I've done some dogs, although I think overall my record is pretty good. Some of my films have been kind of funny and corny, and a few have been really great classics." When asked if there were any in which he felt he didn't give his best performance, the actor replied, "No. There were several I wish I'd had another chance at." Vincent never took his popularity for granted and oversimplified his longevity in a single word: *survival.* "It's awfully easy to get out of the business. It's not easy to stay in. I never felt that the great parts were the only things you should do. That's a great mistake, because there are so many interesting things available."

Although fans consider much of his work to have been tongue-in-cheek (and he himself once claimed to have his tongue "in *both* cheeks"), Vincent was terribly serious about his occupation. "Where do I fit in, in a profession

Caricatures of the popular "Vincent Price image"

VP and his daughter, Victoria, (now a member of the Vincent Price Art Gallery Foundation board of directors) at a 1991 gallery reception (photo courtesy of the Vincent Price Gallery/East Los Angeles College)

"Welcome to My Nightmare" With Alice Cooper and friend

I can see so clearly at fault in so many ways? How do I make a living in it when it dies in my arms at each embrace? And most importantly, how do I make a life in it? Frankly, most of us are in it because we can not imagine any other kind of life. We like to entertain, we like to act, and most of us couldn't hold any other kind of job if we tried or wanted to. . . . I fit in it by my own necessity to be a public servant—to give of my personality and the techniques of that personality something of entertainment to the world. I can justify my being in a popular movie that the critics sneer at by its acceptance by the people at large—or being in a classy artistic flop."

When all was said and done, Vincent Price remained a straightforward, hardworking, down-to-earth midwestern guy who found joy in the smallest things. "Actually, I've had a ball. I've done thirty times more things than most people have, and it's been fun. . . . I have no fear of the ending of life because I think it must be a beginning, too. I don't know where or what or why. I'm a religious person, but I'm *not* going to sit up on a cloud playing a harp, I don't believe that. But I do believe that it is a beginning. I don't believe that life can be useless, or just finished."

A week after Vincent's death, film authority Leonard Maltin wrote: "Other actors may have made better movies, but few lived better lives, or touched so many people with their warmth and gentility."

"You only get one time around," Vincent Price once admonished with a twinkle in his blue eyes. "So why waste a minute of this glorious life?"

The Thirteen Ghosts of Scooby Doo TV cartoon series (photo: TM and © 1985 Hanna-Barbera Productions, Inc.)

Fellow Yale grads: The author, Lucy Chase Williams '77, and Vincent L. Price Jr. '33 (photo by Dan Golden)

Vincent in his West
Hollywood garden, 1991
(photo by long-time
friend William Claxton).

THE FILMS

The *NEW UNIVERSAL* Presents

Constance **BENNETT**
IN

Service de Luxe

with

VINCENT PRICE

CHARLIE RUGGLES

HELEN BRODERICK

MISCHA AUER

JOY HODGES

Directed by ROWLAND V. LEE
Associate Producer EDMUND GRAINGER
Screenplay by Gertrude PURCELL & Leonard SPIGELGASS
Original Story by Bruce Manning and Vera Caspary

A ROWLAND V. LEE Production

Service De Luxe One-sheet poster—Great billing for a film debut

Service De Luxe With Constance Bennett

1. SERVICE DE LUXE

UNIVERSAL

Previewed in Los Angeles October 12, 1938

CREDITS

Associate Producer, Edmund Grainger; *Director*, Rowland V. Lee; *Screenplay*, Gertrude Purcell, Leonard Spigelgass; *Original Story*, Bruce Manning, Vera Caspary; *Cinematography*, George Robinson; *Art Director*, Jack Otterson; *Set Decorator*, R. A. Gausman; *Musical Director*, Charles Previn; *Editor*, Ted Kent; *Miss Bennett's Gowns by* Irene; *Other Gowns by* Vera West; *Running time*, 85 minutes; black and white.

CAST

Constance Bennett (*Helen Murphy*); Vincent Price (*Robert Wade*); Charlie Ruggles (*Scott "Scoot" Robinson*); Helen Broderick (*Pearl*); Mischa Auer (*Serge Bebenko*); Joy Hodges (*Audrey Robinson*); Halliwell Hobbes (*Butler*); Chester Clute (*Chester Bainbridge*); Lionel Belmore (*Wade*); Frances Robinson (*Secretary*); Lawrence Grant (*Voroshinsky*); Nina Gilbert (*Mrs. Devereaux*); Crawford Kent (*Mr. Devereaux*); Raymond Parker, Frank Coghlan Jr. (*Bellhops*).

THE FILM

"A new star is appearing in Hollywood's heavenly bodies . . ."
"Tall, good-looking, and just the type to make the girls' hearts do flip-flops . . ."
"Besides having the qualities of a matinee idol, he impresses with the intelligence of his work. . . . One of the important 'discoveries' of the year . . ."
"'Vince' Price Optical Treat for the Girls . . ."
"Price Glitters in Screen Debut . . . gilt-edged performance presages a brilliant movie career. . . ."

The film debut of Broadway's newest star, matinee idol Vincent Price, had been much anticipated since his storming of the Great White Way in the fall of 1935. When he finally was signed to a contract by Universal, the studio selected a breezy, modern screwball comedy in which to launch its new leading man. *Service De Luxe* gave Price the advantages of an established leading lady, an accomplished supporting cast, and a role which, if unchallenging technically, still permitted him to be dashing and romantic as well as straightforward and sensible.

Service De Luxe With Joy Hodges

Service De Luxe With Constance Bennett and Raymond Parker

66

Chic, capable Helen Murphy (Constance Bennett) heads the Dorothy Madison Service, a superefficient "personal assistance" bureau which handles every aspect of its wealthy clients' affairs, from securing box theater seats to outfitting bridegrooms. Helen loves the superhectic pace but is exasperated with her helpless clientele: "If I ever met a man who could take care of himself, I'd die of delight! I'm so sick of running other people's lives for them that I'd welcome a caveman who'd knock me over the head and drag me off by the hair!" Enter Robert Wade (Vincent Price), neither caveman nor the hayseed described in some synopses, but a determined young inventor raised by a passel of overprotective aunts who just happens to have vowed never again to let his life be controlled by a woman. He's coming to New York City to try and interest capital in his design of a revolutionary new tractor, unaware that his curmudgeonly uncle has commissioned Helen in her capacity of "Miss Madison" to prevent the young man's arrival. On the passenger boat down from Albany, Helen mistakes a nebbish for the inventor and persuades him to jump ship. She then meets the tall, masterful young man she doesn't know is the real Bob Wade and is irresistibly attracted when he matter-of-factly demands her phone number. When he shows up at the Dorothy Madison Service, Helen realizes her mistake; she has her trusty second in command (Helen Broderick) send him away so *he* won't discover that she's the "bossy career-girl type." During his stay in New York, Bob continues to romance the cheerfully vulnerable and demure Helen, who persuades another Madison Service client, Scoot Robinson (Charlie Ruggles), to invest in the tractor. Scoot's flighty daughter, Audrey (Joy Hodges), also takes an immediate interest in the handsome young man and hangs on every nut and bolt as Bob builds a prototype machine in Scoot's cellar. Completely absorbed in his work, he absently agrees to marry the persistent Audrey, and when Helen confesses that she is actually Miss Madison, he gets so angry he decides to go ahead with the nuptials. His tractor is a big hit, but he's still in love with Helen, so he sets up the scatterbrained Audrey to turn her attentions to the Robinsons' Russian prince chef (Mischa Auer). The two elope, and Bob is seemingly left at the altar. But the elaborate wedding arranged by the Madison Service takes place, anyway—with Helen as Bob's bride. "Wade Service from now on?" he asks with a smile. "Yes, boss," she purrs happily.

Service De Luxe, while not a screwball classic of the caliber of *My Man Godfrey* or *Bringing Up Baby*, is a light and amusing movie. In his first scene on film, Vincent is introduced as a polite, earnest young man, coddled and cosseted by well-meaning, elderly aunts. Once out of their clutches, he asserts himself, becoming forceful and authoritative, dominating with his enormous height. His comic scenes with the smitten Joy Hodges are particularly funny, featuring the developing talent for farce which would make his role in *Champagne for Caesar* (1950) one of the best of his career.

Service De Luxe went into production in mid-August 1938. Price considered the story "cute" and his part "swell." He wrote his parents: "It's a marvelous setup, all top-notch people in every field, and the script gets better every day." He was most excited about Rowland V. Lee directing, since he considered him "a superb director . . . he is very interested in me and will work to make my start as good as possible." He was also looking forward to his first paycheck, having laid out "a lot of cash here for clothes, etc."

The picture was completed on September 30 and opened only a couple of weeks later. Newlywed Edith Price wrote a letter to her in-laws, describing the preview as "terribly thrilling and frightening and at last fulfilling." Once in their seats, her husband "looked very pale and still." The theater was standing room only, and when Vincent first appeared on screen, "there was a beautiful reception for him, and from then on he had won their hearts of course. . . . Everyone feels he has a great future in pictures as well as theatre. . . . It is certainly a strange world out here, but Vincent really seems to love it." The St. Louis papers were as quick to herald the young film star as they had been three years earlier when he took Broadway by storm. The proud Price family attended the St. Louis opening of *Service De Luxe*, and Vincent Price Sr. dubbed it "a grand and glorious night for us."

The screen persona of Vincent Price, glorified in the decades to come, might make it difficult to imagine the established star (gray-haired, craggy if still handsome in his sixties, stereotyped as the Master of the Macabre) succeeding in the role of juvenile lead. But this Vincent Price is a natural, charming, leggy twenty-seven-year-old. He slurps a chocolate shake at the soda fountain; lolls on the grass in the park, gazing up at the sky while ruminating on love. He waltzes, he sings, he looks as natural in white tie and tails as he does in overalls and axle grease. Surrounded by a bevy of upper-crust accents and broad New England "a's," he is unaffectedly midwestern, comfortably dropping his "g's" and drawling, "Siddown!" In the film, a captivated Constance Bennett sighs and says "He's got what it takes!" Hollywood agreed, and with a neglected madcap comedy, Vincent Price began a versatile, successful, and above all, popular film career which was to last over half a century.

REVIEWS

[San Francisco] *Standard-Examiner*, August 29, 1938, May Mann

"Feminine Hearts Flutter as Vincent Price Stars—

67

Strikingly Handsome, He Has Charm and Poise on Film Lot. . . . Universal is very enthused with Vincent. . . . He will most likely cause feminine audiences a bit of heart palpitation."

[Review from VP's clipping service which omitted name of paper]: October 13, 1938

"Excellent comedy idea is amusingly exploited. . . . The funning is by turns whimsical and screwball and is given a fast ride by the seasoned troupers . . . with splendid showing by the screen newcomer, Vincent Price. . . . In Vincent Price, Universal has found a promising leading man, assured, a competent actor with an excellent voice, clean cut well mannered and tall above the average. He shows a decided talent for comedy and turns in a very creditable first performance."

Liberty, October 15, 1938

". . . most important of all, watch Price. The Bachelor of Arts from New Haven may be another Gable."

New York Daily Mirror, October 22, 1938

"Blessed with a lucky black cat, six-foot-four of brawn, and a glamorous reputation as Helen Hayes' 'Prince Albert,' Mr. Vincent Price makes his official movie debut. . . . Hollywood blandishments thus have quashed the hope of Broadway that in Mr. Price the theatre at last had a matinee idol exclusively its own."

New York Times, October 24, 1938, B. R. Crisler

"Vincent Price, though a bit hard to get into the camera field vertically, seems a likely screen hero. . . ."

Motion Picture Herald, October 29, 1938

"This is a smoothly coordinated comedy . . . a finely gauged flow of consistently amusing incident . . . [Vincent Price], an impressive recruit from the stage . . . is about the tallest leading man in pictures as of now, and serves up a new and substantial kind of romantic performance. . . . The picture is as modern as today's leaf on the calendar, glib as a Los Angeles realtor, completely sophisticated in the dictionary sense of the word and clean as a spring breeze."

2. THE PRIVATE LIVES OF ELIZABETH AND ESSEX

WARNER BROS.

Released September 27, 1939

CREDITS

Executive Producer, Hal B. Wallis; *Associate Producer*, Robert Lord; *Director*, Michael Curtiz; *Screenplay*, Norman Reilly Raine, Aeneas MacKenzie; *Based on* Maxwell's Anderson's *Elizabeth the Queen*; *Cinematography*, Sol Polito; *Art Director*, Anton Grot; *Music*, Erich Wolfgang Korngold; *Music Director*, Leo F. Forbstein; *Orchestrations*, Hugo Friedhofer, Milan Roder; *Editor*, Owen Marks; *Makeup*, Perc Westmore; *Costumes*, Orry-Kelly; *Dialogue Director*, Stanley Logan; *Special Effects*, Byron Haskin, H. F. Koenekamp; *Running time*, 106 minutes; color.

CAST

Bette Davis (*Queen Elizabeth*); Errol Flynn (*Robert Devereaux, Earl of Essex*); Olivia de Havilland (*Lady Penelope Gray*); Donald Crisp (*Sir Francis Bacon*); Alan Hale (*Earl of Tyrone*); Vincent Price (*Sir Walter Raleigh*); Henry Stephenson (*Lord Burghley*); Henry Daniell (*Sir Robert Cecil*); James Stephenson (*Sir Thomas Egerton*); Nanette Fabares [later Nanette Fabray] (*Margaret Radcliffe*); Ralph Forbes (*Lord Knollys*); Robert Warwick

The Private Lives of Elizabeth and Essex As Sir Walter Raleigh

(*Lord Mountjoy*); Leo G. Carroll (*Sir Edward Coke*); Forrester Harvey, John Sutton, I. Stanford Jolley.

THE FILM

The Private Lives of Elizabeth and Essex was a sumptuous extravaganza and a prestigious assignment for Vincent Price, even if he did accept a demotion in rank to appear in it—in the summer of 1936 he had played the leading role of the Earl of Essex opposite Mildred Natwick in *Elizabeth the Queen*, the free-verse play by Maxwell Anderson on which the film was based. A review described his Essex as "a curious composite of the lover and the soldier, at times soft to the point of an adolescent blinded by his first love, and then again hardened, brave and courageous. . . . [The performance ranks] with the best portrayals of the character in our generation."

The historically stormy relationship between Elizabeth and Essex probably paled in comparison to the animosity that developed between the megastars who portrayed them in this cinema version of their lives. Essex had been younger than Elizabeth, and Flynn was younger than Davis. Bette had two Oscars to her credit; Flynn, self-confessed as not in her league as an actor, nevertheless was earning some $1,000 more per week than Warner's biggest female star. Director Michael Curtiz became so fed up with Flynn's unprofessional behavior, he threatened to replace his male lead with Price. Perhaps the two actors were settling things like gentlemen one afternoon when, still in costume, they were reported playing tennis on the studio court.

Vincent Price left Broadway's *Outward Bound* on a one-picture loan-out to Warners from Universal to film *Essex* around June of 1939. As Sir Walter Raleigh, he enters in an impressive Orry-Kelly doublet and cape, but fares less well at the hands of the screenwriter; he's completely mute, not given even a perfunctory "Yes, Your Majesty" when Elizabeth invests him with the rank she has just stripped from Essex. Later, Price is resplendent in his silver armor but reveals himself as a shifty opportunist, even lily-livered. After the climactic courtroom confrontation between the queen and her rogue subject, Sir Walter is neither seen nor heard from again. While Vincent was making the picture, Edith Barrett Price visited her husband on the set; ten years previously, Bette Davis had had one of her "first good roles" playing Barrett's daughter in summer stock in Massachusetts.

Working titles included *The Lady and the Knight*, *Elizabeth the Queen*, and simply *Elizabeth and Essex*; occasionally, a print in release has one of the alternatives. The film won five Oscars: Art Direction, Cinematography, Original Score, Sound Recording, and Special Effects.

The Private Lives of Elizabeth and Essex Price (*seated second from left*), with Bette Davis and Errol Flynn (standing)

The war forced a venue change from London to Hollywood for the movie's premiere. According to the papers, it was the first time in Beverly Hills that a "rooting section" was erected for fans, accommodating several thousand on tier seats. Traffic was cordoned off for two blocks on either side of the theater, and police estimated more than seventy-five hundred gathered to see "the expensively gowned stars and their escorts." Bad weather kept Davis in New York, and Flynn remained on his yacht off Catalina Island. The "Who's Who of Hollywood" included every celebrated studio head and artists such as Fairbanks, Dietrich, Robinson, Crawford, Burns and Allen, Jane Wyman and Ronald Reagan, and Charles Chaplin and Paulette Goddard. Actresses who played the queen's ladies-in-waiting in the film arrived wearing their costumes. And although he generally eschewed Hollywood dos, Vincent Price also attended.

Leo G. Carroll has only a minor role in *Essex*, but two years later would vie with Vincent for critical honors in the Broadway hit thriller *Angel Street*.

The Private Lives of Elizabeth and Essex was Vincent Price's first color picture; he didn't appear in another until *Wilson* five years later.

REVIEWS

Variety, September 29, 1939

"Done with a magnitude and a spirit thoroughly commensurate with the subject . . . with great entertainment impact . . . [Vincent Price] gives excellent account . . ."

New York Times, December 2, 1939, Frank S. Nugent

"Mr. Flynn is a good-looking young man who should be asked to do no more in pictures than flash an even-toothed smile and present a firm jawline. His Essex lacked a head before the headsman got around to him.... It is a good film, one well worth seeing; how much better it might have been with an Essex worthy of Miss Davis' Elizabeth we can only surmise."

3. TOWER OF LONDON

UNIVERSAL

Released November 17, 1939

CREDITS

Producer/Director, Rowland V. Lee; *Original Screenplay*, Robert N. Lee; *Cinematography*, George Robinson; *Background Photography*, Henry Shuster; *Art Director*, Jack Otterson; *Set Decorator*, R. A. Gausman; *Music Director*, Charles Previn; *Orchestrations*, Frank Skinner; *Editor*, Edward Curtiss; *Makeup*, Jack Pierce; *Gowns*, Vera West; *Fencing Instructor*, Fred Cavens; *Running time*, 92 minutes; black and white.

CAST

Basil Rathbone (*Richard, Duke of Gloucester*); Boris Karloff (*Mord*); Barbara O'Neil (*Queen Elizabeth*); Ian Hunter (*King Edward IV*); Vincent Price (*Duke of Clarence*); Nan Grey (*Lady Alice Barton*); Ernest Cossart (*Tom Clink*); John Sutton (*John Wyatt*); Leo G. Carroll (*Lord Hastings*); Miles Mander (*King Henry VI*); Lionel Belmore (*Beacon*); Rose Hobart (*Anne Neville*); Ronald Sinclair (*Boy King Edward*); John Herbert-Bond (*Young Prince Richard*); Ralph Forbes (*Henry Tudor*); Frances Robinson (*Duchess Isobel*); G. P. Huntley (*Wales*); John Rodion (*Lord DeVere*); Walter Tetley (*Chimney Sweep*); Nigel De Brulier (*Archbishop, St. John's Chapel*); Donnie Dunagan (*Baby Prince*).

THE FILM

Lacking a "monster" per se, *Tower of London* is not one of the better known of Universal's classic 1930s horror films. It should be. Loosely based on the historical legend of the last Plantagenet king, the plot exposes the evildoings of Richard, Duke of Gloucester, as he seeks to attain the throne of England by striding over the corpses of relatives. Aided and abetted by his loyal servant, the executioner/torturer Mord, Richard finally attains the

Tower of London With Ian Hunter (*center*), and Basil Rathbone (*left*)

Tower of London As the Duke of Clarence

crown, only to lose both it and his life at the Battle of Bosworth Field. Thus begins the reign of Henry VII and the introduction to the British monarchy of the Tudor line.

Tower of London went before the cameras on August 11, 1939, officially wrapping September 4. That charmingly familiar Universal back lot, which tourists still marvel at, lends surprising scope to action which is artistically painted with light and shadow. As the sadistic royal executioner, Karloff gives an athletic performance, finding depth in a character who could easily have been one-dimensional. Basil Rathbone, too, displays enormous range, his expressive face mixing righteous jealousy with revealing hypocrisy. (The erudite Rathbone, from a prominent theatrical family, had met Vincent Price in London at the start of the younger man's career.)

As Richard III's brother, the Duke of Clarence, Price makes the most of his smaller role, alternately petulant, devious, arrogant, and cowardly, although the squinty left eye given him by makeup master Jack Pierce is somewhat disconcerting. His final scene with Rathbone, in which Clarence and Richard engage in a drinking duel for the kingdom, is actually one of the meatiest moments Price ever had on film. His drunken arrogance when he believes he has won—the maniacal laughter which, when Rathbone revives, hesitantly becomes hysteria and then fury—are truly eerie. Vincent remembered that much of the "match," which was done in one day, had to be filmed in only a few shots "in order to heighten credibility." Ever afterward, the scene was the source of one of his favorite stories. In the black-and-white movie, Coca-Cola substituted for malmsey in their goblets, which after several takes, had both actors nauseous. Ac-

cording to Price, cohorts Karloff and Rathbone took great glee in tossing empty Coke bottles and cigarette butts into the large barrel (of water) in which Clarence would eventually be drowned. When Price was unceremoniously dumped into the vat, he had to grasp a bar at the bottom and hold on until cut was called, the lid lifted, and the lanky young man yanked out by his heels. Vincent earned a round of applause from the crew, and in commemoration, Rathbone and Karloff presented him with a case of Coke. Price filmed *Tower of London* at Universal at the same time as *Green Hell*; press releases claimed he was drowned one day in medieval England and shot with poison arrows in the Amazon jungle the next.

Basil Rathbone's son, Rodion Rathbone, appears under a partial pseudonym as the first casualty of the picture. Although they had acted together onstage, *Tower of London* was the only film Vincent made with longtime *amour* Barbara O'Neil, whom he had first met in grade school in St. Louis. (Her billing was two places above his!)

In 1962, Roger Corman directed Price in another version of the story of Richard III, a film which eventually had the same title, although strictly speaking it was not a remake.

REVIEWS

Variety, November 16, 1939

". . . *Tower of London* emerges as a spine-chiller with accent on gruesomeness. . . . As a horror picture, it's one of the most broadly etched, but it's still so strong that it may provide disturbing nightmares as aftermath. For biz, it will give a good account of itself in runs where pictures of the type attract. . . . Vincent Price is excellent. . . ."

Review by Harry Mines, November 1939

"As Richard, Basil Rathbone gives a distinguished performance. Likewise Vincent Price as the weak, conniving Duke of Clarence. They have a drunk scene, a terrifying exhibition of debauchery, that proves not only the highlight of *Tower of London*, but one of the acting highlights in the season. Price, in fact, dominates the production until he all too soon is blubberingly drowned in a vat of wine." [This same reporter put Price, along with Thomas Mitchell in *Stagecoach*, Hattie McDaniel in *Gone With the Wind*, John Barrymore in *Midnight*, and Gene Lockhart in *Blackmail*, on his list of ten foremost supporting players in 1939.]

Tower of London Publicity shot with Basil Rathbone and Boris Karloff

Le Retour de l'Homme Invisible (French poster for *The Invisible Man Returns* courtesy Camden House)

The Invisible Man Returns With Nan Grey, Harry Stubbs as police constable, and Forrester Harvey

The Invisible Man Returns
With Nan Grey

72

4. THE INVISIBLE MAN RETURNS

UNIVERSAL

Released January 15, 1940

CREDITS

Associate Producer, Ken Goldsmith; *Director*, Joe May; *Screenplay*, Lester Cole, Kurt Siodmak; *Story*, Joe May, Kurt Siodmak; *Suggested by the novel by* H. G. Wells; *Cinematography*, Milton Krasner; *Art Director*, Jack Otterson; *Set Decorator*, R. A. Gausman; *Music Director*, Charles Previn; *Music*, H. J. Salter, Frank Skinner; *Editor*, Frank Gross; *Gowns*, Vera West; *Special Effects*, John P. Fulton; *Assistant Director*, Phil Karlstein [later Phil Karlson]; *Running time*, 81 minutes; black and white.

CAST

Sir Cedric Hardwicke (*Richard Cobb*); Vincent Price (*Geoffrey Radcliffe*); Nan Grey (*Helen Manson*); John Sutton (*Dr. Frank Griffin*); Cecil Kellaway (*Inspector Sampson*); Alan Napier (*Willie Spears*); Forrester Harvey (*Ben Jenkins*); Ivan Simpson (*Cotton*); Edward Fielding (*Governor*); Frances Robinson (*Nurse*); Harry Stubbs, Cyril Thornton, Rex Evans, Frank Hagney, Ed Brady, Matthew Boulton (*Policemen*); Billy Bevan, Dave Thursby (*Wardens*); Bruce Lester (*Chaplain*); Paul England (*Detective*); Mary Gordon (*Cook*); Ellis Irving, Dennis Tankard, George Lloyd, George Kirby, Harry Cording, George Hyde (*Miners*); Leyland Hodgson (*Chauffeur*); Jimmy Aubrey, Colin Kenny (*Plainclothesmen*); Louise Brien, Hugh Huntley (*Secretaries*); Eric Wilton (*Fingerprint Man*); Mary Field, Ernie Adams, Clara Blore.

THE FILM

The Invisible Man Returns was the first sequel to James Whale's 1933 classic, which had launched the film career of the enormously gifted Claude Rains, who, like Price, had been a Broadway star before he came to Hollywood.

Condemned to hang for a murder he didn't commit, Sir Geoffrey Radcliffe (Price) turns for help to his friend Dr. Frank Griffin (John Sutton), the brother of the man who had created the invisible serum. Facing the inevitable madness which doomed the original "Invisible Man," Radcliffe must discover the identity of the real killer before he, too, succumbs to violent insanity.

At one time, *The Invisible Man Returns* was to have been produced and directed by Rowland V. Lee, who directed Vincent in *Service De Luxe* and *Tower of London*. At the helm instead was Joe May, with whom the

actor would work the following year on *The House of the Seven Gables*. Kurt Siodmak, like May a German émigré, collaborated on the story and screenplay. (He later changed the spelling of his first name to Curt and penned *The Wolf Man*.) Though *The Invisible Man Returns* is more modestly scaled than its predecessor, it received class treatment, from the elegiac cinematography to the surprisingly romantic score. The nifty optical effects and wire work matched and in some instances surpassed the visual magic of the original film; John Fulton was nominated for an Oscar. Although Vincent Price received second billing, his performance in the male lead is highly credible, benefiting (like Rains's) from his rich, theatrically trained voice; when on-camera, the sheer size of him dominates, whether he's in a tweed suit and bandages or "headless" above a flowing dressing gown.

Director Joe May, despite his talent, had considerable difficulty because of his poor command of English. Price remembered: "I, fortunately, spoke German, so I could understand him. He would give me a direction, and I'd say, 'For God's sake, Joe, tell me in German!' I don't think Nan Grey or John Sutton ever understood a word he said!"

The Invisible Man Returns began filming in October 1939 on a reported budget of $250,000. There would be three additional *Invisible* "sequels" as well as the customary late-forties teaming with Abbott and Costello. *The Invisible Man Returns* was one of the last truly fine Universal horror films and for those prone to irony, a harbinger for the twenty-eight-year-old Price of career "Things to Come."

REVIEWS

Hollywood Citizen News, January 1940

". . . The new invisible man is Vincent Price, and his invisibility . . . is the source of drama, comedy and an eeriness which may strain the credulity but which never fails to be highly diverting. . . . Vincent Price's unseen enactment of the title character is expertly done, primarily, of course, with his voice."

Review by James Francis Crow, January 16, 1940

[beneath an empty space with the caption "Vincent Price as the Invisible Man"] ". . . like its predecessor, rich in thrill-and-chill material, and rich in technical novelties. . . . And the reaction of last night's preview audience left no doubt that this new one, again like its predecessor, will be a box office smash. . . . Price . . . does a capital job of the key role, and his resonant Broadway-trained voice stands him in good stead."

New York Times January 16, 1940, Frank S. Nugent

"... a mite on the ghostly side, too, although neither so horrendous nor so humorous as the first one was. . . . It has its fair measure of suspense and excitement and adequate enough performances by Mr. Price (when you can see him). . . .

5. GREEN HELL

UNIVERSAL

Released January 26, 1940

CREDITS

A James Whale Production; *Producer*, Harry Edington; *Director*, James Whale; *Original Story and Screenplay*, Frances Marion; *Cinematography*, Karl Freund; *Art Director*, Jack Otterson; *Set Decorator*, R. A. Gausman; *Musical Director*, Charles Previn; *Editor*, Ted Kent; *Miss Bennett's Gowns by* Irene, Bernard Newman; *Stunts,* Iron Eyes Cody, W. C. Wilkerson; *Running time*, 87 minutes; black and white.

CAST

Douglas Fairbanks Jr. (*Keith Brandon*); Joan Bennett (*Stephanie Richardson*); John Howard (*Hal Scott*); George Sanders (*Forrester*); Alan Hale (*Doctor Loren*); George Bancroft ("*Tex*" *Morgan*); Vincent Price (*David Richardson*); Gene Garrick (*Graham*); Francis McDonald (*Gracco*); Ray Mala (*Mala*); Peter Bronte (*Santos*); Lupita Tovar (*Native Girl*); Bob Fischer (*Explorer*); Noble Johnson (*Indian Chief*); Julian Rivero (*Proprietor*); Yola d'Avril, Nena Quartaro, Anita Camargo (*Native Girls*); Eumenio Blanco (*Well-Dressed Native*); Tony Paton (*Bartender*); Wilson Benge (*Butler*); Kay Linaker, Franco Corsaro.

THE FILM

The all-star cast makes *Green Hell*, director James Whale's last complete feature, worth watching, although its melodramatic script and acting as well are frequently over the top. The original story was supplied by Frances Marion, the woman whom former-agent and producer Harry Edington regarded as "one of Hollywood's greatest writers." Originally titled *South of the Amazon*, the story follows "six well-educated, high-minded young men who go to the Amazon jungles to search for Inca ruins." They are beset by savage natives, wild beasts, searing heat, and worst of all, Joan Bennett (sister of Vincent Price's first leading lady, Constance Bennett), who comes searching

for her husband, played by Price. He, however, has succumbed horribly to the venom on a poisoned arrow ("Carraraca snake, it paralyzes the motor nerves. I've seen men linger for months, in and out of consciousness—it's a filthy death!"), so Joan is free to romance hero Douglas Fairbanks Jr. with impunity.

The title *Green Hell* is the translation of "Inferno Verde," the name given to that section of South America by the natives. The production got no closer to that exotic location than the Universal back lot, where the picture was completed in mid-October 1939, after about ten weeks. Price's character, Richardson, is the quiet intellectual, the introspective member of the party who keeps to himself. Boating down the alligator-infested waterways, he has time to philosophize and inquires of Fairbanks: "Brandy, do you think a man can love two women at the same time, in his heart be faithful to each, and yet want to be free?" The macho hero replies, "What do you want—an answer or a justification?" Vincent was always rather proud of *Green Hell*'s excesses. "About five of the worst pictures ever made were all in that one picture. . . . We all adored making it because we realized that there wasn't a single word in it that was real. . . . I was playing the husband of Joan Bennett, and I never even met her on the picture. James Whale was very contained, very British. And very brilliant. But the story was so preposterous. There was a scene where Joan is brought in after having been lost in the jungle. She has one very neat smudge here [indicating his cheek], that's all. A week in the jungle, she got a smudge. And Alan Hale Sr., who was the doctor of this expedition, leaned over her and said, 'It's all right, fellows, it's just a coma!' The audience fell apart. One line was greater than the other. At the end, George Sanders has one pistol shot left, which he's saving for himself. And he does a whole soliloquy with his gun here [pointing to his head]. Everybody's saying, 'Pull it! Pull the trigger!' Oh, God!"

Price was making *Tower of London* at the same time and reportedly was shot by arrows for this picture one day and the next was drowned in a butt of malmsey by England's Richard III. Iron Eyes Cody and W. C. Wilkerson were hired expressly to perform the archery tricks, and no wires are in evidence when Price gets two in the ribs, so perhaps it was an actual stunt, although Douglas Fairbanks questions whether the insurance company would have permitted the actor to actually be at risk. According to the press kit, "one of the largest interior sets ever built was the jungle set . . . [which] covered approximately 45,000 square feet. Members of the cast had no trouble imagining they actually were in the jungle. They worked right through the worst heat wave to strike Hollywood in more than forty years. Between the heat and the large batteries of lights used to

Green Hell (*from left*) Douglas
Fairbanks Jr., George Bancroft
(*standing behind*), Alan Hale, John
Howard, Price, George Sanders,
and Gene Garrick

illuminate the set, temperatures soared to 130 degrees—
and remained there for a full week."

REVIEWS

Variety, January 15, 1940

"Although *Green Hell* is rather obvious melodrama for
the customers in key runs, it's sufficiently adventurous
and rousing in melodramatic content to satisfy in the
subsequent houses. . . ."

New York Times, February 4, 1940, Frank S. Nugent

". . . manages in its small and screamingly funny way to
include so many of the more flagrant clichés . . . we
cannot remember when we have had a better time at a
worse picture."

St. Louis Post-Dispatch, February 2, 1940

". . . Vincent Price, doing a grand job in a most interesting character role, dies far too early in the picture."
[Slightly biased hometown paper]

DOUGLAS FAIRBANKS

"Hell of a nice guy. Enchanting fellow; couldn't have
been nicer. I loved working with Vincent. *Green Hell*
was voted the worst picture of the year by Harvard University. It was a wonderful cast and a nice idea, but somehow
it didn't come off. It was really a pretty bad picture. I
think we had certain moments of misgivings, hoping
against hope that [producer] Harry Edington could pull
it together. James Whale had a reputation of being very
tough, very mean; I didn't find him so, myself. Maybe
he was scared of *me*, I don't know [laughs]! But it was

pretty much of a chore, we were all anxious to get it
over with. . . . Vincent was a very good leading man, an
excellent one. He was terribly well cast as Prince Albert;
I saw *Victoria Regina* and he was excellent in it. I suppose
I must have seen those horror pictures. [Asked if he had
put them out of his memory, he replied:] I do the best
I can! I was very fond of Vincent, and had great admiration for him, too."

6. THE HOUSE OF
THE SEVEN GABLES

UNIVERSAL

Released early March 1940

CREDITS

Associate Producer, Burt Kelly; *Director*, Joe May; *Screenplay*, Lester Cole; *Adaptation*, Harold Greene; *Based
on the novel by* Nathaniel Hawthorne; *Cinematography*,
Milton Krasner; *Art Director*, Jack Otterson; *Set Decorator*, R. A. Gausman; *Musical Score*, Frank Skinner; *Musical Director*, Charles Previn; "The Color of Your Eyes,"
Music by Frank Skinner, *Lyrics by* Ralph Freed; *Editor*,
Frank Gross; *Gowns*, Vera West; *Running time*, 89 minutes; black and white.

CAST

George Sanders (*Jaffrey Pyncheon*); Margaret Lindsay
(*Hepzibah Pyncheon*); Vincent Price (*Clifford Pyncheon*); Dick Foran (*Matthew Holgrave/Matthew*

The House of the Seven Gables With Margaret Lindsay

The House of the Seven Gables With George Sanders and Margaret Lindsay

The House of the Seven Gables In production shot, with George Sanders and Margaret Lindsay

Maule); Nan Grey (*Phoebe Pyncheon*); Cecil Kellaway (*Philip Barton*); Alan Napier (*Mr. Fuller*); Gilbert Emery (*Gerald Pyncheon*); Miles Mander (*Deacon Arnold Foster*); Charles Trowbridge (*Judge*); Edgar Norton (*Phineas Weed*); Harry Woods (*Wainwright*); Hugh Sothern (*Reverend Smith*); Harry Stubbs (*Jeremiah*); Harry Cording (*Blacksmith Hawkins*); Robert Dudley (*Bailiff*); Etta McDaniel (*Black Woman*); Nelson McDowell (*Courtroom Spectator*); Ed Brady (*Man with Blacksmith*); Russ Powell (*Grocer*); Michael Mark (*Man*); P. J. Kelly (*Man with Rake*).

THE FILM

The House of the Seven Gables is the traditional seat of the Pyncheons, a family whom legend has it was cursed by a man wronged by their ancestor. Tragedy continues through the centuries as Clifford Pyncheon is framed for the murder of his father by jealous brother Jaffrey. After languishing twenty years in prison, Clifford returns to a boarded-up manse and the faithful fiancée who waited for him. He then concocts a scheme in keeping with the tradition of the family curse which brings a fitting justice to his devious brother. Nathaniel Hawthorne's dour 1851 novel of a New England family curse was in public domain, so when Universal decided to adapt the book, the studio kept a low profile prepping the picture. Art director Jack Otterson went east ostensibly to visit relatives when he was actually in Salem inspecting the original house which inspired the atmospheric tale.

In this well-mounted, handsome period piece, which began filming just after New Year's 1940 and wrapped on January 29, the pace is methodical but carried by strong acting.

Robert Cummings, originally cast as Clifford Pyncheon, was replaced by Vincent Price at the last minute because of illness. Price gives a sturdy, believable "dual" performance: buoyant, virile, and romantic as the young lover; weary and tentative when at last he returns to Seven Gables, gray-haired and husky-voiced. The resignation in his face as he sees his much-changed reflection in a mirror is poignant. Later, he sits down at the harpsichord to quietly recapture the memory of the vibrant young couple with a future which he and Hepzibah once were. In his sixth motion picture, the ex–Broadway matinee idol received his first screen kiss, from Margaret Lindsay. And although he'd warbled a bit in *Service De Luxe*, it was also the first (but not the last) time Vincent sang in a film. The ex-member of the Yale Glee Club had a thoroughly pleasant supporting voice, hampered, as men often were in those days, by being forced to sing in a tenor key, higher than his comfortable register. (In college, Price had been a bass.) According to the papers, "carpenters were hurriedly called in to heighten every doorway at least three inches in the 'House of Seven Gables' after the final cast was selected. . . . Reason? Vincent Price, 6 feet 4 inches; George Sanders, 6 feet 3 inches; and Gilbert Emery, 6 feet 2 1/2 inches. . . . After watching prop men 'age' the attic set by draping it with cobwebs and dust, Vincent remarked to the reporter, 'You know, I've watched this being done before, and I estimate that one property man, armed with a studio web-making machine, does the work of ten-thousand efficient and busy spiders.'"

The picture opened in Chicago on February 29, 1940, at the RKO Palace. It was "Mystradrama Week" and "for the first time in screen history, a great *double* world premiere!"—*The House of the Seven Gables* and *Black Friday* (which starred Boris Karloff and Bela Lugosi.) Newspaper ads billed Vincent as "Handsome Star" and Lugosi as "Screen's Man of Horror"; both men appeared in person at the theater for four separate shows. The West Coast premiere was held March 14 at the Orpheum in San Francisco, where due no doubt to proximity to the movie capital, fans met a bevy of their favorite stars: joining Price and Lugosi were Boris Karloff, Mischa Auer, and George Sanders, among others.

REVIEWS

Hollywood Reporter, March 1, 1940

". . . a worthy contribution to the screen. . . . Universal started this almost as a quickie, which accounts for the absence of marquee names in the cast, but a combination of fine performances, good scripting and noteworthy direction make it into a picture considerably more worthwhile. It merits a wide audience, but due to its rather slow pace and its almost unrelieved gloomy tone, its box office prospects are a question . . . with Vincent Price excellent as the hero-victim of [Sanders's] wiles."

Variety, March 8, 1940

"Price clicks as the musical dreamer. . . ."

New Yorker, April 13, 1940, John Mosher

". . . On the screen it seems somewhat droll, I must say, and poor Hepzibah (Margaret Lindsay) with her little shop and her great, loyal love for Clifford (Vincent Price, of all the *jeunes premiers* to select) is beguiling though dusty."

Silver Screen [NY] June 1940

"Vincent Price . . . has at last hit his stride as one of the screen's most romantic leading men."

7. BRIGHAM YOUNG

20th CENTURY-FOX
Released September 27, 1940

CREDITS

Producer, Darryl F. Zanuck; *Associate Producer*, Kenneth Macgowan; *Director*, Henry Hathaway; *Screenplay*, Lamar Trotti; *Story*, Louis Bromfield; *Story Research*, Eleanor Harris; *Cinematography*, Arthur Miller; *Art Directors*, William Darling, Maurice Ransford; *Set Decorator*, Thomas Little; *Music*, Alfred Newman; *Editor*, Robert Bischoff; *Costumes*, Gwen Wakeling; *Running time*, 114 minutes; black and white.

CAST

Tyrone Power (*Jonathan Kent*); Linda Darnell (*Zina Webb*); Dean Jagger (*Brigham Young*); Brian Donlevy (*Angus Duncan*); Jane Darwell (*Eliza Kent*); John Carradine (*Porter Rockwell*); Mary Astor (*Mary Ann Young*); Vincent Price (*Joseph Smith*); Jean Rogers (*Clara Young*); Ann Todd (*Mary Kent*); Willard Robertson (*Heber Kimball*); Moroni Olsen (*Doc Richards*); Marc Lawrence (*Prosecutor*); Stanley Andrews (*Hyrum Smith*); Frank Thomas (*Hubert Crum*); Fuzzy Knight (*Pete*); Dickie Jones (*Henry Kent*); Selmer Jackson (*Caleb Kent*); Russell Simpson (*Major*); Chief Big Tree (*Big Elk*); Tully

Marshall (*Judge*); Ralph Dunn (*Jury Foreman*); Edwin Maxwell (*Leader of Mob*); Edmund MacDonald (*Elder*); Charles Halton (*Prosecutor*); Charles Middleton (*Mobster*); Frank La Rue (*Sheriff*); Paul Burns, Frank Shannon.

THE FILM

It was a junior writer at 20th Century-Fox in May 1938 who came up with the idea of a picture based on the life of the great Mormon leader Brigham Young. Studio head Darryl F. Zanuck dismissed the concept, based predominantly on anticipated problems with the notori-

Brigham Young Dean Jagger (*standing*), John Carradine (*standing with pistol*), and Price (*seated, right*)

Brigham Young With John Carradine (*left*), Tyrone Power, Linda Darnell (*seated behind*), and Moroni Olsen

ous movie Production Code: "There is no way that you can conceivably excuse to audiences of the world the idea of one man having eight or nine bed companions . . . because of religious or economic problems." Ultimately, Pulitzer Prize–winning author Louis Bromfield prepared a viable treatment; five months and seven revisions later, Fox had a screenplay that satisfied most objections. *Brigham Young* went before the cameras in April 1940. Two months of shooting by noted action director Henry Hathaway included second-unit location work in Utah. The picture cost close to $1.5 million and was one of Fox's most expensive to date.

Spencer Tracy had been high on the list for the title role, but because of more than one previous casting as a Catholic priest (*San Francisco* and *Boys Town*, among others), he was eliminated, and the part went to Dean Jagger. The character of Joseph Smith appears only briefly in the film but is integral to the story line. Zanuck apparently favored Preston Foster, but finally the studio announced that ". . . tall, broad-shouldered, handsome Vincent Price, the man the New York critics raved over in *Victoria Regina* and *Outward Bound*, won the role of Joseph Smith after Zanuck had tested twenty-seven players. Price bears a remarkable resemblance to the founder of the Mormon faith."

The initial focus of the film emphasizes the persecution of the Mormons in the 1840s. Price displays quiet forbearance when brought to trial for his religious beliefs; in the flashback sequence in which Brigham comes to Joseph Smith to learn about Mormonism, Price portrays a leader who is dedicated but approachable, a prophet who rolls up his sleeves and chops wood. The biased jury condemns "Holy Joe," and twenty-four minutes into the picture, "justice" is administered by an angry mob: Smith is assassinated awaiting removal to jail. Riddled with shotgun blasts, he gasps out, "Oh, Lord, my God," before he tumbles backward, shattering a huge window in the room and falling two stories to the street below. A resolute Brigham then leads his people out into the wilderness, and the story begins, mixing pioneer spirit with a romance between Tyrone Power and Linda Darnell. (The real Joseph Smith was lynched.)

In an effort to broaden the movie's appeal, the publicity department issued a release insisting "*Brigham Young* is not a biography; it does not profess to explain any religion. It is an epic tale about the adventures, the sufferings, the loves, and the heroic feats of a rugged, hard-hitting pioneer leader and his courageous people who dared the wilderness to found a western empire." Although all release prints retained the two-word title, advertising and publicity materials extended it to three: *Brigham Young—Frontiersman*. The film premiered in Salt Lake City on August 23, 1940.

"Before setting out on the trip the Mormons are shown undergoing religious persecution at the hands of Illinois mobs. Vincent Price, well cast as the muscular prophet Joseph Smith, follows the path of non-resistance to his brutal death. A courtroom scene gives Dean Jagger the opportunity to plead for Smith and deliver a stirring defense of religious freedom, the cornerstone of this country's early settlement."

Silver Screen, November 1940

"20th-Fox's *Brigham Young* was the major epic of the week.... Vincent Price clicked as a convincing and inspiring Joseph Smith.... All critics thought the love interest of Tyrone Power and Linda Darnell an unnecessary addition to an inspiring theme."

8.   HUDSON'S BAY

20th CENTURY-FOX

Released January 1941

CREDITS

Producer, Darryl F. Zanuck; *Associate Producer*, Kenneth Macgowan; *Director*, Irving Pichel; *Screenplay*, Lamar Trotti; *Cinematography*, Peverell Marley, George Barnes; *Art Directors*, Richard Day, Wiard B. Ihnen; *Set Decorator*, Thomas Little; *Editor*, Robert Simpson; *Costumes*, Travis Banton; *Running time*, 95 minutes; black and white.

Hudson's Bay With Virginia Field

CAST

Paul Muni (*Pierre Esprit Radisson*); Gene Tierney (*Barbara Hall*); Laird Cregar (*Gooseberry*); John Sutton (*Lord Edward Crewe*); Virginia Field (*Nell Gwyn*); Vincent Price (*King Charles II*); Nigel Bruce (*Prince Rupert*); Morton Lowry (*Gerald Hall*); Robert Greig (*Sir Robert*); Chief Thundercloud (*Orimha*); Frederick Worlock (*English Governor*); Montagu Love (*Governor D'Argenson*); Ian Wolfe (*Mayor*); Chief John Big Tree (*Chief*); Jody Gilbert (*Germaine*); Jean Del Val (*Captain*); Eugene Borden, Constant Franke (*Sentries*); Lilyan Irene (*Maid*); Keith Hitchcock (*Footman*); Dorothy Dearing (*Girl*); John Rogers (*Sailor*); Reginald Sheffield (*Clerk*); Robert Cory (*Orderly*); Denis d'Auburn, Eric Wilton (*Councillors*); Florence Bates (*Duchess*).

Hudson's Bay With Nigel Bruce (*left*), and Paul Muni (*right*)

THE FILM

In July 1940, while performing a season of summer stock in Skowhegan, Maine, Vincent Price was contacted by 20th Century-Fox mogul Darryl F. Zanuck. Impressed with the young actor's brief appearance in *Brigham Young*, the producer wired him with an offer to test for the part of French-Canadian explorer Pierre Esprit Radisson, the male lead in what was originally titled *Hudson's Bay Company*. Vincent came back to Hollywood to make *Hudson's Bay*, but not in the role of Radisson, which went instead to Paul Muni. In a story of intrepid seventeenth-century explorers carving out a fur-trading company in the new territory of Canada, Price wound up in the framing scenes set in England. He portrays a foppish King Charles II, bewigged and ruffed, equally happy whether stroking his trademark spaniel dogs or his comely mistress. Although a few years younger than the Merry Monarch would have been and more refined of feature, Price conveyed the king's innate intelligence and love of life. Fox apparently went to enormous trouble and expense to import for the picture a pregnant King Charles spaniel all the way from Michigan. The airlines refused to carry the rare breed, and so the animal arrived in Hollywood by rail; whereupon the company stood ready to shoot scenes with the dogs as soon as the pups put in an appearance.

Hudson's Bay was Vincent's first film with Gene Tierney; she had an equally brief role as the love interest of John Sutton's English nobleman turned adventurer. In spite of a budget of over $800,000, not enough was made of the splendor of the great outdoors, and Muni's exaggerated French dialect frequently approached farce. Reviews criticized the picture for being too talky and lacking in real action. Twenty-five years later, screenwriter Lamar Trotti would also script *the Jackals*, Price's South African Western.

REVIEWS

Variety, December 19, 1940

". . . Vincent Price makes a small role as King Charles of Britain notable."

New York Morning Telegraph, January 10, 1941

". . . with only Vincent Price, as King Charles himself, trying to set an example of what good acting should be."

Movie & Radio Guide [Chicago], January 11, 1941

". . . a special mark of recognition is scored by Vincent Price for his portrayal of Charles II of England."

9. THE SONG OF BERNADETTE

20th CENTURY-FOX

(Previewed December 21, 1943, to qualify for the Oscars) Released January 1944

CREDITS

Producer, William Perlberg; *Director*, Henry King; *Screenplay*, George Seaton; *Based on the novel by* Franz Werfel; *Cinematography*, Arthur Miller; *Art Directors*, James Basevi, William Darling; *Set Decorators*, Thomas Little, Frank E. Hughes; *Music*, Alfred Newman; *Orchestrations*, Edward Powell; *Editor*, Barbara McLean; *Costumes*, Rene Hubert; *Makeup*, Guy Pearce; *Special Effects*, Fred Sersen; *Running time*, 156 minutes; black and white.

CAST

Jennifer Jones (*Bernadette Soubirous*); William Eythe (*Antoine Nicolau*); Charles Bickford (*Dean Peyremale*); Vincent Price (*Dutour*); Lee J. Cobb (*Dr. Dozous*); Gladys Cooper (*Sister Marie Theresa Vauzous*); Anne Revere (*Louise Soubirous*); Roman Bohnen (*François Soubirous*); Mary Anderson (*Jeanne Abadie*); Patricia Morison (*Empress Eugenie*); Aubrey Mather (*Lacade*); Charles Dingle (*Commissioner Jacomet*); Edith Barrett (*Croisine Bouhouhorts*); Sig Rumann (*Louis Bouriette*); Blanche Yurka (*Bernarde Casterot*); Marcel Dalio (*Callet*); Pedro de Cordoba (*Dr. Le Crampe*); Jerome Cowan (*Emperor Louis Napoleon*); Linda Darnell (*The Vision*); Charles Waldron (*Bishop of Tarbes*); Moroni Olsen (*Chaplain*); Nana Bryant (*Convent Mother Superior*); Manart Kippen (*Charles Bouhouhorts*); Merrill Rodin (*Jean Soubirous*); John Maxwell Hayes (*Father Pomian*); Jean Del Val (*Estrade*); Tala Birell (*Mme. Bruat*); Frank Reicher (*Dr. St. Cyr*); Alan Napier (*Psychiatrist*); Ian Wolfe (*Minister of the Interior*); Dickie Moore (*Adolar*); Mae Marsh (*Woman*); Nestor Paiva (*Baker*); George Gleboff, Mayo Newhall, Edward Van Sloan, Tom Stevenson (*Doctors*); Arthur Hohl, Fritz Leiber (*Monks*).

THE FILM

The Song of Bernadette is one of the more prestigious credits in Vincent Price's film career. The story was the inspiration of a writer named Franz Werfel, who was among those fleeing the Nazi invasion after the collapse of France in June 1940. Reaching Lourdes, knowing that each day he might become a prisoner condemned to death, Werfel learned of the history of Bernadette Soubirous, a French peasant girl who claimed in 1858 that the Virgin Mary appeared to her in a village grotto. She spent most of her life in a convent and was canonized as a saint in 1933. Werfel made a vow that if he escaped to America, he would "magnify the divine mystery and the holiness of man" as personified in "the song of Bernadette." After it was made, Werfel considered the finished film "a triumph for honesty of artistic purpose and unswerving fidelity to the literary truth."

20th Century-Fox purchased the rights to Werfel's book on April 1, 1942, in advance of publication. The first draft screenplay, dated November 13, was an awkward 266 pages long. After the crew was pulled together, casting began the first week of December, and countless girls were tested for the crucial lead role, including studio player Anne Baxter. Finally, twenty-three-old actress who had made a couple of forgotten late-thirties pictures as Phylis Isley changed her name to Jennifer Jones for her "official" film debut. *Bernadette* went before the cameras on March 29, 1943, after nearly a year of research, design, and construction of sets, a difficult task under wartime restrictions. Final cutting and editing were conducted in June, and by October, Alfred Newman had began to score the picture.

Vincent Price received fourth billing for his pivotal role as the cynical Imperial Prosecutor, contemptuous of religious fanaticism, determined to prove Bernadette's story false. Handsome and elegant, Dutour frequently sniffs into a handkerchief held to his nose, coughing discreetly. It's "the influenza again," he insists, but his hoarse voice betrays the beginnings of the throat cancer which will kill him by degrees. As the years pass, the

The Song of Bernadette As Imperial Prosecutor Dutour

The Song of Bernadette With Alan Napier (*left*), Charles Bickford, and Jennifer Jones

The Song of Bernadette "For those who believe in God, no explanation is necessary. For those who do not believe in God, no explanation is possible."

ministry of the Lady at Lourdes brings miracles to the faithful and hope to the hopeless. "For those who believe in God, no explanation is necessary. For those who do not believe in God, no explanation is possible." And in a grotto now transformed into a holy shrine, lit by the candles of thousands of worshipers, a dying Dutour falls to his knees. Pale, his sunken eyes glistening, he clutches the slender iron gate which preserves the original site and implores, "Pray for me, Bernadette." "One of my best roles," Price would later remark. "I felt at home with the cast of highly competent stage actors."

Vincent Price's wife, Edith Barrett, was one of the dozens of familiar faces among the talented cast, playing a simple village woman with faith in Bernadette's vision whose crippled baby is healed.

Song of Bernadette did very well at the Oscars, with eleven nominations, garnering not only Best Actress honors for Jones but also awards for Art Direction, Cinematography, and Alfred Newman's superb music score.

On April 21, 1946, CBS's popular *Frigidaire Hollywood Star Time* broadcast a radio adaptation of *The Song of Bernadette* starring Vanessa Brown. Although Lee J. Cobb repeated his film role of Dozous, Vincent Price instead played the Dean of Lourdes (who comes to be one of the girl's staunchest supporters).

REVIEWS

Variety, December 21, 1943

". . . an absorbing, emotional and dramatic picturization of Werfel's novel. It's big in every respect; will rate fine critical attention; great in prestige for the industry; and

due for top b.o. reaction. . . . Support is studded with numerous brilliant portrayals, including Charles Bickford, William Eythe, Vincent Price, Lee J. Cobb, Gladys Cooper, Anne Revere, Roman Bohnen, Aubrey Mather, Charles Dingle, Blanche Yurka, Edith Barrett, John Maxwell Hayes and many others. . . . To every person who sees *Bernadette*, there is warmth, inspiration and pause for reflection regardless of creed or non-belief."

P.M. New York, January 27, 1944

"Vincent Price, as the ultra-cynical Imperial Prosecutor, is a perfect symbolization of ruthless intellect."

10. THE EVE OF ST. MARK

20th CENTURY-FOX
Released May 1944

CREDITS

Producer, William Perlberg; *Director*, John M. Stahl; *Screenplay*, George Seaton; *Based on the play by* Maxwell Anderson; *Cinematography*, Joseph LaShelle; *Art Directors*, James Basevi, Russell Spencer; *Set Decorators*, Thomas Little, Frank E. Hughes; *Music*, Cyril J. Mockridge; *Music Director*, Emil Newman; *Editor*, Louis Sacking; *Special Effects*, Fred Sersen; *Running time*, 96 minutes; black and white.

CAST

Anne Baxter (*Janet Feller*); William Eythe (*Quizz West*); Michael O'Shea (*Sergeant Mulveroy*); Vincent Price (*Pvt. Francis Marion*); Ruth Nelson (*Nell West*); Ray Collins (*Deckman West*); Stanley Prager (*Private Glinka*); Henry Morgan (*Private Shevlin*); Robert Bailey (*Corporal Tate*); Joann Dolan (*Lill Bird*); Toni Favor (*Sal Bird*); George Mathews (*Sergeant Ruby*); John Archer (*Private Carter*); Murray Alper (*Sergeant Kriven*); Dickie Moore (*Zip West*); Joven E. Rola (*Pepita*); Harry Shannon (*Chaplain*); Roger Clark (*Captain*); Jimmy Clark (*Neil West*); Harry Carter (*Medical Officer*); Harry Strang (*Military Policeman*); Rod Bacon, Michael Owen, Blake Edwards, John Whitney (*Soldiers*); Milton Kibbee (*Pete Feller*); Matt McHugh (*Cabdriver*); Buddy Yarus (*Polinski*).

THE FILM

The Eve of St. Mark is unknown to most of his fans, but it afforded Vincent Price what was arguably the best role

The Eve of St. Mark With William Eythe

of his film career. His charming, understated, heroic performance in it garnered some of the best critical notices he ever received.

In November 1942, Fox spent $300,000 for the rights to Maxwell Anderson's moving blank-verse play about war and duty. The screen version follows World War II soldiers through service training and weekend leave with girlfriends and at the ballpark. When the GI's are posted to combat duty overseas on a remote Philippine island, they must grapple with the eternal, unanswerable question "How close must a man come to being horizontal before he earns the right to remain perpendicular?"

As Pvt. Francis Marion, Price is a towering, lanky beanpole in fatigues; his fair hair, buzzed short, emphasizes the fine bones of his face. Irresistibly, he creates a thoroughly likable scapegrace full of a humanity and nobility completely lacking in that other attractive southerner *Laura*'s Shelby Carpenter. With a shield of affected cynicism, Marion mocks his own poetic soul by spouting verses to amuse his compatriots and to woo girls. It is an intelligently conceived, entirely honest characterization, proving to just what heights Price could climb when the material was worthy of his gifts.

Pinned down on their island, the Americans are pummeled by enemy fire; rations depleted, their quinine gone, many are racked with malaria. A young Filipino girl has remained to help them. The character of Private Marion figures prominently in the drama of the story when it falls to him, wrapped in blankets and trembling with disease, to relate the title legend—that on St. Mark's eve, if a maiden stands in the door of a church, she will see inside all those who are going to die that year. Glances shift to the ethereal native girl. . . . At last, the remaining soldiers receive orders that release them from their post—unless they feel they can hold on and continue to fight. Fight to the death. And it is Marion who delivers the stirring speech which inspires his comrades to "stick it out another day." In Anderson's play, the soldiers died to a man, sacrificing themselves for the greater good, and it was originally intended for the film to end the same way. At some point, the screenplay was changed and the moral dilemma skirted when enemy fire destroys their antiaircraft gun. The GIs then abandon the island, piling into a tiny raft with clear consciences, knowing they have done their duty.

The Eve of St. Mark was shot around September and October 1943 and completed by mid-November. By the time of release, nearly three years after Pearl Harbor, a few critics felt the film was dated, but the heroism embodied by the characters in it can never be.

The Eve of St. Mark With (*from left*) Henry Morgan, Stanley Prager, William Eythe, Robert Bailey, and George Mathews

REVIEWS

Hollywood Reporter, May 17, 1944

". . . Vincent Price scores a rich hit as the sorrowful Southerner with a weakness for Cuba Libres."

New York Daily News, April 31, 1944

"Price gives an arresting performance in the role of a poetry-spouting soldier. . . ."

New Yorker, June 3, 1944

"[Eythe and Baxter] are extremely well supported, especially it seems to me by Vincent Price. . . . Mr. Price has been, in the course of his acting career, Queen Victoria's Prince Consort, Abraham Lincoln, a murderous jewel thief, and now an amiable GI, which demonstrates a nice flexibility."

[Springfield, MA] News, July 14, 1944

". . . But the credits for acting go, not to Eythe, but to Vincent Price, who is superb. . . . It is Price who somehow gives all the life to the film, who makes it glow with his personality as a soft-speaking, poetry-reading cynic. And it is Price who keynotes the entire story with his ringing question: 'How close must a man come to being horizontal before he earns the right to remain perpendicular?' . . . *Eve* sets a new high in the field of motion pictures, and sets Vincent Price as a promising star on the film horizon."

VINCENT PRICE

(*Saturday Evening Post*, July 13, 1946)

"I think an actor finds much less pleasure in playing himself than he does in playing a person who is com-

pletely different. Basically that is why my favorite role was the literary-minded, poetry-spouting, and sometimes drunken young Southerner, Francis Marion . . . the only character with a completely delightful sense of humor I've played on screen. In contrast, the humor of the imperial prosecutor in *The Song of Bernadette* was so bitter and cynical that you were torn between pity and contempt for such a character. Marion could be cynical, with his pathetically ridiculous quotations, but there was a funny honesty about the guy that I enjoyed. . . ." We worked like the devil, but there wasn't a gayer, happier set anywhere. . . ."

11. WILSON

20th CENTURY-FOX
Released August 1, 1944

CREDITS

Producer, Darryl F. Zanuck; *Director*, Henry King; *Screenplay*, Lamar Trotti; *Cinematography*, Leon Shamroy; *Art Directors*, Wiard Ihnen, James Basevi; *Set Decorators*, Thomas Little, Paul S. Fox; *Music*, Alfred Newman; *Orchestrations*, Edward Powell; *Editor*, Barbara McLean; *Running time*, 154 minutes; color.

CAST

Alexander Knox (*Woodrow Wilson*); Charles Coburn (*Prof. Henry Holmes*); Geraldine Fitzgerald (*Edith Wilson*); Thomas Mitchell (*Joseph Tumulty*); Ruth Nelson (*Ellen Wilson*); Sir Cedric Hardwicke (*Sen. Henry Cabot Lodge*); Vincent Price (*William Gibbs McAdoo*); William Eythe (*Lt. George Felton*); Mary Anderson (*Eleanor Wilson*); Ruth Ford (*Margaret Wilson*); Sidney Blackmer (*Josephus Daniels*); Madeleine Forbes (*Jessie Wilson*); Stanley Ridges (*Admiral Grayson*); Eddie Foy Jr. (*Eddie Foy*); Charles Halton (*Colonel House*); Thurston Hall (*Sen. Edward H. Jones*); Stanley Logan (*Secretary Lansing*); Marcel Dalio (*Clemenceau*); Edwin Maxwell (*William Jennings Bryan*); Tonio Selwart (*Count Von Bernstorff*); John Ince (*Senator Watson*); Arthur Loft (*Secretary Lane*); Robert Barrat (*Secretary Meredith*); George Macready (*William McCoombs*); Francis X. Bushman (*Barney Baruch*).

THE FILM

Wilson opens with a college football game in 1909 in which the Bulldogs of Yale defeat the Tigers of Princeton. The football loss notwithstanding, the president of Princeton, Woodrow Wilson, is fated to do pretty well

Wilson Price as McAdoo looks on as Alexander Knox acts presidential in the title role.

in the political arena. Friends persuade him to run for governor; after a lengthy fight, he wins the nomination from the Democratic National Convention of 1912 and is elected president of the United States.

It is to be presumed that William Gibbs McAdoo, secretary of the treasury, who married Wilson's daughter, played a larger part in the administration than Vincent Price does in portraying him in this picture. Price doesn't appear until thirty minutes into the film; his second scene comes after nearly an hour and a quarter. In all, the actor has less than seven minutes of screen time, most of which consists merely of standing in the background during memorable historical moments and delivering only a handful of lines.

Wilson was a huge, handsome picture, shooting for nearly five months, from November 1, 1943, through the second week in March 1944. Sumptuous re-creations of White House interiors, fascinating black-and-white newsreel footage, and a stirring score of patriotic war songs add immeasurably to what is an unabashedly idealistic depiction of the twenty-eighth president's two terms. Nominated for ten Academy Awards, including one for Alexander Knox, it won five: for Original Screenplay, Art Direction, Cinematography (Color), Editing, and Sound Recording. Rather incredibly, based on the size of the role, Vincent himself received a *Box-Office* Blue Ribbon Award for August 1945 for McAdoo. Perhaps it was more an indication of his growing popularity with audiences.

REVIEWS

New York Times, August 2, 1944, Bosley Crowther

"... an impressive screen biography ..."

Variety, week of August 7, 1944

"*Wilson* is a rah-rah, rousing, 100% American entertainment, which, post-war, can be its own Yankee goodwill-getter abroad. . . . For domestic consumption, it's a must. It will mop up at the box office. . . . Here is history that is entertainment. . . . Vincent Price as McAdoo . . . expertly cast."

ALEXANDER KNOX

(Canadian born, Mr. Knox lived in England for over forty years. In addition to his acting credits, he authored novels, plays, and screenplays and wrote the following memoir exclusively for this book only a few weeks before he passed away.)

"Kenneth Macgowan, when he was setting up his film school at UCLA, remarked to me one day that [Vincent Price] was too intelligent to be an actor.

I never knew Vinnie very well. I met him first when he was playing McAdoo in Col. Zanuck's *Wilson*. In one scene, I and a couple of other actors had to stand on four-inch boxes so that [director of photography] Leon Shamroy could get the angle he wanted over Vinnie's shoulder. I've known four good directors who stood nearly six and a half feet in their socks: H. K. Ayliff, Tyrone Guthrie, John Cromwell, and Henry King. I asked Vinnie if he ever planned to direct a film. He agreed that his stature could lose him interesting parts, but directors of films didn't seem to him to have a very good time and he liked to enjoy himself.

He enjoyed movies and the theater. He read widely. He was fairly well acquainted with music, and his knowledge of painting and sculpture was not only extensive but acute, subtle and full of understanding. When he ran his little gallery in Beverly Hills [1943–45], he sold me an excellent John Sloan etching and a lovely drawing by Mary Cassatt. Later on, when he was buying paintings for a big department store, I used to see him quite often in London. He was a friend of Mildred and Sam Jaffe [later the coproducer of *Theater of Blood*]. I'd see him often at their flat in Eaton Square as well as at some of the less expensive auction houses. I don't think Vinnie ever brought a painting which didn't have some vital quality to recommend it.

As an actor, he had a quality which was special and very useful on the screen, so he always had jobs he could take if he liked. I think that at first he was irritated to discover that his qualities were thought by directors and producers to be too special. Later on, he was, at least to some extent, amused at the direction his career had taken. Directors and producers were naturally delighted to discover an actor with his degree of skill prepared to take on the long list of popular and successful "horror" pictures for which Vinnie will be chiefly remembered. This fact irritated him a bit, but he had the kind of humor which could extract wit even from his irritation.

My own feeling is that, in a better world, Vinnie would have been able to move back and forth from movies to theater. That's easier in the United Kingdom than in the United States. His value to the motion-picture "industry" did, of course, enable him to pursue wider interests with skill and enjoyment. He saw, of course, that there was always a certain irony in the fact that his expertise at "horror" allowed him to enjoy his enjoyments rather more than most people. He didn't like actors who complained. He had a line that went something like this: "Actors are lucky. Most people work hard to earn money so they can play. Actors get paid for playing." That last

Wilson With Mary Anderson

sounds dull. I guess I didn't listen carefully enough. When Vinnie expressed the same "content," it wasn't dull; it was amusing. On the whole, actors in Hollywood behaved in a fairly expected way. Vincent Price was definitely an exception and a most valuable one."

12. LAURA

20th CENTURY-FOX
Released October 11, 1944

CREDITS

Producer/Director, Otto Preminger; *Screenplay,* Jay Dratler, Samuel Hoffenstein, Betty Reinhardt; *Based on the novel by* Vera Caspary; *Cinematography,* Joseph La-Shelle; *Art Directors,* Lyle Wheeler, Leland Fuller; *Set Decorator,* Thomas Little; *Music,* David Raksin; *Musical Director,* Emil Newman; *Editor,* Louis Loeffler; *Costumes,* Bonnie Cashin; *Makeup,* Guy Pearce; *Running time,* 88 minutes; black and white.

CAST

Gene Tierney (*Laura Hunt*); Dana Andrews (*Lt. Mark McPherson*); Clifton Webb (*Waldo Lydecker*); Vincent Price (*Shelby Carpenter*); Judith Anderson (*Ann Treadwell*); Dorothy Adams (*Bessie Clary*); James Flavin (*Sergeant McAvity*); Clyde Fillmore (*Bullitt*); Ralph Dunn (*Fred Callahan*); Kathleen Howard (*Louise the Cook*); Lee Tung Foo (*Servant*); Harold Schlickenmayer, Harry Strang, Lane Chandler (*Detectives*); Frank La Rue (*Hairdresser*); Buster Miles (*Office Boy*); Jane Nigh (*Secretary*); William Forrest (*Man*); John Dexter (*Jacoby*); Alexander Sacha, Dorothy Christy, Aileen Pringle, Terry Adams, Jean Fenwick, Yolanda Lacca, Forbes Murray, Cyril Ring, Nester Eristoff, Kay Linaker, Cara Williams, Gloria Marlin, Beatrice Gray, Kay Connors, Frances Gladwin.

THE FILM

Laura is one of the most highly acclaimed productions in which Vincent Price took part, and the classic film noir remains an all-time cinema favorite.

Laura With Clifton Webb, Judith Anderson, Dana Andrews, and "The Portrait"

In a stylish combination of mystery and twisted romance, a police detective becomes captivated by the woman whose murder he is investigating. None of the intriguing personalities involved—Clifton Webb's vitriolic mentor, Vincent Price's expertly polished playboy fiancé, Judith Anderson's possessive society matron, even Dana Andrews's laconic cop, and Gene Tierney's ice maiden—is what he or she seems. Each is just a little shady, just a little rotten under a glossy exterior.

Rouben Mamoulian was slated to direct the picture, but producer Otto Preminger and studio head Darryl F. Zanuck were unhappy with early rushes. The decision was made to scrap all extant footage, as well as Mamoulian, the cameraman, the designer, and an unsatisfactory portrait of the leading lady which had been painted by Mamoulian's wife. Preminger himself took the helm; it was generally agreed that Mamoulian (the highly successful director of such films as *Becky Sharp* and *The Mark of Zorro*) had been unable to capture the underlying nastiness of the characters. In 1986, Vincent Price was quoted: "I once asked Otto why he did so much better with *Laura* than Rouben. Otto told me: 'Rouben only knows nice people. I understand the characters in *Laura*. They're all heels, just like my friends.'" Original set reference stills prominently display a production slate on which Mamoulian's name is printed as director; in some shots, messily chalked over with the name Preminger.

Opening to mixed reviews, *Laura* nonetheless won the Oscar for cinematography and was up for five other awards, including Best Director and a Best Supporting

Laura With Judith Anderson

Laura (Lobby title card courtesy Camden House)

Actor nod for Clifton Webb in his first "talkie." (Contrary to film legend, Webb did not make his cinema debut in *Laura*, although it was categorically the movie which brought him to prominence; he had made several silent films in the twenties.) Surprisingly, David Raksin's evocative score, with the enduring theme song to which Johnny Mercer later added lyrics, was not even nominated. (Alfred Newman actually conducted, although his brother Emil, who was originally scheduled, received screen credit.)

The casting of Vincent Price to play Laura's scapegrace southern fiancé, Shelby Carpenter, was inspired. Clean-shaven and superbly tailored, the thirty-three-year-old actor was every inch the physical paragon of the novel: "The dark suit chosen for this day of mourning could not dull his vivid grandeur. Male energy shone in his tanned skin. . . . Cigarette smoke curled in flawless circles from Shelby's flawless lips. . . . Mark saw Shelby through the woman's eyes, clothed in the charm he had donned, like a bright domino, for the woman's pleasure.

The ripe color, the chiseled features, the clear, long-lashed eyes . . . the perfect mold of a man."

In the crucial scene in which Detective McPherson (Dana Andrews) prepares to reveal the name of the murderer, and the suspects all react with concern, Preminger had instructed Judith Anderson, as Laura's aunt, to reach for the security of the hand of her toy-boy, Shelby. Vincent, however, kept forgetting to keep his arm at his side and in reach of the considerably shorter Anderson. He was quite taken 'aback when the dignified Australian actress, who would later become a Dame of the British Empire, leaned over to him and muttered, "For crissakes, put it where I can get at it!" Price loved recounting that both he and Anderson became so convulsed every time Preminger called for another take that the exasperated director had to throw them off the stage for about an hour until they regained their composure.

A press release issued by Fox publicity during the very early days of production refers to a scene apparently cut in the final version. "Vincent Price, best known for his keen-edged young character performances . . . gets his opportunity to toss his vocal hat in the ring in his current role. And undeterred by the fact that Sinatra made bobby sox history with 'You'll Never Know,' Price will sing this hit number. Preminger, director Rouben Mamoulian and the studio's music department promptly went into ecstasies over Price's rich baritone. . . . Price makes his vocal bow in films at an informal smart set party." (Obviously, it made for better press copy to conveniently forget that, four years earlier, Vincent had played a songwriter in *The House of the Seven Gables* for another studio and had serenaded fiancée Margaret Lindsay.)

In the spring of 1983, Vincent cohosted *Your Choice for the Film Awards* on television with Barbara Eden. He and the audience were treated to a surprise *Laura* reunion when he was joined on stage by Tierney and Andrews, the first time the three costars had been together since making the picture. It was a rare moment.

Laura (Deleted scene) "Shelby Carpenter" sings "You'll Never Know"

REVIEWS

Variety, October 11, 1944

"A smart murder-mystery, expertly tailored in script, casting and direction, *Laura* is one of the neatest films to come along this season. . . . Vincent Price is convincing as a weak-willed ne'er-do-well."

New York Times, October 12, 1944, Thomas M. Pryor

"When a murder mystery possessing as much sustained suspense, good acting and caustically brittle dialogue as *Laura* . . . comes along, it might seem a little like carping to suggest that it could have been even better. . . . For Gene Tierney simply doesn't measure up to the word portrait of her character. . . . Aside from that principal reservation, however, *Laura* is an intriguing melodrama . . . on the whole close to being a top-drawer mystery."

VINCENT PRICE

("The Villains Still Pursue Me" lecture)

"Every actor longs to be in a classic film—a film that is so well made, so well acted, directed, photographed, written, everything, it remains a classic. And one of those films that I was in, and I'm proud of it, was *Laura*. . . . There were five of us in this picture. And when we were all sent the script, we all knew each other very well. And we all called each other and said, 'Darling! Isn't it wonderful? We're going to be in this wonderful picture together. Isn't it marvelous? And we're going to be with this darling director.' It was repulsive. So we got to the studio, and indeed it was all darling. It was absolutely wonderful. The script was marvelous, the cameraman was marvelous, the director was wonderful, we were wonderful. And finally, after we'd been going it for about a month, we got a call saying everything had been scrapped. And we said, 'But it was so darling!' We were starting all over again. We had a new cameraman, we had a new director. And we all started to work, and we all loved each other. We loved the script, we loved the new cameraman. We liked Otto [audience laughter]. And finally the picture was finished. We all went to see it together. It was extraordinary. It was ostensibly the same picture we had done with the other director, but there was something added. Otto had imbued every single character in this play with an underlying evil. The other director had no knowledge of that, and we had played sort of surface characters."

Laura Reunion 1983: Gene Tierney and Dana Andrews

The Keys of the Kingdom With Gregory Peck

13. THE KEYS OF THE KINGDOM

20th CENTURY-FOX
Released December 15, 1944

CREDITS

Producer, Joseph L. Mankiewicz; *Director*, John M. Stahl; *Screenplay*, Joseph L. Mankiewicz and Nunnally Johnson; *Based on the novel by* A. J. Cronin; *Cinematography*, Arthur Miller; *Art Directors*, James Basevi, William Darling; *Set Decorator*, Thomas Little; *Music*, Alfred Newman; *Editor*, James B. Clark; *Costumes*, Bonnie Cashin; *Makeup*, Guy Pearce; *Running time*, 137 minutes; black and white.

CAST

Gregory Peck (*Father Francis Chisholm*); Thomas Mitchell (*Dr. Willie Tulloch*); Vincent Price (*Monsignor Angus Mealy*); Rosa Stradner [Mrs. Joseph Mankiewicz] (*Mother Maria Veronica*); Roddy McDowall (*Francis as a child*); Edmund Gwenn (*Rev. Hamish MacNabb*); Sir Cedric Hardwicke (*Monsignor Sleeth*); Peggy Ann Garner (*Nora as a child*); Jane Ball (*Nora*); James Gleason (*Dr. Wilbur Fiske*); Anne Revere (*Agnes Fiske*); Ruth Nelson (*Lisbeth Chisholm*); Benson Fong (*Joseph*); Leonard Strong (*Mr. Chia*); Philip Ahn (*Mr. Pao*); Arthur Shields (*Father Tarrant*); Edith Barrett (*Aunt Polly*); Dennis Hoey (*Alex Chisholm*).

THE FILM

The film version of A. J. Cronin's bestselling novel of a Scottish missionary's life in China was Gregory Peck's second picture, and his sincere, spiritual performance garnered him an Academy Award nomination. It was also the second time Vincent Price appeared in a large-scale religious movie; in fact, reviews compared Fox's *The Keys of the Kingdom* both favorably and unfavorably to the studio's *The Song of Bernadette*. Both showcased memorable leading characters, with a strong supporting cast, in moving, sentimental stories. The life and Christian calling of aged Father Francis Chisholm are recounted in a flashback which reveals the enormous influence the humble and courageous cleric had on the lives of those to whom he ministered in rural China over the decades. *The Keys of the Kingdom* was in production from February 1 through May 20, 1944.

Although very prominently billed as Angus Mealy, Francis Chisholm's childhood friend, Vincent Price didn't have a great deal more to do in this inspirational film than he did in *Wilson* earlier in the same year. After a short scene in which he leaves for college with schoolmate Peck, which takes place in the first fifteen minutes of the film, he doesn't put in an appearance for another hour and a half, making quite an entrance riding into Peck's rural Paitan parish perched on a wheelbarrow. Monsignor Mealy is a man overly impressed with his high office, pompous and a bit worldly but genuinely fond of the old friend who has not risen so high. He has a couple of very talky scenes but only ten minutes of actual screen time. (Gregory Peck confirms that several

The Keys of the Kingdom (Deleted scene) with Gregory Peck

91

filmed sequences, at least one at college with Price, were cut from the final print.) Price described his character as "that fat priest." "I had to starve all through *Eve of St. Mark* so I could look heroic," he told a reporter during the filming of *Keys*. "I ate nothing but rabbit food during *Song of Bernadette*. I had some more of the same in *Wilson* so I wouldn't be giving a bay window to William G. McAdoo. Then came this picture with me turning into a big fat bishop, and I started to eat. Boy did I eat. I'm still eating."

Keys was Vincent's second film with wife Edith Barrett, who appeared as Peck's Aunt Polly; however, they do little more than exchange greetings in one short scene. It was the first time Vincent "worked" with Roddy McDowall, who would become a longtime friend, but since they appear in different time frames, they have no scenes together at all.

Although Price's talents were underutilized in *The Keys of the Kingdom*, the young actor apparently made an impression on the film's producer. Two years later, for his next project, and his first as a director, Joe Mankiewicz would offer Vincent the male lead, a role which would prove to be his most important to date.

REVIEWS

Variety, December 13, 1944

". . . takes its place with *Song of Bernadette* and *Going My Way* in inspired, dignified artistic, heart-warming cinematurgy about the Church ... ."

New York World-Telegram, December 29, 1944

"Gregory Peck is the player who dominates the story, but his supporting cast is full of performances to swell Hollywood's pride ... [including] Vincent Price as a bishop whose faith has become submerged in ambition."

New York Morning Telegraph, December 30, 1944

". . . fails in at least two respects: it has neither the majesty or nobility of *The Song of Bernadette* nor the warm, enchanting humanity of *Going My Way*."

GREGORY PECK

"I'm very confident that [I first met Vincent] in the Fox wardrobe department; we were strutting around together in our long cassocks. . . . I had seen Vincent on Broadway with Helen Hayes in *Victoria Regina* when I was starving in New York. I was at the Neighborhood Playhouse school; I graduated from Berkeley and ran straight to New York to try to make something out of myself. We saw all the Broadway shows, but we never saw a first act. We used to mingle with the smokers on the sidewalk after the first act intermission. There'd be a little band

of cigarette smokers on the sidewalk—and somehow, in those days, they did not ask for your stub—and we'd drift back in with them, in a nonchalant fashion, and watch to see where everybody sat. Almost always, there were a few vacant seats. You'd just casually make your way over, make sure that everybody else was in, and just before the lights went down and the curtain went up, ease into a seat. So we used to see the second and third act of everything. And that's how I saw *Victoria Regina*. I remember I thought Vincent was just the *last word* in a cultivated, handsome, well-spoken, aristocratic young *Englishman*. That was the impression he made on me. And spoke beautifully. I was at drama school trying to learn *how* to speak; I had a kind of a lazy Southern California accent when I first went there. So he made a big impression on me. And when we met in the [Fox] wardrobe, I *told* him that. I said, "You know, you're kind of an inspiration to me, and I admired your performance and your speech." I remember being very surprised to learn that he was not an Englishman at all. . . .

We were *busy* [on *The Keys of The Kingdom*]. And I was *slogging* through a six-month schedule, with new scenes every day, and Vincent just *strode* in a couple of times, for a couple of episodes, and he was fresh and vigorous, and I was *slogging* along on scene number two hundred forty-seven [laughs]! There wasn't too much time for just sitting around, hanging out and telling stories, catching up on things; we were just busy working. I remember that he was a big one for jokes. He was a *laughing* man; he had a lot of mischief and humor in him, *always*. And he had a good, self-deprecating sense of humor. . . . He was one of the most charming, and one of the funniest men, that I met. . . .

[Gregory Peck was one of the half-dozen prime movers and shakers behind the founding of the La Jolla Playhouse. The enormously respected theater was created to give actors working in Hollywood in the forties and fifties an opportunity to flex their muscles without having to go back east.] Vincent did *The Cocktail Party* for us, and he was *just marvelous*. *That* was his kind of material; he was *brilliant*. Literate, intelligent writing of a superior quality—that was his meat and drink. That was what Vincent was meant to do. . . . I would just venture to say that had he remained in the theater, he would have become a kind of Alfred Lunt; he would've been a great stage star, and he would have gone on year after year, as the actors in London do. One successful play after another, and played the great classic roles. I'm not so sure Vincent should have focused in on motion pictures. . . . The wonderful voice—and the wonderful delivery—was *demanded* in the theater and *not* demanded in the pictures. I think Vincent was born to do great plays and classic roles and to play kings and princes. . . .

I think, with the stage training behind him, Vincent was audience-conscious, and I doubt if there was ever a moment when he was on-screen that it wasn't in the back of his mind to give the audience a good show for their money. He was a professional. You get a bad piece of material, you do everything you can to improve it. You try to throw a kind of veil over bad dialogue or a clumsily written scene; you reach down and find something to make it more interesting to the audience, tap something inside yourself that'll give it a little life. That's what you're *supposed* to do. That's what Vincent did. I'm sure that he never, in his *life*, phoned it in, so to speak, or did less than his utmost best.... There is a coarse style of acting, and Vincent, by nature, would never fall into that. It's total absence of vulgarity. I think if someone asked me to define Vincent's style, I would say he was incapable of being coarse or of being vulgar. He had his own style. There was no one quite like him.

Of course, it's entirely futile to say so, but I— So often, when people you love move on, you feel a sense of regret that you weren't closer to them, that circumstances took you in different directions. And I have that feeling about Vincent. I loved him and I respected him."

A Royal Scandal With Charles Coburn, Tallulah Bankhead

14. A ROYAL SCANDAL

20th CENTURY-FOX
Released March 16, 1945

CREDITS

Producer, Ernst Lubitsch; *Director,* Otto Preminger; *Screenplay,* Edwin Justus Mayer; *Adapted by* Bruno Frank; *Based on the play The Czarina* by Lajos Biro, Melchior Lengyel; *Cinematography,* Arthur Miller; *Art Directors,* Lyle Wheeler, Mark Lee Kirk; *Set Decorator,* Thomas Little; *Music,* Alfred Newman; *Orchestrations,* Edward Powell; *Editor,* Dorothy Spencer; *Costumes,* Rene Hubert; *Makeup,* Ben Nye; *Running time,* 94 minutes; black and white.

CAST

Tallulah Bankhead (*Catherine II*); Charles Coburn (*Chancellor Nicolai Ilytch*); Anne Baxter (*Countess Anna Jaschikoff*); William Eythe (*Alexei*); Vincent Price (*Marquis de Fleury*); Mischa Auer (*Captain Sukov*); Sig Rumann (*General Ronsky*); Vladimir Sokoloff (*Malakoff*); Mikhail Rasumny (*Drunken General*); Grady Sutton (*Boris*); Don Douglas (*Variatinsky*); Egon Brecher (*Wassilikow*); Eva Gabor (*Countess Demidow*); Frederick

A Royal Scandal With William Eythe and Vladimir Sokoloff (*center*)

Ledebur, Henry Victor, Wilton Graff, Michael Visaroff (*Russian Generals*); John Russell (*Guard*).

THE FILM

Price's next assignment following *Laura* must have been a personal disappointment—a tiny role in a troubled production. *Czarina*, the title under which *A Royal Scandal* was filmed, was Ernst Lubitsch's first picture following a long illness. In order to preserve the "Lubitsch touch," it was decided that he would rehearse the master scenes each day together with Otto Preminger and the actors, and then Preminger would take over the sequence when it went before the cameras—obviously, a working relationship fraught with potential problems. Price considered Lubitsch "the greatest comedy director we ever had. . . . He was a man who could tell you a story and you were on the floor. Unfortunately he had a heart attack, and they wouldn't let him direct, so he had to watch Otto Preminger, who had the sense of humor of a guillotine. Gave him another heart attack." In addition, there had been a tantalizing rumor that Garbo was considering making *Czarina* a comeback vehicle. Because Preminger had refused to drop Bankhead, Lubitsch constantly harangued Tallulah, which made everybody unhappy. "It was an impossible situation," according to Price, "because [Lubitsch] sat on the set the whole time and yet he couldn't do anything. It was difficult for Otto and the actors."

As the French ambassador who comes to woo the legendary royal nymphomaniac on behalf of his country (and himself), Vincent Price had impressive billing considering the size of the role. His character receives quite a buildup in the first quarter hour, but after an introductory scene with the chancellor, he never makes it in to see the czarina and disappears until the final four minutes of the picture! The actual story surrounds Catherine's interest in an earnest young soldier, William Eythe, and *his* interest in lady-in-waiting Anne Baxter. After the ensuing court intrigue has been resolved and Catherine finally inquires, "What happened to the French ambassador?" Vincent Price fans might well wonder. The actor's command of the French language is considerably more convincing than his French accent: "Th's" become "z's," as in "Catherine ze Second." But he is breezy and droll, and given the unpleasant atmosphere of the production, he was probably grateful that so little of the responsibility rested on his shoulders.

REVIEWS

Variety, March 21, 1945

". . . a highly hilarious comedy."

New York Times, April 12, 1945, Bosley Crowther

". . . for all Miss Bankhead's presence, [it] is an oddly dull and witless show."

15. LEAVE HER TO HEAVEN

20th CENTURY-FOX

Released December 19, 1945

CREDITS

Producer, William A. Bacher; *Director*, John M. Stahl; *Screenplay*, Jo Swerling; *Based on the novel by* Ben Ames Williams; *Cinematography*, Leon Shamroy; *Art Directors*, Lyle Wheeler, Maurice Ransford; *Set Decorator*, Thomas Little; *Music*, Alfred Newman; *Orchestrations*,

Leave Her to Heaven With Gene Tierney and Cornel Wilde

Edward B. Powell; *Editor*, James B. Clark; *Costumes*, Kay Nelson; *Makeup*, Ben Nye; *Running time*, 110 minutes; color.

CAST

Gene Tierney (*Ellen Berent*); Cornel Wilde (*Richard Harland*); Jeanne Crain (*Ruth Berent*); Vincent Price (*Russell Quinton*); Mary Philips (*Mrs. Berent*); Ray Collins (*Glen Robie*); Gene Lockhart (*Dr. Saunders*); Reed Hadley (*Dr. Mason*); Chill Wills (*Leick Thorne*); Darryl Hickman (*Danny Harland*); Paul Everton (*Judge*); Olive Blakeney (*Mrs. Robie*); Addison Richards (*Bedford*); Harry Depp (*Catterson*); Grant Mitchell (*Carlson/Bank Vice President*); Milton Parsons (*Medcraft/Mortician*); Earl Schenck (*Norton*); Hugh Maguire (*Lin Robie*); Audrey Betz (*Cook at Robie's Ranch*); Jim Farley (*Conductor*); Charles Tannen (*Man*); Mae Marsh (*Fisherwoman*); Betty Hannon (*Tess Robie*); Kay Riley (*Nurse*); Guy Beach (*Sheriff*).

THE FILM

Being cast in *Leave Her to Heaven* must have been a welcome assignment for Vincent Price, a nice start to 1945, following the little he had to do in *A Royal Scandal*, his previous picture under his Fox contract.

Leave Her to Heaven was a great opportunity for leading lady Gene Tierney as well, giving her a license to kill, literally, in an astounding thriller. She plays a woman so obsessed with her lover that she will lie, cause her own miscarriage, and murder his brother in order to try and keep him all to herself. When he begins to fall in love with her sister, she even takes her own life, framing the girl in order to ensure that if she herself can't have him, no one else will. Tierney's performance garnered her an Oscar nomination for Best Actress.

Price plays Tierney's ex-fiancé who remains bitterly in love with her even though she cruelly, casually dismisses him in the wake of her romance with the bewildered but bewitched Cornel Wilde. The press book made much of this fourth teaming of the two Fox stars. (They both had small roles in *Hudson's Bay*.) "Vincent Price . . . began by pointing out that, as far as he is concerned, Gene Tierney is a *femme fatale*. In *Laura*, he became first her fiancé, then her suspected murderer. In *Dragonwyck*, [in the can but not yet released] for love of her, he committed a murder. Now, in *Leave Her to Heaven*, he is the disappointed suitor who tries to avenge her death. 'But this picture is in Technicolor,' he added. 'That means that audiences also will get the full force of those Tierney eyes. Now maybe they'll understand why scriptwriters have me go off the deep end every time I'm in the same picture with her.'"

When the circumstances of Tierney's suicide frame adopted sister Jeanne Crain for murder, Price is the attorney who prosecutes the case. Despite the conflict of interest this should have been, it gave Vincent a wonderful opportunity to show off as an actor. His savvy, relentless harangue would have reduced any witness to a confession. According to a Fox press release: "For dramatic impact, director John M. Stahl wanted to film the questioning of Cornel as one uninterrupted scene, to be followed by an uninterrupted questioning of Jeanne. So Vincent fired a barrage of questions for five and a half minutes without muffing a line. Then, after time-out for lunch, Vincent went to work again, this time questioning Jeanne. . . . For these two scenes, Vincent learned fifteen solid pages of dialogue." This publicity hype would appear to have a basis in fact. In the screenplay dated February 27, 1945, and marked "final," the interrogation of "Richard" does indeed run ten pages; the questioning of "Ruth," six. Price's ability to learn copious dialogue would stand him in good stead again, garnering him the lead in *Shock* the following year.

Darryl Hickman plays an integral role in *Leave Her to Heaven* as Wilde's crippled younger brother. Although he has no scenes with Price, Hickman remembers the actor as "a cultured man, an accomplished man, and he treated other people that way. When I was a kid in films with adults, I would oftentimes get patted on the head and treated like a child. But the fact that I was a child didn't matter to Vincent—he treated me with a certain amount of grace and respect. I always appreciated that. I loved watching him act when I was on the set, and I loved being around him because he was a nice man and a gentleman." Fourteen years later, the two would play mad scientists together in *The Tingler*. "He hadn't

changed at all," according to Hickman. "As a matter of fact, as Vincent got older, he was even *more* gracious and benign! He was a very pleasant person to be around."

REVIEWS

Los Angeles Times, December 29, 1945

"The picture runs heavily to theatricalism, in fact, too much so in the courtroom scenes, notwithstanding these are brilliantly sustained by Vincent Price whose portrayal merits attention as contending for the Academy supporting honors."

Hollywood Citizen News, December 29, 1945

"Thereafter, the story spins to a rousing climax centering on a murder trial, in which Vincent Price, as the prosecuting attorney, rises to new dramatic heights. His performance—brief as it is—shines like a beacon."

16. SHOCK

20th CENTURY-FOX
Released January 10, 1946

CREDITS

Producer, Aubrey Schenck; *Director*, Alfred Werker; *Screenplay*, Eugene Ling; *Based on a story by* Albert

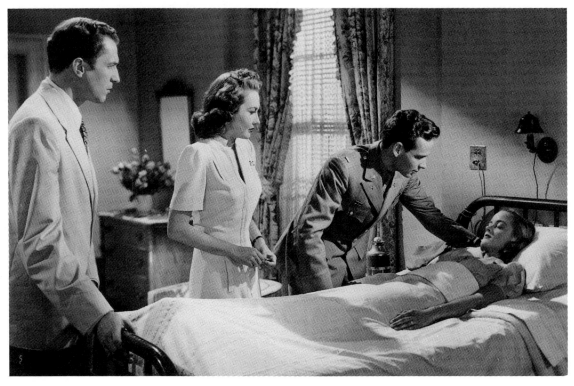

Shock With Lynn Bari, Frank Latimore, and Anabel Shaw

DeMond; *Additional Dialogue*, Martin Berkeley; *Cinematography*, Glen MacWilliams, Joe MacDonald; *Art Directors*, Lyle Wheeler, Boris Leven; *Set Decorators*, Thomas Little, O. Clement Halverson; *Music*, David Buttolph; *Music Director*, Emil Newman; *Orchestrations*, Arthur Morton; *Editor*, Harmon Jones; *Running time*, 70 minutes; black and white.

CAST

Vincent Price (*Dr. Dick Cross*); Lynn Bari (*Elaine Jordan*); Frank Latimore (*Lt. Paul Stewart*); Anabel Shaw (*Janet Stewart*); Michael Dunne (*Stevens*); Reed Hadley (*O'Neil*); Renee Carson (*Mrs. Hatfield*); Charles Trowbridge (*Dr. Harvey*); John Davidson (*Mr. Edwards*); Selmer Jackson (*Dr. Blair*); Pierre Watkin (*Hotel Manager*); Mary Young (*Miss Penny*); Charles Tannen (*Hotel Clerk*); Margaret Brayton, Claire Richards (*Nurses*); Bob Adler (*Male Nurse*).

THE FILM

Shock was Vincent Price's first solo starring role for 20th Century-Fox. Originally a product of the studio's "B" unit, the picture, which was made in mid- to late 1945, did well enough to be "bumped up" to A houses. Price plays an unhappily married psychiatrist who loses control in an argument with his wife and murders her. The crime is witnessed by a hysterical young woman who goes into shock. Her well-meaning husband commits her to a sanitorium for care; unfortunately for her, it's the sanitorium run by Vincent Price. He and his Lady Macbeth mistress (Lynn Bari) try to convince the girl that she imagined the entire incident. Eventually, they inject her with an insulin overdose, but the girl's husband—and the D.A., who was suspicious of the first death—intervene in the nick of time.

There are elements in the plot and drama of *Shock* which are reminiscent of Price's great stage success *Angel Street*—as the smooth, charismatic therapist, Price sits on the girl's bedside, quietly convincing her that she's losing her mind. Fox's creative publicity department sent out the following release: "Price's days at the studio were spent under the supervision of a psychiatric technical advisor. Most of his evenings were spent rehearsing for the *Theatre of Romance* radio show on which he reenacted the same role in *Angel Street* that he made famous on the New York stage. 'So you see,' laughed Price, 'I was a mental case both day and night.' . . . Although Vincent is rapidly becoming known as 'Hollywood's most wicked man,' what with murdering practically every feminine contract player at 20th Century-Fox—for films only, of course—he wants to play comedy. 'Ah yes,' punned Price. 'I'm getting to be quite a lady killer. But

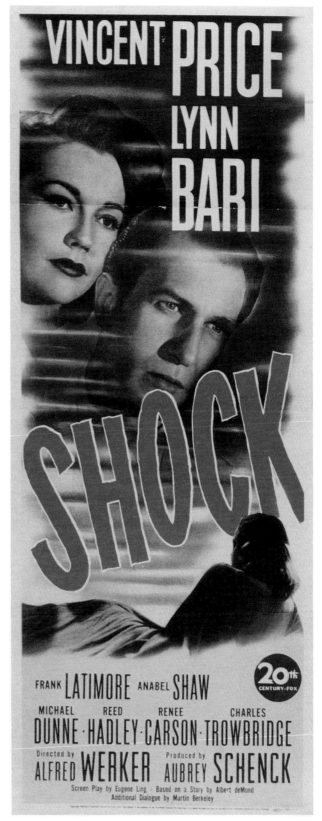

Shock Insert poster

Shock With Lynn Bari

you wait and see, one of these days I'll be killing them with love and murdering women with laughter.'"

Price's performance in *Shock* is considerably more complex than reviews would lead one to believe. Personable, well-spoken, he is genuinely distraught by the initial crime and elicits a measure of sympathy, deserved or not. Wavering between fear of capture and remorse for the murder, he is spurred by intense physical passion for the sexy and devious Bari: "Driving back, there was time to think. I got to thinking about you. I asked myself, is she worth what I've done." "Well?" murmurs Bari provocatively. Price steps forward and kisses her ardently. "That was a very satisfactory answer," she replies. In the end, he can't go through with the second murder, but ends up strangling Bari when she tries to prevent him from reversing the girl's drug overdose.

Producer Aubrey Schenck considered that "Vincent Price was perfect for [*Shock*]. . . . *Anything* Vincent did was great. The movie became an instantaneous hit, and they elevated it to an A picture!"

REVIEWS

Variety, January 16, 1946

". . . all that the title implies in the way of a crime thriller . . . one of those things that keeps an audience on seat-edge from start to finish. Put out unpretentiously as one

for the supporting feature brackets, the show is nevertheless good enough for top billing in many spots and should contribute strongly to box office draw. . . . Price is effective in the male lead. . . ."

Los Angeles Herald Examiner, March 7, 1946

"Here's one of the best of the season—and I'm referring to *Shock*, a terrific little picture that, without any particular ballyhoo, steps into the same category as *Lost Weekend* and *Spellbound* for· intelligent, engrossing entertainment. . . . [Price] is terrific as the psychatrist-murderer—smooth, menacing and as dangerous as a tiger's paw."

VINCENT PRICE

(*Classic Images*, June 1992)

"*Shock* was an experiment, actually. The studio was spending too much money on films and taking too long to make them. Something had to be done to boost output and cut down on costs. So they asked me and Lynn Bari if we could make a film in twenty days and still have it look like a first-class production. I read the script and thought it was pretty good. I said, 'Certainly we can do it, if you don't change the script and louse it up for us.' And so they agreed, and we went ahead and shot it, in exactly twenty days. . . . The film did very well at the box office, so Twentieth was very pleased."

17. DRAGONWYCK

20th CENTURY-FOX
Released April 10, 1946

CREDITS

(*Producer*, Ernst Lubitsch, uncredited); *Writer/Director*, Joseph L. Mankiewicz; *Based on the novel by* Anya Seton; *Cinematography*, Arthur Miller; *Art Directors*, Lyle Wheeler, Russell Spencer; *Set Decorator*, Thomas Little; *Music*, Alfred Newman; *Orchestral Arrangements*, Edward B. Powell; *Editor*, Dorothy Spencer; *Costumes*, Rene Hubert; *Makeup*, Ben Nye; *Special Photographic Effects*, Fred Sersen; *Dances staged by* Arthur Appel; *Running time*, 103 minutes; black and white.

CAST

Gene Tierney (*Miranda Wells*); Walter Huston (*Ephraim Wells*); Vincent Price (*Nicholas Van Ryn*); Glenn Langan (*Dr. Jeff Turner*); Anne Revere (*Abigail Wells*); Spring Byington (*Magda*); Connie Marshall (*Katrina Van Ryn*); Henry Morgan (*Bleeker*); Vivienne Osborne (*Johanna Van Ryn*); Jessica Tandy (*Peggy O'Malley*); Trudy Marshall (*Elizabeth Van Borden*); Reinhold Schunzel (*Count de Grenier*); Jane Nigh (*Tabitha*); Ruth Ford (*Cornelia Van Borden*); David Ballard (*Obadiah*); Scott Elliot (*Tom Wells*); Boyd Irwin (*Tompkins*); Maya Van Horn (*Countess de Grenier*); Keith Hitchcock (*Mr. MacNabb*); Francis Pierlot (*Doctor*).

THE FILM

Dragonwyck is an atmospheric Gothic romance incorporating all the tried-and-true elements of the genre: a naive young heroine, a splendid mansion seat, pounding thunderstorms, restless villagers, murder and madness, ghostly manifestations, and an irresistible lord of the manor, proud and haughty, driven to murder by pride, love, and lust. The film marked the directorial debut of Joseph L. Mankiewicz, who initially hadn't thought much of the book: "The love story is apt to be very unsatisfying in its conclusion. The young doctor cannot be half so glamorous or exciting as his murderous heel/

Dragonwyck "From childhood's hour I have not been / As others were—I have not seen / As others saw—I could not bring / My passions from a common spring . . . And all I lov'd, I loved alone." Edgar Allan Poe

rival. I can imagine no woman preferring the hero to the villain, in this case, for either bed or breakfast. The melodrama must inevitably conflict and suffer in comparison with *Rebecca* and *Suspicion*. The political and economic applications are naive, oversimple, and made unexciting by the times in which we live."

At first, Fox assigned *Dragonwyck* to Ernst Lubitsch. Still recovering from the heart attack which had forced him to withdraw from *A Royal Scandal*, Lubitsch offered Mankiewicz the opportunity to script and direct under the older man's supervision. Despite Mankiewicz's admiration for Lubitsch, conflicts abounded; Lubitsch took his name off the film, and neither man spoke to the other for a long time after. Shot between February 12 and May 4, 1945, *Dragonwyck* is a handsome production. Lighting and camera work are first-rate, and the music score appropriately eerie, as is the nineteenth-century plot. When his unappealing wife cannot supply him with an heir, the wealthy Nicholas Van Ryn, who is "patroon," or lord, of a large estate on the Hudson River, secretly poisons her. He then marries his naive (and beautiful) young cousin Miranda. But Nicholas's growing drug ad-

Dragonwyck With Gene Tierney

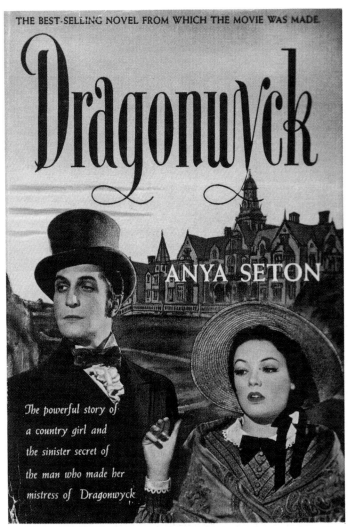

THE BEST-SELLING NOVEL FROM WHICH THE MOVIE WAS MADE

Dragonwyck

ANYA SETON

The powerful story of a country girl and the sinister secret of the man who made her mistress of Dragonwyck

Dragonwyck by Anya Seton—An edition of the book, current with the film's release

diction and the hauntings (real or imaginary) of a long-dead ancestor drive him to try and rid himself of his second bride when their son perishes soon after birth. A suspicious young doctor saves the girl, and Nicholas dies as he lived, elevated in his chair of state, surveying his tenants and the vast lands.

Cast again as expertly as in *Laura*, Vincent Price was the physical incarnation of the glamorous patroon of author Anya Seton's imagination: "He was tall, over six feet and of a slender build. . . . His hair, nearly as black as his boots, was abundant and slightly waving. . . . As for his face, it was so nearly the embodiment of the descriptions of heroes in Miranda's favorite books that she was awed. Here were the full flexible mouth, the aquiline nose with slightly flaring nostrils, the high and noble forehead accented by stern black brows . . . [and eyes of a] particularly vivid light blue." In an interview

on the set, *Look* magazine described Vincent as "lean, razor-jawed and romantic." To achieve that appearance, "he dropped 30 pounds from his 205 pound, 6 foot 4 inch frame."

Nicholas Van Ryn was a wonderful part for Price; a man of great passion and great arrogance. What he cherishes—his birthright, his new young wife—he loves fiercely; what he despises—weakness, self-doubt—he loathes pathologically. In preparing for the role, Vincent found himself having a difficult time relating to the character, a man who could tolerate nothing in his life which was less than perfect, which did not meet his own inflexible standards. The preface to Seton's novel consists of an Edgar Allan Poe poem entitled "Alone"; after reading it, the actor came to understand the terrible, awful isolation in which Nicholas lived his life. (In fact, Nicholas Van Ryn has many of the traits of the antiheroes Price would later portray in AIP's Poe film series.)

Price won the Cine Swiss Award for *Dragonwyck* as well as a *Box-Office* Blue Ribbon Award for May 1946. Intriguingly, although the film was released in black and white, some of the production stills are printed: "20th Century-Fox–Technicolor Production."

REVIEWS

Variety, February 20, 1946 (tradeshow screening)

". . . its box office chances are assured . . . [a] grade-A production in every detail. . . . It is one of [Vincent Price's] best roles to date, and he handles it for all it's worth."

New York Times, April 11, 1946, Bosley Crowther

"Vincent Price gives a picturesque performance . . . clean-shaven and elegantly tailored, he still makes a formidable Bluebeard, and his moments of suave diabolism are about the best in the film."

Look, May 5, 1946

"As *Dragonwyck*'s homicidal aristocrat who tries to murder two wives, [Price] sets a romantic pace which will be a revelation to feminine moviegoers. One of Hollywood's soundest actors, this soft-spoken former member of St. Louis society dominates the picture."

VINCENT PRICE

("The Villains Still Pursue Me" lecture)

"Aristotle wrote a theory of drama that is really quite extraordinary. In it, he says that the villain, the man who has to pay for his sins, should preferably be a man of great intelligence, great charm, great wit, noble birth preferably, rich, well liked—because then, if *this* man has to pay for his sins, you and I, *hoi polloi*, we understand that we have to pay for ours, too. Well, the character of Nicholas Van Ryn is an Aristotelian villain. Jack Manningham in *Angel Street* wasn't because he was kind of common and cheap and tawdry. But Nicholas Van Ryn was everything."

Dragonwyck With Vivienne Osborne and Glenn Langan

Dragonwyck Price as the Patroon is attacked by one of his tenants (Henry Morgan, *back to camera*)

18. THE WEB

UNIVERSAL-INTERNATIONAL
Released May 1947

CREDITS

Producer, Jerry Bresler; *Director*, Michael Gordon; *Screenplay*, William Bowers, Bertram Millhauser; *Based on a story by* Harry Kurnitz; *Cinematography*, Irving Glassberg; *Art Directors*, Bernard Herzbrun, James Sullivan; *Set Decorators*, Russell A. Gausman, William L. Stevens; *Music*, Hans J. Salter; *Orchestrations*, David Tamkin; *Editor*, Russell Schoengarth; *Gowns*, Yvonne Wood; *Makeup*, Bud Westmore; *Hair Stylist*, Carmen Dirigo; *Running time*, 87 minutes; black and white.

CAST

Ella Raines (*Noel Faraday*); Edmond O'Brien (*Bob Regan*); William Bendix (*Lieutenant Damico*); Vincent Price (*Andrew Colby*); Maria Palmer (*Martha Kroner*); John Abbott (*Charles Murdock*); Fritz Leiber (*Leopold Kroner*); Howland Chamberlin (*James Timothy Nolan*); Joe Kirk, William Haade, Ethan Laidlaw (*Plainclothesmen*); Tito Vuolo (*Emilio Canepa*); Patricia Alphin [later Audrey Young] (*Secretary*); Robin Raymond (*Newspaper Librarian*); Wilton Graff (*District Attorney*); Pierre Watkin (*Mr. Porter*); Gino Corrado (*Waiter*).

The Web With Edmond O'Brien

The Web With Edmond O'Brien (*left*), Ella Raines, and John Abbott

THE FILM

Edmond O'Brien had one of his better roles in *The Web*, a melodrama which nonetheless suffers from a cast of predominantly serviceable (i.e., dull) actors playing predominantly uninteresting characters. O'Brien, is an idealistic attorney whom wealthy industrialist Vincent Price hires to look after him. It seems that Price's ex-partner, newly released from prison after serving five years for embezzlement, has threatened his life. O'Brien pulls strings with his police-lieutenant buddy (William Bendix) to get a permit for the gun which he is forced to use that night to protect Price and kill the ex-partner. Soon O'Brien suspects he was set up by Price to get rid of the coconspirator Price double-crossed in the original swindle. He also begins to romance Price's sultry personal assistant, Ella Raines, who is involved with her boss but clearly has an "understanding" with him. Price then makes the cold-blooded decision to murder his faithful second in command and frame both O'Brien and Raines. Unfortunately, the ending is preposterous. Bendix, who has believed O'Brien innocent all along, convinces Price that the victim (whom he shot point-blank) isn't dead and catches the industrialist red-handed when he tries to finish the job.

Shooting, under the production title of *Jeopardy*, took place in February and March 1947. As an attractive, sophisticated villain, Price exhibited some of the self-conscious polish of *Laura*'s Shelby Carpenter; in fact, he's so affable and likable to start that the steely ruthlessness he exhibits at the end seems to come out of left field. Critics certainly seemed to agree he was suave (see below).

The Web was also known as *The Dark Web* and *Black Velvet*.

REVIEWS

New York Herald Tribune, June 5, 1947, Otis Guernsey Jr.

"It owes much to Vincent Price in another of his chilling portraits of suave villainy."

Variety, May 22, 1947

"[Price] gives a compelling reading to the role of a treacherous, suave big-business man."

Los Angeles Examiner, May 26, 1947, Sara Hamilton

". . . the suave and persuasive Vincent Price, than whom there is no suaver when he gets going, smooth as a whistle—he provides nice (Oh, Vinnie Price—you SHOULD be nice) contrast to the sharper, edgier performance of O'Brien."

Los Angeles Herald Express, May 26, 1947, George H. Jackson

"Vincent Price plays this role for all it is worth, giving his usual suave, man of the world portrayal."

19. MOSS ROSE

20th CENTURY-FOX

Released late May 1947

CREDITS

Producer, Gene Markey; *Director*, Gregory Ratoff; *Screenplay*, Jules Furthman, Tom Reed; *Adaptation*, Niven Busch; *Based on the novel by* Joseph Shearing; *Cinematography*, Joe MacDonald; *Art Directors*, Richard Day, Mark Lee Kirk; *Set Decorators*, Edwin B. Willis, Paul S. Fox; *Music*, David Buttolph; *Music Director*, Alfred Newman; *Orchestrations*, Edward Powell, Maurice de Packh; *Editor*, James B. Clark; *Running time*, 82 minutes; black and white.

CAST

Peggy Cummins (*Belle Adair*); Victor Mature (*Sir Alexander Sterling*); Ethel Barrymore (*Lady Sterling*); Vincent Price (*Inspector Clinner*); Margo Woode (*Daisy Arrow*); George Zucco (*Craxton*); Patricia Medina (*Audrey*); Rhys Williams (*Deputy Inspector Evans*); Felippa Rock (*Liza*); Carol Savage (*Harriett*); Victor Wood (*Wilson*); Patrick O'Moore (*George Gilby*); Billy Bevan (*White Horse Cabby*); Michael Dyne (*Assistant Hotel Manager*).

THE FILM

Vincent Price's final assignment under his contract with 20th Century-Fox was a blend of murder mystery and romance. Another period picture, *Moss Rose* opens with an atmospheric re-creation of the London Embankment and Waterloo Bridge. The housemate of chorus girl Peggy Cummins is smothered by a killer who leaves behind a Bible marked with a dried flower, the moss rose. Cummins believes toff Victor Mature murdered her friend and blackmails him into taking her to the family estate for two weeks so she can experience how the other half lives. Mature's mother, Ethel Barrymore, accepts the unusual houseguest, although his fiancée, Patricia Medina, regards the young girl as a rival. She's right—predictably, Cummins falls for Mature, which nearly proves her downfall. It turns out that the killer is not Mature but his psychotic mother, who wants to keep

Moss Rose With (*from left*) Rhys Williams, Peggy Cummins, Ethel Barrymore, and Victor Mature

him all to herself and ritually dispatches any woman in whom her son shows interest. But police inspector Vincent Price and his men have been hot on the trail. Although too late to save Medina, they arrive in time to interrupt the murder of Cummins and capture the delusional Barrymore.

The plot begins well, but ultimately the drama becomes muddled; partly because, as an actor, Mature just isn't sufficiently interesting or enigmatic; and as the character is written, Cummins's intrepid cockney is too naive and trusting. Cummins, who celebrated her twenty-first birthday on December 18, 1946, with a cake on the set, was philosophical: "The script came down, and that was it, and we had to do it. By the time you'd fought your way through to get it changed, the fight was too great, perhaps. Time was money." Only months before, 20th–Century Fox had dropped the English actress from the lead of its Technicolor epic *Forever Amber*, replacing her with the more vixenish Linda Darnell. Colleague Price thought very highly of Hollywood newcomer Cummins—"really sensational, extraordinary," he was quoted after the *Amber* fiasco. "Very special personality, very different." (Price, too, lost out when *Amber* eventually went back before the cameras after several cast and crew changes: He was no longer available, and his meaty costarring role of male star Cornel Wilde's best friend went to Richard Greene.)

As *Moss Rose*'s unassuming, deceptively clever detective, Price alternates between charming affability and deadpan police rhetoric. "Floral geography is a hobby

Moss Rose "Flowers are a hobby with me . . ." Price tells Ethel Barrymore

of mine," he proclaims happily. His knowledge of botany enables him to employ the effective absentminded strategy of Lieutenant Columbo in order to trap the killer: "Oh, by the way, there's something I wanted to ask your ladyship. . . . That's curious, I seem to have completely forgotten it. It couldn't have been very important. . . . Oh, yes! I know what it was!"—embarrassed laugh. "Flowers are a hobby with me. . . ." And Ethel Barrymore proudly shows him her moss roses.

REVIEWS

Hollywood Reporter, May 20, 1947

"Vincent Price scores as a Scotland Yard official."

Variety, May 21, 1947

". . . a good whodunnit, given a lift by solid trouping and direction. . . ."

Los Angeles Examiner, May 31, 1947

"Vincent Price is one actor who can be just as convincing on the side of the law as against it. As the Scotland Yard detective he's outstanding."

San Francisco News, June 20, 1947, Claude LaBelle

"Victor Mature is an odd choice as the young Englishman. He acts well, except that he doesn't act English. It would have seemed smarter to this reviewer to have put Vincent Price, who has a small but magnificently played role as a police inspector, into this part."

PEGGY CUMMINS

"I arrived on the Fox lot in September [of 1945], from England. And I belonged to the studio. I wasn't aware that I belonged to *quite* such an extent [laughs]! . . . Whether he liked it or not, the studio arranged for Vincent to take me to my first Academy Awards; I suppose it was in March of '46. . . . When Fox made *Forever Amber*, they thought they were going to try and outdo *Gone With the Wind*, and no way could they ever have done that, you see. . . . It doesn't matter, but really, I "took the rap," as they say, for [the problems]. Because there were an awful lot of people who came out of that when it was recut; they never made it well known that they changed the director, and they changed this and changed that. Howard Hawks said he would direct it, but he'd only consider doing it with me. There was an awful lot that went on, and good or bad, I got the publicity. But that's life. It wasn't altogether the happiest time. So when we were making *Amber*, Vincent couldn't, of course, have been more sympathetic. It was lovely because he was a stage actor, very different from working with somebody like Cornel Wilde, who was not. It's a different concept altogether. I thought Vincent was excellent as an actor; he was terribly polished. And he looked very good. I'd love to know why they recast *him*. [When informed Price's role was eventually played by Richard Greene:] Oh, my God! [laughs]. I shouldn't say that. I knew Dick very well; he was known as the Brylcreem Boy over here [in England].

In *Moss Rose*, the three of us all got on very well together, Vic and Vincent and myself; we worked very well together. We were all gigglers. Absolutely, *all* gigglers. Here were these two *very* tall men, and I was five feet one and a half, and every scene I had to play, they had ramps. It's nerve-racking enough to try and act as it is; it's not the easiest thing to do, although it may look it at times. Anything can easily set you off, and to walk up these ramps would always make me giggle, and it would make them giggle. I said, "We'll all be sacked if we don't stop, I'm sure!" And then we had one scene in the fog in London, and they put too much fog in, and Vic and I couldn't *see* each other! I think it's a good thing; I think to be *too* serious is terrible. We had, not a coach, but somebody on the set with the script for the English accents. And Ethel Barrymore demanded of [director] Gregory Ratoff, [mimicked in a very grand

104

voice], 'What is this man doing here?' And Gregory looked rather fussed and said [with a pronounced German accent], 'Oh! Ethel, darling, it's to give me English lessons!' Because his English was not very good. . . . Vincent was very warm; he wasn't aloof or standoffish. He could laugh. He wasn't full of self-importance. I think everybody had affection for Vincent."

20. THE LONG NIGHT

RKO RADIO

Released September 16, 1947

CREDITS

Producers, Robert Hakim, Raymond Hakim, Anatole Litvak; *Director*, Anatole Litvak; *Screenplay*, John Wexley; *Based on the story by* Jacques Viot; *Cinematography*, Sol Polito; *Art Director*, Eugene Lourie; *Set Decorator*, Darrell Silvera; *Music*, Dimitri Tiomkin; *Music Director*, C. Bakaleinikoff; *Editor*, Robert Swink; *Assistant Director*, Aaron Rosenberg; *Running time*, 101 minutes; black and white.

CAST

Henry Fonda (*Joe Adams*); Barbara Bel Geddes (*Jo Ann*); Vincent Price (*Maximilian*); Ann Dvorak (*Charlene*); Howard Freeman (*Sheriff*); Moroni Olsen (*Chief of Police*); Elisha Cook Jr. (*Frank*); Queenie Smith (*Janitor's Wife*); David Clarke (*Bill*); Charles McGraw (*Policeman*); Patty King (*Peggy*); Robert A. Davis (*Freddie*); Will Wright (*Janitor*); Ray Teal (*Hudson*); Pat Flaherty (*Sergeant*); Dick Reeves (*Cop*); Jack Overman (*Man*); Byron Foulger (*Man With Bike*); Murray Alper (*Bartender*); Mary Gordon (*Old Lady*).

THE FILM

Broadway's Barbara Bel Geddes made her screen debut in this suspense-filled romance in which Vincent Price played another of his patented attractive cads. *The Long Night* is set against a backdrop of the Pennsylvania-Ohio steel arena. Price's elegant magician exerts a Svengali-like influence over Bel Geddes, an impressionable young woman with whom Henry Fonda has fallen in love, leading to a deadly confrontation between the two men. Fonda kills Price and is left to ponder his fate as he barricades himself in against the gathering police.

RKO borrowed Price from Fox for the picture, which was a remake of a successful Jean Gabin French film, *Le Jour se Leve*, or *Daybreak*. The actor was available because he had been released from Fox's grandiose pro-

The Long Night With Ann Dvorak and "the wonder dogs"

The Long Night With Barbara Bel Geddes

duction of *Forever Amber*, one of several casualties when female lead Peggy Cummins was replaced and all footage scrapped. A late August 1946 gossip column ran: "The original *Forever Amber* cast isn't suffering being cast off from the Peggy Cummins version. Vincent Price, who was the first Lord Almsbury, now on the cutting room floor, goes to RKO with equal star billing with Henry Fonda and Barbara Bel Geddes in *A Time to Kill*, the

The Long Night With Ann Dvorak and Henry Fonda

working title. Price has the satisfaction of being a public-made star after *Leave Her to Heaven* and *Dragonwyck* at 20th, and Anatole Litvak and Robert Hakim, sponsors of the RKO picture, aren't arguing with the fans' decision."

The screenplay of *The Long Night* called for Price to perform two lengthy sequences involving a dozen "wonder dogs." An erudite Pomeranian named Buster was borrowed from a stage act called "Hector and His Dogs" because he could count to ten. On an empty RKO soundstage, Price took instructions from professional magician Charlie Miller, who reportedly taught sleight of hand to Orson Welles. Lessons included complicated card tricks, a magic floating ball, a mind-reading dog, and a feat of levitation. No camera tricks were used; director Litvak elected to "make the tricks as mystifying to the extras in the audience as they would be to people paying actual admission."

Press releases issued by RKO are full of amusing anecdotes about the production: "For the polished gentleman that he is—artist, sculptor, and graduate of Yale and London Universities—Vincent Price is almost convinced he was treated a little roughly. . . . To accomplish the role . . . he fell down a twenty-six-step stairway three times; he was 'shot to death' twelve times by Henry Fonda; he was slapped eighteen times by Barbara Bel Geddes; he was bitten three times by a performing dog." Another claimed: "Doctor Bills Heavy Item for Price"— one would think he played pro football on his Sundays off. First day he suffered from a swollen face caused by repeated slappings called for in the script. Then he

sprained his wrist performing a magic trick for his role, following which he was attacked by a needle-toothed Pomeranian. Worst injury was a fractured rib, incurred when he was required to fall down four steps after a stuntman had tumbled two flights for him. 'I hope my next film assignment calls for a suit of armor,' quoth Price."

REVIEWS

Los Angeles Times, September 25, 1947

". . . a first-class shocker. . . . [But] the motives, the behavior and interactions of the characters . . . simply do not ring true. The effect is one of a kind of distorted realism somehow more alien than American, and I can only conclude that it is the result of trying to adapt a French cinema . . . too literally to the Hollywood mold. . . . Anatole Litvak, who coproduced as well as directed, has lost none of the bravura flair he revealed in Hollywood before the war. . . . The magician is Vincent Price, a glib-tongued but faintly preposterous smoothie and a cad, sir, if ever there was one. . . ."

21.   UP IN CENTRAL PARK

UNIVERSAL-INTERNATIONAL
Released May 1948

CREDITS

Producer/Writer, Karl Tunberg; *Director*, William A. Seiter; *Based on the musical play by* Dorothy Fields, Herbert Fields, Sigmund Romberg; *Cinematography*, Milton Krasner; *Production Designer*, Howard Bay; *Set Decorators*, Russell A. Gausman, Ted Offenbecker; *Music*, Sigmund Romberg; *Orchestrations*, Johnny Green; *Songs*, Dorothy Fields, Sigmund Romberg; *Editor*, Otto Ludwig; *Costumes*, Mary Grant; *Makeup*, Bud Westmore; *Running time*, 88 minutes; black and white.

CAST

Deanna Durbin (*Rosie Moore*); Dick Haymes (*John Matthews*); Vincent Price (*Boss Tweed*); Albert Sharpe (*Timothy Moore*); Tom Powers (*Regan*); Hobart Cavanaugh (*Mayor Oakley*); Thurston Hall (*Governor Motley*); Howard Freeman (*Myron Schultz*); Mary Field (*Miss Murch*); Tom Pedi (*O'Toole*); Moroni Olsen (*Big Jim Pitts*); William Skipper, Nelle Fisher (*Dancers*); Patricia Alphin, Nina Lunn, Bunny Waters (*Guests*); Wayne Tredway, Frank McFarland, Harry Denny, Hal Taggart, Ed Peil

Up in Central Park With Deanna Durbin

Sr. (*Politicians*); G. Pat Collins (*Ward Heeler*); Curt Bois (*Maître d'*).

THE FILM

The musical play *Up in Central Park* had a successful Broadway run in 1945, thanks to master showman Michael Todd. Universal acquired the property as a vehicle for its singing star Deanna Durbin but unaccountably changed the very aspects of the musical which had made it so successful; it dropped most of the songs and basically eliminated the charming period flavor of 1880s New York.

The plot follows the exploits of Irish immigrants Rosie (Durbin) and her father (Albert Sharpe), who arrive in a New York City gripped by a mayoral election being manipulated by William Marcy "Boss" Tweed (Vincent Price). While honest newspaper reporter John Matthews (Dick Haymes) tries to get the goods on Tweed, Rosie is infatuated with the suave politician, who takes advantage of the girl's naïveté and launches her on a singing career. When Tweed's manipulative shenanigans are finally revealed, Rosie unites with hero Matthews.

Another significant variation from the popular stage version was the concept of the character of Boss Tweed, the legendary corrupt politico. As impersonated on stage by Noah Beery, who died shortly before the end of the play's run, Tweed was grim, grizzled, tough, paunchy, and ruthless. For the movie, the part was completely

Up in Central Park With Tom Powers (*left*) and Deanna Durbin

metamorphosed into a debonair individual, romantic enough to be a plausible suitor for Deanna and a rival of good-looking good guy Dick. Consequently, Universal cast Vincent Price—at his most amiable, cultured, slender, and witty.

Reviews generally compared the film version unfavorably to the stage original, and without exception they commented on the "miscasting" of Price, who could hardly be held responsible for the way the film character was restructured.

It was during the filming of *Up in Central Park* that Vincent first met his future wife, Mary Grant; she designed the costumes for the picture.

REVIEWS

Variety, May 26, 1948

". . . [T]he story . . . turns Boss Tweed into a champagne-dispensing wolf. . . . Vincent Price seems a bit unctuous. . . ."

New York Times, May 27, 1948, Thomas M. Pryor

"Since *Up in Central Park* has a lot to do with Boss Tweed and how he bilked the city's pocketbook . . . the juicy role of Tweed is played by Vincent Price and a more inappropriate choice could hardly be imagined. This is not meant to reflect on Mr. Price's acting ability; it's merely a case of the actor not fitting the character."

Cue, May 29, 1948

"Vincent Price, tall, aristocratic and British-accented, is surely the strangest portrait of short, squat, bearded, and grafting Boss Tweed ever offered to a bewildered citizenry."

22. ABBOTT AND COSTELLO MEET FRANKENSTEIN

UNIVERSAL-INTERNATIONAL

Released July 24, 1948

CREDITS

Producer, Robert Arthur; *Director*, Charles T. Barton; *Screenplay*, Robert Lees, Frederic I. Rinaldo, John Grant; *Cinematography*, Charles Van Enger; *Art Director*, Bernard Herzbrun, Hilyard Brown; *Set Decorators*, Russell A. Gausman, Oliver Emert; *Music*, Frank Skinner; *Orchestrations*, David Tamkin; *Editor*, Frank Gross; *Gowns*, Grace Houston; *Makeup*, Bud Westmore; *Special Photography*, David S. Horsley, Jerome Ash; *Running time*, 83 minutes; black and white.

CAST

Bud Abbott (*Chick Young*); Lou Costello (*Wilbur Gray*); Lon Chaney (*Larry Talbot/the Wolf Man*); Bela Lugosi (*Count Dracula*); Glenn Strange (*the Monster*); Lenore Aubert (*Sandra Mornay*); Jane Randolph (*Joan Raymond*); Frank Ferguson (*Mr. McDougal*); Charles Bradstreet (*Dr. Stevens* [called Professor in the film]); Howard Negley (*Mr. Harris*).

THE FILM

Abbott and Costello Meet Frankenstein also pitted Bud and Lou against Dracula, the Wolf Man, and a sultry siren in one of the team's most effective comedies. After animated opening credits, Count Dracula and his assistants attempt to place Costello's brain into the head of the Monster, while a distraught and understandably schizoid Larry Talbot tries to convince the boys they're in danger.

Hold That Ghost (1941), with a screenplay by the same writers as *Abbott and Costello Meet Frankenstein*, had mined so much comedic gold from Costello's fear reactions to a haunted house and its spooky goings-on, that subsequent A & C vehicles continued to incorporate eerie (and unrelated) scenes. By 1947 the comedy team which (together with young Deanna Durbin) had saved Universal from bankruptcy and lifted public wartime morale was in a box-office slump. It was producer Robert Arthur's inspiration to return to the scary-mansion concept with a vengeance.

At first Costello hated the script, which was originally titled *Brain of Frankenstein*. Accustomed to being able to fall back on at least one or two tried-and-true vaudeville or burlesque routines, Lou was concerned about the absence of such bits from the screenplay. Unappreciative and fearful of a structure which relied instead on a stronger story line, he complained, "My daughter could write a better script than that." In the long run, the picture benefited from daily improvisation on the set, and since the monsters play it all straight, the confrontations with Abbott and Costello are even funnier. The end result was a success, Universal's third biggest hit of the year, and returned the duo to Top Ten box office status.

Vincent Price's unbilled "appearance"—a voice-over in the final seconds—provides the capper to the comedy. The boys have escaped from the monsters in a rowboat. "Now that we've seen the last of Dracula, the Wolf Man, and the Monster, there's no one to frighten us anymore," Abbott says overconfidently.

At the other end of the dinghy, unseen hands strike a match and light a cigarette as a smooth, amiable voice bemoans:

"Oh, that's too bad—I was hoping to get in on the excitement."

"Who said that?!" Bud demands as he and Lou look around nervously.

"Allow me to introduce myself—I'm the Invisible Man." At his delighted laughter, which echoes over the water, A & C dive headfirst overboard.

This film was previewed in Los Angeles on June 25, 1948. For U.K. distribution, the title became *Abbott and Costello Meet the Ghosts.*

REVIEWS

Hollywood Reporter, June 28, 1948

". . . a crazy, giddy show that combines chills and laughs in one zany sequence after another. . . . Robert Arthur's production spells out showmanship right down the line, and Charles T. Barton's direction keeps things moving at a lively, vigorous pace. . . ."

Variety, June 28, 1948

"Combination of horror and slapstick should pay off brilliantly. . . . Chaney, Lugosi, Strange and Lenore Aubert as Lugosi's sinister assistant are right in the groove for the numb-skullduggeries. . . . Bud Abbott and Lou Costello work like beavers. . . . [C]halk it up as one of the best for the comedians."

Abbott and Costello Meet Frankenstein

23. ROGUES' REGIMENT

UNIVERSAL-INTERNATIONAL

Released September 28, 1948

CREDITS

Producer/Writer, Robert Buckner; *Director*, Robert Florey; *Story*, Robert Buckner, Robert Florey; *Cinematography*, Maury Gertsman; *Art Directors*, Bernard Herzbrun, Gabriel Scognamillo; *Set Decorators*, Russell A. Gausman, Oliver Emert; *Music*, Daniele Amfitheatrof; *Orchestrations*, David Tamkin; *Songs*, Jack Brooks, Serge Walter; *Editor*, Ralph Dawson; *Costumes*, Orry-Kelly;

Makeup, Bud Westmore; *Choreography*, Billy Daniels; *Running time*, 85 minutes; black and white.

CAST

Dick Powell (*Whit Corbett*); Marta Toren (*Lili Maubert*); Vincent Price (*Mark Van Ratten*); Stephen McNally (*Carl Reicher*); Edgar Barrier (*Colonel Mauclaire*); Henry Rowland (*Erich Heindorf*); Carol Thurston (*Li-Ho-Kay*); James Millican (*Cobb*); Richard Loo (*Kao Pang*); Philip Ahn (*Tran Duy Gian*); Richard Fraser (*Rycroft*); Otto Reichow (*Stein*); Kenny Washington (*Sam Latch*); Victor Sen Yung (*Rickshaw Boy*).

THE FILM

With a locale of Indochina, *Rogues' Regiment* includes skirmishes between French Foreign Legionnaires and Saigon natives as the U.S. Army attempts to chase down a high-ranking Nazi in hiding after the war. Hot on the trail, Military Intelligence agent Dick Powell bumps into Vincent Price, who purports to be a wealthy Dutch antiques dealer but is actually a German involved in gunrunning. Both Powell and Price finger a highly suspicious Stephen McNally, who tries to hide in the middle of the Foreign Legion, which Powell also joins as a cover. When Price realizes that the fugitive is a hunted SS man, he offers (for a fee) to supply money and a passport but is killed when he discovers the Nazi's identity. (McNally's character of Carl Reicher, whose real name is revealed to be Martin Bruner, was a thinly disguised Martin Bormann. Rated as the third-ranking Nazi war criminal, he was still missing at the time of the picture.) Agent Powell saves the day by capturing McNally after a furious battle, and the German is tried and hanged.

Vincent's diary records that he started *Rogues' Regi-*

Rogues' Regiment With Dick Powell (*with newspaper*) and Frank Conroy

ment on April 1, 1948. As an actor, he dresses up the supporting cast, but his role—played with a mild Dutch accent—is no more than a minor heavy of his usual cultured, "white gloves" variety. The picture has a persuasive foreign feel to it and atmospheric lighting, but the action is interrupted by a completely superfluous and improbable romance between Powell and Marta Toren. It's ironic that the story of *Rogues' Regiment*, dealing with closure on the recently ended World War II, is set during the early days of unrest and guerrilla fighting in Vietnam. According to director Robert Florey, the picture was banned in France because it was felt that the Foreign Legion was not respectfully presented.

REVIEWS

Variety, October 1, 1948

"Neat action exploitation feature . . . there is strong menace supplied by Vincent Price as a gunrunning art collector."

New York Times, December 20, 1948, A. H. Weiler

"If credibility is by-passed more than once, it is all done briskly and with good will. . . ."

Rogues' Regiment With Stephen McNally (*in turtleneck*)

24. THE THREE MUSKETEERS

METRO-GOLDWYN-MAYER

Released October 1948

CREDITS

Producer, Pandro S. Berman; *Director*, George Sidney; *Screenplay*, Robert Ardrey; *Based on the novel by* Alexandre Dumas; *Cinematography*, Robert Planck; *Art Directors*, Cedric Gibbons, Malcolm Brown; *Set Decorators*, Edwin B. Willis, Henry W. Grace; *Music*, Herbert Stothart; *Orchestrations*, Albert Sendrey; *Music Director*, Charles Previn; *Editors*, Robert J. Kern, George Boemler; *Costumes*, Walter Plunkett; *Makeup*, Jack Dawn; *Running time*, 125 minutes; color.

CAST

Lana Turner (*Milady Countess de Winter*); Gene Kelly (*D'Artagnan*); June Allyson (*Constance Bonacieux*); Van Heflin (*Athos*); Angela Lansbury (*Queen Anne*); Frank Morgan (*Louis XIII*); Vincent Price (*Richelieu*); Keenan Wynn (*Planchet*); John Sutton (*Duke of Buckingham*); Gig Young (*Porthos*); Robert Coote (*Aramis*); Reginald Owen (*de Treville*); Ian Keith (*de Rochefort*); Patricia Medina (*Kitty*); Richard Stapley (*Albert*); Byron Foulger (*Bonacieux*); Sol Goss (*Jussac*); Richard Simmons (*Count DeWardes*); Robert Warwick (*D'Artagnan Sr.*); William "Bill" Phillips (*Grimaud*); Marie Windsor (*Spy*); Tom Tyler (*Traveler*); Kirk Alyn, John Holland (*Friends of Aramis*); William Edmunds (*Landlord*); Paul Maxey (*Major Domo*); Arthur Hohl (*Dragon Rouge Host*); Gil Perkins (*Guard*); Mickey Simpson (*Executioner*).

THE FILM

Alexandre Dumas's rousing tale of love and adventure in seventeenth-century France has received screen treatment since the first days of film. Over the years, Douglas Fairbanks Sr., Michael York, and Chris O'Donnell have all starred as the earnest country bumpkin turned hero, D'Artagnan. This M-G-M version of the story, beautifully mounted and shot in Technicolor, suffers from wildly varying moods. *The Three Musketeers* soars in its fencing and chase scenes, benefiting from a tongue-in-cheek tone and Gene Kelly's natural exuberance, but flounders and loses momentum in the stretches of dialogue which strand its all-star cast.

Historically, Armand Jean du Plessis, Cardinal Richelieu, was the crafty adviser to France's King Louis XIII; in most cinema interpretations, he is the villain of the piece, devious if not outright evil. *The Three Musketeers'*

The Three Musketeers No Cardinal's robes for Richelieu

costume designer, Walter Plunkett (*Gone With the Wind*), was given the assignment of dressing Vincent Price in a way which would practically disguise the fact that he was portraying a man of the cloth (in order to avoid offending religious-minded audience members.) Thus, Price cuts an imposing figure in thigh-high boots and doublet, draped in a voluminous scarlet cloak, sword at his side and a sweepingly plumed hat on his head; in fact, he's nearly as dashing as the musketeers. Perhaps producers had read author Dumas's description of Richelieu, which begins: "At first sight there was nothing about him to indicate that he was a cardinal, so that those who did not know him had no way of guessing who he was when they saw him." Most reviewers were quick to carp. One wrote: "It is notable that Vincent Price appears in no clerical trappings and is never addressed by his ecclesiastical title. In fact, if it were not for his doublet and hose, you could hardly tell him from the standard Hollywood version of a Fifth Columnist or crooked used car dealer." Despite the wardrobe anomaly, the actor creates another of his magnificent, elegant villains. Intellectual, with a fine sense of irony when he is bested at the end, Price delivers most of his lines to coconspirator and enemy alike in a seductive murmur.

Vincent had several costume tests in the weeks preceding and then began the picture the second week in February 1948. Upon release of the film, he received another Box Office Blue Ribbon Award for December 1948 for his role of Richelieu.

REVIEWS

Variety, October 20, 1948

". . . a swaggering, tongue-in-cheek treatment of picturesque fiction, extravagantly presented to capture the fancy of any high romanticist . . . with a multi-star cast to brighten marquees, there is every indication it will cut a socko box office swath right down the line. . . . Wise casting has Vincent Price bringing his suave leer and menace to the role of Richelieu. The part is short in total footage. . . ."

New York Times, October 21, 1948, Bosley Crowther

". . . [an] onrush of million-dollar cliches and star-steam-rollering. . . . Vincent Price is Hollywood-haughty as Richelieu, conspicuously without his Cardinal's robes."

ANGELA LANSBURY

"I saw Vincent do *Angel Street*. That's when he landed fairly and squarely in our midst, as an actor. He just had tremendous authority on stage. Of course, he acted much older than he was, he was like me in that respect. He played very mature roles, and very effectively. He had such authority and strength on screen. He was a wonderful villain. . . . I went through many years at M-G-M being a young character actress. [For *The Three Musketeers*] I went to see Louis B. Mayer in his office, and I said, 'You know, this would be a wonderful opportunity for me if you let me play Lady de Winter. Don't make me play the Queen of France, with darling Frank Morgan as my husband. You're putting me in this old mold again.' One of the few times in my career that I *really* went after something. . . . But we laughed a lot. I think Vincent and I took it all with a big grain of salt. This was M-G-M's idea of the court of Louis; we just did our best to make it as palatable as possible. It was kind of a fun version, when you think about it. It was really almost sort of a musical version of French history. . . . Vincent was the consummate actor. Most giving and sharing. Prepared to rehearse, and make it wonderful for everybody. Ready to go. Knew his lines; we all did in those days. There was no such thing as coming stumbling into a scence, not knowing your lines. He certainly was an extremely professional person. He was also great fun. Charming. . . . I knew him with Mary. She was an excellent designer, a great cook. [Years later, Vincent and I] got to see each other a great deal, through a mutual friend. We used to meet at his house many, many times, for dinner, in the 1980's. [As a couple, Vincent and Coral] were marvelous. They matched each other wonderfully. They seemed to have a great sense of each other, enjoy each other tremendously. They were the most comfortable pair you could possible imagine. She came from London, she had an incredible career there. She was a very, very *funny*, sophisticated, caustic woman. Terribly *funny*; I mean she was *hilarious*. She would have us all on the floor, including Vincent—she certainly made *him* laugh. [Coral passed away in May 1991, and less than six weeks later actress Lee Remick died.] I was unable to go to Lee Remick's funeral. She died of cancer also. My husband went, and Vincent was there. I though it was rather wonderful he was able to get himself together and go . . .

We would have *loved* to have had Vincent [as a guest star on her popular TV series, *Murder She Wrote*.] He was not always available; he was out on the circuit so much. During the years I've been doing the show, he was *not* sitting around [laughs]! The problem was always to find a part that was really *good enough* for him. He had an elegance; he looked like a man out of another time, another period. He definitely had a period appearance, and he always dressed that way, you know, he never looked like your average guy. He dressed in a rather cultivated, and rather studied way, I always thought. He had the air of somebody who—he was extremely literate, he had a marvelous education—and it showed. One was always awed by Vincent, one always felt, my gosh, here was a man one could listen to, and give pause."

25. THE BRIBE

METRO-GOLDWYN-MAYER
Released late January 1949

CREDITS

Producer, Pandro S. Berman; *Director*, Robert Z. Leonard; *Screenplay*, Marguerite Roberts; *Based on the story by* Frederick Nebel; *Cinematography*, Joseph Ruttenberg; *Art Directors*, Cedric Gibbons, Malcolm Brown; *Set Decorator*, Edwin B. Willis; *Music*, Miklos Rozsa; *Song*, Nacio Herb Brown, William Katz; *Editor*, Gene

The Bribe

Ruggiero; *Ava Gardner's costumes by* Irene; *Makeup*, Jack Dawn; *Running time*, 98 minutes; black and white.

CAST

Robert Taylor (*Rigby*); Ava Gardner (*Elizabeth Hintten*); Charles Laughton (*J. J. Bealer*); Vincent Price (*Carwood*); John Hodiak (*Tug Hintten*); Samuel S. Hinds (*Dr. Warren*); John Hoyt (*Gibbs*); Tito Renaldo (*Emilio Gomez*); Martin Garralaga (*Pablo Gomez*); Pepe Hernandez (*Bellboy*); Nacho Galindo (*Clerk*); Marcel de la Brosse, Albert Pollet (*Frenchmen*); Walter A. Merrill, Frank Mayo (*Americans*); Robert Cabal, David Cota, Richard Lopez (*Bellboys*); Fernando Alvarado (*Flute Player*); Peter Cusanelli (*Rhumba Dancer*); Jerry Pina (*Stunt Juggler*); Harry Vejar (*Indian*); Felipe Turich (*Clerk*); William Haade (*Walker*); Joe Dominguez (*Waiter*); Julian Rivero (*Boatman*); Ernesto Morelli (*Bartender*); Albert Morin (*Jose the Waiter*).

The Bribe With Charles Laughton

THE FILM

Despite the promise of its star cast, *The Bribe* is a fairly routine crime drama about smuggling. Robert Taylor plays a U.S. Justice Department agent assigned to put an end to the Caribbean-based war-surplus racket which Vincent Price runs with a little help from a deliciously seedy Charles Laughton. Playing coconspirator John Hodiak's wife, Ava Gardner provides the glamour as the unwilling lure used to undermine Taylor's resolve. In the end, he undermines hers, and with husband and bad guy both dead, they've got each other.

According to his diary, Vincent was shooting the picture on June 28, 1948. Although he was only thirty-eight, his hair is unconvincingly grayed at the temples; he refers to Taylor as a "young fella." The two deep-sea marlin fish; well, pretend to, anyway, in front of a blue screen. In real life, Price was an avid fisherman, although more of the stream and lake variety. His character of Carwood is icier, more completely evil, than most of his "suave villain" roles. In the picture's denouement, he and Taylor participate in a wild gun chase through the streets of the village during a fireworks festival—the first but by no means the last occasion in his screen career in which Price had to dodge homicidal pyrotechnics. However, it's an extremely unrealistic dummy which takes the death fall down the steps of a building.

Only a few years later, Price took over Laughton's role of the Devil in the tour of George Bernard Shaw's *Don Juan in Hell*, which the English actor was also directing.

In the unusual *Dead Men Don't Wear Plaid* (1982), director Carl Reiner used clips from *The Bribe*, including Price's smothering of Hodiak and the chase scene.

REVIEWS

Variety, January 28, 1949

". . . pretty standard melodramatic filmfare . . . star value of Vincent Price [is wasted]."

Hollywood Reporter, February 4, 1949

"Vincent Price is excellent as the brains of the outfit."

Newsweek, February 14, 1949

"Vincent Price in the role of archvillain . . . acquires his comeuppence amid more fireworks than the fire commissioner of even an island like Carlota would be likely to condone—fiesta or no fiesta."

VINCENT PRICE

("The Villians Still Pursue Me" lecture)

"*The Bribe* had two superstars in it, I mean, really big, big stars—a famous, famous actress and a famous actor. And the thing that made the picture really a success was

The Bribe Fishing on the backlot with Robert Taylor

that it had three villains—three entirely different kinds of villains. The first was a fellow named John Hodiak, who had slick black hair and flashing eyes and teeth that went a-a-a-l-l the way around his head [audience laughter]. And then there was a fellow, short and fat and kinda stubby, with funny little twinkly eyes, named Charles Laughton—the great Charles Laughton. And then, of course, the ultimate, the suave, the perfect villain, myself. . . . The leading lady, the superstar of her time—I wanna pay a tribute to this woman. I have had the pleasure of working with—I was going to say playing with, but it was working with—some of the most famous sex idols in the movie business, like Jane Russell and Lana Turner and Maureen O'Hara. But the only one that ever really seemed to me to live up to her reputation as a sex object was this lady Ava Gardner . . . *mmmm*. . . . Every time I think about her, I just go limp. . . . No, I don't mean that [audience laughter]. It's just a question of semantics, isn't it? But Ava Gardner, my *God* she was sexy, let me tell ya."

26. BAGDAD

UNIVERSAL-INTERNATIONAL
Released November 1949

CREDITS

Producer, Robert Arthur; *Director*, Charles Lamont; *Screenplay*, Robert Hardy Andrews; *Story*, Tamara Hovey;

Cinematography, Russell Metty; *Art Directors*, Bernard Herzbrun, Alexander Golitzen; *Set Decorators*, Russell A. Gausman, John Austin; *Music*, Frank Skinner; *Songs*, Frank Skinner, Jack Brooks; *Editor*, Russell Schoengarth; *Costumes*, Yvonne Wood; *Makeup*, Bud Westmore; *Assistant Director*, Jesse Hibbs; *Choreography*, Lester Horton, Bella Lewitsky; *Running time*, 82 minutes; color.

CAST

Maureen O'Hara (*Princess Marjan*); Paul Christian (*Hassan*); Vincent Price (*Pasha Ali Nadim*); John Sutton (*Raizul*); Jeff Corey (*Mohammed Jad*); Frank Puglia (*Saleel*); Fritz Leiber (*Emir*); Otto Waldis (*Marengo*); Leon Belasco (*Beggar*); David Wolfe (*Mahmud*); Ann Pearce (*Tirza*); Paul Maxey (*Fat Clothes Merchant*); Dewey Robinson (*Fat Drunk Black Robe*); Trevor Bardette (*Soldier*); Tom Browne Henry (*Elder*); Dale Van Sickel.

THE FILM

> "Bagdad—city of intrigue and mystery!"
> "She risked her honor to avenge her father's name."

Bagdad concerns a nineteenth-century power struggle for the desert city, officially ruled by Turks and under the command of the Pasha Ali Nadim (Vincent Price).

Bagdad As Pasha Ali Nadim

Bagdad With Maureen O'Hara and Paul Christian

The pasha is secretly in league with the tribal leader of the Black Robes, Prince Raizul (Price's longtime costar John Sutton.) When English-educated Princess Marjan (Maureen O'Hara) returns to avenge the death of her father, a rival tribal leader, she blames Hassan (Paul Christian), who is Raizul's cousin. Of course, the handsome Christian is really the good guy. Sutton is unmasked as the real culprit, Price is summarily and discreetly dispatched in a raid, and sheikh gets princess.

Director Lamont was responsible for one of Abbott and Costello's best comedies, *Hit the Ice*, and several of the Ma and Pa Kettle films, but *Bagdad* is surprisingly slow-moving and contains little humor. It's a toss-up who looks least like an Arab—the Welsh-by-way-of-Missouri Price, Irish O'Hara, German/Swiss Christian, or stiff-upper-Brit Sutton. The picture was filmed in Lone Pine, California, the location for countless Hollywood Westerns and the classic *Gunga Din*. The cast of 150 does their best to depict a horde, and there's a lot of dashing around in the sand, but interior sets are minimal and uninspired, considering the so-called exotic locale. In a singularly gruesome and incongruous scene, captives are buried up to the neck so that mounted tribesmen can ride by, jabbing at their heads with lances. (Fortunately, it's filmed in long shot.)

Soft-spoken and silky, Price's military governor is another of his patented educated, elegant villains. He is resplendent in a spectacular wardrobe of colorful uniforms, complete with fez, knee-length scarlet sash, and medals. His demise, however, is quite ordinary; a quick gunshot from an anonymous soldier in the middle of the climactic melee, without the courtesy of a final death close-up generally afforded a movie's chief villain (Basil

Rathbone in *Captain Blood*, Margaret Hamilton in *The Wizard of Oz*, and Price's own dramatic last shot in *Pit and the Pendulum*).

Price also speaks the brief opening narration which sets the scene: "Bagdad—Scheherazade's fabulous city of the thousand and one nights. . . . Legend has it that Adam and Eve built Bagdad when they were expelled from the Garden of Eden. It may be true, for in Bagdad all unbelievable things are possible."

REVIEWS

Variety, November 23, 1949

". . . Overseeing all the dirty work is Vincent Price, no mean leerslinger himself as the Pasha of Bagdad. . . . Price, who is called upon to slap many of the cast in a manner reminiscent of the Three Stooges in their heyday, is swamped in the ridiculous role."

New York Times, December 24, 1949, Thomas M. Pryor

"Vincent Price is friendly as a cobra as the Pasha. . . ."

Los Angeles Examiner, December 26, 1949

"Vincent Price is the familiar snooty heavy with an added touch—one eye droops throughout the picture, and it's an annoying quirk."

VINCENT PRICE

(*The Book of Joe*, 1961)

"[I] did once develop a one-sided romance with . . . a camel. It seems that camels become enormously attached to certain individuals and not necessarily their owners or caretakers, and this happened to me on a desert location for a film called *Bagdad*. All through one week's filming in the blistering sun, take after take was being ruined by the inhuman howls of a lady camel. No one could make her stop, and the furious reprimand of the sound man to the animal owner brought out the news that the camel must have fallen in love with one of the cast. . . . [My costars] apparently had caused her no emotional upset whatsoever, but the moment I appeared the great lumpy beast gave forth with the most disturbing screams of passionate anguish. I was the object of her affection and also the friendly derision of the entire company, but the film was able to continue by eliminating this camel from any scene I was in. One evening after work, I thought I'd just see if my camel appeal was for real, so I casually sauntered by their corral. Sure enough, the lusty love call rang through the evening calm, and I strode away, smug in the knowledge that it's not every man who could find a camel willing to walk a mile for him."

Bagdad With John Sutton, Jeff Corey, Maureen O'Hara, and player

115

MAUREEN O'HARA

"Vincent had a wonderful sense of humor, and he was a *pleasure* to work with. Just before he started *Bagdad*, he was lighting a cigarette and the match exploded and burned his eye. It was terribly painful, he couldn't open his eye, so he had to play the role with it swollen closed. But halfway through the movie it started to get better, and he had one helluva time trying to keep it closed [to match the earlier footage]! He really should have put a patch on it and then he wouldn't have had so much trouble. He was complaining and laughing. He made a big, big joke out of the whole thing. . . . It was terribly, terribly hot; we used to sit in this one little trailer with buckets of ice to try and keep ourselves cool. One day, we were sitting in there and Vincent got called in to work. I was left by myself, and a tre-*men*-dous wind came through the desert and blew the trailer upside down! I was in it, and Vincent escaped! It was a mess! But I remember his sheer delight that he wasn't in the trailer when it went over. . . . In another scene, we were both sitting on horseback and his horse let loose—did everything, EVERYTHING, from every department—and I just turned to the whole crew and I said, 'You know, it's amazing what these actors will do to try and steal a scene!' I thought Vincent was going to fall off the horse. He had a tremendous sense of humor. . . . [When reminded that Price used to tell bawdy limericks, she confirms:] Oh, GOD, yes. He was *outlandish*! Loved to joke around! He was a great, charming, wonderful person; no matter what happened, he'd make a funny remark under his breath that no one else could hear, and nobody could understand why you were falling down laughing—he kept you laughing and having fun all the time. A totally professional professional. Acted and behaved at all times in a professional manner. A joy to know and fun to be near. A fine actor; I wish we'd made other pictures together."

27. CHAMPAGNE FOR CAESAR

UNITED ARTISTS
Released January 27, 1950

CREDITS

Executive Producer, Harry M. Popkin; *Producer*, George Moskov; *Associate Producer*, Joseph H. Nadel; *Director*, Richard Whorf; *Story and Screenplay*, Hans Jacoby, Fred Brady; *Cinematography*, Paul Ivano; *Art Director*, George Van Marter; *Set Decorator*, Jacques Mapes; *Music*, Dimitri Tiomkin; *Editor*, Hugh Bennett; *Costumes*, Maria Donovan; *Makeup*, William Knight, Ted Larson; *Technical Assistants*, John Claar, Robert H. Forward, by arrangement with CBS-KTTV; *Running time*, 99 minutes; black and white.

CAST

Ronald Colman (*Beauregard Bottomley*); Celeste Holm (*Flame O'Neil*); Vincent Price (*Burnbridge Waters*); Barbara Britton (*Gwenn Bottomley*); Art Linkletter (*Happy Hogan*); Gabriel Heatter, George Fisher (*Announcers*); Byron Foulger (*Gerald*); Ellye Marshall (*Frosty*); Vici Raaf (*Waters's Secretary*); Douglas Evans (*Radio Announcer*); John Eldredge (*Executive No. 1*); Lyle Talbot (*Executive No. 2*); George Leigh (*Executive No. 3*); John Hart (*Executive No. 4*); Mel Blanc (*Voice of Caesar*); Peter Brocco (*Fortune Teller*); Brian O'Hara (*Buck, T-Man*); Jack Daly (*Scratch, T-Man*); Gordon Nelson (*Lecturer*); Herbert Lytton (*Chuck Johnson*); George Meader (*Mr. Brown*); Robert Clarke (*Actor in Drive-in Movie*).

THE FILM

Vincent Price's first of two films with his idol Ronald Colman proved to be a cult classic and one of the actor's own favorites. With reason. *Champagne for Caesar* is a funny, insightful satire and afforded Price one of his most memorable roles.

Colman plays Beauregard Bottomley, a gentleman and a scholar who "knows everything" but can't find gainful employment. He shares a home with his sister Gwenn (Barbara Britton) and Caesar, an alcoholic parrot whom they found one night leaning up against a lamppost and unable to remember where he lived. To the proverbial inquiry "Polly want a cracker?" Caesar replies, "Polly wants a drink! Let's get loaded!" Beauregard and Gwenn are probably the only two Americans not lined up in front of their TV sets watching *Masquerade for Money*, the hugely popular quiz show emceed by the irrepressible Happy Hogan (Art Linkletter). Contestants impersonate their favorite person, thing, or animal and receive money for each question on the subject they answer correctly. The show is sponsored by "Milady, the soap that sanctifies." Ironically, it's to the Milady Soap Company that the state employment department sends an earnest Beauregard, who applies for a research job. When vain, pompous president Burnbridge Waters (Vincent Price) summarily dismisses him as "an intellectual type," Beauregard conceives the scheme of appearing on *Masquerade for Money* as the *Encyclopaedia Britannica*. Since he knows everything, he can't be stumped, and week after week he continues to win. At first, Waters

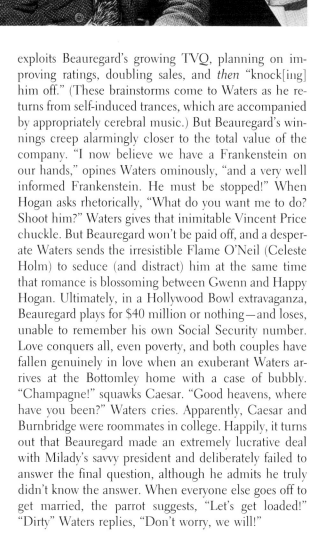

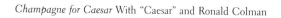
Champagne for Caesar With "Caesar" and Ronald Colman

Champagne for Caesar "Mr. Waters is not with us. He's concentrating. He's on a higher plane," With Ronald Colman and John Eldredge.

exploits Beauregard's growing TVQ, planning on improving ratings, doubling sales, and *then* "knock[ing] him off." (These brainstorms come to Waters as he returns from self-induced trances, which are accompanied by appropriately cerebral music.) But Beauregard's winnings creep alarmingly closer to the total value of the company. "I now believe we have a Frankenstein on our hands," opines Waters ominously, "and a very well informed Frankenstein. He must be stopped!" When Hogan asks rhetorically, "What do you want me to do? Shoot him?" Waters gives that inimitable Vincent Price chuckle. But Beauregard won't be paid off, and a desperate Waters sends the irresistible Flame O'Neil (Celeste Holm) to seduce (and distract) him at the same time that romance is blossoming between Gwenn and Happy Hogan. Ultimately, in a Hollywood Bowl extravaganza, Beauregard plays for $40 million or nothing—and loses, unable to remember his own Social Security number. Love conquers all, even poverty, and both couples have fallen genuinely in love when an exuberant Waters arrives at the Bottomley home with a case of bubbly. "Champagne!" squawks Caesar. "Good heavens, where have you been?" Waters cries. Apparently, Caesar and Burnbridge were roommates in college. Happily, it turns out that Beauregard made an extremely lucrative deal with Milady's savvy president and deliberately failed to answer the final question, although he admits he truly didn't know the answer. When everyone else goes off to get married, the parrot suggests, "Let's get loaded!" "Dirty" Waters replies, "Don't worry, we will!"

Champagne for Caesar With Ronald Colman, Barbara Britton, Art Linkletter, and Lyle Talbot

According to his diary, Price was working on *Champagne for Caesar* from September 9 to 29, 1949. The picture was way ahead of its time as a satire on television quiz shows and of course was an ironic precursor of the Charles Van Doren *Twenty-One* scandal nearly a decade later.

Price is completely deranged in the role of Burnbridge Waters. It's difficult to single out a representative scene, since every minute he has on-screen is hilarious. The

117

performance is a masterful combination of physical comedy, timing, and joke delivery unlike anything else Vincent did on film. His unmitigated glee as he watches Beauregard stumble over Einstein's space-time continuum—his horrified shriek as the scientist himself telephones to corroborate Beauregard's answer—are unforgettable moments in a movie filled with gems from every participant. Price always professed that he was completely tongue-tied on meeting Colman, whose work he had revered as a young man; so much so that he asked director Richard Whorf to arrange that their first scene together would be one in which Price had no dialogue. Whorf was no mean actor himself, having played opposite James Cagney in *Yankee Doodle Dandy* as George M. Cohan's producing partner, Sam Harris. In 1953, the multi-talented Whorf designed the sets for José Ferrer's Broadway production of *Richard III*, in which Vincent Price played Buckingham. *Champagne for Caesar* was the inspiration for another job for Price thirty-five years later. In 1985, when Disney animators were preparing the storyboards for *The Great Mouse Detective*, they discovered the perfect voice for nemesis Professor Ratigan after watching Vincent's larger-than-life performance as Burnbridge Waters.

Champagne for Caesar went quickly to television but unaccountably is not widely available on home video—the biggest scandal of all!

The Baron of Arizona As James Addison Reavis

REVIEWS

Hollywood Reporter, February 5, 1950

"*Champagne for Caesar* is a light and frothy comedy with a clever, original idea. Vincent Price broadly caricatures the executive to results that frequently approach the hilarious."

Fortnight, March 31, 1950

"Vincent Price sheds his usual sinister roles long enough to have the time of his life as the advertising genius. He overacts sometimes but is so funny you will hardly notice."

28.   THE BARON OF ARIZONA

LIPPERT PRODUCTIONS
Released March 1, 1950

CREDITS

Presented by Robert L. Lippert; *Producer*, Carl K. Hittleman; *Writer/Director*, Samuel Fuller; *Cinematography*, James Wong Howe; *Art Director*, F. Paul Sylos; *Set Decorator*, Otto Seigel; *Music*, Paul Dunlap; *Editor*, Arthur Hilton; *Wardrobe*, Alfred Berke, Kitty Major; *Makeup*, Vernon Murdoch; *Running time*, 96 minutes; black and white.

CAST

Vincent Price (*James Addison Reavis, "the Baron"*); Ellen Drew (*Sofia de Peralta-Reavis*); Beulah Bondi (*Loma Morales*); Vladimir Sokoloff (*Pepito Alvarez*); Reed Hadley (*John Griff*); Robert H. Barrat (*Judge Adams*); Robin Short (*Lansing*); Barbara Woodell (*Carry Lansing*); Tina Rome (*Rita*); Margia Dean (*Marquesa*); Edward Keane (*Surveyor Miller*); Gene Roth (*Father Guardian*); Karen Kester (*Sofia as a child*); Jonathan Hale (*Governor of Arizona*); Angelo Rossitto (*Angie*); Stanley Price (*Mr. Reynolds*); Joseph Green (*Gunther*); Fred Kohler Jr. (*Demming*); Tristram Coffin (*McCleary*); I. Stanford Jolley (*Secretary of the Interior*); Terry Frost (*Morelle*); Zachery Yaconelli (*Greco*); Adolfo Ornelas (*Martinez*); Wheaton Chambers (*Brother Gregory*); Robert O'Neil (*Brother Paul*); Stephen Harrison (*Surveyor's Assistant*); Edward D. Wood Jr. (*Stunt Double*).

THE FILM

"The lustiest adventure a man ever lived!"
"The half-mad, half-genius romantic lover who parlayed three women into a $300 million swindle!"

One of Vincent Price's personal favorites, *The Baron of Arizona* is an unusual film, the largely fictionalized account of a clever man's scheme to swindle the U.S. government out of the entire territory of Arizona. Real-life James Addision Reavis was an ex-Confederate soldier, born, like Price, in Missouri. An employee of the Federal Land Office in Sante Fe in 1872, Reavis laid claim to some 66,000 square miles in the Southwest on the basis of forged Spanish land grants which attempted to prove that his wife was a direct descendant of a nobleman who had been granted the land by the Spanish crown.

Lippert Productions' vice president, Murray Lerner, conceived the idea for the story, and chief Robert L. Lippert assigned "his best team," writer-director Samuel Fuller and producer Carl K. Hittleman, to explore its possibilities. Fuller based his screenplay on historical truth, building up dramatic elements of love, adventure, and pathos. *Baron* had a seven-month prep and filmed at Nassour Studio Stages in October and November 1949. Price described Samuel Fuller as "a very flamboyant character, very much like an old-time director. He wore puttees and a megaphone and everything. But I thought he was very good."

As the "Baron of Arizona," Vincent grew a beard and took on what the film's press kit called "a slight Missouri twang." The script gave Price an opportunity to stretch as an actor. Soft-spoken, he masquerades as a monk; exchanging clerical robes for a Gypsy's silks, he romances several women at one time, all with the same irresistible come-on: "I have known . . . *many* women, but with you . . . I'm afraid!" In the end, Reavis is tripped up and sent to prison, but is reunited with his wife and devoted old friend after serving his term. The Department of the Interior agent who exposes Reavis is played by Reed Hadley, who had equal success nailing Price's killer-psychiatrist four years earlier in *Shock*.

Price was already being referred to in publicity material as a "Film Actor and Authority on Art." "Suave, handsome Vincent Price, noted for film villainy and most recently as a romantic lover following his combining a few dastardly deals with a little *amour* in *The Baron of Arizona*, is also one of the nation's most noted art critics and experts. During the year 1949, Vincent, under the name Vincent L. Price, spoke to more than seventy-five thousand students at schools in Los Angeles on the subject of modern art. Billed merely as a board member of the Modern Museum of Art, at his first lecture students were surprised to discover that Vincent L. Price was in

The Baron of Arizona With Wheaton Chambers and players

The Baron of Arizona "I have known many women, but with you—I'm afraid," Price assures Tina Rome.

119

The Baron of Arizona (VP is clean-shaven in one-sheet art, but bearded in one-sheet photos and film)

fact the famed film actor. . . . Though not everyone came to hear about art, Price believes the lectures were worthwhile, for the students must have absorbed something about American culture in addition to ogling a real, live movie star."

REVIEWS

Hollywood Reporter, February 9, 1950

". . . top players may be found in the leading roles. And as a story it would be hard to find anything better . . . but the script and direction of Samuel Fuller makes it

120

The Baron of Arizona With Beulah Bondi (*left*) Ellen Drew, Reed Hadley, Vladimir Sokoloff (*hands clasped*), Robert Barrat, and players

impossible for them to jell in acceptable fashion. . . . It may be that the parts afford [Price and Ellen Drew] little opportunity for convincing acting, but the impression remains that they are just walking through on cue. . . ."

Independent Film Journal, February 11, 1950

". . . an absorbing, beautifully-acted, impressive film that would reflect credit on any studio. While the star value isn't very strong, word-of-mouth on the solid merit of *The Baron of Arizona* should cause busy box offices. Film is capably directed and offers a fine blend of drama, action and amusement. Vincent Price is a suave combination of rascal and lover. . . . Skillfully acted, produced, written, and directed, *Baron of Arizona* should go over big in any situation."

Los Angeles Times, April 17, 1950

[Fuller] and star Vincent Price make the Baron a brilliantly resourceful, fascinating fellow, and his adventures absorbing . . ."

29.   CURTAIN CALL AT CACTUS CREEK

UNIVERSAL-INTERNATIONAL
Released May 1950

CREDITS

Producer, Robert Arthur; *Director*, Charles Lamont; *Screenplay*, Howard Dimsdale; *Story*, Stanley Roberts,

Howard Dimsdale; *Cinematography*, Russell Metty; *Art Directors*, Bernard Herzbrun, John F. DeCuir; *Set Decorators*, Russell A. Gausman, Ruby R. Levitt; *Music*, Walter Scharf; *Editor*, Frank Gross; *Costumes*, Rosemary Odell; *Makeup*, Bud Westmore; *Dance Director*, Louis DaPron; *Running time*, 89 minutes, color.

CAST

Donald O'Connor (*Edward Timmons*); Gale Storm (*Julie Martin*); Walter Brennan (*Rimrock*); Vincent Price (*Tracy Holland*); Eve Arden (*Lily Martin*); Chick Chandler (*Ralph*); Joe Sawyer (*Jake*); Harry Shannon (*Clay*); Rex Lease (*Yellowstone*); I. Stanford Jolley (*Pecos*).

THE FILM

Curtain Call at Cactus Creek is a likable comedy Western which gave Vincent Price his first opportunity to play a ham actor, and even a mainstream publication like *Newsweek* magazine recognized the comedic gifts he displayed in it.

Donald O'Connor plays the general dogsbody of the Tracy Holland Repertory Company, a traveling theatrical troupe in the Old West. Desperado Walter Brennan robs the local bank and evades the law by joining up with them, assisting O'Connor with his dream of leaving backstage behind and treading the boards and also in his stalled romance with determined ingenue Gale Storm. Brennan's men organize another job during the company's performance in a neighboring town, and O'Connor is jailed as an accomplice. But Brennan, who has

Curtain Call at Cactus Creek With Eve Arden, Chick Chandler, and Donald O'Connor

121

Curtain Call at Cactus Creek With Harry Shannon (*wearing sheriff's badge*), Paul Maxey, and players

become genuinely fond of the earnest young man, arranges things so that O'Connor captures the notorious gang and becomes the inadvertent hero. Not only the hero but the star of his own company—advertised up and down the street by Tracy Holland (Vincent Price) in white tie, tails, and sandwich board.

The theatrical vignettes presented by the company, including English music-hall songs and an "I can't pay the rent!" tearjerker, are the best part of the film. O'Connor races around in the wings and up in the flies like a demon, providing piano accompaniment, curtain pulling, snowflake dropping, whipping wind, and thunderclap noises as the drama warrants. These Buster Keatonesque antics and Brennan's portrayal of the outlaw, who worships stage star Eve Arden (a takeoff on his Oscar-winning role in 1940's *The Westerner*), combine to create an irresistible atmosphere of silly fun.

Tracy Holland is a wonderful role for Price. Vain and pompous in his black silk topper and mink-collared overcoat, Tracy sniffs at the rowdy cowboys, "Uncouth rabble!" Affecting a voice so theatrical he practically sings his dialogue and employing the enormous posturing to go with it, he spouts Shakespeare for every occasion. "Tracy, you're a very romantic man," comments Arden dryly, "You're conducting one of the great love affairs of all time—with yourself." In the outrageous sketch "Ruined by Drink," Price staggers in as the drunkard father, a shaggy wig hanging in his eyes, overcome by

remorse and the effects of demon rum. Then he makes a quick change in the wings into the white satin–lined cape and drooping mustache of the sneering landlord; when the audience boos, he bows.

Universal announced *Curtain Call at Cactus Creek* as a vehicle for O'Connor in January 1949, and filming began on February 14. In Britain, the picture was called *Take the Stage*.

REVIEWS

Hollywood Reporter, May 24, 1950

"Vincent Price's ham actor is artfully overplayed."

Newsweek, June 19, 1950

"Recently both Bob Hope (*The Paleface*) and Yvonne De Carlo (*The Gal Who Took the West*) have poked fun at the routine sagebrush epic. But in *Cactus Creek*, Donald O'Connor outparodies both. . . . Price [wading] pompously through an old-time melodrama called 'Ruined by Drink' is alone worth the price of admission."

[Los Angeles] *Daily News*, June 29, 1950, Darr Smith

"Actor Vincent Price plays the consummate 'ham,' the head of the little troupe, the man who spouts a classical quotation to fit any occasion. . . . Everybody is very funny. And the Technicolor is beautiful."

30. HIS KIND OF WOMAN

RKO RADIO

Released September 1951

CREDITS

Producer, Robert Sparks; *Director*, John Farrow; *Screenplay*, Frank Fenton, Jack Leonard; *Based on the original story* "Star Sapphire" *by* Gerald Drayson Adams; *Cinematography*, Harry J. Wild; *Art Director*, Albert S. D'Agnostino; *Production Designer*, J. McMillan Johnson; *Set Decorators*, Darrell Silvera, Ross Dowd; *Music*, Leigh Harline; *Music Director*, C. Bakaleinikoff; *Songs*, Sam Coslow, Harold Adamson, Jimmy McHugh; *Editors*, Eda Warren, Frederick Knudtson; *Miss Russell's Gowns*, Howard Greer; *Makeup*, Mel Berns; *Hair Stylist*, Larry Germain; *Running time*, 120 minutes; black and white.

CAST

Robert Mitchum (*Dan Milner*); Jane Russell (*Lenore Brent*); Vincent Price (*Mark Cardigan*); Tim Holt (*Bill*

Lusk); Charles McGraw (*Thompson*); Marjorie Reynolds (*Helen Cardigan*); Raymond Burr (*Nick Ferraro*); Leslye Banning (*Jennie Stone*); Jim Backus (*Myron Winton*); Philip Van Zandt (*José Morro*); John Mylong (*Martin Krafft*); Carleton G. Young (*Hobson*); Erno Verebes (*Esteban*); Dan White (*Tex Kearns*); Richard Berggren (*Milton Stone*); Stacy Harris (*Harry*); Robert Cornthwaite (*Hernandez*); Jim Burke (*Barkeep*); Paul Frees (*Corle*); Sally Yarnell (*Wife*); Anthony Caruso (*Tony*); Joan Olander [later Mamie Van Doren], Joy Windsor, Jerri Jordan, Mary Brewer (*Girls*).

THE FILM

His Kind of Woman is frequently broadcast on television, and the *TV Guide* log line always includes the comment "Vincent Price—fine comic job." Indeed, he gives one of his most enjoyable performances in a picture that is exciting and entertaining.

Robert Mitchum plays Dan Milner, a laconic gambler who becomes involved in a scheme to get deported racketeer Nick Ferraro (Raymond Burr) back into the States. Waiting for his instructions in a resort south of the border, he runs into cafe singer Lenore Brent (Jane Russell) who is having a laissez-faire affair with Vincent Price. As popular, if second-rate, movie star Mark Cardigan, Vincent is called upon to provide comic relief, genuine

His Kind of Woman "Explain to them the survivors will get parts in my next picture. 'Now soldiers, march away—and how thou pleasest God, dispose the day.'"

romance, and action-packed derring-do. In fact, when Milner finds out who his "employer" really is and tries to back out of the deal, Cardigan helps save the day and Milner's life. The bad guys are routed, Dan and Lenore get each other, and Mark Cardigan gets the media attention he craves.

The picture began shooting around May 1950 under the title *Smiler With a Gun*. (Price's copy of the final-draft screenplay is credited to Roy Huggins, who later produced *Maverick* and *77 Sunset Strip* for television.) Long after the film was in the can, RKO mogul Howard Hughes decided that the last reel needed more action and hired Richard Fleischer (later *Barabbas*, *The Boston Strangler*, *Dr. Dolittle*) to direct a handful of new scenes, many of which involved Hughes's favorite character, Mark Cardigan. Incredibly, Hughes also decided he didn't like the actor playing the chief villain, Ferraro; after the original actor was recast and his scenes reshot, Hughes *still* wasn't happy; Raymond Burr was brought in, and they tried again. That spring, Vincent Price threw a party on the stage to celebrate his first year on the picture! The end result was a professional coup for Price, and he made the most of the extra screen time.

Price has a field day as ham actor Cardigan: applauding with a schoolboy's tentative pride at a screening of one of his own swashbucklers; looking endearingly "dismal" (in girlfriend Russell's words) when she begins to grow tired of him. But as spoiled and childishly conceited as he may be, if we cannot seriously regard Mark Cardigan as a lover worthy of Jane Russell and as a marksman capable of saving Robert Mitchum's life, then

His Kind of Woman With Robert Mitchum and Jane Russell

much of the drama of the climactic battle would be ineffective. Price manages to make both sides of the all-too-human character believable. The scene in which he stands dramatically in the bow of the overloaded rescue rowboat as it slowly sinks remains a comedy classic.

Advertising for *His Kind of Woman* included "the world's largest outdoor mural" mounted in September 1951 at Wilshire Boulevard and Fairfax in Los Angeles. The thirty-ton framework stood three stories high and was forty-five feet wide, supporting a painting by Marc Zamparelli depicting Russell draped over a prone Mitchum. Posters based on the artwork were nixed in the United Kingdom when the picture was released there. The British Board of Film Vendors ordered the top of Russell's dress to be "raised" six inches to diminish the cleavage, and the teaser ad copy, "The Hottest Combination Ever," changed to "The Greatest Combination Ever."

Vincent and Jane met making this picture, which was typical of the glamorous (and underrated) Russell's RKO/Howard Hughes vehicles. They remained close friends until his death.

REVIEWS

Motion Picture Herald, July 21, 1951

"Price shows himself a consummate comedian as an egocentric film star who proves to himself that he is quite as heroic in real life as on celluloid."

Los Angeles Daily News, September 1, 1951

". . . the best part of the picture, as far as we are concerned, is Vincent Price. He is deliciously funny . . ."

Los Angeles Times, September 1, 1951

"Vincent Price is a cast as a 'ham' screen actor spouting Shakespeare and strutting so preposterously that after a while, perversely, you begin to recognize some truth in the character."

Newsweek, September 10, 1951

"Helping Mitchum in killing scores of mobsters is Vincent Price as a fading movie idol who carries screen heroics into the real fray with fervor and quotations. He is very funny. . . ."

VINCENT PRICE

(*Gazette-Journal*) [Reno, NV] November 25, 1979

"In the middle of the picture, Howard fell in love with this character I was playing . . . We finished the film and I went to Rome for another picture. But he called us back for some new scences. We all crowded in the boat and sailed off to save Mitchum from this fate worse than death. [The boat slowly sinks] but I'm still standing in the prow. I look around. All the people are underwater, hats are floating around and bubbles are coming up. And I say, 'Don't stand there gabbering—abandon ship!' Howard wrote that line—and others equally wild."

JANE RUSSELL

"Vinnie, Vinnie, Vinnie! He was absolutely crazy. He had great, sharp humor, and he was laughing all the time; but in pictures, they always made him so stiff. He just had lots of fun. One evening, we were still making [*His Kind of Woman*], but Vinnie wasn't working, and we were all sitting around in Mitch's dressing room, and I said, 'Where's Vinnie? We gotta get him here!' We called, and he was home, but Mary wasn't. And he came down to the studio, and we were all sitting there drinking and carrying on, and all of a sudden we had to get Vinnie home. Mary was mad as the dickens at him because Vinnie was down at the studio getting loaded with all the actors!"

ROBERT MITCHUM

[When asked for his most enduring memory of Price, Mitchum's immediate response was:] "Tall!." [About *His Kind of Woman*:] "We did the picture, it was very interesting, very good really. We were all very harmonious. Earl Fenton, the writer, was a maniac. It was a great 'love-in,' the whole thing, really—with old Vinnie, Janey, me. I'd known him slightly before I worked with him. Very studious and literate. He did it all with great flair—the old Buster Keaton thing with the boat sinkin'. And the great hammy gestures. . . . [He was a believable love interest for Jane] because he was very glamorous—it was exaggerated, certainly—and she was playing a sort of available mercenary. He had great charm. He was totally free of any affectation at all, really, personally. He was a very caring person. . . . He was very versatile and demonstrated it. . . . I just show up, say the lyrics, and clock out. . . . Vincent was a pleasure to know."

31. ADVENTURES OF CAPTAIN FABIAN

REPUBLIC PICTURES
Released September 1951

CREDITS

A Silver Films Production; *Producer/Director*, William Marshall; *Associate Producer*, Robert Dorfmann; *Screen-*

Adventures of Captain Fabian As George Brissac

play, Errol Flynn; *Based on the novel* Fabulous Ann Madlock *by* Robert Shannon; *Cinematography*, Marcel Grignon; *Production Supervisor*, R. E. Marshall; *Sets*, Eugene Lourie, Max Douy; *Music*, Rene Cloerec; *Editor*, Henri Taverna; *Costumes*, Arlington Valles; *Running time*, 100 minutes; color.

CAST

Errol Flynn (*Capt. Michael Fabian*); Micheline Prelle (*Lea Marriotte*); Vincent Price (*George Brissac*); Agnes Moorehead (*Aunt Jesebel*); Victor Francen (*Henri Brissac*); Jim Gerald (*Constable Gilpin*); Helena Manson (*Madam Pirott*); Howard Vernon (*Emil*); Roger Blin (*Phillipe*); Valentine Camax (*Housekeeper*); George Flateau (*Judge Jean Brissac*); Zanie Campan (*Cynthia Winthrop*); Reggie Nalder (*Constant*); Charles Fawcett (*Defense Attorney*); Aubrey Bower (*Mate*); Marcel Journet; Gilles Queant.

THE FILM

This anachronism—inconceivably released the same year as *An American In Paris*, *The African Queen*, and *A Streetcar Named Desire*—was dated before it was even produced. Set in New Orleans in 1860, *Adventures of Captian Fabian* involves a dashing sea captain (is there any other kind?), a fiery Creole adventuress, and a

wealthy philanderer in deception, blackmail, seduction, and murder.

Price was a little old for his role of the privileged ne'er-do-well, but a younger costar would have contrasted unfavorably with the dissipated Flynn. When the two men square off as rivals for the same conniving woman—curiously, Price performs considerably more on-screen lovemaking than Flynn—it's difficult to believe that their previous film together, *The Private Lives of Elizabeth and Essex* was only just over a decade earlier. The thirty-nine-year-old Vincent is attractive, confident, and mature; at forty-one but looking fiftyish, there is little left in aging swashbuckler Errol of Captain Blood, Robin Hood, or Essex.

Shooting on what was originally called *The Bargain* was scheduled for the south of France in August 1950, but the starting date was held up pending issuance of work permits from the French Labor Department for the American stars. There were problems on location; reports that Marshall had violated several French government coproduction regulations, including ignoring a requirement that every English-language film made in France had also to be shot in French. (Originally, respected director Robert Florey was hired to lens a foreign-language version. Florey remained on the film as an unofficial consultant to Marshall.)

Meanwhile, Warner Bros. was regarding Flynn's appearance as a breach of contract, since the actor was permitted to make outside films only for major release.

Adventures of Captain Fabian With Micheline Prelle

125

Similar notice was served on costar Prelle (Marshall's wife) by 20th Century-Fox, the studio which had "discovered" her and changed the spelling of her last name from the original "Presle." (According to the trade papers, Prelle's costumes were designed by an uncredited Mary Grant, Price's wife.)

Flynn himself received sole screen credit for writing the screenplay of *Captain Fabian*, but his associate Charles Gross filed suit in Superior Court in July 1951, asserting that he had been hired in June 1950 to adapt the story and was owed back pay and expenses. Price also brought legal action against producer Marshall and Flynn in September 1954 for the balance due of his own salary. It wasn't until two and a half years later, in March 1957, that the actor obtained a default judgment against them.

The picture had various release titles, including *Fabulous Ann Madlock*, *Bloodline*, and *La Taverne de N.O.*, presumably for France.

REVIEWS

Variety, September 22, 1951

"Though this pic has some name calibre in Errol Flynn, Vincent Price and Micheline Presle [sic], contrived scripting, static direction and generally weak production values give this slight chance for scoring in first-runs. . . ."

New York Times, December 14, 1951, Howard Thompson

". . . an absurd, yawn-provoking hodgepodge of romance, intrigue and swashbuckling capers. Possibly to give authentic Gallic backgrounds and flavoring to this heavy-handed tale of Old New Orleans, producer William Marshall packed the stars off to France. . . . Neither the trip nor this foundering fiasco was necessary."

32.   PICTURA— ADVENTURE IN ART

PICTURA FILMS

Released December 21, 1951

CREDITS

A Pictura Films Presentation; *Planned and Produced by* Leonid Kipnis, Herman Starr; *Framing Sequences Directed by* E. A. Dupont; *Cinematography*, Ernest Haller, Mario Caveri, Ubaldo Marelli, John Lewis; *Editors*, Chester Schaeffer, Reine Dorian, Robert S. Robinson, Mark Sorkin; *Running time*, 80 minutes; black and white.

Featuring Vincent Price
Episode 1: "The Lost Paradise" by Hieronymus Bosch (1450–1516). *Producer/Director*, Luciano Emmer; *Research and Story Plan*, Luciano Emmer, Enrico Gras; *Commentary*, King James version of the Old Testament; *Music*, Roman Vlad; *Performed by* Orchestra of Santa Cecilia Academy in Rome; *Narrator*, Vincent Price.
Episode 2: "The Legend of St. Ursula" by Vittore Carpaccio (1460–1526). *Coproducer*, Sergio Amidei; *Director*, Luciano Emmer; *Special Camera work and Effects*, Mario Bava; *Screenplay*, Richard Nickson; *Music*, Roman Vlad; *Performed by* Orchestra of Santa Cecilia Academy in Rome; *Conducted by* Willy Ferrero; *Narrator*, Gregory Peck.
Episode 3: Francisco Goya (1746–1828). *Producer*, Luciano Emmer; *Director*, Lauro Venturi; *Screenplay*, Harry Marble; *Music*, Isaac Albeniz; *Guitar*, Andres Segovia; *Narrator*, Harry Marble.
Episode 4: Henri de Toulouse-Lautrec (1863–1901). *Producer*, Pierre Braunberger; *Directors*, Robert Hessens, Olga Lipska; *Screenplay*, Herman Starr; *Music*, Guy Bernard; *Narrator*, Lilli Palmer.
Episode 5: Paul Gauguin (1848–1903). *Producer*, Pierre Braunberger; *Director*, Alain Resnais; *Research*, Gaston Diehl; *Music*, Darius Milhaud; *Narrator*, Martin Gabel.
Episode 6: Grant Wood (1892–1942). *Producer*, Leonid Kipnis; *Director*, Mark Sorkin; *Research*, Jules Schwerin; *Camera*, John Lewis; *Music*, Lan Adomian; *Musical Direction*, Jack Shaindlin; *Narrator*, Henry Fonda.

THE FILM

Pictura—Adventure in Art was a unique concept in feature films, consisting of six episodes based on the lives and works of six of the world's great artists. Not surprisingly, since his passion for art was well known even by 1950, Vincent Price was signed to contribute; in addition to recording voice-over narration for one of the segments, he was the only actor featured on-screen, talking about art with young listeners in the framing sequences. Price's sequences were directed by E. A. Dupont, who had several German silent films to his credit.

In 1949, Leonid Kipnis brought to America from France a short film on the life and works of Van Gogh which he supplied with English-language commentary spoken by Martin Gabel. *Van Gogh* was acclaimed at public showings for cultural groups and art museums, and in 1949, it received the Academy Award for Best Two-Reel Short Subject. Based on the success of the short, producers Kipnis and partner Herman Starr planned a full-length film—artists were selected, scripts were developed, commentaries prepared, musical scores written and performed—in a tricountry (France, Italy, and the United States) collaboration. With a framework filmed in Hollywood (consisting of Vincent Price's discussions with eager young art students) to hold together the vignettes, the feature was completed. The director of the Metropolitan Museum of Art, Francis Henry Taylor, wrote a letter to producer Herman Starr, commenting: "I found myself completely entranced with the wonders of this picture.... Your discriminating selection of famous stage and screen stars as narrators and the wonderful music scores especially composed for it have made *Pictura* a production which provides fascinating entertainment and real excitement for every movie goer. Your company should be congratulated for its courage and accomplishment."

In 1954, Price's segment on Bosch was released as an eleven-minute short.

REVIEWS

Variety, December 20, 1951

"... explores a new field for motion pictures in combining visual displays of painting masterpieces by famous artists with explanatory narrative of the creators and suitable mood music for the subjects presented.... Opening scene, in which Vincent Price discusses art with a group of university students, sets the stage for presentation and explanation of six noted artists from year 1500 to modern days...."

Los Angeles Daily News, December 22, 1951

"... And to hurdle any chilling unfamiliarity with the 15th century world of Hieronymus Bosch and Vittore Carpaccio, the reassuring 20th Century profile of Vincent Price and the equally comforting tones of Gregory Peck, Henry Fonda, Lilli Palmer and Martin Gabel have been liberally written into the script. Price, as a kind of a garrulous Sunday painter given to park bench disquisitions before a cluster of young students, agreeably etches the transitions between the several episodes and, with his unseen but audible thespian colleagues, provides an entertaining narrative account of the temper and circumstances that conditioned the several palettes...."

33. THE LAS VEGAS STORY

RKO RADIO
Released January 1, 1952

CREDITS

Presented by Howard Hughes; *Executive Producer*, Samuel Bischoff; *Producer*, Robert Sparks; *Director*, Robert

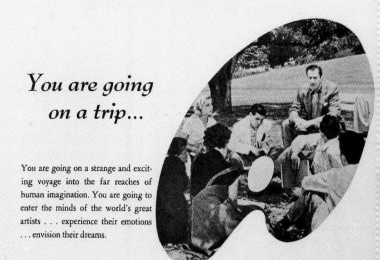

You are going on a trip...

You are going on a strange and exciting voyage into the far reaches of human imagination. You are going to enter the minds of the world's great artists . . . experience their emotions . . . envision their dreams.

You will feel, as they felt, love and anger . . . tragedy . . . futility . . . exaltation. The artist's painted figures will be the actors in this dream world which will unfold itself before scenery imagined by the painter. There will be guides on this voyage, voices and music.

Pictura—Adventure in Art Original program

Stevenson; *Screenplay*, Earl Felton, Harry Essex (Paul Jarrico, uncredited); *Based on a story* by Jay Dratler; *Cinematography*, Harry J. Wild; *Art Directors*, Albert S. D'Agostino, Field Gray; *Set Decorators*, Darrell Silvera, John Sturtevant; *Music*, Leigh Harline; *Music Director*, C. Bakaleinikoff; *Songs*, Hoagy Carmichael, Harold Adamson; *Editors*, George Shrader, Frederic Knudtson; *Gowns*, Howard Greer; *Makeup*, Mel Berns; Miss Russell's necklace by Cartier, Inc.; *Running time*, 88 minutes; black and white.

CAST

Jane Russell (*Linda Rollins*); Victor Mature (*Dave Andrews*); Vincent Price (*Lloyd Rollins*); Hoagy Carmichael (*Happy*); Brad Dexter (*Thomas Hubler*); Gordon Oliver (*Drucker*); Jay C. Flippen (*Capt. H. A. Harris*); Will Wright (*Mike Fogarty*); Bill Welsh (*Martin*); Ray Mont-

The Las Vegas Story
Print ad

The Las Vegas Story With (*from left*) Will Wright, Hoagy Carmichael (*in hat*), Jane Russell, Victor Mature, Jay C. Flippen, Brad Dexter (*seated*), Paul Frees (*in glasses*), and players

gomery (*Desk Clerk*); Colleen Miller (*Mary*); Robert Wilke (*Clayton*); Syd Saylor (*Matty*); Paul Frees (*District Attorney*); Clarence Muse (*Pullman Porter*); Milton Kibbee (*Coroner*); George Hoagland, Roger Creed, Jimmy Long, Bert Stevens, Norman Stevens, Ben Harris, Ted Jordan, Philip Ahlm, Mary Bayless, Diana Mumby, Marg Darby, Barbara Freking, Barbara Thatcher, Beverly Thomas, Jean Corbett, Hazel Shaw, Sue Casey, Evelyn Lovequist, Betty Arlen, Jeane Cochran, Carole Morton (*Bits*).

THE FILM

In *The Las Vegas Story*, his second picture with the sultry Jane Russell as a love interest. Vincent Price again lets her slip through his fingers, figuratively speaking. En route to Los Angeles from the East Coast, Price and Russell stop off in Vegas, where a few years earlier Jane had been a nightclub singer involved in a torrid affair with Victor Mature. There Price racks up gambling debts, desperately trying to make some quick big bucks, while Mature, a member of the sheriff's department, hurls recriminations at Russell until they fall back into each other's arms. Then the unpopular casino owner argues with Price and turns up dead; Russell's expensive diamond necklace, which Price has hocked for credit, goes missing. This time, though, Vincent is innocent of the killing, which was committed by an insurance agent gone bad. However, Price goes to jail, anyway, on charges of embezzlement and fraud back east. Russell had already made the decision to stay in Las Vegas with her old job and her old beau.

At first, Price is an understanding and sympathetic husband, encouraging his wife to confront the demons of her Vegas past. And, initially, Russell is genuinely concerned about his problems, entreating him to trust her. It's his unwillingness to confide in her that really drives her back to Mature. Price interrupts them renewing their acquaintance out on a balcony and purrs, "What a beautiful picture. Moonlight—sagebrush—my wife with a stranger." Unfortunately, the script denies him a final confrontation with her before the police cart him off, but Price and Russell are terrific together, both tall, dark, and cynical.

REVIEWS

Hollywood Reporter, January 2, 1952

"Vincent Price, smooth and handsome, is fine as the crooked promoter."

Variety, January 2, 1952

"A neat b.o. cast and what should have been the right ingredients for a good melodrama ... however, pic is

The Las Vegas Story With Jane Russell

only average.... Price is too animated, but good, in third spot."

JANE RUSSELL

"Vinnie was a consummate actor. I remember in *Las Vegas Story*, he was upset at one point and tried to talk to the director, because he was saying, 'There doesn't seem to be any reason for us to be together, and if we are, it's like, *why*, unless I do something overt to make her go back to her old love. I've got to give her more reason to go.' There were a couple of changes made [in the script], but maybe not enough, I don't know. But he was saying, 'Here's a husband and wife, and she's taking off, and I've gotta show people *why* she's taking off. Otherwise, she's just being a pain in the ass.'"

34. HOUSE OF WAX

WARNER BROS.

Released April 10, 1953

CREDITS

Producer, Bryan Foy; *Director*, Andre de Toth; *Screenplay*, Crane Wilbur; *Based on a Story by* Charles Belden; *Cinematography*, Bert Glennon, J. Peverell Marley; *Art Director*, Stanley Fleischer; *Set Decorator*, Lyle B. Reifsnider; *Music*, David Buttolph; *Orchestrations*, Maurice de Packh; *Editor*, Rudi Fehr; *Wardrobe*, Howard Shoup; *Makeup*, Gordon Bau; *Natural Vision Supervision*, M. L. Gunzburg; *Visual Consultant*, Julian Gunzburg, M.D.; *Natural Vision Consultant*, Lothrop Worth; *Running time*, 89 minutes; color and 3-D.

House of Wax VP's first trial by fire

CAST

Vincent Price (*Prof. Henry Jarrod*); Frank Lovejoy (*Lt. Tom Brennan*); Phyllis Kirk (*Sue Allen*); Carolyn Jones (*Cathy Gray*); Paul Picerni (*Scott Andrews*); Roy Roberts (*Matthew Burke*); Angela Clarke (*Mrs. Andrews*); Paul Cavanagh (*Sidney Wallace*); Dabbs Greer (*Sgt. Jim Shane*); Charles Buchinsky [later Charles Bronson] (*Igor*); Reggie Rymal (*Barker*); Ned Young (*Leon Averill*); Philip Tonge (*Bruce Alison*); Darwin Greenfield (*1st Lodger*); Jack Kenney (*2nd Lodger*); Riza Royce (*Ma Flanagan*); Ruth Warren (*Scrubwoman*); Richard Benjamin (*1st Detective*); Jack Mower (*2nd Detective*); Grandon Rhodes (*Surgeon*); Frank Ferguson (*Medical Examiner*); Eddie Parks (*1st Morgue Attendant*); Jack Woody (*2nd Morgue Attendant*); Oliver Blake (*Pompous Man*); Leo Curley (*Portly Man*); Mary Lou Holloway (*Millie*); Joanne Brown (*Girl Friend*); Shirley Whitney (*2nd Girl Friend*); Merry Townsend (*Ticket Taker*); Terry Mitchell (*Woman*); Ruth Whitney (*Woman*); Trude Wyler (*Woman*); Lyle Latell (*Waiter*).

THE FILM

House of Wax is the feature film which changed the direction of Vincent Price's career. For several years

prior, following the lapse of his movie contract with 20th Century-Fox, Price had freelanced, appearing in a variety of films, mostly playing comedy. Landing the lead in *House of Wax* established him as the quintessential (predominantly sympathetic) villain and set him on the professional path which would be both a curse and a blessing for the rest of his life.

House of Wax was a remake of *Mystery of the Wax Museum* (1933), which had been directed by Michael (*Casablanca*) Curtiz and starred Lionel Atwill. It was Vincent's first horror film since starring in *The Invisible Man Returns* in 1940 (apart from his voice-over cameo in the Abbott and Costello movie). Gentle, idealistic sculptor Henry Jarrod is presumed dead in the flames of his wax museum when his greedy partner commits arson for the insurance money. But Jarrod returns, wheelchair bound, his hideous burns hidden by a clever mask, and the artist who can no longer create beauty opens a horrific and enormously popular Chamber of Horrors. Jarrod himself supplies the displays, murdering people who resemble his "children" destroyed in the fire and covering their bodies with wax. He attempts to re-create Marie Antoinette out of his unsuspecting assistant's fiancée (Phyllis Kirk), but when the police burst into his laboratory at the crucial moment, he becomes a victim of his own twisted genius. (Interestingly, the original script ended with Jarrod falling into the hissing vat of boiling wax and not with the existing comedy tag which inappropriately wraps things up, similar to the equally unsatisfying ending of the Claude Rains version of *The Phantom of the Opera*.)

Jack Warner saw the 3-D *House of Wax* as the means to save his studio (and, by association, the movie industry) from the doldrums imposed by the growing television incursion. Phyllis Kirk had great trepidation about appearing as the female lead, Sue Allen. "I told Jack Warner that I didn't really want to be in this monster film," she remembers, "and I had no desire to be the Fay Wray of my time. In any event, all of my complaining and moaning, I knew was of no avail. What Jack Warner wanted to do, he did." Kirk's heroine is no scream queen, however. Intelligent and intrepid, Sue Allen maintains her wits about her and actually is the only one rightfully suspicious of the goings-on at the House of Horrors. As for Vincent Price in a decision that he never suspected would be a turning point in his life, he accepted the film assignment over a Broadway play with colleague José Ferrer.

Since director Andre de Toth had only one eye, he couldn't perceive the much heralded 3-D special effects. Probably because of that, he didn't overdo them, and the result is a restraint in the gimmickry that makes it all the more effective and fun. Who can forget the street hawker and his paddle-ball? De Toth was equally successful with his supporting players. Carolyn Jones's dumb blonde who is not so dumb is charming and memorable; the talented actress makes the most of a too brief role. And, of course, a pre-Bronson Charles, with his granite face, is effective as the deaf-mute assistant.

Price's original script, titled *The Wax Works*, is dated January 14, 1953. During the filming, Hollywood reporter Vernon Scott claimed that Price had been "banished from the studio commissary" and was being "kept hidden from fellow actors and the public alike" on account of "the hideous mask" he sported in the picture. "The handsome Price, who usually plays suave sophisticates, arrives at the studio at six A.M. daily and remains in the makeup chair until nine for his first horror role." Price was quoted as saying: "'This cold-shoulder treatment started when I walked into the commissary for lunch the first time. The girl at the cash register turned green and almost fainted. Then the patrons got up and headed for the door. It was bad for business, to say nothing of the indigestion it must have caused a couple of hundred people.'" Because he was head of the studio makeup department, Gordon Bau received credit for the brilliant design. Actually, it was his brother, George, who created and applied the makeup.

Vincent Price was no mean sculptor himself, despite lifelong protestations of his lack of artistic talent. In December 1940, his lovely terra-cotta bust of Pan was included in an exhibition of art by film industry professionals at a noted Los Angeles gallery. The show received full-page coverage in *Time* magazine.

House of Wax opened in New York at the Paramount Theatre on April 10, 1953. For the April 16 premiere at the downtown Los Angeles Paramount, Warners pulled out all the stops. Local transit lines were involved in a tie-in, calling out "Sixth and Hill, change for *House of Wax*!" as buses and streetcars approached the theater. (The film opened without fanfare the same day at the Hollywood Paramount.) Warners set a round-the-clock premiere, with twelve opening ceremonies scheduled during the twenty-four-hour period, starting with a midnight "spook premiere." (Members of the Mystery Writers of America announced they would be on hand for that one.) All the screenings had catchy names, including: four A.M., milkman's matinee; six A.M., breakfast premiere; eight A.M., career girls' matinee; twelve noon, luncheon club; four P.M., school matinee; eight P.M., screen stars' premiere; ten P.M., daters' premiere. Warner Bros. even concocted a deal with the Schick Co. to actually make electric razors available in the lobby for any men attending the six A.M. screening. Admission was $1.25, which included a pair of cardboard 3-D glasses.

On initial release across the country, *House of Wax* chalked up some of the "heftiest" box-office returns in years. In the decades since its premiere, the picture has

House of Wax With Charles Buchinsky (Bronson) and Paul Cavanagh

House of Wax "There is a pain beyond pain, an agony so intense it shocks the mind into instant oblivion." Makeup by George Bau

had several successful "comebacks;" the one in 1972 merited mention by *Time* magazine. In 1990, Price himself made a personal appearance at a special 3-D screening at a revival theater in Los Angeles.

REVIEWS

Hollywood Reporter, April 10, 1953

"Warner Bros.' *House of Wax* proves once and for all that true stereo combined with perfect color and directorial sound is truly a visually new and exciting medium.... *House of Wax* is great entertainment, an exciting, diverting thriller.... Exhibitors can count on this to pay off their bill for 3-D equipment installation, and then some.... Vincent Price, aided and abetted by the expert makeup of Gordon Bau, gives the part of the sculptor as much ghoulishness as the audience can stand. He makes his blood-curdling brothers, Herr Frankenstein and Mr. Hyde, seem like friendly folk.... Andre de Toth's direction makes the best possible use of all effects, without throwing too many things at the audience...."

Variety, April 10, 1953

"This will knock 'em for a ghoul.... Vincent Price is capital as the No. 1 menace...."

PHYLLIS KIRK

"I had known Vincent's work for a long time. I adored *The Eve of St. Mark* and his southern soldier. If you saw that, you can't believe that that actor could ever give a bad performance. He was very generous with other performers—helpful, not forever hogging everything—he was a gentleman. He was adorable.... The only thing I objected to was that they padded my bosom. They always did that in Hollywood. Because I was a small-bosomed female, I didn't blame them for doing it, but I was never really comfortable with that—ever. There was a scene in the film where I am lying on a slab, supposedly nude, with Vincent's monster character going to do something, and all I had over me was a piece of gossamer, like chiffon. And I kept saying to Andre, 'Andre, there ain't nothin' to hold this chiffon up—it's going to fall off.' My chest was very vulnerable, let's put it that way.... Everybody was paranoid about something that could happen to hold up or stop production. Jack [Warner] didn't want any of us to go anywhere. And because I was under contract to him, he made me sleep on the lot in my dressing room. They were afraid I'd get into an accident, or something would happen, and I'd hold up the production. I was living in Beverly Hills. I know that I slept in my dressing room a lot...."

35. DANGEROUS MISSION

RKO RADIO
Released February 1954

CREDITS

Producer, Irwin Allen; *Director*, Louis King; *Screenplay*, Horace McCoy, W. R. Burnett, Charles Bennett; *Story*, Horace McCoy, James Edmiston; *Cinematography*, William Snyder; *Art Directors*, Albert S. D'Agostino, Walter Keller; *Set Decorators*, Darrell Silvera, John Sturtevant; *Music*, Roy Webb; *Music Director*, C. Bakaleinikoff; *Editor*, Gene Palmer; *Costumes*, Michael Woulfe; *Makeup*, Mel Berns; *Hairstylist*, Larry Germain; *Running time*, 75 minutes; color and 3-D.

CAST

Victor Mature (*Matt Hallett*); Piper Laurie (*Louise Graham*); William Bendix (*Joe Parker*); Vincent Price (*Paul Adams*); Betta St. John (*Mary Tiller*); Steve Darrell (*Katoonai*); Marlo Dwyer (*Mrs. Elster*); Walter Reed (*Dobson*); Dennis Weaver (*Pruitt*); Harry Cheshire (*Elster*); George Sherwood (*Mr. Jones*); Maureen Stephenson (*Mrs. Jones*); Fritz Apking (*Hawthorne*); Ken Dibbs (*Johnny Yonkers*); Bert Moorehouse (*Piano Player*); Roy Engel (*Hume*); Frank Wilcox (*Jeremiah Kern*).

Dangerous Mission With Victor Mature and Piper Laurie

THE FILM

Dangerous Mission is a tale of murder and intrigue set and partially filmed in Montana's Glacier National Park. A good-looking picture, it can't live up to the glory of the location's natural beauty.

After witnessing a gangland murder, Piper Laurie flees to a remote Glacier National Park hotel where she takes a job as a cashier in the newsstand/gift shop. When Victor Mature and Vincent Price arrive, she can't be sure which is the officer from the D.A.'s office and which the hit man hired to silence her. (She obviously hasn't seen many movies.) Mature is an ex-marine with a gun in his glove compartment; Price, a magazine photographer who is already squiring Laurie around when Mature turns up and begins to woo her away. Price finally makes his move before Mature can make his, and the climax comes with a dangerous chase across the treacherous glaciers.

In addition to the so-called mystery, there are a lot of "ordinary people caught in a disaster" scenes, which became producer Irwin Allen's trademark: An avalanche during a square-dance party sends people leaping for cover as boulders smash through windows of the building and live power lines spark outside. When a forest fire gets out of hand, the park rangers speed to the rescue; even Mature and Price are handed jumpsuits and hard hats and conscripted to fight the blaze. They barely make it through the flames alive. (So soon after *House of Wax*, Vincent must have thought it was déjà vu!)

Price is the villain once again, but at least he doesn't look the part. Casually clad in cuffed blue jeans and sporting Clark Kent thin-framed glasses, he appears much younger than his forty-three years. The plot also gives him another opportunity for romance—with a young Indian girl (Betta St. John) who has a crush on him. In hunting the girl's father, who is suspected of murder, park ranger William Bendix and his men end up tracking down Price when he takes the girl as a hostage out onto the glacier in pursuit of Laurie. And instead of fire, it's ice that spells doom, as Price is buried in a miniavalanche caused by his own attempts to shoot Mature. Reportedly, RKO spent $45,000 to convert their two largest soundstages into a replica of a nothern glacier, bringing in three wind machines and grinding up fifty tons of ice daily.

Fellow actor Walter Reed remembers that Vincent dubbed the picture *She Lost It in the Crevasse*. During filming, cast and crew stayed in a hotel full of "staid, sedate people. . . . That hotel was on an Indian reservation, and down the street about two miles, *off* the reservation, was a gambling and drinking place. You couldn't drink at the hotel because that was on Indian territory.

Dangerous Mission An icy death in Glacier National Park

On the weekend, we'd get bored, so Vic Mature, Bill Bendix, Dennis Weaver, Vincent Price, and myself used to hitchhike our way down there at night—people would pick us up; they hadn't the slightest idea who we were!"

In preproduction as *The Glacier Story*, the movie got a title change to *Rangers of the North* while filming (in 3-D!) during the summer of 1953. It became *Dangerous Mission* only just prior to release.

REVIEWS

Harrison's Reports, February 27, 1954

". . . suitable for undiscriminating patrons who like action melodramas. For thrills it has much hokum but dependable situations. . . . The story itself is a routine affair."

New York Times, March 6, 1954, Bosley Crowther

". . . a tale that hasn't the vitality or intelligence of a good comic-strip episode. It is a miserably dull and mixed-up fable about a hunt for a missing witness to a crime, with Vincent Price eventually emerging as some sort of villain, which is obvious all along."

36. CASANOVA'S BIG NIGHT

PARAMOUNT PICTURES
Released March 1954

CREDITS

Producer, Paul Jones; *Director*, Norman Z. McLeod; *Screenplay*, Hal Kanter, Edmund Hartmann; *Based on a story by* Aubrey Wisberg; *Cinematography*, Lionel Lindon; *Art Directors*, Hal Pereira, Albert Nozaki; *Set Deco-*

Casanova's Big Night With Joan Fontaine and Bob Hope

rators, Sam Comer, Ross Dowd; *Music Score*, Lyn Murray; *Song*, "Tic-A-Tic-A-Tic" *by* Jay Livingston and Ray Evans; *Editor*, Ellsworth Hoagland; *Makeup Supervision*, Wally Westmore; *Women's Costumes*, Edith Head; *Men's Costumes*, Yvonne Wood; *Dances staged by* Josephine Earl; *Running time*, 86 minutes; Color.

CAST

Bob Hope (*Pippo Popolino*); Joan Fontaine (*Francesca Bruni*); Audrey Dalton (*Dona Elena*); Basil Rathbone (*Lucio*); Hugh Marlowe (*Stefano di Gambetta*); Arnold Moss (*The Doge*); John Carradine (*Minister Foressi*); John Hoyt (*Maggiorin*); Hope Emerson (*Duchess of Castelbello*); Robert Hutton (*Raphael, Duke of Castelbello*); Lon Chaney Jr. (*Emo*); Raymond Burr (*Bragadin*); Frieda Inescort (*Signora di Gambetta*); Primo Carnera (*Corfa*); Frank Puglia (*Carabaccio*); Paul Cavanagh (*Signor Alberto di Gambetta*); Romo Vincent (*Giovanni*); Henry Brandon (*Captain Rugello*); Natalie Schafer (*Signora Foressi*); Nestor Paiva (*Gnocchi*); Lucien Littlefield, Douglas Fowley (*Prisoners*); Kathryn Grant, Marla English (*Girls on Bridge*).

THE FILM

Casanova's Big Night actually concerns the adventures of Casanova's tailor's apprentice. Reviews were mixed, but the comedy gave an unbilled Vincent Price, as Casanova, the chance to play predominantly straight the type of swashbuckling hero he lampooned in the movie-within-a-movie in *His Kind of Woman*.

The penniless Casanova deserts both his home in Parma and his creditors, unaware that wealthy patrons have just arrived with a lucrative offer for his services. The Duke of Castelbello and his formidable mother want to test the fidelity of the duke's fiancée, and who better to attempt to seduce the maiden than the world's most famous lover? But because the genuine article has fled, his valet (Basil Rathbone) and the grocer lady (Joan Fontaine) pass off tailor's apprentice, Pippo (Bob Hope), in order to try and earn the princely sum offered for proof of the lady's virtue—the petticoat monogrammed with the Castelbello family crest. Much comedy ensues as Hope attempts to match the exploits of the legendary Casanova, kiss for kiss, quip for quip, duel for duel, and in the end, everyone lives happily ever after.

The movie was origially announced as *Mr. Casanova* and was much touted as Basil Rathbone's first film in five years. In 1948, the actor returned to the stage to appear in *The Heiress*, remaining with the production for three solid years. He followed that with some television and preparation for a new play about Sherlock Holmes written by his author wife, Ouida Bergere.

Vincent Price has some fun in his two early scenes, which include athletic dueling with a jealous husband and verbal banter with Fontaine and Hope. Production notes say that he agreed to make the "guest appearance" as a "special favor to his good friend Hope." "[Vincent] always enjoyed a good joke," the comedian remembers. "And he was gentleman enough to laugh at some that weren't so good."

REVIEWS

Motion Picture Exhibitor, March 10, 1954

"This shapes up as one of the better Hopes. It is slow in getting started, but once it hits its pace, it should be responsible for plenty of laughter."

Saturday Review, April 10, 1954

". . . Like [Danny] Kaye, Hope can be a very comical fellow, but his chances to prove it here are rare indeed. . . . What makes *Casanova's Big Night* acutely distressing, however, is the awareness that these peanuts of humor are banging around in the shell of a lavish and gorgeous and expensive production. The settings, a cross between 18th-century Venice and 20th-century Paramount, are opulent beyond belief; while the supporting cast, headed by Joan Fontaine and Basil Rathbone, includes such costly but generally dependable performers as Hugh Marlowe, Arnold Moss, John Carradine, Frieda Inescort, and, making the briefest appearance, Vincent Price. Everything considered, Price made out best of all."

37. THE MAD MAGICIAN

COLUMBIA PICTURES

Released March 1954

CREDITS

An Edward Small Production; *Producer*, Bryan Foy; *Director*, John Brahm; *Story and Screenplay*, Crane Wilbur; *Cinematography*, Bert Glennon; *Art Director*, Frank Sylos; *Set Decorator*, Howard Bristol; *Music*, Emil Newman, Arthur Lange; *Editor*, Grant Whytock; *Makeup created by* Gustaf Norin and George Bau; *Wardrobe*, Robert Martien; *Special Effects*, David Koehler; *Magical Effects*, Bob Haskell; *Running time*, 72 minutes; black and white and 3-D.

CAST

Vincent Price (*Don Gallico*); Mary Murphy (*Karen*); Eva Gabor (*Claire Ormond*); John Emery (*Rinaldi*); Donald Randolph (*Ross Ormond*); Lenita Lane (*Alice Prentiss*); Patrick O'Neal (*Lt. Alan Bruce*); Jay Novello (*Frank Prentiss*); Corey Allen; Roy Engel; Lyle Talbot; Robert B. Williams; Conrad Brooks; Mickey Golden.

THE FILM

The Mad Magician, can only suffer in comparison with its inspiration, *House of Wax*. Both shot in 3-D, the films have much in common: producer, scriptwriter, makeup artist, and cameraman; as well as a turn-of-the-century murder mystery plot and fantastic, lurid murders committed by a deranged artist driven over the edge when he loses all he holds dear. But there the similarity ends, and although there are memorable moments in *The Mad Magician*, it can't be compared with the movie which Vincent Price was proud to remind people was one of Hollywood's biggest moneymakers.

Price plays Gallico the Great, a gifted, burgeoning creator of stage magic whose concepts are commandeered by a more celebrated performer. Stripped of "everything—everything I ever had . . . my wife, my brains, my self-respect—everything but the air I breathe!" the gentle Gallico goes berserk and decapitates the haughty employer who orchestrated the confiscation of his illusions. The magician then assumes a myriad of disguises to cover up that crime and the ones which inevitably follow, until he receives his comeuppance, consumed

The Mad Magician Mary Murphy, with Price as Gallico the Great masquerading as the Great Rinaldi

The Mad Magician "The Lady and the Buzz-Saw" illusion

135

in the flames of his greatest creation, the "Crematorium."

Gallico has a lot to learn in the "successful psychotic killer" department. He leaves the first victim's head in a bag which someone mistakes for their own and makes off with; he rents a room for one of his "alter egos" from a nosy biddy who writes bestselling murder mysteries in her spare time; and to top it off, his assistant is dating a resourceful police detective! Unfortunately, Price's own voice is dubbed every time he's in disguise, and of course, because of the actor's height, Gallico is several inches taller than the various men he impersonates so "successfully." But in the first scenes Vincent creates a believable portrait of a vulnerable, shy genius, speaking softly and earnestly, biting his thumb and pulling on a curly forelock in anxious thoughtfulness.

Sensing that the as-yet-unreleased *House of Wax* was going to be a hit, producer Bryan Foy hired his scriptwriter, Crane Wilbur, to knock out *The Mad Magician*, which was intended to be shot in color and "Natural Vision 3-D" in a codeal with Edward Small. Vincent's script was dated July 7, 1953; the film went into production on the Samuel Goldwyn lot on September 14, wrapping on October 3. The picture wasn't released until May 1954.

In May 1982, Elvira, Mistress of the Dark, hosted *The Mad Magician* in the original 3-D on her syndicated *Movie Macabre*. Some of her outrageously funny commentary segments and an original catchy theme song were also shot in 3-D. In the summer of 1990, during the filming of *Edward Scissorhands*, Vincent recognized a member of the crew as the prop man from *The Mad Magician*. "He put me in a crematorium, that's why I remembered him," the actor explained. "Damn near burnt me to death. I've always loved so much the technical end of the movie business. I knew [the crew on the picture] a lot better than I knew a lot of the actors. Because actors talk about just one thing—most of them— acting and themselves. Because it ain't the actor, it's the director and the cameraman and the prop man and the special effects."

REVIEWS

Harrison's Reports, March 27, 1954

"In certain respects it is even more gruesome than *House of Wax*.... There is considerable suspense in the story.... Vincent Price gives his usual skillful performance."

Los Angeles Daily News, April 8, 1954

"Vincent Price carries the acting load in this grim little film of murder by hacksaw and crematory furnaces.... [You] get the impression that Price is a laboratory techni-

cian for Murder, Inc. If you're the type who likes your murders in bizarre style, you will find some imagination in the film . . ."

38. SON OF SINBAD

R K O   R A D I O
Released June 1, 1955

CREDITS

A Howard Hughes presentation; *Producer*, Robert Sparks; *Director*, Ted Tetzlaff; *Screenplay*, Aubrey Wisberg, Jack Pollexfen; *Cinematography*, William Snyder; *Art Directors*, Albert S. D'Agostino, Walter E. Keller; *Set Decorators*, Darrell Silvera, John Sturtevant; *Music*, Victor Young; *Music Director*, C. Bakaleinikoff; *Editors*, Roland Gross, Frederic Knudtson; *Costumes*, Michael Woulfe; *Makeup*, Mel Berns; *Hairstylist*, Larry Germain; *Choreography*, Olga Lunick; *Running time*, 91 minutes; color and Superscope.

CAST

Dale Robertson (*Sinbad*); Sally Forrest (*Ameer*); Lili St. Cyr (*Nerissa*); Vincent Price (*Omar Khayyam*); Mari Blanchard (*Kristina*); Leon Askin (*Khalif*); Jay Novello (*Jiddah*); Raymond Greenleaf (*Simon*); Nejla Ates (*Dancer in Market*); Kalantan (*Dancer in Desert*); Ian MacDonald (*Murad the Tartar*); Donald Randolph (*Councillor*); Larry J. Blake (*Samit*); Edwina Hazard (*Lota*); Paul Frees (*Seer*); Kim Novak (*Raider*).

THE FILM

Cynics should not be in such a hurry to dismiss *Son of Sinbad*, which is a funny, exciting, and entertaining romp.

This Sinbad (Dale Robertson) is the son of the famous sailor, and his romantic exploits in the harem of the khalif of Bagdad have him headed for beheading, together with his much put upon buddy, Omar Khayyam (Vincent Price), tentmaker and sometime poet. Also in the doghouse (literally, since Omar is initially scheduled to be thrown to the dogs) are an old man and his daughter, Kristina (Mari Blanchard.) They have the secret of Greek fire, an explosive which could turn the tide against the imminent Tartar invasion. When Kristina is kidnapped by the Tartars the secret goes with her, so Sinbad and Omar offer to recover both in exchange for their lives. With the help of palace handmaiden Ameer (Sally Forrest), and the "Brotherhood," female descendants of the original Forty Thieves, the Tartars are routed and the

Son of Sinbad With Nejla Ates

Son of Sinbad Price and Dale Robertson (*second right*) kneel before Khalif Leon Askin (*in turban*) as his right-hand man Jay Novello looks on.

Greek fire is recovered. Promoted second in command to the khalif, Sinbad promises to try and confine his attentions to Ameer. The verses of the new poet plenipotentiary have captured for Omar the heart of Kristina. And the khalif can patch things up with the luscious Nerissa (stripper Lili St. Cyr) if only he can remember those effective rhymes of Omar's!

Son of Sinbad: Dale Robertson, Mari Blanchard, VP

137

It was reputed that Howard Hughes used the picture as an opportunity to placate starlets who were under professional contract to RKO (many of whom probably had a close personal acquaintance with Mr. Hughes). Besides giving roles to an inordinate number of beautiful women, the story combines humor and adventure with genuine intrigue, complemented by a superb score by Victor Young. And at the end it's the women who save the day and Vincent Price who dispatches the villain!

The casting supplement describes Omar as "a tall man in his late thirties, with the physique of a laborer and the soul of a dreamer." As the legendary poet, Price provides much more than mere comic relief in a supporting role which is basically the same size as that of Sinbad. His dry, casual delivery of caustic asides is genuinely funny; his brief quotations of the timeless poetry are tantalizing: ("A Book of Verses underneath the bough / A Jug of Wine, a Loaf of Bread—and Thou / Beside me singing in the wilderness—Oh, Wilderness were Paradise enow—a little something I concocted on the spur of the moment . . .") It's an athletic performance, too, as he canters on horseback alongside Robertson and engages in a wild fight with a Tartar swordsman.

Son of Sinbad was shot in the spring of 1953. But when it was completed, the maiden-laden movie was denied a seal by the Production Code office because of "some bad dances," according to a Motion Picture Association of America spokesman. Howard Hughes (who was suspected of having orchestrated the controversy in order to generate publicity) had the picture trimmed, but the "gyrations" of Lili St. Cyr still prompted the Legion of Decency to slap a "C," for "Condemned," rating on it. (They also didn't like Leslie Caron's Hong Kong ballet number in *Daddy Long Legs*.)

The world premiere of *Son of Sinbad* wasn't until May 31, 1955. RKO instituted a three-week "transcontinental tour of four costumed Harem Beauties" to "create advance publicity." Other books have listed an alternative title, *A Night in a Harem* or *Nights in a Harem*, but there is no official record of it.

The reviews are nearly as entertaining as the film itself!

REVIEWS

Hollywood Reporter, May 31, 1955, Jack Moffitt

"This movie, in its story and in its approach to sex, seems to be made for (and by) adolescents of all ages. . . . In this laboriously sensual municipality, it never occurs to anyone, including one of the great lyric poets of the world, Omar (as played by Vincent Price), to consider love a part of sex and sex a part of love. Here sex is just sex. Even the women[!] plunge into its exploitation without seeming to have given much thought to it. They never use the winsome smile, the fluttered eyelid or the glimpsed ankle to catch the attention of men . . .; they woo by a series of bodily gyrations that makes them seem to be trying to erase a blackboard with a nonexistent bustle. . . ."

Los Angeles Examiner, June 2, 1955, Ruth Waterbury

"If for one split second you take *Son of Sinbad* seriously, you'll go out of your mind. But if you follow the line of its advertising, which admonishes you to 'hold on to your turban,' and regard it as a big, colorful, crazy romp, you'll really have a ball. The story doesn't make a lick of sense—but never have I seen so many pretty girls on the screen in one single film. . . . *Son of Sinbad* thus belongs in the category of the old Ziegfeld Follies and similar stage extravaganzas. Whoever noticed the plot of one of those things when they brought on the dolls? . . . Vincent Price hams it up even more broadly (and deliberately). . . . So, go laugh."

Variety, May 31, 1955

"Vincent Price seems to enjoy his unrestrained portrayal of Omar, the Poet. Audiences, too, will get a chuckle from his tongue-in-cheek handling of the worries his wall-climbing friend causes."

VINCENT PRICE

[San Francisco] *Times Tribune*, April 15, 1985

"They sent me the script and asked me how I liked it. I said, 'I think it's the worst script I've ever read.' They said (Price smiles his Cheshire cat smile), 'It *is*, isn't it?' I said, 'Are you going to fix it?' They said (a Price chuckle), 'Well . . . no.'. . . . For some reason, [Hughes] liked me, though I never met him. He used to call me up from Las Vegas—he was deaf as a post, so I had to shout—and he'd say, 'What happened on the set today?' With 250 women on the set, I always had a lot to tell him."

SALLY FORREST

"*Son of Sinbad* was a riot. The first day of the shooting, Dale came walking in when Lili St. Cyr was taking a bath in a sunken tub, and I don't know what he was looking at, but he fell right in the tub! I was so naive in those days; I was taking my career so seriously. I was the only girl who was a trained ballet dancer, and everybody *else* was getting these dances to do. Of course, two of them were strippers! But at any rate, I was furious, and I asked Mr. Hughes for a number, too. And mine ends up being the one that was really censored, because I showed my navel, with an amber in it. Vincent said it looked like a Luden's cough drop! Vincent had *such* a sense of humor. He was so funny. He would say the darnedest things to keep everything happy on the set. One very hot day, at lunchtime, he and Dale climbed up way high in the catwalks and threw down bags of water. And they had squirt guns! Oh, my! They were like two kids. And those catwalks were *high*—it was quite a chore to go up there and do it.... The *warmth* of Vincent's personality is what I think of most often. I think he was the nicest man I ever worked with. He was it."

39. SERENADE

WARNER BROS.

Released March 29, 1956

CREDITS

Producer, Henry Blanke; *Director*, Anthony Mann; *Screenplay*, Ivan Goff, Ben Roberts, John Twist; *Based on the novel by* James M. Cain; *Cinematography*, J. Peverell Marley; *Art Director*, Edward Carrere; *Music*, Nicholas Brodszky; *Original Songs*, Nicholas Brodszky, Sammy Cahn; *Editor*, William Ziegler; *Costumes*, Howard Shoup; *Makeup Supervisor*, Gordon Bau; *Operatic Adviser*, Walter Ducloux; *Operatic Coach*, Giacomo Spadoni; *Running time*, 121 minutes; color.

CAST

Mario Lanza (*Damon Vincenti*); Joan Fontaine (*Kendall Hale*); Sarita Montiel (*Juana Montes*); Vincent Price (*Charles Winthrop*); Joseph Calleia (*Maestro Marcatello*); Harry Bellaver (*Monte*); Vince Edwards (*Marco Roselli*); Silvio Minciotti (*Lardelli*); Frank Puglia (*Manuel*); Edward Platt (*Carter*); Frank Yaconelli (*Giuseppe*); Mario Siletti (*Sanroma*); Maria Serrango (*Rosa*); Eduardo Noriega (*Felipe*); Jean Fenn (*Soprano*); Joseph Vitale (*Baritone*); Victor Romita (*Bass*); Norma Zimmer (*Mimi in* "**La Boheme**"); Licia Albanese (*Desdamona in* "**Otello**"); Francis Barnes (*Iago in* "**Otello**"); Lilian Molieri (*Tosca in* "**Tosca**"); Laura Mason (*Fedora in* "**Fedora**"); Richard Cable (*Shepherd Boy in* "**L'Arlesiana**"); Richard Lert (*Conductor*); Creighton Hale (*Assistant Stage Manager*).

THE FILM

"The story of a farmhand who won fame as a singer and nearly lost his soul as a man."

The James M. Cain novel on which *Serenade* was based was published in 1937. Bringing it to the screen had a

Serenade With Joan Fontaine and Mario Lanza

Serenade With Sarita Montiel, Mario Lanza, and Harry Bellaver

long history, not the least reason for which was censorship problems, since the Svengali-pupil relationship detailed in the book was between two men. In the movie, Mario Lanza's Northern California vineyard worker gets his big break as an opera singer when he attracts the eye of wealthy socialite Joan Fontaine and noted concert manager Vincent Price. Fontaine's modus operandi is to sniff out talented young men, make love to them, and then dump them on the eve of their professional triumphs. Despite witnessing the humiliation of a young boxer (Vince Edwards), and her frank self-assessment ("Damon, don't you understand? I always hurt people. That's my talent."), Lanza is captivated by Fontaine. Completely distraught when she is a no-show for his New York debut (in Verdi's *Otello*), he storms off the stage in the middle of the performance, throwing away his career before it has officially begun. Lanza flees to Mexico, a broken man. Convinced he has lost the ability to sing, he is nursed back to health and professional confidence by the fiery daughter of a dead local matador (Sarita Montiel). Married, they return to the States, where Joan Fontaine attempts to seduce Lanza back into her web. True love triumphs, however, and on stage with the San Francisco Opera, the new star proves he's still got what it takes.

Warner Bros. purchased the screen rights to the book in February 1944, and a variety of people were associated with the project over the next decade. At one time, Ann Sheridan and Dennis Morgan wre set to costar; once, Michael Curtiz was attached as director. Finally, it was announced as a vehicle for Mario Lanza in 1954, and Nicholas Brodszky, composer of some of Lanza's biggest hits, was assigned to write the musical score. Vincent Price was announced as a cast member in July 1955; his character, Charles Winthrop, was described as a concert manager and "man about the world." Vincent's script had the printed final date of August 19, but he penned in under it "October 19, 1955." If nothing else, the film is a fest for Lanza fans. Genial and likable, if bland, the undeniably gifted tenor does what he does best in a number of famous and original numbers. The Mexican location sequences, complete with spirited dancing, festivals and bullfighting, also supply some nice atmosphere. Unfortunately, several members of the Hollywood crew, unaccustomed to the food and water, were so terrifically sick it made the papers!

Serenade received very good and very bad reviews, but across the boards, Vincent Price's concert manager was lauded. The sophisticated, attractive, witty impresario was the type of role for which he was ideally suited.

REVIEWS

Hollywood Reporter, March 13, 1956

"Mario Lanza makes a smashing screen comeback in this musical drama which combines the appeal of both operatic arias and popular ballads with a passionate love story.... Vincent Price scores with some scintillatingly witty dialogue as a world weary concert manager."

Variety, March 13, 1956

"... Vincent Price, equipped with some sharp, brittle dialog by the scripters, stands out...."

Cue, March 24, 1956

"... [Lanza's] ringing golden tenor is the only thing that makes this pic at all endurable.... The acting is, for the most part, on a par with the story. Vincent Price alone—with a sneer on his face and a quip on his lips—manages to emerge with thespianic honor intact."

New Yorker, March 31, 1956

"*Serenade*, an etude for tenor and castanets by James M. Cain, has been extensively watered down in its adaptation for the movies. The novel, you may recall, dealt with homosexuality in the American male, impotence in the same, and prostitution as practiced in shanty towns in old Mexico...."

40. WHILE THE CITY SLEEPS

R K O   R A D I O
Released May 1, 1956

CREDITS

Producer, Bert Friedlob; *Director*, Fritz Lang; *Screenplay*, Casey Robinson; *Based on the novel* The Bloody Spur *by* Charles Einstein; *Cinematography*, Ernest Laszlo; *Art Director*, Carroll Clark; *Set Decorator*, Jack Mills; *Music*, Herschel Burke Gilbert; *Orchestrations*, Joseph Mullendore, Walter Sheets; *Editorial Supervision*, Gene Fowler Jr.; *Sound Editor*, Verna Fields; *Costumes by* Norma; *Makeup Supervision*, Gus Norin; *Hairstylist*, Cherie Banks; *Assistant Director*, Ronnie Rondell; *Technical Advisor*, Mike Kaplan; *Running time*, 100 minutes; black and white.

CAST

Dana Andrews (*Edward Mobley*); Rhonda Fleming (*Dorothy Kyne*); Ida Lupino (*Mildred Donner*); George Sanders (*Mark Loving*); Howard Duff (*Lt. Burt Kaufman*); Thomas Mitchell (*Jon Day Griffith*); Vincent Price (*Walter Kyne*), Sally Forrest (*Nancy Liggett*); John Barrymore Jr. (*Robert Manners*); James Craig (*Harry Kritzer*); Vladimir Sokoloff (*George Pilski*); Robert Warwick (*Amos Kyne*); Ralph Peters (*Meade*); Larry Blake (*Police Sergeant*); Edward Hinton (*O'Leary*); Mae Marsh (*Mrs. Manners*); Sandy White (*Judith Felton*); Celia Lovsky (*Miss Dodd*); Pitt Herbert (*Bartender*); Andrew Lupino.

While the City Sleeps

While the City Sleeps With Dana Andrews

THE FILM

While the City Sleeps begins in "New York City . . . Tonight." A psychopathic sex murderer, dubbed "the Lipstick Killer," preys on young women. Publisher Walter Kyne (Vincent Price) offers the top executive position in his multimedia corporation to any staff member who can bring in a scoop on the slayings. The veteran manag-

ing editor of the newspaper (Thomas Mitchell), the head of the wire service (George Sanders), and the chief of the photo department (James Craig) all engage in a frantic competition for the post—with and without the aid of participating secretaries, mistresses, and girlfriends. The TV news commentator/ex-reporter (Dana Andrews) remains aloof from the proceedings, a wry observer, but ultimately cannot help getting involved. In the dual pursuit of killer and career, everyone reveals the depth of their own loyalty, greed, ambition, and morality. Blind to the infidelity of his contemptuous wife, Rhonda Fleming, Price succumbs to blackmail by her lover, the photographer, and awards him the big post, even though Andrews and Mitchell bring in an exclusive on the killer's capture. But when Andrews mocks his boss, pointing out how saving face has stripped him of integrity, Price proves in a surprise ending to be a man of honor, after all—wife is dumped, lover banished, Mitchell is appointed to the job he coveted, and Andrews is offered a return to journalism as the new editor of the paper.

Producer Bert Friedlob and writer Casey Robinson acquired the Charles Einstein story in May 1954 and announced a shooting title of *News Is Made at Night*. Filming began in June under the direction of the great Fritz Lang, and while it is not one of his better pictures, the main story element of the sexual psychopath killer harkens back to Lang's immortal *M*, starring Peter Lorre. Vincent Price remembered Fritz as "such a wonderful man. Charming, cultured, a really intelligent man. An artist." As a playboy "killed by kindness—polo ponies, yachts, women," Price creates the portrait of a resentful, ambitious son, determined to make his own mark on his

While the City Sleeps With Rhonda Fleming

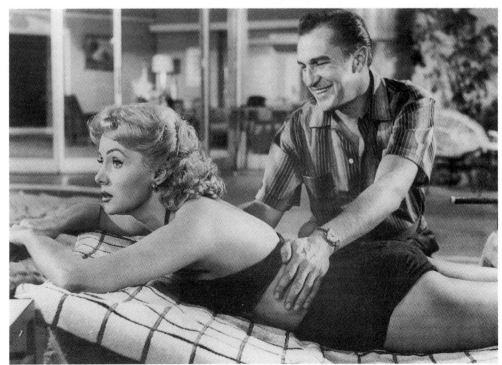

142

deceased father's empire. Pondering the job scramble he has instigated, he has a wonderful "soliloquy" on the merits of each candidate, representing them as cocktail peanuts which he makes into a shell game before popping them casually into his mouth.

Producer Friedlob made news during production by inviting a U.S. Senate subcommittee investigating the effect of comic books on juvenile delinquents to use the movie as "a weapon in the growing battle against the corrupting force of comic books on young minds." The film's killer, played by John Barrymore Jr., is depicted as an avid fan. Distribution negotiations apparently held up release of *While the City Sleeps* until the next year. Curiously, most previously published sources incorrectly list Price's character as Walter Kyne *Junior*, and also misspell several other names.

REVIEWS

Variety, May 1, 1956

"The old-fashioned 'stop-the-presses' newspaper yarn has been updated with intelligence and considerable authenticity and further brightened with crisp dialogue. . . . Presence of an 'all-star' cast of ten good marquee names also helps. . . ."

Hollywood Reporter, May 2, 1956

"A very commercial attraction . . . a down-to-earth murder yarn of the type that has proven staple fare among the masses and a good part of the class clientele as well. Since it is a tabloid-style story, Fritz Lang has directed it astutely in tabloid style, with short vignettes keeping the action going at a good clip, and the cast is studded with fine troupers, some of them with much less to do than their fans might like but all acquitting themselves with commendable conformity to the requirements of the story. . . . This is perhaps the most sex-preoccupied newspaper layout ever seen on the screen, with three romances going all the time. . . . Price makes the role of the playboy publisher entertaining. . . ."

41. THE VAGABOND KING

PARAMOUNT

Released August 29, 1956

CREDITS

Producer, Pat Duggan; *Director*, Michael Curtiz; *Screenplay*, Ken Englund, Noel Langley; *Based on the operetta,* *music by* Rudolf Friml, *book and lyrics by* William H. Post, Brian Hooker; *From the play by* Justin Huntly McCarthy; *Additional songs*, Rudolf Friml, Johnny Burke; *Cinematography*, Robert Burks; *Art Directors*, Hal Pereira, Henry Bumstead; *Set Decorators*, Sam Comer, Grace Gregory; *Music Scored by* Victor Young; *Vocal adaptations/arrangements*, Charles Henderson; *Orchestral arrangements*, Leo Shuken, Gus Levene, Albert Sendrey; *Editor*, Arthur Schmidt; *Costumes*, Mary Grant; *Makeup*, Wally Westmore; *Special Effects*, John P. Fulton; *Choreography*, Hanya Holm; *Running time*, 88 minutes; color and VistaVision.

CAST

Kathryn Grayson (*Catherine De Vaucelles*); Oreste (*François Villon*); Rita Moreno (*Huguette*); Sir Cedric Hardwicke (*Tristan*); Walter Hampden (*King Louis XI*); Leslie Nielsen (*Thibault*); William Prince (*Rene*); Jack Lord (*Ferrebone*); Billy Vine (*Jacques*); Harry McNaughton (*Colin*); Florence Sundstrom (*Laughing Margot*); Lucie Lancaster (*Margaret*); Raymond Bramley (*The Scar*); Gregory Morton (*General Antoine De Chabannes*); Richard Tone (*Quicksilver*); Ralph Sumpter (*Bishop of Paris and Turin*); C. Thomas Duggan (*Burgandy*); Gavin Gordon (*Majordomo*); Joel Ashley (*Duke of Normandy*); Ralph Clanton (*Duke of Anjou*); Gordon Mills (*Duke of Bourbon*).

THE FILM

If one discounts Disney's snazzed-up remake of *Babes in Toyland* (1961), then *The Vagabond King* has a claim to being the last Hollywood operetta. The art form gained great popularity in the Depression through the M-G-M team of Jeanette MacDonald and Nelson Eddy and experienced a new lease on life with the emergence at the same studio of Mario Lanza. However, by the mid-1950s, the singer's weight gain and other personal problems had damaged his career to the point where he merely dubbed the voice of the leading man in *The Student Prince* (1954).

Hoping to fill the void with a tenor of their own, Paramount starred a young Maltese singer named Oreste Kirkop in a second version of Rudolf Friml's musical *The Vagabond King*. François Villon, the real-life fifteenth-century poet who was the subject of the work, had been portrayed by William Farnum in *If I Were King* (1920), John Barrymore in *The Beloved Rogue* (1926), Dennis King in *The Vagabond King* (1930), and by Ronald Colman in *If I Were King* (1938). Paramount commissioned Friml to add new songs with lyrics by Johnny Burke and hired Michael Curtiz, who had just wrapped *White Christmas*, to direct. The look of the picture is lush, but the dialogue seems stagy. The film's lead had his billing

144   *The Vagabond King*

shortened, but unfortunately he proved to be no "Garbo" and no "Karloff." Oreste became a single-named star with a single-movie filmography. The audience for operettas had dwindled away, as eventually would the audience for musicals in general.

Uncredited on the official cast list, Vincent Price provided a melodramatic thirty-second voice-over after the opening credits to set up the historical framework of the story. His wife, Mary Grant, designed the costumes which contributed so much to the handsome look of the production.

REVIEWS

Variety, August 29, 1956

". . . lavishly produced pageantry combining with battle movement and the music of Rudolf Friml to colorfully backdrop the story of François Villon, vagabond poet. From an entertainment standpoint, however, the Technicolor picture has few high levels and seldom rises above a monotone. . . ."

Hollywood Reporter, August 30, 1956

". . . a big, colorful presentation . . . that serves as the screen debut of the singer, Oreste. Lavish sets, costumes and production numbers provide considerable visual beauty. Oreste has a magnificent voice although, like many singers, he is a rather stiff actor. There have been reports that some of his dialogue was dubbed, due to his unfamiliarity with English, but if so it is not noticeable nor is it important to moviegoers." [Oreste's speaking voice is certainly dubbed.]

42. THE TEN COMMANDMENTS

PARAMOUNT

Released October 5, 1956

CREDITS

Producer/Director, Cecil B. DeMille; *Associate Producer*, Henry Wilcoxon; *Screenplay*, Aeneas MacKenzie, Jack Gariss, Jesse L. Lasky Jr., Fredric M. Frank; *Adapted from the novels* **Prince of Egypt** *by* Dorothy Clarke Wilson, **Pillar of Fire** *by* Rev. J. H. Ingraham, *and* **On Eagle's Wings** *by* Rev. A. E. Southon; *Based on the ancient texts of* Josephus, Eusebius, Philo, the Midrash, and the Holy Scriptures; *Cinematography*, Loyal Griggs; *Additional Photography*, J. Peverell Marley, John Warren, Wallace Kelley; *Art Directors*, Hal Pereira, Walter Tyler, Albert Nozaki; *Set Decorators*, Sam Comer, Ray

Moyer; *Music*, Elmer Bernstein; *Editor*, Anne Bauchens; *Costumes*, Edith Head, Ralph Jester, John Jensen, Dorothy Jeakins, Arnold Friberg; *Makeup*, Wally Westmore, Frank Westmore, Frank McCoy; *Hairstylist*, Nellie Manley; *Special Effects*, John P. Fulton; *Running time*, 221 minutes; color and VistaVision.

CAST

Charlton Heston (*Moses*); Yul Brynner (*Rameses*); Anne Baxter (*Nefretiri*); Edward G. Robinson (*Dathan*); Yvonne De Carlo (*Sephora*); Debra Paget (*Lilia*); John Derek (*Joshua*); Sir Cedric Hardwicke (*Sethi*); Nina Foch (*Bithiah*); Martha Scott (*Yochabel*); Judith Anderson (*Memnet*); Vincent Price (*Baka*); John Carradine (*Aaron*); Olive Deering (*Miriam*); Douglass Dumbrille (*Jannes*); Frank De Kova (*Abiram*); Henry Wilcoxon (*Pentaur*); Eduard Franz (*Jethro*); Donald Curtis (*Mered*); Lawrence Dobkin (*Hur Ben Caleb*); H. B. Warner (*Amminadab*); Julia Faye (*Elisheba*); Lisa Mitchell, Joanna Merlin, Joyce Vanderveen, Noelle Williams, Pat Richard, Diane Hall (*Jethro's Daughters*); John Miljan (*the Blind One*); Francis J. McDonald (*Simon*); Ian Keith (*Rameses I*); Joan Woodbury (*Korah's Wife*); Woodrow Strode (*King of Ethiopia*); Fraser Heston (*the Infant Moses*); Touch [later Mike] Connors (*Amalekite Herder*); Clint Walker (*Sardinian Captain*); Michael Ansara (*Taskmaster*); Robert Vaughn (*Spearman Hebrew*); Kathy Garber (*Child Slave*); Carl Switzer (*Slave*).

THE FILM

Cecil B. DeMille's directorial swan song was propelled by the legendary master's craft and force of personality. The wide-screen Technicolor blockbuster was just the thing to lure audiences away from their tiny black-and-white television screens, and the scope of the film—the enormous cast, awesome sets, groundbreaking special effects—made for pure entertainment. DeMille first brought *The Ten Commandments* to the silent screen in 1923. This version had a tentative shooting schedule of 194 days; Vincent Price's script is dated March 1, 1955.

It's almost easier to remember who *isn't* in *The Ten Commandments* than who is. As Baka, the pharaoh's master builder, Vincent Price has half a dozen brief but memorable appearances ("I was the only blue-eyed Egyptian in the picture," he claimed hyperbolically), and it is his murder which causes Moses to become the leader of the Hebrews. Price delivers his first lines, discussing with Heston the dispensability of worker slaves, with silky fastidiousness. Later, driven by passion for a beautiful slave girl, Baka displays an aristocratic lechery, dictating which flower she should wear in her hair. He is poetic in his analogies; when the girl's lover,

The Ten Commandments As Baka, the Pharaoh's master builder

Price had worked previously with Charlton Heston in the very first *Playhouse 90*, an episode about a close call with the Russians called "Forbidden Area" which was broadcast October 4, 1956, on CBS-TV.

REVIEWS

Motion Picture Exhibitor, October 17, 1956

"Cecil B. DeMille will long be remembered for this outstanding work of entertainment, for it is among the greatest films produced in the history of the industry. . . . No one will mind the length because every moment is packed to overflowing with drama, intense settings, as well as a sense of historical accuracy."

Los Angeles Mirror News, November 10, 1956 Dick Williams

Joshua, starts a blaze in the stable, he dictates: "No—no, your wings must not be singed, my dove; at least not by *that* fire." She escapes when Joshua breaks in, but the young man is overpowered and spreadeagled between the columns of the master builder's love nest as Baka elegantly removes his wide bracelets, the better to wield his whip. "You've seen me drive my chariot. I can flick a fly from my horse's ear without breaking the rhythm of his stride." But after only a few strokes, the rebel Moses intercedes, and Baka dies in the strong grip of God's chosen one. Thus, the great trek begins. . . .

Vincent Price, the inveterate storyteller, frequently related a wonderful anecdote about filming the scene in which he was called upon to describe "the city of Sethi's glory." Director DeMille interrupted the take, complaining, "You don't deliver that line with much conviction, Vincent." "I don't know what the hell I'm talking about, Mr. DeMille!" the actor protested, since, of course, all the "glory" would be added later by the special effects department. So DeMille took Price and other cast members to a screening room to view the Egyptian second-unit footage, depicting hordes of extras laboring to build the enormous sets, in order to impress upon the actors just how glorious the city would actually be. "Eleven thousand people did make you read it a little differently," Price agreed. (Unfortunately, this anecdote is probably

The Ten Commandments With Charlton Heston and player

146

"... At least an hour of this footage could have been cut out and never missed. ... Less effective are the heavies. Villains, under DeMille's characteristic flowery approach, inevitably become unbelievable blackguards of an old and outdated school of melodrama. Edward G. Robinson, as the evil Hebrew informer Dathan, looks ludicrously like Little Caesar in a turban. Vincent Price as the effete, whip-cracking master builder Baka is equally overdone. ..."

VINCENT PRICE

(*Classic Images*, June 1992)

"I think all of us, you know, Eddie Robinson, myself, Judith Anderson, we all really wanted to be in a DeMille picture. We really felt that you couldn't call yourself a movie [star] unless you had been in a DeMille picture! So we all took these sort of small, but rather arresting parts. DeMille was a wonderful director to work with,

The Ten Commandments With John Derek and Charlton Heston

unlike any other in the business. He was one hundred percent visually minded. Really, his stories were very thin, but the visual effects he pulled off were marvelous. ... The script was of secondary importance to him. What he was interested in was what was on the screen—the use of crowds, particularly. He was really fond of putting hundreds, even thousands, of people in a shot and then pulling if off. Spectacle! That was DeMille."

CHARLTON HESTON

"Vincent was a very professional actor. He did some very important work on the stage with Miss Hayes in *Victoria Regina*, and in *Angel Street*. (I appeared in *Angel Street* in summer stock myself.) That he gained his greatest fame in a series of horror films is another thing. ... [Price] was very good in *Ten Commandments*. He had quite a large part until I killed him. [When asked if Moses was strangling Baka or breaking his back, Heston replies:] Your choice [laughs]! My idea is that I was breaking his neck. It takes longer than that to strangle someone. I've done it several times—really, it takes at *least* two or three minutes to do it! I'm kidding. ... He was playing it appropriately, as an aristocratic Egyptian who had an important job and was very proud of having

147

The Ten Commandments CD soundtrack

it; was high in the structure of Egyptian society. Moses and Baka were both part of the same class at that point, colleagues on the project. . . . Vincent was a *good actor.* I had great respect for him, and great admiration for his abilities, which were considerable, there's no question of that."

43. THE STORY OF MANKIND

WARNER BROS.

Released October 1957

CREDITS

Producer/Director, Irwin Allen; *Associate Producer,* George E. Swink; *Screenplay,* Irwin Allen, Charles Bennett; *Based on the book by* Hendrik van Loon; *Cinematography,* Nick Musuraca; *Art Director,* Art Loel; *Set Decorator,* Arthur Krams; *Music,* Paul Sawtell; *Editor,* Gene Palmer; *Costumes,* Marjorie Best; *Makeup Supervisor,* Gordon Bau; *Technical Adviser,* Ruth K. Greenfield; *Running time,* 100 minutes; color.

CAST

Ronald Colman (*Spirit of Man*); Hedy Lamarr (*Joan of Arc*): Groucho Marx (*Peter Minuit*); Harpo Marx (*Sir*

Isaac Newton); Chico Marx (*Monk*); Virginia Mayo (*Cleopatra*); Agnes Moorehead (*Queen Elizabeth*); Vincent Price (*Mr. Scratch*); Peter Lorre (*Nero*); Charles Coburn (*Hippocrates*); Cedric Hardwicke (*High Judge*); Cesar Romero (*Spanish Envoy*); John Carradine (*Khufu*); Dennis Hopper (*Napoleon*); Marie Wilson (*Marie Antoinette*); Helmut Dantine (*Mark Antony*); Edward Everett Horton (*Sir Walter Raleigh*); Reginald Gardiner (*Shakespeare*); Marie Windsor (*Josephine*); Cathy O'Donnell (*Early Christian Woman*); Franklin Pangborn (*Marquis de Varennes*); Melville Cooper (*Majordomo*); Francis X. Bushman (*Moses*); Henry Daniell (*Bishop of Beauvais*); Jim Ameche (*Alexander Graham Bell*); Dani Crayne (*Helen of Troy*); Anthony Dexter (*Columbus*); Austin Green (*Lincoln*); Bobby Watson (*Hitler*); Reginald Sheffield (*Caesar*); Nick Cravat (*Mr. Scratch's Apprentice*); George E. Stone (*Waiter*); Alexander Lockwood (*Promoter*); Leonard Mudie (*Chief Inquisitor*); Don Megowan (*Early Man*); Melinda Marx [Groucho's daughter] (*Early Christian Child*); David Bond, Richard Cutting, Toni Gerry, Eden Hartford [Groucho's wife], Bart Mattson, Marvin Miller, Nancy Miller, Burt Nelson, Tudor Owen, Ziva Rodann, Harry Ruby, William Schallert, Abraham Sofaer.

THE FILM

In *The Story of Mankind,* Vincent Price is superbly attired in a black cutaway coat, gray vest, and dark gray trousers, with a red silk tie and red gloves. Goateed, with cynical eyebrow arched, he arises in a cloud of red smoke, brandishing a pitchfork—who else could he be playing but the Devil? (The actor could boast previous work experience, having appeared in the same role on stage in Shaw's *Don Juan In Hell*.)

As the Spirit of Mankind, Ronald Colman argues before a heavenly high tribunal for the salvation of Man in the face of self-annihilation from the "Super 'H' Bomb." His worthy opponent, Mr. Scratch (Price), brings his own witnesses to illustrate the essential evil and unworthiness of the race. With a host of quaint, curious, and affecting cameos by some of Hollywood's famous and infamous and relying on stock footage from a variety of previous pictures, *The Story of Mankind* disappointed contemporary critics but makes for fun celebrity spotting. Price is clearly at home amid fire and brimstone; with his sense of panache and his bad jokes, Mr. Scratch would have been a great villain on *Batman*.

The trades announced in 1953 that Broadway agent and producer Bernie Foyer had acquired "complete performing rights" to Hendrik Willem van Loon's bestseller *The Story of Mankind*. At that time, Foyer was planning to produce several feature films based on the book as well as a TV series. However, when *The Story of Mankind* went into production in November 1956, Irwin Allen was in charge.

Price's script is 153 pages long and has an elaborate printed cover with a sketch of the book and small ink sketches of scenes from history. (Ronald Colman's last name, scrawled at the top, is crossed out!) There were appended pages marked "Added Scenes—Vincent Price" dated January 8, 1957. He had a separate script marked "Devil—wild lines." The preponderance of stars posed such a difficult billing and credit problem that it was decided to list the stars alphabetically, apart from Ronald Colman. Surprisingly, even Vincent Price was relegated to the annoying indignity.

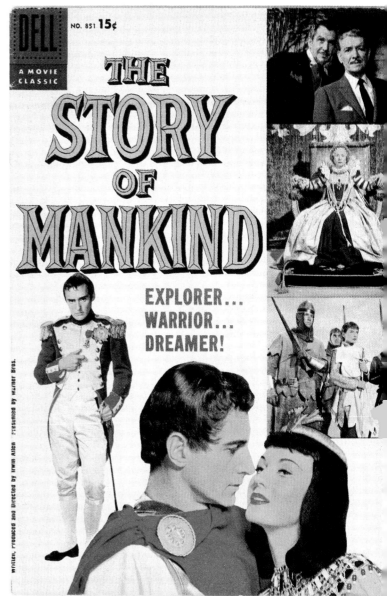

The Story of Mankind Dell comic book

The Story of Mankind With Ronald Colman and Nick Cravat

149

The Story of Mankind With "Leonardo Da Vinci" and Ronald Colman

The papers reported that Allen "would not attempt to encompass the book's six hundred pages: 'Where we can't do justice to a time and place, we won't brush them off summarily. We just won't use them. There have been four hundred or more giants of history in all fields. Our big problem has been to bring them down to some fifty, asking about each: Was what he or she did lasting—and how long did it last?'" Most critics felt: too long.

REVIEWS

Los Angeles Mirror News, October 14, 1957

"Hendrik van Loon's monumental work . . . tracing earthlings from the Pleistocene Age to the present has now been made into a Technicolor movie and it is anything but monumental. . . . A swarm of stars are employed in vignettes in the style made popular in *Around the World in 80 Days*, but all but a handful of the thirty or so used shoddily enact their roles. . . . The picture fails completely in its purpose of showing to what heights and depths man has risen and fallen in his stay on earth to date."

Variety, October 15, 1957

". . . Ronald Colman, as always, is a dignified personification of the Spirit of Man, and Vincent Price is the sophisticated, sneering embodiment of Old Scratch."

New Yorker, November 16, 1957

"As the Devil, Vincent Price has, as usual, the suave and sinister air of a headwaiter in a backs-to-the-wall supper club, and as the Spirit of Man, Ronald Colman has the suave and sanguine air of a D.A.R. lecturer booked solid for the season."

44.   THE FLY

20th CENTURY-FOX
Released July 1958

CREDITS

Producer/Director, Kurt Neumann; *Screenplay*, James Clavell; *Based on a story by* George Langelaan, *Cinematographer*, Karl Struss; *Art Directors*, Lyle R. Wheeler, Theobold Holsopple, *Set Decorators*, Walter M. Scott, Eli Benneche, *Music*, Paul Sawtell; *Editor*, Merrill G. White, *Executive Wardrobe Designer*, Charles Le Maire; *Costumes*, Adele Balkan; *Makeup*, Ben Nye; *Hairstyles*, Helen Turpin; *Special Effects*, L. B. Abbott; *Running time*, 94 minutes; color and CinemaScope.

CAST

Al Hedison [later David Hedison] (*André Delambre*); Patricia Owens (*Helene Delambre*); Vincent Price (*François Delambre*); Herbert Marshall (*Inspector Charas*); Kathleen Freeman (*Emma*); Betty Lou Gerson (*Nurse Anderson*); Charles Herbert (*Philippe Delambre*); Eugene Borden (*Dr. Ejoute*); Torben Meyer (*Gaston*); Harry Carter (*Orderly*); Charles Tannen (*Doctor*); Franz Roehm (*Police Doctor*); Arthur Dulac (*French Waiter*).

THE FILM

"Once it was human—even as you and I!"

"The monster created by atoms gone wild!"

One of the films for which Vincent Price is best remembered, *The Fly* is an affectionate favorite among many movie buffs. Ironically, of course, Price isn't the title "monster," the scientist whose genes become entangled with those of an insect in his matter-transference machine. As the scientist's good-guy brother, Vincent spends the picture consoling his distraught sister-in-law, jailed for "killing" her husband. Ultimately, he and Inspector Herbert Marshall discover the scientist's "fly alter ego," destroying it and the telltale evidence of his experiments.

The original story, "The Fly," written by noted science-fiction author George Langelaan, appeared in the June 1957 issue of *Playboy* and received the magazine's award for best story of the year. When 20th Century-Fox bought the screen rights, Michael Rennie, who had starred to such effect in *The Day the Earth Stood Still,* rejected a leading role. Production on the film began March 17, 1958.

Al Hedison's "fly" head represented ten weeks' work by makeup artist Ben Nye. (In 1986, a collector sold the head of the creature to SFX creator Lyle Conway [*Dark Crystal*] for $500.) The great press used for crushing the scientist was an authentic prop—a metal press obtained from a Los Angeles machinery dealer, capable of exerting pressure of 150 tons; it weighed nearly 50 tons itself. According to the production notes, the lab set cost $28,000 to build, although it contained surplus army and air force equipment worth a quarter of a million dollars, which Fox bought for a song. (The $3,500 oscillograph cost them $25.)

The simulated electronic integrator, which was modeled on IBM's famous electronic brain, was built under the direction of the studio's electronics expert, Dr. Frank Creswell, at a cost of $18,000. The production team was quite pleased with the results, with 396 lights indicating proper function and the recording tapes and switches. Producer/director Kurt Neumann felt that "the things we do must *seem* possible. Thus it is possible to give reality to the most unscientific idea, if your setting and machinery has the texture, if not the actuality, of scientific equipment. . . ." Technical adviser Creswell set the flashing lights of one panel to spell "Pat [Owens] is a doll," although not during the takes. Despite all this technical equipment, *The Fly* was made for under $500,000; reportedly, it grossed over $3 million.

The Fly With Patricia Owens

And yes, the original script actually contains the (in)famous dialogue:

"Over comes the faintest, thinnest, spine-chilling scream of frenzy. . . .
Andre's Voice: "Helpppp . . . get away frommm Mmeeee!
Again and again the minute scream pulsates:
Andre's Voice: "Helpppp me—Helpppp meeee!"

The Fox press department touted Price's reputation as "[perhaps] the leading popular authority on art. . . . Price now divides himself between films, television, making dramatic recordings, doing stage plays and lecturing. 'They are all different aspects of the same profession,' Price says, 'and I find it a most stimulating way to live.' In *The Fly*, Price is not directly associated with the horror aspects of the picture, but he thinks that the role will build the general public impression that horror is his favorite medium. 'I've done only three horror films prior to *The Fly*, but one of them, *House of Wax*, was so tremendously successful, I've been pretty well identified with this sort of thing ever since. I've done more comedy parts than villains; more straight parts than either, but the odor of evil seems to cling to me.'" Little did he know it was to cling for the next three and a half decades!

The Fly's producer/director Kurt Neumann died only

The Fly "Helppp meee!" With Herbert Marshall and Charles Herbert

a month after the picture was released, on August 21, 1958. There were two sequels, of course; Price had the good sense to star in only one. Less than a decade after the original classic, he did a guest stint on *Voyage to the Bottom of the Sea*, again costarring with Hedison, who had by that time changed his first name to David. *The Fly* was remade in 1986, starring a couple of big Price fans (see letter below).

REVIEWS

Hollywood Reporter, July 11, 1958

"This whole first third of the film is seen through the eyes of Price, who firmly establishes a convincing mood of bewilderment, incredulity and shock."

New York Times, August 30, 1958, Howard Thompson

"It flew in yesterday, *The Fly* did—and folks, hang on to your hair. . . . Believe it or not, *The Fly* happens to be one of the better, more restrained, entries of the 'shock' school . . . a quiet, uncluttered and even unpretentious picture, building up almost unbearable tension by simple suggestion. . . . By deftly easing some nice people in and out of a situation as pathetic as it is horrible, Mr. Neumann has wrought the most originally suggestive hair-raiser since *The Thing*."

VINCENT PRICE

("The Villains Still Pursue Me" lecture)

". . . I turned to the detective and said, 'There, there you see, I told you.' So we go out into the garden and sure enough, there's a great big spider web. And in one corner is a great big spider going chompety chompety chomp. And down here is my nephew [sic] who is a fly with a human head, and the little fly is saying, 'Help me . . . help me . . .' Now, Herbert Marshall, the detective, one of the great actors, and I had to play a very serious scene in front of this little tableau. Well, we'd start the scene and Marshall would say, 'Ah, monsieur, I see what you mean, I have doubted you all along . . .' and he'd start to giggle. And the little voice would say, 'Help meee, help meeee.' I'd say, 'Don't worry, Bart [Marshall's nickname], I've been chasing that damn fly all through the picture.' I'd say, 'There, Inspector, you see—I've been telling you that my nephew is . . .' and I'd start to giggle. Little voice says, 'Help meee, help meeee.' Finally, Herbert Marshall said, 'Help *you*! To hell with you! Help *us*!'"

Dial, July 1987

"I thought Jeff Goldblum was wonderful [in the remake]. I thought the picture had great humor, which ain't easy when you're doing something like that."

JEFF GOLDBLUM AND GEENA DAVIS

(October 7, 1986 personal letter)

"Dear Mr. Price: As you must know by now, we recently co-starred in a re-make of your classic movie, *The Fly*. We have been considering writing you ever since we began the project, because we want you to know what big fans of yours we both are! We've enjoyed watching you in so many movies, and one of our favorites is of course your *Fly*. The plot in our version is very different, so in a sense it's not really a re-make. . . . There's no reason to re-do what's already terrific. We just thought we'd like to let you know how much we like your work, and send our regards . . . and we want to say what great affection we have for the First Fly. Best wishes."

45. HOUSE ON HAUNTED HILL

ALLIED ARTISTS
Released December, 1958

CREDITS

A William Castle/Robb White Production; *Producer/Director*, William Castle; *Associate Producer/Writer*, Robb White; *Cinematography*, Carl E. Guthrie; *Art Director*, David Milton; *Set Decorator*, Morris Hoffman; *Music Composed and Conducted by* Von Dexter; *Theme* "House on Haunted Hill" *by* Richard Kayne and Richard Loring; *Editor*, Roy Livingston; *Men's Wardrobe*, Roger J. Weinberg; *Ladies' Wardrobe*, Norah Sharpe; *Makeup*, Jack Dusick; *Hairstylist*, Gale McGarry; *Special Effects*, Herman Townsley; *Running time*, 75 minutes; black and white.

CAST

Vincent Price (*Frederick Loren*); Carol Ohmart (*Annabelle Loren*); Richard Long (*Lance Schroeder*); Alan Marshal (*Dr. David Trent*); Carolyn Craig (*Nora Manning*); Elisha Cook (*Watson Pritchard*); Julie Mitchum (*Ruth Bridgers*); Leona Anderson (*Mrs. Slydes*); Howard Hoffman (*Jonas Slydes*); Skeleton (*Himself*).

THE FILM

Vincent Price made only two films for showman extraordinaire William Castle, but they're among his (and the producer's) most popular. *House on Haunted Hill* can still elicit screams of delight from today's jaded audiences.

Allied Artists had a huge success with Castle's first independent picture, *Macabre*, and was keen for him to produce again for them—preferably a movie with another of his soon-to-be-trademark exhibition gimmicks. Castle came up with an idea for a "good, old-fashioned ghost story, complete with a haunted house." To carry the picture, he felt that "the male lead had to be someone special—elegant, fey, with an offbeat personality." Castle stumbled on Vincent Price, "the perfect lead," seated alone in a small coffee shop near Samuel Goldwyn studios, "attacking" a slice of pie. "Mr. Price," declared Castle, launching into the pitch, "fate has brought us together this rainy night." The actor found Castle's description of the story line, especially the part when his wife would try to throw him into a vat of boiling acid, "charming!" and over a second slice of pie agreed to a deal.

Millionaire Frederick Loren (Price) invites five strangers to participate in his "haunted house party"—the test pilot–hero (Richard Long), a newspaper columnist (Julie Mitchum, Robert's sister!), the owner of the house (Elisha Cook), a psychiatrist interested in hysteria (Alan Marshal), and one of Loren's employees (Carolyn Craig). (The remarkable exterior of the mansion was actually a famous Frank Lloyd Wright home north of Los Feliz Boulevard in Los Angeles, erected during the architect's "Mayan" period.) He offers $10,000 to anyone who will stay in the house overnight—if they survive, since, in the century since it was built, seven people have been murdered there. Loren's bitchy wife (Carol Ohmart) puts in an appearance, and the doors are locked just before midnight, but the hauntings start before then—blood drips, ghosts spook, a severed head pops up, and a hanged body drops down. But just who's trying to scare whom to death?

Price's script of *House on Haunted Hill* is dated July 22, 1958; according to his diary, he wrapped his scenes on September 16. In his role as the sarcastic host of the evening, Price's humor is sardonic, less tongue-in-cheek than in later films; the verbal fencing with his trampy wife is acidic and bitter. Price shared equal billing with the gimmick Castle dubbed "Emergo," which capitalized on one of the film's creepiest moments—the famous sequence in which a skeleton rises from the acid vat and terrorizes one of the participants. Theater owners rigged up prop skeletons in their own houses, and at the appropriate moment they were run out on wires into the audience. It prompted one contemporary critic to comment: "The movies might be better off if there were more producers like Bill Castle. Castle is not only a producer—he is a showman . . . ."

There was a problem with the print ad when *House on Haunted Hill* went into release. The *Los Angeles*

House on Haunted Hill With Julie Mitchum (Robert's sister), Alan Marshal, and Elisha Cook

House on Haunted Hill With Carol Ohmart

House on Haunted Hill Rehearsing "Emergo"

Times and the *Mirror-News*, both owned by the Chandler family, censored the art and notified Allied Artists that a layout for *House*, which they had already placed in papers all over the country, was unacceptable. (The Hearst-owned *Examiner* and *Herald-Express* had both accepted and printed it.) The art consisted of a sketch of a skeleton dangling a rope around the neck of a figure of a woman. To placate the Chandler papers, AA eliminated the skeleton and rope and substituted another figure of a woman, screaming.

In the 1960s, William Castle would claim that *House on Haunted Hill* cost $150,000 to produce and made $4 million. Whatever the exact figures, it's certainly a viable example of filmmaking at its most successful—and entertaining!

REVIEWS

Film Daily, December 3, 1958

"Vincent Price, whose career in melodramatic stories has been of a kind to keep his audience this time completely unsure whether he's on the good side or the bad side of the plot, holds central interest. . . . His is the top name for marquee purposes, except in engagements where Emergo, the Castle invention optionally available to exhibitors playing the picture, is used."

Motion Picture Herald, December 6, 1958

"A very commercial piece of nerve-wracking horror entertainment. . . . The surprise element and clever effect [Emergo] rated a round of applause from the highly responsive audience who reacted audibly to the weird, shocking business on the screen. . . . [Castle's] timing of the acting will have the audience on the edges of their seats. . . . Contributing to the shocking fun is a cast headed by Vincent Price, who lends a touch of whimsy to his role of a very clever, sadistic millionaire. . . ."

Beverly Hills Citizen, May 14, 1959

"If you ask me, Price is wasted in such a role, but no doubt these excursions give him capital with which to add to his already large art collection." [Busted!]

Los Angeles Examiner, May 14, 1959, Ruth Waterbury

"If you want the living daylights scared out of you, go visit *House on Haunted Hill*. . . . [It] probably won't be mentioned by next year's Academy Awards, but take my word: it's a lot more thrilling and funny than many a film that will. When the ads say, 'See it with somebody with warm hands,' they're not fooling. You really ought to see it with somebody who has their arms around you. . . . Price, as always, is a standout. . . . Who needs art? *House*

on Haunted Hill is that tingly kind of fun you had on your first Halloween, the chill that made Poe's raven a household pet for several generations. Go get a charge out of it."

ROBB WHITE

(*Science Fiction Stars and Horror Heroes*, 1991)

"Vincent was a professional get-along-with-er. He knew his lines, he knew what to do, he didn't need much direction and he gave nobody any trouble. . . . Whenever you killed Vincent Price in a movie, he was always so dramatic about it—he'd writhe around and scream and holler and carry on. I remember I told Vincent, when he got shot in *House*, 'When someone gets hit with a .45 caliber bullet, they fall backwards. You always fall forwards when you get hit.' And Vincent said, 'My boy, no actor falls *away* from the camera!' [laughs]." [For the record, Vincent grimaces and silently clutches at his chest, staggers back a couple of steps into the wall, and then slumps down, crumpling forward onto his face.]

CASSANDRA PETERSON ("Elvira, Mistress of the Dark")

"I was a *huge* Vincent Price fan, my whole life. . . . When I was a little kid, probably seven or eight, I went to see *House on Haunted Hill*, and I'll never get over that movie as long as I live! I actually had horrible, recurring nightmares for the longest, longest, longest time. I mean, I thought I was going to have to go to the loony bin or something! But I kept wanting to see it over and over again. I was totally mesmerized by Vincent Price, so every time he was in a movie, I had to go see it. . . . And I saw every one of those [Roger Corman/Poe] movies when I was a kid growing up. . . . It started with *House on Haunted Hill*—that's the day my *film* interest started, not just my horror movie interest; it hit me like a ton of bricks. I guess it's really not a coincidence I became Elvira; I guess I was really heading down that path. . . . Vincent himself didn't scare me; I was fascinated by his character. I thought, Ooooh, he's so wonderful, he's so great. I always told people he was kind of my idol."

46. THE BIG CIRCUS

ALLIED ARTISTS
Released June 1959

CREDITS

Producer, Irwin Allen; *Director*, Joseph M. Newman; *Screenplay*, Irwin Allen, Charles Bennett, Irving Wallace; *Based on a story by* Irwin Allen; *Cinematography*, Winton C. Hoch; *Production Supervisor*, Lowell Farrell; *Art Director*, Albert S. D'Agostino; *Set Decorator*, Robert Priestley; *Music*, Paul Sawtell, Bert Shefter; *Title Song*, Sammy Fain, Paul Francis Webster; *Editor*, Adrienne Fazan; *Costumes*, Paul Zastupnevich; *Makeup*, William Tuttle; *Hairdresser*, Sydney Guilaroff; *Choreographer*, Barbette; *Technical Adviser*, Jimmie Wood; *Running Time*, 108 minutes; color and CinemaScope.

CAST

Victor Mature (*Hank Whirling*); Red Buttons (*Randy Sherman*); Rhonda Fleming (*Helen Harrison*); Kathryn Grant (*Jeannie Whirling*); Vincent Price (*Hans Hagenfeld*); Peter Lorre (*Skeeter*); David Nelson (*Tommy Gordon*); Adele Mara (*Mama Colino*); Gilbert Roland (*Zach Colino*); Steve Allen (*Himself*); Howard McNear (*Mr. Lomax*); Charles Watts (*Jonathan Nelson*); *The World's Most Famous Circus Acts*: Hugo Zacchini, the Human Cannonball; Dick Walker's World-Famous Lion Act; the Flying Alexanders; Gene Mendez, World's Greatest Wire-Walker; the Ronnie Lewis Trio, High-Ladder Equilibrists; the Jungleland Elephants; Tex Carr and his Chimpanzees; Dick Berg's Movieland Seals.

THE FILM

Without the script, the cast, or the enormous budget of Cecil B. DeMille's *The Greatest Show on Earth*, *The Big Circus* still provides sufficient spectacle on a smaller scale. Playing the circus ringmaster must have been a welcome relief for Vincent Price, coming as it did in the midst of a plethora of horror roles.

To secure badly needed financial backing for his circus, owner Victor Mature is saddled with capable press agent Rhonda Fleming and the penny-pinching of new financial adviser Red Buttons. While trying to keep the show on the road, Mature must discover the identity of the double-crosser in their midst who is trying to sabotage Whirling Circus on behalf of a rival owner. At the end, Mature manages to snag a live broadcast on Steve Allen's TV show, and David Nelson (!) is unmasked as the criminally insane bad guy.

The Big Circus involved three years of preparation and production on the part of impresario Irwin Allen. When the film went into production early in 1959, Vincent Price worked twenty-three days, from January 12 through February 16. The ubiquitous Hedda Hopper visited the set during filming and described it in her *Los Angeles Times* column: "The Big Circus Set Magnificent. . . . No circus ever had a ringmaster like Vincent Price, whose six feet four in top hat, scarlet coat, white tights and high black patent boots, literally stops the show. . . ." Price

The Big Circus

was cast as the ostentatious prime suspect but was provided with little motivation; in fact, he creates quite a likable character in Hagenfeld. Nonetheless, in the wake of near deadly arson, when Mature says pointedly that the double-crosser who set the fire "could be anyone— anyone at all," instead of a series of close-ups of the entire cast, only Price is fingered. In fact, every time something bad happens, the camera lingers accusingly on Vincent. On the title page of his script, Vincent made some notes: "Page 59—Red Herring—Why not some real reason Hans could be suspect."

The Big Circus teamed Price for a third time with Victor Mature and was the first picture in which he acted together with Peter Lorre (since they had no common scenes in *The Story of Mankind*.) *Box Office* awarded Vincent a Blue Ribbon Plaque in July 1959 for his role of ringmaster Hagenfeld.

REVIEWS

Variety, June 26, 1959

". . . a rousingly lavish film. . . . Vincent Price is perfect as the ringmaster, his voice bellowing through the big tent with precision and authority."

Beverly Hills Citizen, August 5, 1959

"Vincent Price delivers his usual fine performance."

VINCENT PRICE

("The Villains Still Pursue Me" lecture)

"Villains have a very definite role in acting. It is absolutely necessary for the villain in the first place to create the most essential thing in drama, which is *suspense*! If the man or woman who is playing the villain gives himself or herself away, right at the beginning of the picture, there's nowhere to go. . . . Consequently, the actor playing the villain always has to keep himself very diversified. It is an enormous challenge. You have to be witty, charming, sexy, ah, subtle, intelligent, bright. You have to be everything so that the audience won't guess right away that you are the villain. After I got started playing a few villains, I was often cast in movies as a kind of red herring. They'd put me in a movie, and then when the murder happened, everybody'd say, 'Oh, Vincent Price did it.' Well, I was in one circus picture where I was the ringmaster and I was very cruel and there was a murder happened and everybody said, 'Oh, Vincent Price did it.' Well, it wasn't me. It turned out to be Ricky [*sic*] Nelson [audience laughter]. God, I mean, you know, nobody would ever have thought of him as a villain—or even an actor, so [laughter and applause] . . . but he, he sings very nicely."

47. RETURN OF THE FLY

20th CENTURY-FOX
Released July 1959

CREDITS

Associated Producers, Inc; *Producer*, Bernard Glasser; *Writer/Director*, Edward L. Bernds; *Suggested by the short story by* George Langelaan; *Cinematography*, Brydon Baker; *Art Directors*, Lyle R. Wheeler, John Mansbridge;

Set Decorators, Walter M. Scott, Joseph Kish; *Music*, Paul Sawtell, Bert Shefter; *Editor*, Richard C. Meyer; *Makeup*, Hal Lierley; *Running time*, 80 minutes; black and white and CinemaScope.

CAST

Vincent Price (*François Delambre*); Brett Halsey (*Philippe Delambre*); David Frankham (*Alan Hinds*); John Sutton (*Inspector Beacham*); Dan Seymour (*Max Berthold*); Danielle De Metz (*Cecile Bonnard*); Janine Grandel (*Madame Bonnard*); Richard Flato (*Sergeant Dubois*); Barry Bernard (*Lt. John Maclish*); Francisco Villalobas (*Priest*); Jack Daly (*Granville*); Michael Mark (*Gaston*); Gregg Martell, Rick Turner, Courtland Shepard (*Policeman*); Pat O'Hara (*Detective Evans*); Joan Cotton (*Nurse*); Florence Strom (*Nun*); [Ed Wolff and Joe Becker uncredited as the Fly].

THE FILM

Vincent always joked that they should have called this inevitable follow-up *The Zipper*. If only the film had been that inventive, it would have been vastly improved. *Return of the Fly* belongs in that crowded inventory of sequels which fail to live up to the original, a major reason for its inferiority being that it was shot in black and white.

The son of the original scientist who lost his head in *The Fly* continues Dad's matter-transference experiments despite the warnings of his uncle, Vincent Price (the only returning main actor/character from the first film.) A wicked assistant arranges for the son to follow in his father's fly-footsteps, although Uncle François comes to the rescue and reverses the process after a minimal amount of mayhem.

Producer Bernard Glasser remembers that "Price was always a gentleman, always ready and prepared, but as I recall he was not overly enthusiastic about the screenplay!" Small wonder, since it called for the long-suffering actor to deliver such undeliverable lines as: "Inspector— when this same ghastly thing happened to my brother, he still had a *human* mind and a *human* conscience. What if Philippe does not have the mind of a human, but the murderous brain of the fly!" The cover of Price's script has a tiny *Musca domestica* printed on the lower right corner.

Price's longtime costar John Sutton is the dignified Inspector Beacham, assisting him with a scientific experiment just as he did nearly twenty years earlier in *The Invisible Man Returns*. (The first picture's inspector, Herbert Marshall, was recovering from an illness; Sutton's character has a different name.) There was a second sequel, *Curse of the Fly*, filmed in Britain in 1965. Starring Brian Donlevy, it, too, was filmed in black and white. It seems film producers aren't any better at learning from past mistakes than mad scientists.

REVIEWS

Variety, July 9, 1959

"... it will be unfavorably compared with the first, which was a superior horror film."

Hollywood Reporter, July 13, 1959

"Unlike *The Fly*, this film stresses plot gimmicks at the expense of honest human values. But the acting of Price goes a long way toward making it believable. Though not a classic, it is considerably better than the run-of-the-mill B horror picture."

Los Angeles Mirror News, August 27, 1959

"There were few empty seats in the house and that's a rarity these days. . . . The audience, composed of young folk and old, enjoyed the picture. They sat there stoned during the creepier sequences, shrieked in mock terror or laughed loudly at other moments."

Return of the Fly Battling "the Fly"

Return of the Fly One-sheet poster

EDWARD L. BERNDS

(*B Movie Makers*, 1988)

"Vincent Price liked my script. . . . Sometime later a problem came up. What Vincent read was a first draft, and like many first drafts it was a little overlong, and some cuts were made to trim it down, and some changes were made to bring about budget economies. Vincent liked some of the scenes we had cut, and he objected. If I recall correctly, they were mostly scenes with Danielle De Metz—scenes of warmth and charm, but when you're pressed for footage, not truly essential to the progression of the story . . . [Working with Price was] a delight, no less. Thoroughly professional, always prepared, giving his best to every scene. His wasn't even the biggest part in *Return of the Fly*, but his star status and the strength he brought to his performance lifted it out of the B category it might have fallen into. . . ."

48. THE TINGLER

COLUMBIA PICTURES
Released July 29, 1959

CREDITS

Producer/Director, William Castle; *Screenplay*, Robb White; *Cinematography*, Wilfrid M. Cline; *Art Director*, Phil Bennett; *Set Decorator*, Milton Stumph; *Music*, Von Dexter; *Editor*, Chester W. Schaeffer; *Sound*, John Livadary, Harry Mills; *Makeup Supervisor*, Clay Campbell; *Assistant Director*, Herb Wallerstein; *Running time*, 81 minutes; black and white.

CAST

Vincent Price (*Dr. Warren Chapin*); Judith Evelyn (*Martha Higgins*); Darryl Hickman (*David Morris*); Patricia Cutts (*Isabel Chapin*); Pamela Lincoln (*Lucy Stevens*); Philip Coolidge (*Ollie Higgins*); Gail Bonney (*Woman #1*); Amy Fields (*Woman #2*); Clarence Straight (*Man #1*); Pat Colby (*Man #2*); Dal McKennon (*Projectionist*); Bob Gunderson (*Prisoner*).

THE FILM

"Guaranteed: The Tingler will break loose in the theatre while you are in the audience. As you enter the theatre you will receive instructions . . . how to guard yourself against attack by The Tingler!"

Made in 1959, *The Tingler* is still a regular feature at New York Film Forum's annual Summer Festival of Fantasy, Horror & Science Fiction, where it is screened in the original "Percepto!" and brings new dimensions to audience participation.

The wonderfully outrageous story line sets up Vincent Price as a surgeon-scientist researching the psychological and physical causes and effects of fear. Autopsies and brainstorming with young partner Darryl Hickman have led him to discover a creature he names the Tingler—a hideous, overgrown centipede-like thing which materializes along a person's spinal column when they experience intense fear. Unless that fear is dispelled by scream-

ing, the vertebrae are crushed. In the course of his work, (Price) meets a married couple who manage a silent-movie theater and learns that the phobic wife (Judith Evelyn) is a deaf-mute. He can't help speculating on the result of uncontrollable fear for a person who *cannot* scream; of course, we're meant to believe there's nothing Vincent wouldn't do for science. . . . Evelyn is literally frightened to death by scary apparitions (including a delightfully lurid "color" sequence in which red blood gushes into the bathroom sink and tub). When the Tingler is removed from her body and gets loose in the cinema below, Price entreats the audience to "scream, scream for your lives!" They aren't the only ones! For the release of *The Tingler*, innovative filmmaker William Castle improved on the *House on Haunted Hill*'s "Emergo" and invented "Percepto," an effect cinema exhibitors created by rigging theater seats with electric motors to selectively buzz bums in simulated Tingler attacks. When the creature has been paralyzed by our shrieking, it turns out that Evelyn's husband is the culprit, and in a last-minute surprise ending, he gets what's coming to him.

Chapter 20 in Castle's autobiography, *Step Right Up! I'm Gonna Scare the Pants Off America*, is titled "Scream for Your Life." After a confab with the Columbia art department about exactly what their title monster should look like, it was off to convince a star. Castle writes: "'Vinnie, you've got to play the doctor in it. You'll be perfect!' 'Bill, I don't want to be typecast.' Vincent Price puffed on his long, slender cigar." In the understatement of a lifetime, Castle replied: "Vinnie, with the success of *House on Haunted Hill*, I think it'll open up a whole new career for you."

Vincent's script is dated April 21, 1959; for a time, in March, the proposed title of the project was *The Chiller*. The film begins with director Castle himself delivering his caveat about the Tingler to "unfortunate, sensitive" people in the audience, a warning which is partially excised in Vincent's screenplay by a large "Top Secret" stamp. The far-out premise of the story is juxtaposed with bleak reality as the picture begins with an execution by electric chair and Price's performance of an autopsy. Fans generally find amusing the LSD "trip" Price takes in an effort to scare himself sufficiently to cause the Tingler to appear. After injecting himself with the drug, he describes his physical symptoms into a tape recorder until paranoia sets in and he begins to hallucinate. "I wasn't much good at that," Price admitted, "because I don't know what the effect's meant to be." Despite the histrionics required when he's under the influence, Price's performance in *The Tingler* is remarkably underplayed; he discusses the most preposterous "science" completely straight-faced and matter-of-fact. He's better

The Tingler "This man's vertebrae are cracked, and nearly splintered in two. . . , There's a force in all of us that science knows nothing about—the force of fear. . . , Never had a name for it until now. Now I think I'll call it the 'Tingler.'"

trading insults with slutty wife Patricia Cutts; on-screen Price excelled at sarcasm and conveying personal bitterness, although in real life his disposition was remarkably even-tempered.

Costar Darryl Hickman had to wear lifts for the only time in his career for his scenes opposite Price, who was nearly six inches taller. The important role of the deaf-mute woman went to Vincent's 1941 Broadway costar from *Angel Street*, Judith Evelyn. Price himself was instrumental in her casting, and it's somehow touching to watch the two of them, united by their great Broadway success, maneuvering through the movie's outlandishness. *The Tingler's* budget was set at $400,000, but the addition of the gimmicks and the exploitation brought the overall cost up to $1 million. Special cues for projectionists (when to "tingle," when to turn theater lights on and off) were issued to participating theaters. And audiences screamed, screamed for their lives, during one of Vincent Price's most ridiculous, most enjoyable, and most popular films.

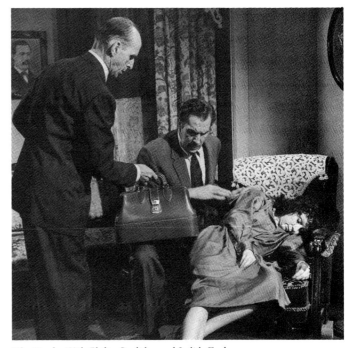

The Tingler With Philip Coolidge and Judith Evelyn

159

". . . Overall, it's a highly entertaining property. . . . Price appears perfectly sinister, and when it's found he's not really bad after all, it becomes obvious he has left just the right loopholes in his actions and personality."

The Tingler Insert poster

49.   THE BAT

ALLIED ARTISTS

Released Early August 1959

CREDITS

A Liberty Pictures Production; *Producer,* C. J. Tevlin; *Director,* Crane Wilbur; *Screen Story and Screenplay,* Crane Wilbur; *Based on the* Wagenhals-Kemper *play by* Mary Roberts Rinehart and Avery Hopwood; *Cinematography,* Joseph Biroc; *Art Director,* David Milton; *Set Decorator,* Rudy Butler; *Musical Score,* Louis Forbes; *"The Bat" theme played by* Alvino Rey; *Editor,* William Austin; *Costumes,* Roger J. Weinberg, Norah Sharpe; *Makeup,* Kiva Hoffman; *Running time,* 80 minutes; black and white.

CAST

Vincent Price (*Dr. Malcolm Wells*); Agnes Moorehead (*Cornelia Van Gorder*); Gavin Gordon (*Lieutenant Anderson*); John Sutton (*Warner*); Lenita Lane (*Lizzie Allen*); Elaine Edwards (*Dale Bailey*); Darla Hood (*Judy Hollender*); John Bryant (*Mark Fleming*); Harvey Stephens (*Carter Fleming*); Mike Steele (*Jack Bailey*); Riza Royce (*Mrs. Patterson*); Robert B. Williams (*Detective Davenport*).

THE FILM

"When it flies . . . someone dies!"

Mary Roberts Rinehart's novel *The Circular Staircase* was published in 1908. Adapted for the stage as *The Bat,* it was a big success in the 1920–21 Broadway season, running for two years and grossing more than $9 million. The granddaddy of comedy-mystery thrillers had been filmed three times by the late 1950s.

Actor/director/playwright Crane Wilbur had written two other Vincent Price films, the hugely successful *House of Wax* and the derivative *The Mad Magician.* With his screenplay for *The Bat,* he was said to have "modernized" the story, because "audiences are more sophisticated than they used to be." Unfortunately, the film was terrifically creaky, even in 1959, with stagy dialogue and completely improbable action.

An intrepid mystery writer (Agnes Moorehead) and her companion (Lenita Lane, director/writer Crane Wilbur's wife) rent a country mansion, only to be terrorized by a hooded mad killer loose in the neighborhood. In between murders, he's searching the house for a hidden fortune embezzled by a dead banker. There are sneaky suspects galore—guests, a chauffeur, a couple of detectives, the embezzler's doctor. Film advertising admonished: "Warning! Keep the secret! Anyone who reveals who I am will have to answer to [signed] The Bat." The picture's title referred to the mysterious mad killer. Vincent Price plays a doctor studying the genuine article, and he's the one who cold-bloodedly murders the banker, but he's not the real bat-man.

Shooting began on April 27, 1959. Reviews for the movie were extremely mixed; the picture has completely failed to hold up today.

REVIEW

Variety, August 7, 1959

"The mystery that made a classic out of Mary Roberts Rinehart's *The Bat* has been all but muffled in this sluggish film version.... As in nearly every other film he has made in the past two years, Vincent Price casts enough furtive glances to register as the ghoul when, indeed, he isn't.... [H]e plays the role with his usual skill and relish...."

Box Office, August 17, 1959

"... [Emphasis has been placed] on mystery rather than the oft-fantastic gimmicks that freight today's abundant supply of chillers. Such old-fashioned garb should prove an asset, because, asserting a nostalgic appeal, it will attract hordes of oldsters... At the same time there are sufficient backbone-freezing elements to satisfy younger ticket buyers, educated to a more modern type of horrific celluloid."

The Bat One-sheet poster

The Bat (from left) Riza Royce *(standing)*, Lenita Lane, Agnes Moorehead, John Sutton, and Darla Hood

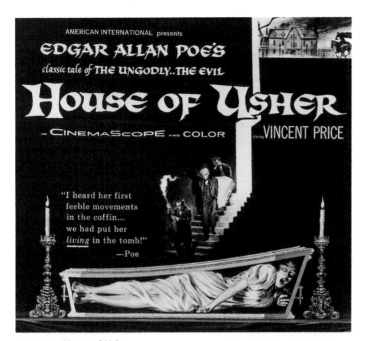

House of Usher

House of Usher As Roderick Usher

50. HOUSE OF USHER

AMERICAN INTERNATIONAL
PICTURES

Released June 22, 1960

CREDITS

Alta Vista Productions; *Presented by* James H. Nicholson and Samuel Z. Arkoff; *Executive Producer,* James H. Nicholson; *Producer/Director,* Roger Corman; *Screenplay,* Richard Matheson; *Based on* "The Fall of the House of Usher," *by* Edgar Allan Poe; *Cinematography,* Floyd Crosby; *Production Design/Art Director,* Daniel Haller; *Set Decorator,* Harry Reif; *Music,* Les Baxter; *Editor,* Anthony Carras; *Wardrobe,* Marjorie Corso; *Makeup,* Fred Phillips; *Paintings by* Burt Schoenberg; *Assistant Director,* Jack Bohrer; *Production Manager,* Bartlett A. Carre; *Properties,* Dick Ruben; *Special Effects,* Pat Dinga; *Running time,* 79 minutes; color and CinemaScope.

CAST

Vincent Price (*Roderick Usher*); Mark Damon (*Philip Winthrop*); Myrna Fahey (*Madeline Usher*); Harry Ellerbe (*Bristol*); Bill Borzage, Mike Jordan, Nadajan, Ruth Oklander, George Paul, David Andar, Eleanor Le Faber, Geraldine Paulette, Phil Sylvestre, John Zimeas (*Ghosts*).

THE FILM

To quote *Casablanca,* "I think this is the beginning of a beautiful friendship. . . ." *House of Usher* was the first of eight motion pictures (seven starring Price) based on the works of Edgar Allan Poe directed by young cult auteur Roger Corman, and it launched Vincent Price's historic association with American International Pictures. His understated performance as the hypersensitive Roderick Usher is regarded as one of his best horror roles. With it began the development of the "horror persona," which, the more celebrated Price became, would frequently be confused with the actor's real-life personality.

Because *Usher* was based on an Edgar Allan Poe story with substance and not, as in other films, on a poem or even just a title, screenwriter Richard Matheson was able to be faithful not only to the ambience of Poe but to his plot as well. When Philip Winthrop arrives at the family home to claim the hand of the vivacious young woman he met months earlier in Boston, he discovers that both the literal and the figurative House of Usher are "tainted" and decaying. Madeline, his betrothed, is frail and drained; her intensely protective brother, Roderick, tries to convince Winthrop that Madeline cannot be removed from her surroundings. The history of the Ushers is a history of savage degradations, and always in the same house, brought over generations before from England. If Madeline were to wed and bear children, the Usher evil would spread anew. In order to ensure against that, Roderick will even exploit the Usher predilection to catalepsy and inter his sister alive. When the deranged young woman claws her way out of her crypt, she and her brother die as they lived, locked in an embrace, and the House of Usher meets a fiery destiny.

Legend has it that when asked by Sam Arkoff, "Where's the monster?" Roger Corman replied, "The house is the monster." Roderick Usher has a line in the film: "The house lives, the house breathes." "What does that mean," Price asked his director. "That's the line that allowed us to make this movie" was the honest reply. "'Well, fine,' he said reasonably," Corman remembers, "'I suppose I can breathe some life into it, then.' Vincent breathed plenty of life and Gothic horror into all the lines and action." Handsome hero Mark Damon came from a different school; writer Matheson recalled one day of filming: "Mark Damon was playing, I guess, at being a method actor, and before he went on the set he would run in place and huff and puff [laughs]! Then he'd

House of Usher With Myrna Fahey and Mark Damon

walk in on a scene where Price would be chatting with somebody, and Price would outact the hell out of him!"

Usher boasted elements which would become trademarks of the popular Poe series: imaginative production design (by Daniel Haller) convincingly creating a mood and a style on a "modest" budget; atmospheric camera work (by Floyd Crosby); a plot heavy with a pervasive, frequently perverse sexuality, manifested in adultery, obsession, covetousness, or incest; star Vincent Price as a tormented, haunted (often literally) hero/antihero; and a blazing "wow" finish. *Usher* was also Les Baxter's first assignment for Corman, one which the composer enjoyed: "An old castle and Price and the castle finally burning and sinking into the mud—what more could I ask for? It was a composer's dream. . . . think *Usher* was one of the most sensual scores. It was very sensitive for a horror film."

Production rolled on January 13, 1960. The picture had a handful of production designations, including *Mysterious House of Usher*, *Haunted House of Usher*, and *The Fall of the House of Usher*. For the film's 1994 letterbox release on laser disc, the title was restored to *The Fall of the House of Usher*.

Vincent Price was the first choice for the male lead, although the film was not specifically tailored for him, as were many of the subsequent pictures. The character description of Roderick Usher in the original script is very different from Price's eventual on-screen appearance: "In his middle forties . . . he is handsome in a darkly, almost Hebraic manner with a Van Dyke beard, black brooding eyes, dark hair with a dusting of ash-grey at the temples, mouth lean and harsh yet somehow beautiful. His skin has the pallor of deep illness." As Usher, Price is an immense, towering figure, broad-shouldered and robust despite his disability of a "morbid acuteness of the senses." "If you lived in that house, you'd be *very* strange!" commented the actor. Roderick's emotions are palpable, his angst pitiable even in the face of his ghastly treachery when faced with releasing his sister to the love of another man. As he sinks onto her bedside and takes her tenderly by the shoulders, murmuring, "Oh, my dear, *hate* you? Don't you know that I love you more than anything in the world? Can't you see it's my *love* for you makes me act as I do . . . ," the undercurrent of unnatural eroticism in unmistakable. Offset by snow-white hair, Price's expressive blue eyes are startling in a pale, smooth face—Roger Corman confirms that the suggestion for the "albinoism" was Price's. (Later, Vincent admitted that it was "real agony" stripping the color from his hair and described his appearance when the roots began to grow out as "like a zebra.")

Roger Corman's Edgar Allan Poe series has been praised, panned, discussed and analyzed; been the subject of fan magazine articles and midnight movie retrospectives, as well as major university theses and European film festivals. Its influence on the career of Vincent Price is inescapable—for better and for worse.

REVIEWS

Hollywood Reporter, June 22, 1960

"... a class horror picture.... It has the same visual elegance and attempt at story depth as the superior horror films made in recent years by Hammer.... [*Usher*] is in the grand tradition of the horror film, with rich and lavish settings, a great horror of a house slowly disintegrating, guttering candles flickering in the wind, murky secret passageways and cobwebbed burial crypts.... Vincent Price creates a baroque portrait as the ancestor-obsessed aristocrat...."

Los Angeles Examiner, July 17, 1960, Harold Hildebrand

"... brings together two masters of the macabre. And when you see Vincent Price starring for the first time in

Die Verfluchten (German poster for *House of Usher*, courtesy of Camden House)

an Edgar Allan Poe classic, you'll ask why these two had not met sooner.... Price, who has lately become the master of horror films, animates his roles with a special brand of authoritative menace. His power stems from the sincerity he injects into each characterization. Although you will be shocked by his deeds in *House of Usher*, you nonetheless feel compassion for the distorted reasoning behind them. To the tall, handsome actor, theatrical terror and death are not new...."

ROGER CORMAN

"In Vincent, I found a man of cultural refinement for Usher. This was partly his reputation and partly his persona as I had seen it in many of his films. He was a first-rate actor and handsome leading man who had a distinguished career. I felt audiences had to fear the leading man but not on a conscious, physical level based on strength. I wanted a man whose intelligent but tormented mind works beyond the minds of others and who thus inspires a deeper fear.... In *Dragonwyck*, particularly, there had been this romantic quality to him.... Vincent was the consummate professional. He had been trained in a classical manner, but he had also worked a little bit with the Method. He and I would discuss the role before shooting; there wouldn't be that much discussion on the set because we had already worked out the main characteristics. Vincent *would* prepare, but ... I think it was more of an internal thing. Immediately before a shot, he would not be making party conversation and then get up and jump into it. He would sit quietly and think about it and be ready. When there was *time*, he would chat and be friendly on the set, but he would fully prepare for his scene without the outward look of doing it. We had no problems whatsoever. It was as congenial and as friendly and as professional a method of working with an actor as I've ever had."

51. MASTER OF THE WORLD

AMERICAN INTERNATIONAL PICTURES

Released May 1961

CREDITS

Executive Producer, Samuel Z. Arkoff; *Producer*, James H. Nicholson; *Coproducer*, Anthony Carras; *Associate Producers*, Bartlett A. Carre and Daniel Haller; *Director*, William Witney; *Screenplay*, Richard Matheson; *Based on the novels* Master of the World *and* Robur, The Conqueror *by* Jules Verne; *Cinematography,* Gil Warrenton; *Production Design/Art Direction,* Daniel Haller; *Set Decorator,* Harry Reif; *Music,* Les Baxter; *Song "Master of the World"* by Les Baxter, Lenny Addelson; *Sung by* Darryl Stevens; *Editor,* Anthony Carras; *Wardrobe,* Marjorie Corso; *Makeup,* Fred Phillips; *Special Effects,* Tim Baar, Wah Chang, Gene Warren; *Special Props and Effects,* Pat Dinga; *Aerial Photography,* Kay Norton; *Running time,* 104 minutes; color.

CAST

Vincent Price (*Robur*); Charles Bronson (*John Strock*); Henry Hull (*Prudent*); Mary Webster (*Dorothy Prudent*); David Frankham (*Phillip Evans*); Richard Harrison (*Alistair*); Vito Scotti (*Topage*); Wally Campo (*Turner*); Steve Masino (*Weaver*); Ken Terrell (*Shanks*); Peter Besbas (*Wilson*); Gordon Jones (*Townsman*).

THE FILM

This entertaining, moralistic adventure story teamed Price for the second time with by-now leading man Charles Bronson. The script combined Jules Verne's two novels about Robur the Conqueror, a nineteenth-century philosopher/inventor determined to put an end to war. With the invincible, zeppelin-like airship he has designed, Robur intends to destroy the weapons of all countries until they agree to put aside their arms in peace. Unwilling passengers he is forced to take on board agree with his motive but not his means and bring about the end of the *Albatross,* her crew and her captain, the *Master of the World.*

Price had already been set to star when the casting of Charles Bronson was announced in March 1960; the picture rolled at Republic Studios around September 14. Although the trades printed AIP press releases that aerial sequences were being filmed over the U.S. eastern seaboard and the coast of Ireland, in fact director William Witney and a cameraman shot all the process plates over the High Sierras. Stock footage sufficed for shots of the ground below, which in two lengthy sequences display a clearly pre–Industrial Revolution, even Elizabethan, London. A standing Globe Theatre—Shakespeare's playhouse—is clearly identifiable in the foreground. According to the film's press kit, the *Albatross* was a scale model complete in all respects, with thirty-nine practical propellers, mechanized trap doors, rocket devices, controls, etc. The only life-size portion built was the rear deck, which was on lifts to simulate motion. The sound of the flying machine was accomplished by combining the noises of different sized wooden paddles being twirled at various speeds.

The opening sequence of the film, a history of aviation,

Master of the World As Robur, the Conquerer

is frothy and fun, similar to *Those Magnificent Men in Their Flying Machines,* and the introductory musical themes are very gay, full of adventure. Makeup by Fred Phillips (who did *House of Usher* and later television's *Star Trek*) had Vincent squinting under peculiarly thick false eyebrows. Price's Robur is an educated man, completely dedicated to the cause of world peace; in fact, committed enough to die for it. He is also an inspiration to his crewmen, who disobey orders to abandon ship when the *Albatross* is plummeting out of the skies. In a moving climax, Robur reads from the Bible as his comrades solemnly bow their heads. Then the airship crashes into the ocean and explodes.

According to screenwriter Richard Matheson, Charles Bronson "was miscast, and he knew it. He was very unhappy. Testy is more the word. . . . Vincent Price, who could make friends with a dead man—and very often *has* in his movies [laughs]—said, 'I can't get through to this guy. I cannot make friends with him.' I guess Bronson's always been that way. Very strange. . . ."

REVIEWS

Box Office, May 15, 1961

"Topliner Vincent Price is his characteristic suave, sinister and convincing self. . . ."

Hollywood Citizen News, June 1, 1961

". . . 'that specialist' in the odd, unusual, eerie and fantastic—Vincent Price—is playing (again) a tailored role as the mad 'master' of the film's title."

VINCENT PRICE

[In response dated January 12, 1962 to a letter from the parent of young fans, Price wrote:] "I'm glad your kids liked *Master of the World*, and I loved their drawings of that kookie airship—much better I must say than I liked it in the picture, since it made me slightly seasick."

52. PIT AND THE PENDULUM

AMERICAN INTERNATIONAL PICTURES

Released August 12, 1961

CREDITS

Alta Vista Productions; *Executive Producers*, James H. Nicholson, Samuel Z. Arkoff; *Producer/Director*, Roger Corman; *Screenplay*, Richard Matheson; *Based on the story by* Edgar Allan Poe; *Cinematography*, Floyd Crosby; *Production Design/Art Director*, Daniel Haller; *Set Decorator*, Harry Reif; *Music*, Les Baxter; *Editor*, Anthony Carras; *Wardrobe*, Marjorie Corso; *Makeup*, Ted Cooley; *Assistant Directors*, Jack Bohrer, Lou Place; *Production Manager*, Bartlett A. Carre; *Special Effects*, Pat Dinga; *Scenic Effects*, Tom Matsumoto; *Running time*, 85 minutes; color and Panavision.

CAST

Vincent Price (*Nicholas Medina*); John Kerr (*Francis Barnard*); Barbara Steele (*Elizabeth Barnard Medina*); Luana Anders (*Catherine Medina*); Antony Carbone (*Dr. Charles Leon*); Patrick Westwood (*Maximillian*); Lynn Bernay (*Maria*); Larry Turner (*Nicholas as a child*); Mary Menzies (*Isabella Medina*); Charles Victor (*Bartolome Medina*).

THE FILM

Perhaps more than any other film in the series, *Pit and the Pendulum* is quintessential Edgar Allan Poe. While the plot owes no more than its horrific apparatuses to the Poe story, the ambience created is completely faithful, intertwining habitual Poe characters (submissive male, dominant female) in a foreboding atmosphere of despair and death.

Francis Barnard (John Kerr) arrives at the castle of grieving brother-in-law, Don Nicholas Medina (Vincent Price), to learn more about the mysterious death of his sister, Elizabeth Barnard Medina (Barbara Steele). Nicholas is distraught, anguished, consumed with guilt. Barnard learns that the grieving nobleman was traumatized as a child when he witnessed his Spanish inquisitor father (Price in a dual role), torture his adulterous wife and then entomb her alive. For that reason, Nicholas is convinced that Elizabeth suffered the same fate, but his best friend, Dr. Leon (Antony Carbone), assures him that "if Elizabeth Medina walks these corridors, it is her spirit and not her living self." Then Elizabeth's room is ransacked and her portrait slashed, and mysterious harpsichord playing is heard in the night. To satisfy Francis's mounting suspicions and Nicholas's gnawing guilt, Elizabeth's crypt is opened, and the agonized posture of the decaying corpse seems to confirm that she was indeed buried alive. Dazed, numb, Nicholas awaits his wife's vengeance, following the sound of her voice down into the castle catacombs, becoming increasingly demented with every step. What he eventually finds in the dungeon leads to his total madness and to more torture and death, as history repeats itself.

Vincent Price is far from the villain of the picture. Nicholas Medina, gentle, sensitive, racked with remorse, is a husband like Othello who "loved not wisely, but too well." His wife is everything to him; betrayed by her, he loses everything, including, ultimately, his sanity. Price gives a full-throttle performance, meticulously and skillfully crafting a character growing unstable by degrees through the drama of the story (and the continuity of a speedy Corman production).

The success of *House of Usher* made a second Poe film an obvious decision; *Pit and the Pendulum* was announced in August 1960 and began filming the first week of January 1961. Price's script, signed with a flourish "V. Price II," is dated December 12, 1960. The sixteen-day shoot cost close to $1 million. It was the first American film of the luscious British actress Barbara Steele, whose voice had to be dubbed prior to the film's release; the rushes had convinced Corman that her thick "working-class" English accent "didn't blend with the other actors."

Pit and the Pendulum "While we were up here mourning her, she was alive—struggling to be free . . . I can never leave. I must accept whatever vengeance Elizabeth chooses to inflict upon me . . ."

Pit and the Pendulum As Nicholas Medina

Pit and the Pendulum As Sebastian Medina

Pit and the Pendulum With Barbara Steele and Antony Carbone

There are many variations in the screenplay as it was written and as it was shot. Vincent himself made numerous suggestions for changes in his lines. When Francis Barnard is introduced to Nicholas in the catacombs and asks questions about the terrifying noise he has just heard, the script called for Don Medina to respond simply, "Uh . . . an apparatus, Mr. Barnard. (*turning*) What brings you to us?" Price penned in a "?" in the margin and the suggestions, "that must be kept in repair" and "that cannot be stopped?" Later in the story, when Nicholas describes his father's torture chamber, Price inserted several alternate explanations of Sebastian Medina's brutality.

The final shot of Nicholas in the bottom of the pit originally included dialogue. Sprawled like a rag doll, "his expression one of dying agony, suddenly, his mind clears and he remembers everything. He tries to get up; cannot." He asks in a horrified voice, "Elizabeth. What have I done to you? (*beat*) What have I done to you?" Then the camera was to come back on the face of his unfaithful wife, contorted with horror, trapped in the iron maiden. As filmed, Nicholas has no lines; Corman felt that the picture should be very visual at that point and dialogue would have destroyed the mood.

In the formal application to the Motion Picture Academy in connection with the 34th Annual Awards, the creation of *Pit*'s special effects was described in detail: ". . . the most impressive and nerve-wracking was the operation of the huge pendulum itself [which consisted of adjusting] the height of the swinging blade progressively nearer to the principal until it actually cut through his shirt and scored the metal flesh-colored protective plate worn on his chest. . . . Cobwebbing of the sets was a continuous operation for weeks. As each set was

photographed, the webs were renewed between takes. About sixty oakum torches were expended in the pendulum set alone. . . . Being out of the realm of one's everyday experience [!], sounds for [the pendulum] sequence had to satisfy the imagination and credulity of each person who heard them. [A] conglomeration of things—windmills, drawbridges, waterwheels, steamboat paddles, ratchets, blow torches, even rail click—these were speeded up and slowed down, echoed and squeezed. The final effect was achieved using sixteen sounds of different intensities and pitches. . . ."

When *Pit and the Pendulum* was broadcast on television in 1968, it was deemed too short for the standard two-hour network time slot, and ten minutes of additional footage was shot by Corman assistant Tamara Asseyev. Of the original cast, only Luana Anders was available; the new scenes depicted Catherine Medina alone in a madhouse, telling her terrible tale in a flashback.

REVIEWS

Motion Picture Herald, August 12, 1961

"Vincent Price, rapidly acquiring a first class monopoly on this type of role, is his usual excellent self in the lead. . . ."

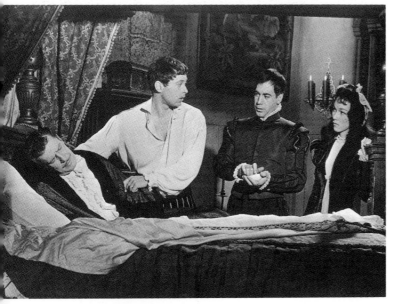

Pit and the Pendulum With John Kerr, Antony Carbone, and Luana Anders

Pit and the Pendulum: One-sheet poster (release print title does not include the word *The*)

Hollywood Reporter, August 14, 1961, James Powers

"... a class suspense-horror film of the calibre of the excellent ones done by Hammer.... It is carefully made and has full production values ... Vincent Price gives a characteristically rococo performance as the slightly mad Spanish aristocrat.... Matheson's elaboration of the Poe story is sound, suffering from only one flaw and that not of his making: ... American actors, particularly of the modern school, often sound awkward with the orotund lines [of period dialogue], although Price, with his stage and platform experience, has no such handicap ..."

Los Angeles Times, September 29, 1961, Charles Stinson

"If ... *Pit and the Pendulum* does nothing else of merit, it does at least ... reveal just how well Vincent Price manages a swoon. Ladies and gentlemen, Mr. Price faints away more gracefully than a reviewer can describe.... The uncredited[?] scenario violates Poe's gothic style with passages of flat, modernized dialogue.... But the peccadilloes of the script pale beside the acting. Price and [John] Kerr should get some sort of joint award.... Price mugs, rolls his eyes continuously and delivers his lines in such an unctuous tone that he comes near to burlesquing the role. His mad scenes were just ludicrous. The audience almost died laughing. After he had moaned: "Elizabeth, where are you?" five or six times, an adolescent male voice, somewhere down front and distinctly unsympathetic, rasped, 'Right here, dear.' ..." [Vincent's personal papers contain a letter he most likely never sent to this reviewer; instead, it would have gone in his "Letting Off Steam File." It reads: "I find I must break a 25 year determination never to answer a critic. Since your review of *The Pit and the Pendulum* was obviously not meant to be instructive, and therefore con-

169

structive, but only to hurt and humiliate, I'm sure you would enjoy the satisfaction of knowing it did." A P.S. adds: "My only consolation, and I add this with no intention of justifying the picture or myself, is that at present it is the second greatest box office attraction in the country. There you are, dear." And for the record, each of Nicholas's faints is written into Matheson's screenplay. *There you are, dear.*]

New Yorker, September 9, 1961, Brendan Gill

"... the result is a thoroughly creepy sequence of horrors.... The star of the picture is the well-known art historian and collector Vincent Price...."

ANTONY CARBONE

"I direct plays at the American Academy of Dramatic Art. Certain actors have an instinct; there's always something else going on that they're not sharing with the audience. Vincent had that gift. He was always thinking of two or three things at the same time, and that keeps you guessing, will he do this or will he do that? That element keeps you totally focused on the image.... He also was one of the most professional people I've ever worked with. He knew his lines better than anyone else, he was always ready to go. He could get *in* there— wonderful, just wonderful. If I had a scene to do [and Price's lines were delivered off camera], he was always there. He had a wonderful sense of humor, wonderful stories. You could sit around and talk to him for hours.... It's almost unfortunate that Vincent was so good in this kind of film, because he could have done anything. He was a wonderful actor. I'm sure anyone has to have a great deal of affection and respect for the man."

ROGER CORMAN

[The original script called for a flashback with exterior shots depicting Nicholas and Elizabeth horseback riding and enjoying a picnic prior to her decline. Corman explains why these were deleted:] "I had a lot of theories I was working with when I did the Poe films. Vincent commented to somebody, something about, 'I didn't necessarily believe everything Roger said, but it was really *interesting* to listen to [laughs]!' One of my theories was that these stories were created out of the unconscious mind of Poe and the unconscious mind never really sees reality, so until *Tomb of Ligeia*, we never showed the real world. Mark Damon rode through a burned-out landscape in *Usher* [the result of Corman's resourcefullness in dashing out with his crew the day after a forest fire in the Hollywood Hills]. In *Pit*, John Kerr arrived in a carriage against an ocean background, which I felt was more representative of the unconscious. That horse-

back interlude was thrown out because I didn't want to have a scene with people out in broad daylight."

53. NAKED TERROR

DISTRIBUTED BY JOSEPH BRENNER ASSOCIATES
Released November 1961

CREDITS

Narration: Vincent Price; *Running time*, 74 minutes; color.

THE FILM

Independent distributor Joseph Brenner picked up this feature documentary, which was described as "a colorful, candid, concise study of the savage native Zulus of Africa, tribes persistently adhering to past superstition and ancient tradition despite the admittedly tremendous inroads by foreign powers, manners and morals."

REVIEWS

Motion Picture Herald, December 6, 1961

"... It's for the adult crowd—and the squeamish must be warned that what happens on the screen wouldn't necessarily be incorporated into a wholesome-toned screen glimpse of Yellowstone National Park.... Last remnants of uncivilized society in a rapidly-changing continent are poignantly captured for the documentary screen."

54. CONVICTS 4
(Reprieve)

ALLIED ARTISTS
Released March 1963

CREDITS

Kaufman-Lubin Productions; *Producer*, A. Ronald Lubin; *Writer-Director*, Millard Kaufman; *Based on the autobiography* **Reprieve** by John Resko; *Cinematography*, Joseph Biroc; *Art Director*, Howard Richmond; *Set Decorator*, Joseph Kish; *Music*, Leonard Rosenman; *Editor*, George White; *Wardrobe*, Roger J. Weinberg, Wally Harton, Norah Sharpe; *Makeup*, William Turner; *Hairstyles*, Janette Marvin; *Location Manager*, James E.

Henderling; *Technical Adviser*, John Resko; *Running time*, 105 minutes; black and white.

CAST

Ben Gazzara (*John Resko*); Stuart Whitman (*Principal Keeper*); Ray Walston (*Iggy*); Vincent Price (*Carl Carmer*); Rod Steiger (*Tiptoes*); Broderick Crawford (*Warden*); Dodie Stevens (*Resko's Sister*); Jack Kruschen (*Resko's Father*); Sammy Davis Jr. (*Wino*); Naomi Stevens (*Resko's Mother*); Carmen Phillips (*Resko's Wife*); Susan Silo (*Resko's Daughter*); Timothy Carey (*Nick*); Roland LaStarza (*Duke*); Tom Gilson (*Lefty*); Arthur Malet (*Storekeeper*); Lee Krieger (*Stanley*); Myron Healey (*Gunther*); Josip Elic (*Barber*); Jack Albertson (*Art Teacher*); Robert H. Harris (*Commissioner*); Andy Albin (*Con*); Burt Lange (*Gallery Man*); John Kellogg, Adam Williams, Robert Christopher, Warren Kemmerling, Kreg Martin, John Close, Billy Varga (*Guards*); Reggie Nalder (*Greer*); John Dennis (*Cell Block Guard*).

THE FILM

It's hard to get further away from Gothic terror and period costume than the real-life horror of prison life. *Convicts 4* chronicles the true story of John Resko, an imprisoned murderer who discovers a talent for painting which eventually is the source of his rehabilitation. His work is introduced to the general public by a noted art critic, who circulates petitions to have the convict released, and after eighteen years in prison, he is paroled.

Kaufman-Lubin bought the rights to the 1956 autobiography *Reprieve: The Testament of John Resko* in July 1960, and Gazzara was signed for the lead role of the convict/artist the following April 1961. In late October, Vincent Price was set as one of the guest stars of the picture, which was lensed (and initially released) as *Reprieve*. Location scenes were actually filmed at Folsom Prison; eighty guards played prisoners, and one thousand actual convicts who had volunteered to work as extras were used in other scenes. The film has a gritty feel about it, thanks to the starkness of the black-and-white photography, an aggressive "beat" soundtrack, and the hard-line story which mixes comedy with the drama.

In the script Price's role is identified simply as "Tall Man." Entering the prison art class in the company of the warden and an unsympathetic parole-board member, he surveys Resko's paintings while sucking thoughtfully on the tip of his glasses, acknowledging, "They're pretty damn good." After his exit a guard bursts back into the classroom to inform Resko that the "big wheel" was influential author Carl Carmer, who "not only knows all about art; he even knows what he likes," a line which must be a deliberate reference to Price's popular 1959

book *I Like What I Know*. Cast as an art expert, Vincent must have enjoyed acting on-screen the role he filled so adroitly offscreen. (Although Carmer played an enormously important part in the real Resko's life, Price's appearance in this film is little more than a walk-on, with only three minutes of screen time.)

In September 1962, only six months after the picture's original release, *Variety* reported: "It's high hopes for *Reprieve* snuffed out by the results from a handful of playdates, distributor Allied Artists is rising to the challenge by changing the title and campaign for the film and giving it a fresh start with trade and public. Henceforth *Convicts 4*. Allied Artists concedes that the original title simply wasn't a 'plus factor.'"

Convicts 4 "Hollywood art apostle Vincent Price (he's a member of the White House Art Commission and lectures on art between pictures) shows early John Resko oil, painted on mattress covering which the artist wove in Dannemora prison mill, using brushes he made from slivers of wood, pigments he extracted from the earth. Scene is in his cell block. Another inmate had just killed himself by leaping from high tier of cells . . . Imaginatively, the pent-up Resko also painted the dead man's departing soul, titled the picture 'Escape.'"

Box Office, April 9, 1962

"Vincent Price, as well-known author and art critic Carl Carmer, registers well in brief scenes in which he accredits Gazzara's release from prison as rehabilitated for civilian life."

Newsweek, May 14, 1962

"Unfortunately, the story is overrun by an all-star cast. . . . Vincent Price drips charm as Resko's art sponsor."

55. TALES OF TERROR

AMERICAN INTERNATIONAL PICTURES
Released May 1962

CREDITS

Executive Producers, James H. Nicholson and Samuel Z. Arkoff; *Producer/Director*, Roger Corman; *Screenplay*, Richard Matheson; *Based on stories by* Edgar Allan Poe; *Cinematography*, Floyd Crosby; *Production Design/Art Director*, Daniel Haller; *Set Decorator*, Harry Reif; *Music*, Les Baxter; *Editor*, Anthony Carras; *Wardrobe*, Marjorie Corso; *Makeup*, Lou LaCava; *Assistant Director*, Jack Bohrer; *Running time*, 85 minutes; color and Panavision.

CAST

"Morella": Vincent Price (*Locke*); Maggie Pierce (*Lenora*); Leona Gage (*Morella*); Edmond Cobb (*Coachman*). "The Black Cat": Vincent Price (*Fortunato*); Peter Lorre (*Montresor Herringbone*); Joyce Jameson (*Annabel*); Wally Campo (*Bartender*); Alan DeWit (*Chairman*); John Hackett (*Policeman*). "The Case of M. Valdemar": Vincent Price (*Valdemar*); Basil Rathbone (*Carmichael*); Debra Paget (*Helene*); David Frankham (*Dr. Elliot James*); Scotty Brown (*Servant*).

THE FILM

In the opening voice-over of the trilogy *Tales of Terror*, Vincent Price informs us that this anthology is concerned "with death and dying. What happens at the point of death? What happens after it?"

In the first story, Price plays yet another brooding, haunted widower possessed by yet another dead wife who reaches from beyond the grave to destroy both him and the long-lost daughter she holds responsible for her untimely demise. The second segment, which has elements of humor, also incorporates the denouement from Poe's *Cask of Amontillado*. When wine-bibber Lorre discovers his neglected wife having an affair with celebrated oenologist Price, he entombs the couple in the cellar, together with an incriminatingly vocal black cat. The final offering is genuinely creepy, with Price as a terminally ill man whose death is forestalled when he is placed in a hypnotic state by mesmerist Rathbone. He finally breaks free of the trance to save his wife from the clutches of the covetous doctor and then rots away into a "mass of loathsome, of detestable putrescence." (One of the handful of times Price wore extensive effects makeup, although the on-screen depiction of Poe's vision wasn't all *that* putrid. "I said, 'Roger, how precisely does one putrify?'" Price remembers inquiring of his director. "He said, 'That's *your* problem!'")

Like most of the films in the Corman/Poe series, *Tales* was briskly produced in sixteen days, beginning on November 28, 1961. It did slightly less well at the box office, which the director attributed to the trilogy format. Vincent had a ball perfecting his wine-tasting technique under the advice of Harry H. Waugh of John Harvey & Sons, Ltd., Bristol, England. The mesmerism sequences were supervised by William J. Bryan Jr., M.D., the executive director of the American Hypnosis Institute.

Excerpts from the shooting schedule for the picture are more amusing and clever than most screenplays. Roger Corman believes it came from the pen of assistant director Jack Bohrer: "He made up the shooting schedule; he was a funny guy."

"*Black Cat* segment. Monty's Bedroom—Monty enters & sees bed messed up. He's quite suspicious, has an evil mind, I guess. Annie in with cat. Big row ensues & she tells him off—says she's gonna quit him and marry Forty. 'Oh, yeah,' he says.

"*Morella* segment. Lenora's Room—Morella's soul (?) slips into Lenora, lying in bed. She screams & Locke comes flying in & finds her in pain. She apparently dies, wavers back & forth, and then becomes Morella, if you can believe it. (Poe did.) Morella scares the hell out of Locke & he dashes out of there.

"Morella's Room—close on Morella's mummified body as her soul (?) prepares to leave her body for Lenora, and does. . . . Lenora takes its place with mummy makeup. She tells Locke of her intended revenge, and as candle slips to floor & ignites bedclothes, she grabs him and tries to strangle him. She succeeds and metamorphoses back into Lenora on the bed & becomes the mummy-dummy as the fire consumes all. Pleasant finish, no? Poe at his best—or worst. Note: Mr. Nicholson says we have enough [fire] stock for scenes 175 & 176.

Tales of Terror "Morella": with Leona Gage

Tales of Terror "The Black Cat": Price (*seated at table left*), Peter Lorre (*seated at table right*), and players

Tales of Terror "The Black Cat": Harry H. Waugh of John Harvey & Sons, Ltd. teaches VP the fine art of wine tasting: "(He showed us) the whole thing about testing the wine and breathing it in, and doing all that stuff, then Peter and I just went a little further. I was trying to do it in an exaggerated fashion, which made it so funny."

Tales of Terror Publicity shot: Peter Lorre, VP, Basil Rathbone

Tales of Terror "The Case of M. Valdemar": "A mass of loathsome, of detestable putrescence": with Debra Paget

"*Valdemar* segment. Int. Bedroom—7 months later as Carmichael in & gives orders old Val who begs release. Nothing doing & he lets the Doc & Helene in. James threatens Carmike with gun but he just laughs at him since only he can release Val. Carmichael tries to take advantage of Helene. This is too much for old Val, dead as he is & he comes back from over yonder & goes after Carmichael, finally dissolving in a decomposed mess all over him as Dr. James rushes in. Fini la guerre!

The film is sometimes titled *Edgar Allan Poe's Tales of Terror* or just *Poe's Tales of Terror*.

REVIEWS

Hollywood Reporter, June 4, 1962

". . . a class picture. . . . A richly mounted, slick collection . . . that is superior to anything in its category in years. . . . The format of three stories instead of one actually works out better than stretching one Poe story to full-length. . . . Vincent Price plays in all three stories, ranging from Grand Guignol macabre to some very funny broad comedy. . . ."

Kinematograph Weekly [England], March 14, 1963

"Massive macabre 'club sandwich' . . . Points of Appeal: Gripping, if lurid, stories, strong and attractive cast, title."

56. CONFESSIONS OF AN OPIUM EATER

ALLIED ARTISTS
Released June 1962

CREDITS

An Albert Zugsmith Production; a Production of Photoplay Associates, Inc.; *Producer/Director*, Albert Zugsmith; *Associate Producers*, Robert Hill, Eugene Lourie; *Screenplay*, Robert Hill; *Based on the novel by* Thomas de Quincey; *Cinematography*, Joseph Biroc; *Art Director*, Eugene Lourie; *Set Decorator*, Joe Kish; *Music*, Albert Glasser; *Editors*, Roy Livingston, Robert Eisen; *Wardrobe*, Roger J. Weinberg and Norah Sharpe; *Makeup*, Bill Turner; *Choreography*, Jon Gregory; *Stunt Director*, Paul Stader; *Running time*, 85 minutes; black and white.

CAST

Vincent Price (*Gil de Quincey*); Linda Ho (*Ruby Low*); Philip Ahn (*Ching Foon*); Richard Loo (*George Wah*); June Kim (*Lotus*); Yvonne Moray (*Child*); Alicia Li (*Ping Toy*); John Mamo (*Auctioneer*); Arthur Wond (*Kwai Tong*); Jo Anne Miya (*1st Dancing Girl*); Geri Hoo (*2nd Dancing Girl*); Keiko [Keiko Nishimura] (*3rd Dancing Girl*); Carol Russell (*Slave Girl*); Terence De Marney (*Scrawny Man*); Vincent Barbi (*Captain*); Caroline Kido (*Lo Tsen*); Gerald Jann (*Fat Chinese*); Vivianne Manku (*Catatonic Girl*); Miel Saan (*Look Gow*); Victor Sen Yung (*Wing Young*); Ralph Ahn (*Wah Chan*), Richard Fong.

THE FILM

On his script cover for *Confessions of an Opium Eater*, Vincent scratched out the author's name after the word "by" and penned in "Peking Noodle Co. Inc." Under the signature of his initials "V.P." he added "The Death of Me" and superscribed an ornate flourish.

Gil de Quincey comes to San Francisco at the turn of the century, "perhaps to keep a predestined rendezvous." Sporting the tattoo of the dragon and the crescent moon on the inside of his forearm, he infiltrates the Tong in order to assist a crusading newspaper editor/renegade Tong leader in his battle against the auctioning of slave girls. Voice-over monologues laden with Oriental philosophy are interspersed with scenes of derring-do and debauchery (opium smoking and suggestive dancing); the end result is both seedy and silly.

In its October 29, 1958, issue, *Variety* reported that William Castle would produce and direct a film version of de Quincey's 1822 semiautobiographical classic. The picture was to be filmed in color in Japan in early 1959 and was expected to be one of that year's "top films" from the company. In the summer of 1961, while Price was working on *Queen of the Nile*, his agent forwarded various drafts of a screenplay to be produced by Albert Zugsmith, soliciting the actor's comments about wardrobe: "Zugsmith likes the idea of trousers, a sort of naval-type jacket over a turtleneck sweater and a well-used navy skipper's cap. The thought is that after the action gets going the coat would be discarded and the rest of the action would be just in slacks and sweater. Other thoughts are matching trousers and coat with the coat being the Norfolk type which was of the period. Whatever thoughts you and [costume designer/wife] Mary might have which you think are best, tell me and I will see that such wardrobe is organized and ready for fittings on your return."

Confessions was shot during October 1961. Earlier in the year, the L.A. Committee Against Defamation of the Chinese had protested the making of the film; they were persuaded that they had "an erroneous impression of what was going into the final script." The merits of the picture (or lack of same) aside, this is a peculiar, even unique, role for Vincent Price in what is basically an action movie. The plot calls for him to be athletic (climb up the side of a building, break a window with his elbow), tough and sarcastic (get into slugfests, be chased by bad guys), rescue Chinese virgins from the slave trade, and, at the end, apparently to drown in a watery embrace with the Asian "Mata Hari" who has been both his neme-

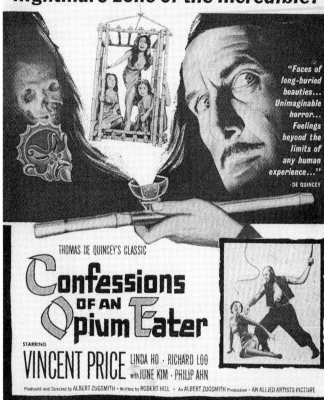

Confessions of an Opium Eater

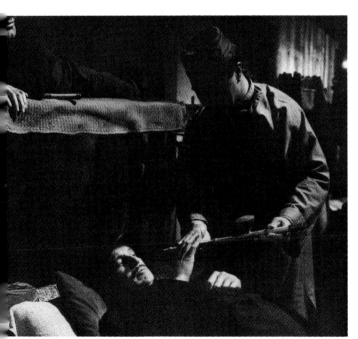

Confessions of an Opium Eater The opium den

sis and romantic interest. (And he keeps that cap on throughout it all.) It's the kind of part one would expect to go to Robert Mitchum, or at least Jack Palance.

The picture's press kit has a doozy of a publicity idea: "Oriental Slave Girls in Bamboo Cage—a sure stopper for Lobby or Store Window! . . . If you cannot obtain bamboo, have your artist simulate the bamboo shoots on beaver board. If an Oriental girl is not available, have a white girl made up to look like one. She is to occupy the cage during peak show hours."

Confessions of an Opium Eater had a number of titles: *Souls for Sale, Secrets of a Soul,* and for U.K. release, *Evils of Chinatown.*

REVIEWS

Monthly Film Bulletin, October, 1963

"This crude piece of claptrap has to be seen to be believed."

Film Comment, May/June, 1983, [Film director] Joe Dante

"... sheer, ingenuous, and possibly unintentional pop-poetry ... [a] triumphantly surreal parade of seemingly inexplicable images. ... The relentlessly sententious dialogue begins to make almost cosmic sense by the end of the picture, in which Price is last glimpsed floating down a sewer, embracing the dragon-lady heroine, and still pondering the Meaning of It All [in a voice-over]: 'Was this just another girl in my arms—or was she a kind of Destiny for me?' I couldn't tell you, and I've seen it plenty. But take my word for it, this is good stuff."

Tower of London

57. TOWER OF LONDON

UNITED ARTISTS
Released October 24, 1962

CREDITS

Admiral Pictures; *Producer*, Gene Corman; *Director*, Roger Corman; *Screenplay*, Leo V. Gordon, Amos Powell, and James B. Gordon; *Story*, Leo V. Gordon, Amos Powell; *Cinematography*, Arch R. Dalzell; *Art Director*, Daniel Haller; *Music*, Michael Andersen; *Editor*, Ronald Sinclair; *Dialogue Director*, Francis Coppola; *Running time*, 80 minutes; black and white.

CAST

Vincent Price (*Richard, Duke of Gloucester*); Michael Pate (*Sir Ratcliffe*); Joan Freeman (*Lady Margaret*); Robert Brown (*Sir Justin*); Justice Watson (*Edward IV*); Sarah Selby (*Queen Elizabeth*); Charles Macaulay (*Duke of Clarence*); Eugene Martin (*Edward V*); Sandra Knight (*Mistress Shore*); Richard Hale (*Tyrus*); Donald Losby (*Prince Richard*); Bruce Gordon (*Earl of Buckingham*); Joan Camden (*Anne*); Sara Taft (*Richard of Gloucester's Mother*); Morris Ankrum (*Archbishop*); Gene Roth (*Tailor*); Paul Frees (*Opening Narration*).

THE FILM

"Do you have the courage to spend 83 minutes in the Tower of London?"

This version of Shakespeare's account of history followed the plot line of the famous play even less than did the 1939 Universal film of the same name. Vincent Price got a promotion from duke in 1939 to king in 1962, but horror was still the order of the day as Richard III tortures and murders his way to the English crown.

A Dream of Kings, described as a "psychological study

Tower of London With Joan Camden

of Richard III," was announced in February 1962 by Roger Corman's brother, Gene. Construction of sets at Producers Studios began ten days later, and shooting commenced in mid-March despite Roger's dissatisfaction with budgetary restrictions. The decision to film in black and white was Admiral Pictures' and came as a surprise to the Cormans. It proved to be a crucial weakness of the final picture both on release and for television distribution. Price's script was titled *The Tower of London*; over "London" he penned in the words "Doom" and "Death," as if suggesting alternates. On the cover he made many textual comments, one repeated: "Where's the threat of Bosworth," "[scenes] 18 & 52 chance for Bosworth again," and "no prediction of Bosworth," referring to the battlefield on which the king lost his crown and his life. In this version, Richard also has no opportunity to drown brother Clarence in a butt of malmsey; the script calls for him to stab the duke and then hide the corpse in the open cask. (Price's script annotations include: "Why not drown Clarence.") He himself meets a nonhistorical end by falling on a battle-ax and then staggering into a sort of a deep puddle, into which he sinks, the water slowly closing over his face. The budget being what it obviously was, Richard reigns over a pretty tiny kingdom, rather like Prospero's cult in *The Masque of the Red Death*. Either retakes were at a premium, or continuity wasn't a priority; after the first ghostly appearance of one of his victims and a supernatural attempt on his life, Vincent runs off the balcony wearing a hat and dashes immediately into another room without it. Price received sole billing over the title of the picture and has a few nice moments—silky and seductive as he attempts to persuade a lady-in-waiting to betray her queen; anguished when his growing hallucinations lead him to strangle his own wife.

REVIEWS

Hollywood Citizen News, November 1, 1962

"... And what would they do without Vincent Price leering his way through these epics? He's getting so good at his macabre portrayals, I'm afraid I would jump if he were suddenly to smile—a nice, clean, wholesome smile, that is. Oh, well, with all their stereotyped characteristics—low budget, small cast, big castle and one expression: malevolent—I get kind of a kick out of these pictures, and I'm not the only one. If past box office figures are any criterion, then citywide theatres ... should do a whale of a business."

Los Angeles Times, November 3, 1962, John L. Scott

"... goes all out for thrills with the redoubtable Vincent Price playing King Richard III. ... Mr. Price has a field day as the miserable monarch, particularly when his ghostly 'pals' return to taunt him. There's a strong possibility that you might chuckle here and there at the hysterical goings-on, but dyed-in-the-wool horror devotees should have a quivering good time. ..."

58. THE RAVEN

AMERICAN INTERNATIONAL PICTURES

Released January 25, 1963

CREDITS

Alta Vista Productions; *Executive Producers*, James H. Nicholson, Samuel Z. Arkoff; *Producer/Director*, Roger Corman; *Screenplay*, Richard Matheson; *Cinematography*, Floyd Crosby; *Art Director*, Daniel Haller; *Set Decorator*, Harry Reif; *Music*, Les Baxter; *Editor*, Ronald Sinclair; *Costumes*, Marjorie Corso; *Makeup*, Ted Coodley; *Special Effects*, Pat Dinga; *Raven Trainer*, Moe Disesso; *Running time*, 86 minutes; color and Panavision.

CAST

Vincent Price (*Dr. Erasmus Craven*); Peter Lorre (*Dr. Adolphus Bedlo*); Boris Karloff (*Dr. Scarabus*); Hazel Court (*Lenore Craven*); Olive Sturgess (*Estelle Craven*); Jack Nicholson (*Rexford Bedlo*); Connie Wallace (*Maidservant*); William Baskin (*Grimes*); Aaron Saxon (*Gort*); Jim Jr. (*Raven*).

THE FILM

Fans are enormously, perhaps overly, sentimental about this spooky comedy. An earlier Roger Corman/Poe film, *Tales of Terror*, had featured a single story segment high in humor; with *The Raven*, the director went all out, partly in a concerted effort to vary the tone and look of the series. Cast as sorcerers of varying abilities, Vincent Price and costars Peter Lorre and Boris Karloff trade quips, insults, magic spells, and even women, all in an atmosphere of good-natured, tongue-in-cheek silliness.

Universal had (loosely) based a 1935 picture on Poe's famous poem which starred Boris Karloff and Bela Lugosi, and in 1952 the producer of that picture announced a remake to star Vincent Price. But in January 1962, Richard Matheson was signed to deliver two screenplays as costarring vehicles for Price and Peter Lorre for American International. *The Raven* was to be the first; the second, "an untitled comedy," became *The Comedy of Terrors*.

Filming on *The Raven* began on September 21, 1962;

The Raven

himself, Price often acted as a balance between the two actors. And Vincent himself was no mean contributor to the proceedings: When Karloff's magic appears to have dissolved Lorre into a scarlet viscous mess, his original line was simply "Oh, dear." Price penned in the additional words "raspberry jam," which he delivers after sticking his finger in the glop and licking it!

The famous sorcerers' "duel to the death" between Price and Karloff is an imaginative sequence lasting nearly eight minutes. Les Baxter's score is a mixture of sounds and cues perfectly in keeping with the charmingly simple effects, which include a snake becoming a scarf, a cannonball exploding with confetti, stone animals roaring into life, Price elevating his chair with waves of his hands, and Karloff tossing fireballs. The movie, of course, also featured a young Jack Nicholson, who held his own in the remarkable company, even if he seemed too contemporary a type for costume pictures. "Roger gave me one direction," he remembers. "Try to be as funny as Lorre, Karloff, and Price. I loved those guys."

The costliest Poe film to date, reputedly $350,000, *The Raven* went on to earn $1.4 million after distribution costs. The cost-conscious Corman shrewdly determined a way to get his money's worth out of Daniel Haller's attractive standing sets. A script was quickly pulled together, and the beleaguered Karloff was hired for an additional forty-eight hours, since Price had left immediately after *The Raven*'s wrap for an art lecture tour. Corman shot the remaining footage of the picture, called *The Terror*, in the next few months. He also got the most mileage out of his own previous footage: *The Raven* ends with the ubiquitous "mansion in flames" shots from *House of Usher*.

REVIEWS

Hollywood Reporter, January 30, 1963

". . . another healthy contender in the class horror-comedy . . . should make more money in a week at one first-run house than Edgar Allan Poe made in his lifetime. . . . Price, Lorre and Karloff perform singly and in tandem like what they are, three seasoned pros who can take a gentle burlesque and play it to the end of its values without stretching it past the entertainment point. They are performances, in their way, that are virtuoso."

Motion Picture Herald, February 20, 1963

". . . With a tongue-in-cheek sort of script, a lively and effective production, and a trio of real "names" to head the cast, this AIP presentation emerges as an engaging item of entertainment. . . . Roger Corman, as producer-director, extracted a deal of suspense, excitement and general fun from the lively screenplay by Richard Mathe-

in keeping with Corman's reputation for speed, fourteen and three-quarter pages of dialogue were shot that day! Peter Lorre's well-known tendency to improvise, a by-product of his training in Germany with Bertolt Brecht, reputedly led to some of the best lines in the film: Surveying the dust in the dungeon, he comments, "Hard place to keep clean, huh?" But according to Roger Corman, Lorre's ad-libbing "kept everyone on their toes," particularly the seventy-eight-year-old Karloff, whose training was strictly by the book. Although occasionally frustrated

son, while the men who handled the special effects are entitled to a deep bow for the magic they impart to the sorcerers' magic tricks."

Films and Filming, October 1963, Allen Eyles

"Once again it's time to rendezvous with Vincent Price and a sturdy supporting cast on those well-trod sets for another affectionate parody by Roger Corman and his associates of the Edgar Allan Poe world of romantic torment."

VINCENT PRICE

[In 1991, Price was asked if he could think of another performer who could respond to the challenge of so-called horror pictures. He replied immediately:] "Yes, Jack Nicholson. I think Jack has a great sense of the dramatic and of the obscure, of the sick and fantastic. He's larger than life. If he doesn't become afraid of being Jack Nicholson, he'll go on to be one of the greats. I don't know him that well personally, but I feel this about him. He still has this . . . trembling vitality. Very eccentric — he's not everybody's cup of tea. I'm also very eccentric. But I think Jack's the only one I know; the rest take themselves too seriously. I've worked with a lot of them, some of the great stars, superstars. They were the most boring people to be around. My God, they were boring. But the villains were always kind of fun."

HAZEL COURT

"Here you have *three* very good *minds*. Peter, Boris, and Vincent — they were all interested in art; they all had stories to tell. And oh! I used to sit and listen to them! Peter was absolutely fascinating, although he was very sick all the time. He was always pinching me on the behind! [laughing]. Today he'd be sued! [Asked if she minded:] *No-o-o-o*, of course not! Boris had a bad hip. He was a very gentle man, very soft, very kind. A real English gentleman. Vinnie was the healthy one, although he did frequently groan, 'Ohhh, my knees . . .' He always had a dirty story. And Jack Nicholson — he was always going home to write. I'll never forget his pantaloons; I mean, they just didn't suit him. It was so incongruous with him. I don't think the picture was really meant to be a comedy; it evolved into one on the set. The interesting thing was, Vincent would joke and laugh and tell stories. And the *minute* he went into these characters, it was very serious. Very real. There was never any fooling around in the actual character — not from the moment they said, 'Action!' until they said 'Cut!' *Afterward*, yes. The days were wonderful. They just rolled on. Sheer bliss . . . I'd been painting all my life, but I'd always kept it very quiet. I would never have dreamed

The Raven The sorcerer's duel: (note film equipment, upper left)

The Raven With one of his least favorite costars

of saying [*laughing*], 'Look at my etchings.' But I think it was when we were on *The Raven*, Vincent came back one night to have a drink. My husband, [director Don Taylor], had just hung up two paintings. Vincent said, 'Who did those?' Don said, 'Mum' [laughs]; Hazel did them.' And he looked at them and said, 'I want to buy *that* one!' I said, 'You can't, that's a special one.' 'Then,' he said, 'I'll buy *that* one!' So when he was buying for that big Sears collection, he purchased about thirty of my paintings. From then, I did a show in Palm Springs, and I went on to sculpt—I'm still exhibiting—and Vincent really was responsible."

59. DIARY OF A MADMAN

UNITED ARTISTS

Released March 6, 1963

CREDITS

Admiral Pictures; *Writer/Producer*, Robert E. Kent; *Director*, Reginald LeBorg; *Based on stories by* Guy De Maupassant; *Cinematography*, Ellis W. Carter; *Art Director*, Daniel Haller; *Set Decorator*, Victor Gangelin; *Music*, Richard LaSalle; *Editor*, Grant Whytock; *Costumes*, Marjorie Corso; *Special Effects*, Norman Breedlove; *Running time*, 96 minutes; color.

CAST

Vincent Price (*Simon Cordier*); Nancy Kovack (*Odette Duclasse*); Chris Warfield (*Paul Duclasse*); Elaine Devry (*Jeanne D'Arville*); Stephen Roberts (*Rennedon*); Lewis Martin (*Priest*); Ian Wolfe (*Pierre*); Edward Colmans (*Andre D'Arville*); Mary Adams (*Louise*); Harvey Stephens (*Louis Girot*); Nelson Olmstead (*Dr. Borman*); Joseph Ruskin (*Voice of the Horla*); Dick Wilson, Gloria Clark, George Sawaya, Wayne Collier, Don Brodie, Joseph Del Nostro Jr.

THE FILM

When the *Diary of a Madman* is read, it unfolds the tragic story of turn-of-the-century French magistrate Simon Cordier. Attacked in prison by a confessed murderer whom he condemned to death, Cordier accidentally kills in self-defense. He thereby "inherits" the Horla, an evil spirit which compels its unwilling host to commit crimes. Cordier, too, is driven to slaughter, dispatching the opportunistic model who has been sitting for his amateur sculptures. In the end the magistrate retains enough of his true self to set fire to his house, thus putting an end to the Horla's existence—and his own.

Diary of a Madman leads to yet another fiery end for Vincent Price, who plays well against the disembodied voice of the Horla (a very effective Joseph Ruskin). In a sincere and low-key performance, Price is suitably bewildered and confused as the immoral creature begins to take control of his life. The script gave him considerably more duality to wrestle with than he later had in *The Haunted Palace*; he makes believable the magistrate's possession by the evil entity, even to crushing his pet canary in his hand.

Admiral Pictures was the same outfit responsible for Roger Corman's *Tower of London*. In June 1962, Reginald LeBorg was signed to direct Price in a picture based on a Guy de Maupassant short story called "The Horla." Production began on July 11 at Goldwyn Studios and lasted into August, drawing much inspiration from the ambience of the Poe films but lumbered with a talky screenplay and dull supporting cast. Special footage was

Diary of a Madman Magistrate Simon Cordier under the influence of the Horla

shot for the trailer: the script had Price seated at a table with a flickering candle and a human skull before him, inquiring: "Would you know the terrible secret of the Horla's mysterious powers? Come, then, and let me lead you into the dwelling-place of evil itself . . . where you too will be possessed by . . . the Horla. . . .' He beckons to camera—then blows out candle . . . screen goes dark— segue into balance of trailer." Whether for time constraints or budgetary reasons, the promo was actually shot on the graveyard set.

The film's title change to *Diary of a Madman* was announced at the end of December 1962, a few months prior to release.

REVIEWS

Film Daily, March 6, 1963

". . . standard horror fare which is not particularly scary, covers absolutely no new ground, but is a competent rehashing of the old. [With] Vincent Price, in all his mid-Victorian splendor . . . good production values. . . ."

Box Office, March 18, 1963

"Vincent Price, that master delineator of horror films on the screen, has another shuddery field day. . . . Price has played in so many period pictures that he would almost seem out of place in modern dress."

NANCY KOVACK

(*Science Fiction Stars and Horror Heroes*, 1991)

"I enjoyed working with Vincent Price. He was very respectful, and I found that unusual. I knew that I wasn't known, and yet he was very respectful of me and kindly—he didn't have to be. He was professional, and I appreciated that. I remember that just before the scene where he kills me with the knife, he was tickling me and I was laughing, and I couldn't stop laughing after that!"

REGINALD LEBORG

(*B Movie Makers*, 1988)

"Vincent Price I found to be entirely professional and very, very nice, and I enjoyed working with him very much. I was surprised how brave he was in the fire scene. I was scared for him, because there was fire all around him in that scene. I asked him if he wanted a double, and he said no. I said, 'Well, it might get really hot, so be careful,' and he said, 'Don't worry, I've done things like this before.' He was a brave guy."

Diary of a Madman With Nancy Kovack

60. BEACH PARTY

AMERICAN INTERNATIONAL PICTURES

Released July 14, 1963

CREDITS

Alta Vista Productions; *Executive Producer*, Samuel Z. Arkoff; *Producers*, James H. Nicholson, Lou Rusoff; *Associate Producer*, Robert Dillon; *Director*, William Asher; *Screenplay*, Lou Rusoff; *Cinematography*, Kay Norton; *Production Design/Art Director*, Daniel Haller; *Set Decorator*, Harry Reif; *Music Score*, Les Baxter; *Songs*: "Beach Party," "Swingin' and A-Surfin'," "Secret Surfin' Spot," Gary Usher, Roger Christian; *Songs*: "Promise Me Anything (Give Me More)," "Treat Him Nicely," Guy Hemric, Jerry Styner; *Song*: "Don't Stop Now," Bob Marcucci, Russ Faith; *Editor*, Homer Powell; *Costume Supervisors*, Marjorie Corso, Tom Welsh; *Makeup*, Carlie Taylor; *Hairdresser*, Scotty Rackin; *Running time*, 101 minutes; color and Panavision.

CAST

Bob Cummings (*Prof. Jason Sutwell*); Dorothy Malone (*Marianne*); Frankie Avalon (*Frankie*); Annette Funicello (*Dolores*); Morey Amsterdam (*Cappy*); Harvey Lembeck (*Eric Von Zipper*); Eva Six (*Ava*); John Ashley

Beach Party Not Price but his "sit-in" double

(*Ken*); Jody McCrea (*Deadhead*); Dick Dale and the Del Tones (*Themselves*); David Landfield (*Ed*); Dolores Wells (*Sue*); Valora Noland (*Rhonda*); Bobby Payne (*Tom*); Duane Ament (*Big Boy*); Andy Romano (*J.D.*); John Macchia, Jerry Brutsche, Bob Harvey (*Motorcycle Rats*); Linda Rogers, Alberta Nelson (*Motorcycle Mice*); Candy Johnson (*Perpetual Motion Dancer*); Roger Bacon (*Tour Guide*); Yvette Vickers, Sharon Garrett (*Yogi Girls*); Mickey Dora, John Fain, Pam Colbert, Donna Russell, Mike Nader, Eddie Garner, Laura Lynn, Susan Yardley, Brian Wilson (*Surfers*); Lorie Summers, Meredith Mac-Rae, Luree Nicholson, Paulette Rapp, Marlo Baers (*Beach Girls*); John Beach, Bill Slosky, Brent Battin, Roger Christian, Gary Usher, Bill Parker (*Beach Boys*).

THE FILM

Beach Party was the first of American International's enormously successful teen-oriented series (with many of the same crew from the Poe films!). Once again, Vincent Price was in on a trend, his cameo cementing his position as a groovy icon for the young and hip.

Bob Cummings is a square anthropologist studying the behavior peculiar to young people with no visible means of support who spend their time surfing, dancing, singing, and trying to make time with the opposite sex. (Annette Funicello is the only girl on the beach not wearing a skimpy bikini. Walt Disney, to whom she was still under long-term contract, insisted that she not ruin her image by exposing her navel.)

The cast-and-credits sheet in the press kit has a separate page for "Uncredited guest appearance by Vincent Price as Big Daddy." Big Daddy is the official beach guru. Bearded and barefoot, wearing a loose white suit, blue-and-white-striped T-shirt, he spends the entire picture seemingly comatose, slumped in an oversize chair in the corner of the bar with his face hidden by a full-brimmed straw hat. The kids are waiting for him someday to deliver "the word." At the very last moment he stirs. Everyone gathers around excitedly. In the original script, Big Daddy's "Word" was "(in a bellow of pain): I can hear the scratch of rats within the walls!" On the cover of his script, Vincent penned in an alternative: "Bring me my pendulum—I'm going to swing!" In the actual film Big Daddy raises his head, snaps up the brim of his hat, and intones ominously: "The Pit! Bring me my pendulum, kiddies—I feel like swingin'!" Then, like the Dormouse in *Alice in Wonderland*, he collapses once again.

As the credits of the picture roll, the very last one is superimposed over a shot of Price's face: "Special thanks to: Vincent Price as Big Daddy." There follows a gorgeous matte painting of a castle and the sea and the legend "Soon to be seen in Edgar Allan Poe's *Haunted Palace*."

REVIEWS

Hollywood Reporter, July 15, 1963

"Comedy With Music Has Youth Appeal . . . a strong summer attraction and one that will carry over into later dates. . . . Takes a fairly routine teenage situation and elevates it by handling things with class and taste.

The Film Daily, July 17, 1963

". . . a slick, commercial, well-made picture for the teen-age set. . . . Exhibitors will find it a powerful means of getting vacationing youngsters off the street and into the movie theatres where they belong. . . . Les Baxter's musical score like swings, man."

Films and Filming, September 1964, Robin Bean

". . . AIP (which has in recent years been providing a steady diet of Corman/Poe films) has found itself with a profitable new cycle of films. . . . [*Beach Party* is] slickly professional; the script may not be worthy of detailed examination but its dialogue is snappy, its humour well-timed. . . . But wait a minute; there's a familiar character disguised as a beachcomber sleeping in the background—it is supposed to be Big Daddy who when he wakes is to utter 'The Word,' the word that is to put a significance on life for these young people. He wakes and silence falls. The head jerks up suddenly, why it's Vincent. And the word? But you must go and hear for yourself . . . it made my day."

61. RAGE OF THE BUCCANEERS

COLORAMA FEATURES

Released August 1963

CREDITS

A Max Production; *Producer*, Ottavio Poggi; *Director*, Mario Costa; *Screenplay*, Ottavio Poggi, John Byrne; *Cinematography*, Mario Bellero; *Art Directors*, Ernesto Kromberg, Amedeo Mellone; *Music*, Carlo Rustichelli; *Editor*, Renato Cinquini; *Fencing Masters*, Andrea Fantasia, Franco Fantasia; *Running time*, 90 minutes; color and CinemaScope.

CAST

Ricardo Montalban (*Gordon, the Black Buccaneer*); Vincent Price (*Romero*); Guilia Rubini (*Manuela*); Liana Orfei (*Luana*); Mario Feliciana (*Tortuga*); Gisella Sofio, Giustino Durano, José Jaspe, Edoardo Toniolo, Andrea Fantasia, Gino Marturano.

THE FILM

More slave trading for Vincent Price, this time in *Rage of the Buccaneers*, an Italian-made swashbuckler in which he plays the secretary of the governor of San Salvador who is secretly the head of the slave traffic. In his spare time, Vincent lusts after the governor's daughter. At least in this movie, he manages to avoid being dispatched by the hero (Ricardo Montalban) and instead is packed off to prison.

Montalban was signed to star in *The Black Pirate* in December 1960, and the project was scheduled to film in Italy the following spring. The picture opened in Rome in July 1962 as *Gordon II Pirata Nero* and became *The Black Buccaneer* for the United Kingdom. Producer Ottavio Poggi was also responsible for *Nefertite, Regina del Nilo* (U.S. title: *Queen of the Nile*), which Price made around the same time, although it was released a year later. Much of the crew also worked on both movies. Vincent's foreign films were often an excuse to travel and to ferret out new acquisitions for his art collection. "As a matter of fact," Price would admit, "it was the only

Rage of the Buccaneers With Guilia Rubini

way I could [afford to buy] 'cause I had no money behind me to begin with. Everything I ever had in my life I earned. So I would buy a picture—maybe two or three, depending on the price of them—for each [film] I made. And I made some dreadful pictures in Italy. They were terrible. . . . But I had the best time, and I bought so much good art. Oh, I had a wonderful time!"

REVIEWS

Box Office, September 16, 1963

"Ricardo Montalban, as handsome as ever, and Vincent Price, still sneering unsympathetically at heroes and heroines alike, are teamed with a predominantly Italian cast. . . . The film is of obvious appeal and attraction to the mass market audience, which asks no more of its screen entertainment than constant movement, much spiritedness and the allure-and-appeal of lithesome love-lies in the throes of emotional turbulence. . . ."

RICARDO MONTALBAN

"Terrible picture [laughs]! Those are the times when work was a little scarce here, and Italy offered all those "spaghetti Westerns" and this kind of adventure story.

They were terrible, but I guess they served a purpose: they paid us reasonably well, and we wanted to make an honorable living. . . . We were in Porto Ercole, which was a *delightful* little town, a sleepy town. The society of Rome had discovered this little port, and they [whispers] kept it very quiet, because they didn't want anybody to *spoil* it. I was supposed to have this *wonderful*, invincible ship, the fastest ship—and they came out with a fishing boat from Napoli that was the fattest, smelliest, most *awful* thing. I used to get kind of seasick in that boat! It was awful. That was the great pirate ship. . . . [laughs] I remember that we caught Vincent, and he was down in the hull, way down, below deck, where they kept the fish, and it was smelling [laughing], and he was down there yelling, 'You'll pay for this!' or one of those things, in the hull, with it *stinking* of fish! That was so funny. . . . A couple of times I went with Vincent [on excursions to buy art]. There wasn't much in Porto Ercole, but then in Rome, of course, I would lose—I would never see Vincent because he was always hunting for things with his wife. . . . He also bought a little convertible, a Fiat. He didn't know how to drive it very well, and I had to show him; I think he had to double-clutch to shift the thing. I remember going on rides with his brand-new car. And he had *extremely* long legs, Vincent—you know, when I sat next to him, I was a little taller, but when we stood up, he just towered over me, towered over me. Had the longest legs I've ever seen in my life. And that little Fiat, he could hardly fit in there. . . . We had first met briefly at M-G-M in the late forties. After Italy and that terrible boat, we became quite close. My wife, Georgiana, and I used to see Vincent and Coral at communion every Sunday. Sometimes we would join them for luncheon. Coral was delightful, wonderful sense of humor, very dry, very caustic. But very lovable. Both my wife and I loved Coral and Vincent both. My wife said that Coral was the one of the best-dressed women she ever saw. She could get dressed in the most elegant fashion in the most casual way, and she was always impeccable, with the best taste ever. Her conversation was very amusing; when she didn't like somebody, boy, you knew it! But I think she was a good friend; a good, loyal friend. She and Vincent were very happy together; they complemented each other beautifully. . . . Just a few months before Vincent passed away, in July 1993, I had this very serious operation on my spinal cord. I suffered a hemorrhage, and Vincent sent notes, hoping that I was better and praying for me, with such concern over my condition—such *compassion*. I felt almost very small, thinking, Yes, I'm in bad shape, but here's a man who, well, is *dying*, and he doesn't show any pity for himself in these notes, just hoping that I would get well and inserting a little humor to make

me feel better. It was wonderful, very thoughtful. Very thoughtful. I think he did find enormous consolation and peace in his religion; I really believe that. Vincent was very kind; he was a gentle man, Vincent. . . ."

62. THE HAUNTED PALACE

AMERICAN INTERNATIONAL PICTURES

Released August 28, 1963

CREDITS

Alta Vista Productions; *Executive Producers*, James H. Nicholson, Samuel Z. Arkoff; *Producer/Director*, Roger Corman; *Associate Producer*, Ronald Sinclair; *Screenplay*, Charles Beaumont; *Based on the poem by* Edgar Allan Poe *and the story* "The Case of Charles Dexter Ward" *by* H. P. Lovecraft; *Cinematography*, Floyd Crosby; *Art Director*, Daniel Haller; *Set Decorator*, Harry Reif; *Music*, Ronald Stein; *Editor*, Ronald Sinclair; *Wardrobe Supervisor*, Marjorie Corso; *Makeup*, Ted Coodley; *Hairdresser*, Lorraine Roberson; [*Uncredited Dialogue Supervisor*, Francis Coppola]; *Running time*, 85 minutes; color and Panavision.

CAST

Vincent Price (*Charles Dexter Ward/Joseph Curwen*); Debra Paget (*Ann Ward*); Lon Chaney (*Simon Orne*); Frank Maxwell (*Dr. Marinus Willet*); Leo Gordon (*Edgar Weeden*); Elisha Cook (*Micah Smith/Peter Smith*); John Dierkes (*Jacob West/Benjamin West*); Milton Parsons (*Jabez Hutchinson*); Cathie Merchant (*Hester Tillinghast*); Guy Wilkerson (*Gideon Leach*); Harry Ellerbe (*Minister*); I. Stanford Jolley (*Mr. Carmody*); Darlene Lucht (*Young Woman Victim*); Barboura Morris (*Mrs. Weeden*); Bruno Ve Sota (*Bartender*).

THE FILM

In an attempt to find inspiration outside of Edgar Allan Poe, Roger Corman came up with the idea for *The Haunted Palace* during his independent production of *Premature Burial*, the only one of his Poe films with a star other than Vincent Price (Ray Milland, since Price's contract with AIP called for exclusivity for horror pictures). The plot was based on a story by H. P. Lovecraft; the title only came from Poe, who suffered the further indignity of having his middle name misspelled "Allen" in the opening credits. The tenuous Poe tie-in was the

The Haunted Palace Warlock Joseph Curwen meets his fate

idea of producer Jim Nicholson, based on the commercial success of the previous films.

Warlock Joseph Curwen curses the villagers of Arkham who condemn him to be burned at the stake. One hundred and ten years later, Curwen's descendant, Charles Dexter Ward, arrives in the village and is possessed by the spirit of the sorcerer, who uses the living body to exact revenge on the townspeople.

The Haunted Palace began filming in April 1963. Although Curwen sets a few townspeople on fire along the

The Haunted Palace Publicity shot: (*On lower staircase, top to bottom*) Frank Maxwell, Lon Chaney, Debra Paget, and Price

The Haunted Palace Debra Paget, and Price among the cursed villagers

185

way (an appropriate revenge for a man burned at the stake), the film doesn't have much action, and special-effects makeup on villagers born with facial deformities is unconvincing. Nevertheless, it is superior to later Poe series pseudoentrants, such as *The Oblong Box* and *Cry of the Banshee*. Its title music theme by Ronald Stein is particularly sinister. Vincent Price must have appreciated the flexibility afforded him by playing a Jekyll and Hyde. He moves seamlessly between the dual characters—the gentle, good nature of Ward and the intense confidence of Curwen's sensual "spirit." As he prepares the dungeon setting for a hellish sacrifice—lighting torches, tossing herbs onto a pyre—Price is casual and unaffected. Intoning the lyrical, hypnotic Latin of the satanic ritual, he is power and assurance itself, until the deadly peril to Ward's wife brings him to his senses and he saves all their lives. But is it Ward or Curwen who survives?

REVIEWS

Hollywood Reporter, August 29, 1963

"*The Haunted Palace* is a class horror picture . . . it should do well and deserves to. . . . Mood is important, and so is story, but the acting is equally so, and the repeated use of Vincent Price in these AIP films is interesting in this connection. . . . Using Price, a handsome, intelligent, distinguished-looking individual, for this kind of part is skillful casting against type. His humor and detachment make him seem an unlikely 'mad scientist'. . . ."

Newsweek, September 9, 1963

". . . a well-made horror film, weirdly enough, a healthy specimen with black blood coursing through its veins. . . .

The evil is burned away, but we know it will be back. We have the evidence not only of Price's face in a chilly smile, but of the news from AIP that Corman will soon be starting on *Masque of the Red Death*."

Films and Filming, April 1966

". . . a powerful and unified surrealist fantasy. . . . Vincent Price gives a masterly performance with no trace of self-parody."

63. TWICE-TOLD TALES

UNITED ARTISTS
Released September 1963

CREDITS

Admiral Pictures; *Writer/Producer*, Robert E. Kent; *Director*, Sidney Salkow; *Based on stories by* Nathaniel Hawthorne; *Cinematography*, Ellis W. Carter; *Art Director*, Franz Bachelin; *Set Decorator*, Charles Thompson; *Music*, Richard LaSalle; *Supervising Film Editor*, Grant Whytock; *Costumes*, Marjorie Corso, Tom Welch; *Makeup*, Gene Hibbs; *Hairstylist*, Jane Shugrue; *Assistant Camera*, Bert Eason; *Special Effects*, Milt Olsen, Pete Faga; *Running time*, 119 minutes; color.

CAST

"Dr. Heidegger's Experiment": Vincent Price (*Alex Medbourne*); Sebastian Cabot (*Dr. Carl Heidegger*); Mari Blanchard (*Sylvia Ward*). "Rappaccini's Daughter": Vincent Price (*Dr. Giacomo Rappaccini*); Brett Halsey (*Giovanni Guastconti*); Abraham Sofaer (*Prof. Pietro Baglioni*); Joyce Taylor (*Beatrice Rappaccini*); Edith Evanson (*Lisabetta*). "The House of the Seven Gables": Vincent Price (*Gerald Pyncheon*); Beverly Garland (*Alice Pyncheon*); Richard Denning (*Jonathan Maulle*); Jacqueline De Wit (*Hannah*); Floyd Simmons (*Matthew Maulle*); Gene Roth (*Cab Driver*).

THE FILM

Subtitled "A Trio of Terror," *Twice-Told Tales* is a trilogy of episodes based on stories by Nathaniel Hawthorne. The first involves an experiment to restore youth to the aged and life to the lifeless, complicated by adultery and jealousy. In the second, a new angle on "Rapunzel," a scientist imprisons his daughter in her own body by making her poisonous to any man who touches her. The final segment is another adaptation of *The House of the*

Twice-Told Tales "Rappaccini's Daughter": with Brett Halsey and Joyce Taylor

Seven Gables, but no more faithful to the novel than Universal's 1940 feature in which Vincent Price co-starred. In the climax of this version, Price fulfills the family curse which promises that every male Pyncheon will die with blood on his lips as he is strangled by a ghostly, skeletal hand.

Incomprehensibly, the project was announced as *The Corpse Makers*, which is the title of Vincent's working script, dated September 21, 1962. Under the direction

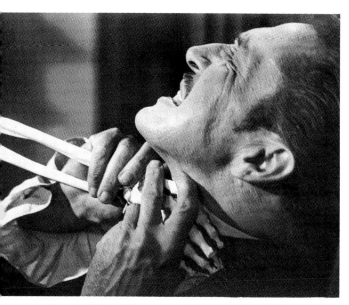

Twice-Told Tales "The House of the Seven Gables": The curse of the Pyncheons

of *The Last Man on Earth*'s Sidney Salkow, the picture was shot in the fall; the title wasn't changed to (*Nathaniel Hawthorne's*) *Twice-Told Tales* until mid-December. The film received favorable contemporary reviews, but compares *unfavorably* to the AIP-Poe films. It also suffers from that telling aspect of low budgets, a small cast; Roger Corman could make it work for him, but here it leads to an improbably unpopulated universe. Additionally, there is the unavoidable claustrophobia which results when unrelated stories take place on less than a dozen sets. Price creates distinct characters in his three different roles, but the script gives him considerably less to work with than Matheson's *Tales of Terror*. Additionally, the supporting cast, apart from Sebastian Cabot, supplies little support.

REVIEWS

Variety, September 25, 1963

"Vincent Price has a chance to display the virtuosity which has made his name a must in first-class horror fare."

Hollywood Reporter, October 4, 1963

". . . an anthology horror film, each a good story in itself and the three adding up to a strong package. . . . The picture has good production values and should be a profitable booking. . . . Vincent Price plays the lead . . . with his usual authority and dispatch."

Newsweek, November 4, 1963

"Vincent Price has almost singlehandedly restored the works of Edgar Allan Poe to the screen, but one man can't carry everybody. Now . . . Price has tried to make a horror writer out of Nathaniel Hawthorne. Despite a strenuous lot of tinkering with the material, Hawthorne clearly doesn't have the stuff. There's a pretty good moment in part two when Joyce Taylor, whom Price has made radioactive through inoculations, touches a lizard and fries it purple."

64.   THE COMEDY OF TERRORS

AMERICAN INTERNATIONAL PICTURES
Released December 25, 1963

CREDITS

Producers, James H. Nicholson, Samuel Z. Arkoff; *Coproducer*, Anthony Carras; *Writer/Associate Producer*, Richard Matheson; *Director*, Jacques Tourneur; *Cinematography*, Floyd Crosby; *Producer Designer/Art Director*, Daniel Haller; *Set Decorator*, Harry Reif; *Music*, Les Baxter; *Editor*, Anthony Carras; *Costume Supervisor*, Marjorie Corso; *Makeup*, Carlie Taylor; *Hairstyles*, Betty Pedretti, Scotty Rackin; *Special Effects*, Pat Dinga; *Running time*, 84 minutes; color and Panavision.

CAST

Vincent Price (*Waldo Trumbull*); Peter Lorre (*Felix Gillie*); Boris Karloff (*Amos Hinchley*); Joyce Jameson (*Amaryllis Trumbull*); Basil Rathbone (*John F. Black*); Joe E. Brown (*Cemetary Keeper*); Beverly Hills (*Mrs. Phipps*); Paul Barselow (*Riggs*); Linda Rogers (*Phipps's Maid*); Buddy Mason (*Mr. Phipps*); Rhubarb the Cat (*Cleopatra*); Alan De Witt, Douglas Williams, Harvey Parry, Luree Holmes.

THE FILM

Sillier than *The Raven*, *The Comedy of Terrors* is also funnier. Waldo Trumbull (Vincent Price) and Felix Gil-

The Comedy of Terrors

The Comedy of Terrors Publicity shot: with Basil Rathbone, Peter Lorre, and Boris Karloff

The Comedy of Terrors With Peter Lorre

lie (Peter Lorre) are a couple of turn-of-the-century underworked undertakers who supplement the meager call for their services by knocking off elderly townspeople and recycling the sole coffin in the mortuary. Mr. Black (Basil Rathbone), the landlord determined to collect unpaid rent from the duo, has "Candidate" written all over him, but despite their best homicidal endeavors, he keeps popping back up to plague them, and in the end it is only the unredeemable Trumbull who meets his maker.

The Comedy of Terrors went into production on September 4, 1963, on a fifteen-day shooting schedule. Boris Karloff, who plays Price's endearingly senile father-in-law, Amos Hinchley, was originally cast in the larger role of Mr. Black. At seventy-five, two of the actor's best professional moments were still in his future: TV's animated classic *How The Grinch Stole Christmas* and Peter

Bogdanovich's feature tribute *Targets*. But here, suffering terribly from arthritis, "King" Karloff would never have been able to manage the physically demanding role of the landlord, who chases and is chased around a mansion brandishing a sword and is then unceremoniously dragged down stairs and stuffed into a coffin. (Karloff's pasty-faced appearance in the film was the result of heavy character makeup.)

As the drunken rogue Trumbull, Price has a truly uproarious time, making the most of the fabulously insulting dialogue given him by screenwriter Matheson, who was free to completely indulge his imagination with the story line. Price's verbal abuse of the somehow cuddly Lorre and his sparring matches with his unappreciated, buxom spouse, Amaryllis, played by Joyce Jameson, are great fun. With a sneering leer, he repeatedly offers to slip poison to his father-in-law, although comedy being the order of the day, he's the only one who kicks the bucket.

However, in the original script, ninety-two-year-old Amos Hinchley was the sole survivor; Felix, Amaryllis, Black, and Trumbull are all dispatched in the climactic melee. Surveying the corpses littering the house, the old man mutters, "Nothing ever happens around here. Day in, day out, the same old thing. No excitement, no variety. Now when I was young, we knew how to live. . . ." He heads up the stairs. "See you in the morning." In the filmed version, and in keeping with the overall humor of the picture, the bodies are merely "apparently dead," and all revive except the undeserving Trumbull. And, of course, the much-abused Mr. Black, who continues to inquire plaintively from within the coffin, "What place is this??"

A year after the initial release, in March 1965, AIP reissued the picture as *Graveside Story*, the title on the working script Vincent used during the filming. It was double-billed with the Ray Milland shocker *Panic in Year Zero!*, retitled *The End of the World*.

REVIEWS

Hollywood Reporter, December 26, 1963, James Powers

"It will be one of AIP's reliable moneymakers. . . . *Comedy of Terrors* is a smart film. . . . Without overstressing it, it is a good comedy, too. There is not much about timing and attack to be learned by such as Price, Lorre, Boris Karloff and Basil Rathbone. . . . Although these actors are all now in the character range, their names—particularly in combination—still have potency at the box office."

VINCENT PRICE

"I once went around and asked a priest and a rabbi and a child psychologist if they thought horror movies were bad for children, and not one of them had a bad thing to say about them. They said they were like a catharsis, like a fairy tale, and they have the effect of shifting the child's hate away from the parent and transferring it to the villain. . . . I personally think that the only way these pictures come off is to have a slight element of camp. But I don't think you can kid them to the point where they aren't frightening, because that's what people came to see them for. . . . Boris, Peter, Basil, all of us, we used to talk about what really scares people. One time, we were trying to figure it out, and Boris said, 'Cobwebs.' And I said, 'Oh, come on, Boris, cobwebs don't scare anybody!' And he said, 'They scare *men*. Men *hate* cobwebs!' And it's absolutely true, you know; they're *sticky*. Women don't mind them; they just think you're a bad

housekeeper. But men *hate* 'em! So we rigged up this huge cobweb, and I walked right into it, and this thing went right across my face, and the whole male audience went 'Yeeech!' "

65. QUEEN OF THE NILE

A MAX PRODUCTION
Previewed in New York City, January 15, 1964

CREDITS

Producer, Ottavio Poggi; *Director*, Fernando Cerchio; *Director, English-language version*, Richard McNamara; *Screenplay*, John Byrne, Ottavio Poggi, Fernando Cerchio; *Story*, Emerico Papp, Ottavio Poggi; Cinematogra-

Queen of the Nile

phy, Massimo Dallamano; *Art Directors*, Ernesto Kromberg, Amedeo Mellone; *Set Decorator*, Gianfranco Lowley; *Music*, Carlo Rustichelli; *Editor*, Renato Cinquini; *Costumes*, Giancarlo Bartolini Salimbeni; *Makeup*, Eligio Trani; *Running time*, 97 minutes; color and Super-Cinescope.

CAST

Jeanne Crain (*Nefertiti*); Vincent Price (*Benakon*); Edmund Purdom (*Tumos*); Amedeo Nazzari (*Amenophis IV*); Liana Orfei (*Merit*); Carlo d'Angelo, Clelia Matania, Alberto Farnese, Piero Palermini, Giulio Marchetti, Umberto Raho, Luigi Marturano, Raffaele Baldassarre, Romano Giomini, Adriano Vitale, Gino Talamo.

THE FILM

A few years after *The Ten Commandments*, Vincent Price was back in Egyptian tunic and sandals for *Queen of the Nile*, but the small-scale Italian quickie wasn't up (or down) to the standards of Steve Reeves's most enjoyable muscle epics.

"The night began in deceptive quiet, in Thebes, along the banks of the river Nile. On this night, two lovers planned to meet; a meeting that would affect their destiny, and the destiny of Egypt." Despite being "groomed for the temple," Tanit (Jeanne Crain) is in love with handsome sculptor Tumos (Edmund Purdom). They hope for the royal support of Tumos's boyhood friend Amenophis, who has been away at war and is now pharaoh. But Tanit is ceremonially transformed with a new name, Nefertiti, by the high priest, Benakon (Vincent Price), who reveals that she is, in fact, his daughter. He

has counterfeited a mandate from the god Amon which decrees that Nefertiti is destined to become a priestess and the bride of the pharaoh. Blackmailed by a threat on the life of Tumos, Nefertiti reluctantly marries Amenophis, although she and the sculptor meet periodically in the shadows to pledge their undying love for each other. When Amenophis begins to favor the "one god" Aton over his own priesthood, a religious uprising ensues; the powerful Benakon determines to eradicate not only the followers of Aton but the pharaoh as well. The high priest leads a revolt on the palace, and Amenophis takes his own life, but just as the throne room is stormed, Tumos arrives with reinforcements, and Benakon is killed. Nefertiti remains queen, with her lover by her side.

Vincent Price was attached to the project when Jeanne Crain was announced to star in December 1960; the two had costarred once before, in *Leave Her to Heaven*. *Queen of the Nile*'s love interest, Edmund Purdom, had previous experience in the locale; he was the hero of *The Egyptian* (1954).

Vincent cuts an impressive figure in his priest's robes, leopard-skin cape, black ceremonial braids, and dramatic kohl eye makeup. Production took place in Italy around March and April of 1961, and the film opened in Rome in June of the following year as *Nefertite, Regina del Nilo* with a running time of 106 minutes. It had no American theatrical distribution but was broadcast on television as *Queen of the Nile* (also the U.K. title) through Warner Bros./Seven Arts. The Italian video version runs 101 minutes; the U.S. video release is shorter (90 minutes), sequences are in a different order, and many of Price's scenes are different takes. Even the music track is not laid in the same way. The two versions, viewed together, offer an interesting opportunity to study slight variances in Price's blocking and delivery of dialogue, even in such a mediocre vehicle—for example, "In the name of Amon, attack!" gets a little more conviction in the Italian version.

REVIEWS

Films and Filming, July 1963

"Directed by Fernando Cerchio, whose work seems better with each import, this is an attractive film pictorially and it even improves as it goes along.... There is also Vincent Price, at first unrecognizable beneath his priest's robes, but still his cunning old evil self. A very respectable spectacular this, but more for the politician who likes to mix romance with affairs of high state. Give me musclemen and mythology."

Queen of the Nile "In the name of Amon, attack!"

190

The Last Man on Earth "Another day to live through . . . Is that all it has been since I inherited the world? Three years? Seems like a hundred million."

66. THE LAST MAN ON EARTH

AMERICAN INTERNATIONAL PICTURES
Released May 1964

CREDITS

Associated Producers, Inc. presentation in conjunction with Produzioni La Regina; *Producer*, Robert L. Lippert; *Associate Producer*, Harold E. Knox; *Director, U.S. version*, Sidney Salkow; *Director, Italian version*, Ubaldo Ragona; *Screenplay*, Logan Swanson [*pseudonym*, Richard Matheson], William P. Leicester; *Based on the novel* I Am Legend *by* Richard Matheson; *Cinematography*, Franco Delli Colli; *Art Director*, Giorgio Giovannini; *Music*, Paul Sawtell, Bert Shefter; *Orchestration*, Alfonso

D'Artega; *Editor*, Gene Ruggiero; *Makeup*, Piero Mecacci; *Running time*, 86 minutes; black and white.

CAST

Vincent Price (*Robert Morgan*); Franca Bettoia (*Ruth Collins*); Emma Danieli (*Virginia Morgan*); Giacomo Rossi-Stuart (*Ben Cortman*); Umberto Rau, Christi Courtland, Tony Corevi, Hector Ribotta.

THE FILM

"Do you dare imagine what it would be like to be . . . the last man on earth . . . or the last woman? Alive among the lifeless . . . alone among the crawling creatures of evil that make the night hideous with their inhuman craving!"

This strangely atmospheric picture was one of the few times in his film career that Vincent Price was pitted against a traditional "monster"—in this case, a populace

The Last Man on Earth With vampires

infected with a mysterious plague which has killed and transformed them into vampires. Apparently the only living creature immune to the disease, Price can only mark time in a desolate, mechanical existence, ferreting out and dispatching the undead. However, he doesn't know that some plague victims have discovered a way to survive without entirely losing their humanity; but because they fear the avenger who destroys their kind as well as the undead, they chase Price into a church and there murder *The Last Man on Earth*.

In August 1962 it was announced that Robert L. Lippert would go to Europe to scout talent to costar with an American cast for a Rome production of Richard Matheson's novel *I Am Legend*. Price's script was a revised final draft dated January 16, 1963; by March, American director Sidney Salkow was adding music, narration, and looping of the Italian cast members. Despite the noticeable dubbing, *The Last Man on Earth*'s documentarylike black-and-white photography, and a resigned, restrained, matter-of-fact performance from Price convincingly create the monotony of despair. The Italian title of the picture was a literal translation: *L'Ultimo Uomo Della Terra*.

Matheson's story was remade in 1971 as *The Omega Man* starring Charlton Heston.

REVIEWS

Hollywood Citizen News, May 7, 1964

"Director Sidney Salkow has kept the pace generally swift in this better than average science-fiction fantasy. The first hour is particularly engrossing. . . . Later, however, Salkow allows the movie, which showed promise of being a superior horror film, to peter out during the final reels. Vincent Price delivers his most restrained performance in some time."

Los Angeles Times, May 9, 1964

"Vincent Price continues his macabre film adventures as the star of a shocker called *The Last Man on Earth*. . . . His portrayal almost becomes a one-man show and this versatile actor makes the most of it."

VINCENT PRICE

("*Fangoria* Weekend of Horrors," personal appearance, 1990)

"Actually, I thought [*The Last Man on Earth*] wasn't too bad. . . . The problem was that it was supposed to be set in Los Angeles, and if there's a city in the world that doesn't look like Los Angeles, it's Rome! We would get up and drive out at five o'clock in the morning, to beat the police, and try to find something that didn't look like Rome. Rome has flat trees, ancient buildings—we had a terrible time! And I never was so cold in my life as I was in that picture. I had a driver, and I used to tip him a big sum to keep the car running so I could change my clothes in the backseat."

67. THE MASQUE OF THE RED DEATH

AMERICAN INTERNATIONAL PICTURES

Released June 24, 1964

CREDITS

Alta Vista Productions in association with Anglo-Amalgamated Productions; *Producer/Director*, Roger Corman; *Associate Producer*, George Willoughby; *Screenplay*, Charles Beaumont, R. Wright Campbell; *Based on the story by* Edgar Allan Poe *and* Poe's story "Hop-Frog"; *Cinematography*, Nicolas Roeg; *Production Designer*, Daniel Haller; *Art Director*, Robert Jones; *Set Dresser*, Colin Southcott; *Music*, David Lee; *Editor*, Ann Chegwidden; *Costume Supervisor*, Laura Nightingale;

Makeup, George Partleton; *Hairstyles*, Elsie Alder; *Choreography*, Jack Carter; *Special Effects*, George Blackwell; *Running time*, 90 minutes; color and Panavision.

CAST

Vincent Price (*Prince Prospero*); Hazel Court (*Juliana*); Jane Asher (*Francesca*); David Weston (*Gino*); Patrick Magee (*Alfredo*); Nigel Green (*Ludovico*); Skip Martin (*Hop Toad*); John Westbrook (*Man in Red*); Gaye Brown (*Señora Escobar*); Julian Burton (*Señor Veronese*); Doreen Dawn (*Anna-Marie*); Paul Whitsun-Jones (*Scarlatti*); Jean Lodge (*Scarlatti's Wife*); Verina Greenlaw (*Esmeralda*); Brian Hewlett (*Lampredi*); Harvey Hall (*Clistor*); Robert Brown (*Guard*); David Davies, Sarah Brackett.

THE FILM

The Masque of the Red Death, regarded as one of the best in the AIP Poe series, was the first of a number of films Vincent Price would shoot in England over the next decade. The rather surreal story is set in twelfth-century Italy. Philosopher Prince Prospero (Vincent Price), a worshiper of Satan, holds a macabre masked ball in the midst of a deadly plague. The hedonistic nobles believe that Prospero's castle walls will keep out not only the countryside's peasants but the lethal Red

The Masque of the Red Death As Prince Prospero

The Masque of the Red Death With Hazel Court and Jane Asher (*in bath*)

Death as well—until a mysterious uninvited guest in a hooded scarlet robe reveals his identity. The story has a different quality from the Poe scripts written by Richard Matheson; it is darker, more complicated, with a heavy accent on sadism. On arrival in London, director Roger Corman felt that "Chuck Beaumont's script was good, but wasn't exactly what I wanted," so he "brought on Bob Campbell to go over a final polish of the script." Campbell contributed the scenes derived from a lesser known Poe story "Hop Frog" and additional dialogue as well.

The rights to the picture were to become a source of controversy. In August 1958 producer Alex Gordon announced Edgar Allan Poe's *Mask of the Red Death* under his independent banner. But in February 1961, Roger Corman signed Charles Beaumont to script *Masque of the Red Death*. Star Vincent Price was connected first with the *Mask* project, which was to be scripted by writing team Gordon and Mildred Gordon; Price's wife, Mary Grant, was to be executive wardrobe designer. Alex Gordon was reported to be "overturing" director Ingmar Bergman (!) to direct that project in the summer of 1962. According to the trade papers, the picture was "set in the fourteenth century, the period in which Bergman specializes. Should Bergman accept the offer, Gordon would be willing to shift production to Europe if the direct prefers working there. If deal jells it would be Bergman's first U.S. film."

Nothing actually happened with either script until October 1963, when AIP formally announced *The Masque of the Red Death* starring Vincent Price and the film went before the cameras in London on November

The Masque of the Red Death
The Masque: Price with Jane Asher

The Masque of the Red Death "Continue with your merrymaking. Act according to your natures . . . You are small and insignificant, no more than a worm. Can you be a worm? . . . As for the rest of you, use your imaginations. Show me the lives and loves of the animals!"

18. James Nicholson and Sam Arkoff had a coproduction deal with Anglo-Amalgamated, which distributed AIP's Poe films in Britain, and so it was decided to make the next picture in the United Kingdom. The film was shot in Elstree, England, in five weeks, about one and a half times as long as Corman's normal shoot, which Corman expected would permit him to make "a bigger picture." Actually, the English crews (which Corman is quick to point out are just as capable as their American counterparts) worked much more slowly, so the end result was the same. Some of the enormous *Masque* sets were magnificent flats left over from previous pictures, including the recently completed *Becket*, and the picture's ambience owed much to Corman's inspiration from Ingmar Bergman's *The Seventh Seal*.

Price's working script is heavily annotated with comments, question marks, and dialogue changes, more so than almost any other of his extant screenplays. His comments, as usual, are perspicacious: "We shall have a masquerade. The wardrobes of the castle are yours to use," he added the line in the margins: "But I beg of you, even for the humor of it, not to wear red." He also queried: "Am I the Man in Red too? Shouldn't be." The comment was crossed out when he learned he was not dual cast. (Actor John Westbrook, who plays the part in a hood which hides his face, has a voice which sounds remarkably like Christopher Lee's.)

Prince Prospero is a complex character, a mixture of lordly sadist and sensual philosopher. Educated, refined, he holds his guests spellbound with his exotic views:

"The knowledge of terror is vouchsafed only to the precious few." Unlike the boorish nobleman Alfredo (Patrick Magee), Prospero takes his pleasure "not in corrupting" but "instructing." He is genuinely disgusted when Alfredo slaps the tiny dancer who has annoyed him; contemptuously, he bids his guests act out the antics of the animals they truly are. His cynicism is affected by the simple faith of the young Christian girl (Jane Asher) and she whom he planned to defile he ultimately entreats the Man in Red to spare. But the castle revelers succumb to the final dance, and Prospero's life is forfeit, too, together with the soul he had long ago surrendered.

In June 1964, just before *The Masque of the Red Death* was to be released, Alex Gordon Productions filed suit in Los Angeles superior court against AIP, Anglo-Amalgamated Film Distributors, Ltd., Vincent Price, and others, asking for an injunction against the release. The complaint for plagiarism alleged that *Masque* "copied and appropriated substantial parts and portions" of the Mildred and Gordon Gordon script *Mask of the Red Death*. Upon consideration, the judge denied the petition, "holding that any similarities beyond those contained in Poe's story from which both scripts were derived [and which was in public domain] may merely reflect standard ingredients for every Vincent Price horror performance, for which each script was designed."(!)

REVIEWS

Variety, June 24, 1964

"... Price is the very essence of evil, albeit charming when need be.... In Price is the perfect interpreter, too, of the Poe character, and he succeeds in creating an aura of terror...."

Hollywood Reporter, June 24, 1964, James Powers

"... not up to AIP's past films in this genre. It suffers from a thin, underdeveloped story.... There isn't the humor of some of AIP's other pictures of this sort, and there isn't the out-and-out horror of the other kind of film in this category.

Hollywood Citizen News, June 25, 1964

"... [T]he name of Vincent Price, who is rapidly becoming the leader of the modern day horror film, should carry the picture into the ranks of financial hits ..."

Newsweek, June 29, 1964

"... a stylish excursion into demonology. In Great Britain, in fact, it was so convincing that most of the Black Mass sequence has been excised by censors ..."

SAMUEL Z. ARKOFF

"When we moved to England, we argued out with Vincent the stipend he would get for his living expenses. We all had illusions that Vinnie was living like an Oriental potentate in some deluxe London penthouse. One day, I called him up and asked him if he wanted to look at a new script and give us an opinion. He said, 'Drop it off and we'll have a cup of coffee.' Driving into what seemed to me to be the worst part of London, and I'm looking around and thinking, Jesus Christ, Vincent's getting all this money a week. We come to the seediest block of all, and there's a run-down hotel; I can't believe it. I go inside; there's no elevator in the damn place. No room service. No elaborate suite, just one seedy room with no bathroom. I said, 'For God's sake, Vincent, why don't you even have a bathroom?' He said, 'Well, you really don't use a bathroom too much.' I thought he probably peed out the window or something. Anyway, it turns out, he was buying artwork with the expense money!"

HAZEL COURT

"Vincent loved London. We'd have a bite on the way home. But we did work *awfully* hard — it was fast and furious. It was wonderful. I was staying with my sister, and Vincent was at the Cadogan Hotel. He loved it; he had a particular room he liked on the corner. [When informed of Sam Arkoff's contention that Price stayed in "hovels" in London to save his per diems to buy art, she scoffs:] He stayed at Cadogan on Sloane Street! I suppose to Arkoff, who always stayed at the Ritz or somewhere, maybe it was a hovel! It's a nice hotel, turn of the century.... I liked Vincent best as a heavy. He had a sinister quality which he could portray which was quite marvelous and penetrating. He was a *sexy* man; he had an aura about him, a sensuality. The other side was fun, the comedies, but the dramatic qualities that he always brought to the movies should have been put to use in pictures that were *not* horror films."

68. THE TOMB OF LIGEIA

AMERICAN INTERNATIONAL PICTURES

Released January 20, 1965

CREDITS

Alta Vista Productions; *Producers*, Pat Green, Roger Corman; *Assistant Producer*, Paul Mayersberg; *Director*,

The Tomb of Ligeia As Verden Fell

Roger Corman; *Screenplay*, Robert Towne; *Based on the story by* Edgar Allan Poe; *Cinematography*, Arthur Grant; *Art Director*, Colin Southcott; *Music*, Kenneth V. Jones; *Played by* Sinfonia of London; *Editor*, Alfred Cox; *Wardrobe*, Mary Gibson; *Makeup*, George Blackler; *Special Effects*, Ted Samuels; *Cat Trainer*, John Holmes; *Running time*, 81 minutes; color and WideScreen Colorscope.

CAST

Vincent Price (*Verden Fell*); Elizabeth Shepherd (*Lady Ligeia/Lady Rowena Trevanion*); John Westbrook (*Christopher Gough*); Oliver Johnson (*Kenrick*); Derek Francis (*Lord Trevanion*); Richard Vernon (*Dr. Vivian*); Ronald Adam (*Parson*); Frank Thornton (*Peperel*); Denis Gilmore (*Livery Boy*); Penelope Lee.

THE FILM

The Tomb of Ligeia was the last in Roger Corman's eight-film Poe cycle; the director decided he "wanted a rest" from the series. The picture was a fitting swan song; expensive looking, with a more psychologically driven script, it benefited from superb location photography and a subdued performance by Vincent Price. As the Byronic figure of Verden Fell, Price is clean-shaven for the second time in the series, clad in black frock coat, flowing cravat, and crisp white blouse. A tousled black wig adds to the allure of the character; both Corman and Price considered the movie "to a large extent a love story as well as a horror film."

In an attempt to escape from the spell placed upon him by his late wife, Ligeia, Verden Fell woos and marries lookalike Lady Rowena, the blond beauty from the estate next door. Then she, too, begins to be haunted by the dead woman's spirit, and a mysterious black cat endangers her life and her very soul. Price dominates the picture early on but unaccountably takes a backseat to the cat's stalking of costar Elizabeth Shepherd. He is missed. The actual intricacies of Rowena's possession were extremely complicated; during the filming, even Corman had to refer to notes to figure out whether Shepherd, who played both women, was supposed to be Rowena or Ligeia.

Price arrived in London on June 25, 1964, and production began on June 29. The picture was known at various stages by a variety of titles, including *Ligeia, House at the End of the World, Last Tomb of Lygeia, Tomb of the Cat,* and *Edgar Allan Poe's Tomb of Ligeia.* John Westbrook essayed the rather thankless standard-hero role; he (and his voice) had been put to better use as "The Man in Red" in *The Masque of the Red Death.* The location scenes for *Ligeia* were shot in the village of Swaffham near the Deer Leap Woods of Norfolk, England; Rowena and Verden married in the nine-hundred-year-old Church of St. John.

Frequently asked by reporters if his horror pictures frightened him, Price once replied, "I was never frightened by the plots. The scariest thing was all those fires blazing! Symbolical cleansing by fire is a horror-tale tradition. I have been singed many times. . . . But then Roger's a fire fiend. He's a firebug." An inordinate number of Price's pictures end with everything going up in smoke—but supposedly just for make-believe. Price the actor had experienced a close call during *House of Wax* and he took a flaring torch right in the face on-camera in *Adventures of Captain Fabian*. An accident on the set of *Ligeia* was more serious. While filming the climactic scenes in which Verden wrestles with his demented (ex-)wife, the fire effects got away from the technicians, and the set was quickly blazing for real. As the crew got the flames under control with extinguishers, Price, his arms protectively around costar Shepherd, dashed for safety. "It was just one wall," Roger Corman insists innocently. "I had a whole *set* I was ready to burn up! I was envisioning a Great Fire!"

The Tomb of Ligeia opened in London in November 1964 and had its American premiere in Los Angeles simultaneously in forty theaters on January 20, 1965. There was a wonderful publicity stunt the night before the L.A. release. Price, Elsa Lanchester (the *Bride of Frankenstein*), Maila Nurmi, who gained fame as "Vampira," and *Mark of the Vampire*'s Carroll Borland were chauffeured in a motorcade down Hollywood Boulevard—preceded by a horse-drawn hearse—to "Hollywood's first 'Ghoul Premiere'" at the Pix Theatre. Front-of-house festivities included a contest to select Miss Ghoul and Mr. Gruesome; prizes included dinner for two in a haunted house, a five-pound bucket of quicksand, and a "do it yourself" guillotine.

The Tomb of Ligeia "Nor lie in death forever . . . " with John Westbrook

The Tomb of Ligeia Discussing a line with Roger Corman and script person

The Tomb of Ligeia Verden strangles Ligeia—or is it Rowena? With Elizabeth Shepherd

197

The Tomb of Ligeia Taking a (black) cat nap

The Tomb of Ligeia American Premiere: with Carroll Borland, Maila Nurmi ("Vampira"), Fred Stuthman ("Jeepers Creepers") and Elsa Lanchester

"After *Ligeia*, AIP wanted me to do another Poe picture," Roger Corman remembers, "and I said, 'That's it. It's time to move on.'"

In pace requiescat....

REVIEWS

London Times, December 3, 1964

"Here at last Mr. Corman has done what it always seemed he might be able sometime to do: make a film which could without absurdity be spoken of in the same breath as Cocteau's *Orphee* (1950).... Vincent Price has one of his best performances as the tormented Verden."

Los Angeles Times, January 22, 1965

"*Tomb of Ligeia* succeeds in two ways: as entertainment, it's a satisfying scare show; as art, it's a stylish rendition of Edgar Allan Poe in the unabashed Romantic tradition.... The fluid camerawork, first-rate color, sumptuous period sets and an impassioned performance from Vincent Price blend perfectly to bring a great Gothic tale of terror to life on the screen.

ELIZABETH SHEPHERD

(*Scarlet Street*, Summer 1992)

"Aside from having the most eloquent voice on earth, he has enormous personal charm and charisma. I loved working with Vincent Price; he made everything seem easy. He is such a superb actor, and extraordinarily generous.... He was very open to working on our scenes together, which certainly put me at ease. But I must say, for all of his intensity in the film, offscreen he had a wickedly witty sense of humor. He kept us laughing."

ROGER CORMAN

"Because *Ligeia* was the closest thing to a love story, I specifically cast a woman [opposite Price] who was mature enough to make the relationship believable yet young enough to be beautiful. Vincent wore a wig and a little more makeup than normal, and I used a little bit of diffusion on the lens in the close-ups. I didn't use much, but I felt a light amount would make him look younger, better, more romantic, but not be heavy enough to take away the masculinity.... I would say that Vincent gave *full* performances. He was not afraid to go all the way with an emotion, but I wouldn't call it hammy. He was very flexible. He could modify lines, improvise to a certain extent, come up with bits of business on his own. He was a great gentleman. He was one of the finest actors I've ever worked with."

69. TABOOS OF THE WORLD

AMERICAN INTERNATIONAL
PICTURES
Released April 1965

CREDITS

A Royal Film Production; *Producer*, Guido Giambartolomei; *Director*, Romolo Marcellini; *Screenplay*, Romolo Marcellini, Ugo Guerra; *Story*, Romolo Marcellini, Virgilio Lilli, Ettore Della Giovanna, L. De Marchi, Bonacina Lansmann; *Cinematography*, Rino Filippini; *Music*, Francesco Lavagnino, Armando Trovajoli; *Music/U.S. version*, Les Baxter; *Editor*, Otello Colangeli; *Running time*, 97 minutes; color; [Narrator U.S. version, Vincent Price].

THE FILM

In the wake of the success of *Mondo Cane*, a "pseudo-documentary" or "shockumentary," James Nicholson and Samuel Arkoff announced in August 1964 that AIP had acquired distribution rights to an Italian color documentary called *Tabu*, which was slated for U.S. release in October of that year. A lawsuit filed against AIP regarding distribution rights held up proceedings; it was not until March 1965 that Vincent Price completed his narration for the "shock-doc feature," which had been retitled *Taboos of the World*. Price made many changes in the script copy he was given; after the line "For those with queasy stomachs or weak nerves, I'd advise you to turn your eyes away," he penciled in a comment in his own style: "*I'm not looking.*"

According to the trades, *Taboos of the World* opened with "unusually large grosses across the country," and played at theaters and drive-ins on a double bill with Price's *War-Gods of the Deep*. The original film had been released in Rome in December 1963 as *I Tabu*, with a running time of 100 minutes.

REVIEWS

Box Office, April 19, 1965

". . . should have an irresistible appeal to American curiosity seekers . . . highlighted by the commentary of Vincent Price, sophisticate and connoisseur . . . [whose] narrating adds interest and humor. [E]ducational, if not enjoyable. . . . "

Los Angeles Times, July 30, 1965 Kevin Thomas

"Once again human suffering and ignorance are ex-ploited and exotic customs patronized to make a fast buck at the box office. As usual, the result is a large dose of grisly and pointless trash. . . . Perhaps the picture's greatest surprise is that it is being released by AIP, which takes such pains to explain how it keeps sex and even smoking out of its beach movies. Indeed, their great horror film star, Vincent Price . . . serves as narrator. He tries to bring wit, compassion and taste to this shapeless, shoddy footage but it is a task doomed from the outset."

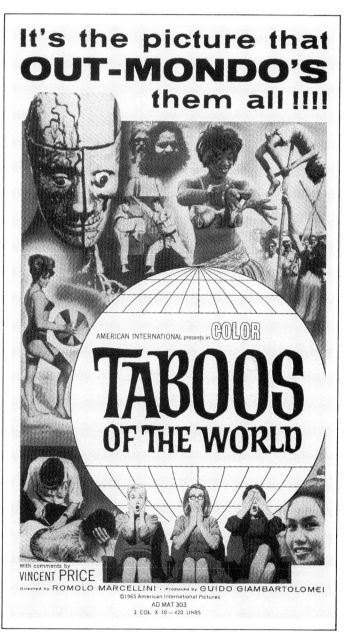

Taboos of the World

199

70. WAR-GODS OF THE DEEP

AMERICAN INTERNATIONAL
PICTURES

Released May 26, 1965

CREDITS

An Anglo-Amalgamated production; *Executive Producer,* George Willoughby; *Producer,* Daniel Haller; *Director,* Jacques Tourneur; *Screenplay,* Charles Bennett, Louis M. Heyward; *Suggested by the* Edgar Allan Poe *poem* "The City in the Sea"; *Additional Dialogue,* David Whitaker; *Cinematography,* Stephen Dade; *Director of Underwater Photography,* John Lamb; *Art Director,* Frank White; *Set Decorator,* Colin Southcott; *Music,* Stanley Black; *Editor,* Gordon Hales; *Wardrobe,* Ernie Farrer; *Makeup,* Geoff Rodway, W. T. Partleton; *Special Effects,* Frank George, Les Bowie; *Running time,* 85 minutes; color and WideScreen Colorscope.

CAST

Vincent Price (*Sir Hugh Tregathion, "the Captain"*); Tab Hunter (*Ben Harris*); Susan Hart (*Jill Tregellis*); David Tomlinson (*Harold Tufnell-Jones*); John Le Mesurier (*Rev. Jonathan Ives*); Henry Oscar (*Mumford*); Derek Newark (*Dan*); Roy Patrick (*Simon*); Anthony Selby (*George*); Michael Heyland (*Bill*); Steven Brooke (*Ted*); William Hurndell (*Tom*); Jim Spearman (*Jack*); Dennis Blake (*Harry*); Arthur Hewlett, Walter Sparrow, John Barrett (*Fishermen*); Barbara Bruce, Hilda Campbell Russell, Bart Allison, George Ricarde (*Guests*); Herbert the Rooster.

THE FILM

The ad campaign for *War-Gods of the Deep* promised "a fantastic journey to a lost empire one thousand fathoms beneath the sea!" In 1903, the eruption of a volcano off the coast of Cornwall endangers air pumps which supply the long-lost underwater city of Lyonesse. The "Captain" of its inhabitants sends ashore raiding parties of his slave-like gill-men in a desperate attempt to find a solution to the dilemma. When the Captain orders the kidnapping of a young woman (Susan Hart) who resembles his dead wife, her friends (Tab Hunter and David Tomlinson) come to her rescue and become unwilling participants in vain efforts to save the city.

War-Gods of the Deep As the Captain

AIP announced production of three upcoming Poe films—*City in the Sea, Descent Into the Maelstrom,* and *Ligeia*—in October 1963. It wasn't until the following August that Susan Hart was signed for the female lead of *City in the Sea* and production was scheduled at Pinewood Studios in England. Only on his November 3 arrival did Price receive a copy of the final revised script, and the picture began six days later. During the four-week shoot Price spent over 25,000 British pounds purchasing fine art for Sears, Roebuck in America. He also had a chance to socialize: a "midnight-'til-dawn welcome-to-London party" attended by Ringo Starr, American actor Martin Balsam, and BBC comedian Bob Monkhouse, among others was thrown for Price and Tab Hunter at a private home in posh St. John's Wood. The last shots Price filmed on *War-Gods* were the effects sequence during the eruption of the volcano in which the Captain struggles up through the underwater tunnels to the surface and reverts to his true age of over a century.

This tedious, unfunny adventure was another pseudo-entry in AIP's Poe series which owed next to nothing to the frequently maligned source. If anything, the ambience created is reminiscent of Jules Verne. (The Poe poem "The City in the Sea" was rendered in a Price voice-over.) Perhaps the fault lay with director Jacques Tourneur, who fared better helming *The Comedy of Terrors*; AIP's London executive Louis M. "Deke" Heyward remembers problems with the script. Curiously, the usually elegant and bright-eyed Price looks drawn, weary, and older than his years here, at one point even appearing to be at a loss for his line (although explanation of the ludicrous gill-men might have stuck in anyone's throat). Perhaps he was despondent because the Captain never got to change his clothes, spending the entire film and presumably the centuries in the same green frock coat.

The title change to *War-Gods of the Deep* was announced in February 1965, although it became *City Under the Sea* (not *City in the Sea*) for U.K. release. It was the "Yank" entry and the opening film at the Fourth International Trieste Science Fiction Fest in July.

REVIEWS

Hollywood Reporter, June 2, 1965

". . . not up to the other AIPers in this field. Dialogue is fumbling and except for the last half hour there isn't enough menace and suspense. . . . [A] touch of comedy has been attempted, and it isn't very good comedy. . . . Price seems a little subdued, playing with less than his customary flamboyance. The picture needs that kind of color."

Variety, June 16, 1965

"Bright and tight sci-fi exploitationer. Good performances, excellent direction and special effects. Marquee lure in Vincent Price and other stars."

Films and Filming, December 1965

"Jacques Tourneur gets the film off to a strong, atmospheric start . . . but the director is defeated by a script of considerable ineptitude. . . . Vincent Price has been given, in outline, a strong character for a change. Despite his size and commanding manner, he has most often been seen as a weak and haunted figure; in fact, even here, he has the familiar delusion that his wife, her memory preserved by an oil painting, has been reincarnated in the form of the heroine . . . a real disappointment, especially compared to the excellence of its director's last work, *Comedy of Terrors*."

LOUIS M. HEYWARD

"Vincent and I had a community of interests [art and cooking, among others] to keep us busy talking between takes. Occasionally, he would read a line, then look at me and say, 'Deke—dear, sweet Deke—you are screwing my career into the ground!' And indeed I may have [laughs]! But I appreciated his frankness about it. He was a delight to work with."

71. DR. GOLDFOOT AND THE BIKINI MACHINE

AMERICAN INTERNATIONAL PICTURES

Released November 1965

CREDITS

Producers, James H. Nicholson, Samuel Z. Arkoff; *Coproducer*, Anthony Carras; *Director*, Norman Taurog; *Screenplay*, Elwood Ullman, Robert Kaufman; *Story*, James Hartford; *Cinematography*, Sam Leavitt; *Art Director*, Daniel Haller; *Set Decorator*, Clarence Steensen; *Music*,

Dr. Goldfoot and the Bikini Machine The Bikini Machine at work

Les Baxter; *Title song by* Guy Hemric and Jerry Styner; *Performed by* the Supremes; *Wailing by* Al Simms; *Editors*, Ronald Sinclair, Fred Feitshans; *Costumes*, Richard Bruno; *Makeup*, Ted Coodley; *Hairstylist*, Ray Foreman; *Special Hairstyles for Miss Hart*, Jon Peters; *Choreography*, Jack Baker; *Main Title*, Art Clokey; *Running time*, 90 minutes; color and Panavision.

CAST

Vincent Price (*Dr. Goldfoot*); Frankie Avalon (*Craig Gamble*); Dwayne Hickman (*Todd Armstrong*); Susan Hart (*Diane*); Jack Mullaney (*Igor*); Fred Clark (*D. J. Pavney*); Alberta Nelson (*Reject No. 12*); Milton Frome (*Motorcycle Cop*); Hal Riddle (*News Vendor*); Kaye Elhardt (*Girl in Nightclub*); William Baskin (*Guard*); Vincent L. Barnett (*Janitor*); Joe Ploski (*Cook*); Introducing Sam and the Ape Men with Diane De Marco; Annette Funicello, Deborah Walley, Harvey Lembeck, Aron Kincaid (*Guest Stars*); Patti Chandler, Salli Sachse, Sue Hamilton, Marianne Gaba, Issa Asnal, Pam Rodgers, Sally Frei, Jan Watson, Mary Hughes, Luree Holmes, Laura Nicholson, China Lee, Deanna Lund, Leslie Summers, Kay Michaels, Arlene Charles (*Robots*); David Sharpe, Bob Harris, Ronnie Rondell, Carey Loftin, Louis Elias, Troy Melton, Mari Ann Leslie, Ronnie Dayton, Paul Stader, Harvey Parry, Jerry Summers, Fred Stromsoe.

THE FILM

Anyone who hasn't actually seen *Dr. Goldfoot and the Bikini Machine* may be surprised to learn that it's an enjoyable, unabashedly silly movie, with wonderful individual elements which combine to create an extremely successful whole. (Just look at the reviews!) The mysterious Dr. Goldfoot's plan is to ensnare a dozen of the world's wealthiest men in traps baited with beautiful bikini-clad robots which he gleefully manufactures in an electronics laboratory in his medieval castle. It may not be art, but it's enormous fun. Audiences loved it, and AIP laughed all the way to the bank.

At the end of February 1965 the trade papers were announcing that AIP had set *Dr. Goldfoot and the Sex Machine* for summer production. Vincent looks like he's having a ball in this picture. He has a natty wardrobe, including a gold smoking jacket and gold slippers; Goldfoot is a very elegant mad scientist, owing much to Price's developing "Poe persona." Judging by the notes in his script, many of the worst jokes were Vincent's suggestions. Female lead Susan Hart is considerably less robotic than she had been in *War-Gods of the Deep*—she's an entirely different, capable actress/comedienne in *Goldfoot*. (Maybe she was happier; she had married producer Jim Nicholson.) The picture is full of in-gags spoofing popular advertising of the time (a line about a razor bleeps the product name), and there are half a dozen cameos by other AIP stars. *Goldfoot* even spoofs the company's other films, utilizing the same setup from *Pit and the Pendulum*'s climax as well as clips from the actual picture. Unfortunately, the production was marred by a terrible accident: On August 17, 1965, grip Alva Roy Hicks, thirty-nine, was fatally injured during preparations at Producers Studio for the afternoon shoot. He fell thirty-five feet from a catwalk while relocating lights and died shortly after being taken to the hospital.

Goldfoot was American International's most expensive film to date, with a price tag of around $1 million. (The budget included higher production values and the San Francisco location.) AIP promoted the movie with a "Travelling Bikini Machine" which caught fire on the Hollywood freeway; the papers reported that "after installation of a new generator and a quick paint job to hide scorch marks," it was safely back on the road. *Variety* figured that AIP had a pretty safe bet with the picture based on the title alone, noting that it traded on "the always popular *Doctor*, the current fad for *Gold* as in *Goldfinger*, and the bestseller of all, *Sex*." In fact, the title went through several incarnations, becoming *Dr. Goldfoot and the Bikini Machine* during production, partially in order to minimize exhibitor trouble in placing ads in locales where broadcast and print media were "sensitive to certain words." For U.K. release, a couple of medicos actually named Goldfoot protested, and the film became *Dr. G. and the Bikini Machine*.

Ever in the vanguard of trends, American International set a movie/TV precedent on November 18, 1965, by airing a half-hour "teaser" show called *The Wild Weird*

Dr. Goldfoot and the Bikini Machine With Frankie Avalon (*lower left*), Jack Mullaney, and Dwayne Hickman

World of Dr. Goldfoot on the 150-station ABC network. It was produced by Louis M. Heyward, who coauthored the script with prolific *Batman* writer Stanley Ralph Ross. Price starred as Goldfoot with Harvey Lembeck as his assistant and Susan Hart played a robot named Diane. Heroic support came from Tommy Kirk, who wasn't in the film, and Aron Kincaid, who had only a cameo in the feature.

Not surprisingly, the last titles to roll on *Dr. Goldfoot and the Bikini Machine* are the words "The End?"

REVIEWS

Hollywood Citizen News, November 12, 1965

"Highly imaginative from start to finish, *The Bikini Machine* cleverly combines elements of sf, horror and beach films with a spoof on James Bond.... [It is] certain to make it a hit with teeners. And surprisingly enough, adults will enjoy it too. All players performed well, but Vincent Price, as always, stole the show."

Box Office, November 22, 1965

"By teaming Vincent Price, AIP's master-of-horror, with several of the company's 'Beach' boys and girls, notably the popular Frankie Avalon, who leaves the singing chores to the current warbling craze, the Supremes, and the lovely Susan Hart, in a thrill-packed but completely fantastic spoof of the James Bond films, AIP has a sure-fire boxoffice hit.... Price plays it straight to strong laugh returns. It's all grand fun."

Motion Picture Herald, November 24, 1965

"*Dr. Goldfoot and the Bikini Machine* is a money machine.... This addition to the AIP procession of box-office bonanzas is bigger, budget-wise, longer, running-time wise, and funnier, inch for inch, than any of its predecessors.... Price, as Dr. Goldfoot, has a ball for himself as the villainous scientist ... [and] is, as always, the anchor man of the picture.... Rating: "Excellent.""

72. DR. GOLDFOOT AND THE GIRL BOMBS

AMERICAN INTERNATIONAL PICTURES

Released November 1966

CREDITS

American International Productions/Italian International Film; *Producers*, Fulvio Lucisano, Louis M. Hey-

Dr. Goldfoot and the Girl Bombs

ward; *Director*, Mario Bava; *Screenplay*, Louis M. Heyward, Robert Kaufman, Castellano & Pipolo; *Story*, James Hartford; *Cinematography*, Antonio Rinaldi; *Art Direction*, Gastone Carsetti; *Music*, Les Baxter; *Title Song*, Guy Hemric, Jerry Styner; *Performed by* the Sloopys; *Editor*, Ronald Sinclair; *Production Supervisor*, Antonio Raffa; *Running time*, 85 minutes; color.

CAST

Vincent Price (*Dr. Goldfoot*); Fabian (*Bill Dexter*); Franco Franchi (*Franco*); Ciccio Ingrassia (*Ciccio*); Laura Antonelli (*Rosanna*); Moana Tahi (*Goldfoot's Assistant*); Francesco Mule (*Colonel Benson*).

THE FILM

"Meet the girls with the Thermo-Nuclear Navels!"

Dr. Goldfoot and the Bikini Machine had received wonderful reviews and did very well at the box office. Unfortunately, Dr. G's return to the screen was as disappointing a cinematic comeback as that of Dr. Phibes. The opening sequence of *Dr. Goldfoot and the Girl Bombs* is extremely promising—groovy music, fun clips from the first picture, and an engaging narration by Vincent Price—but the film quickly becomes a slapstick farce involving the distribution of gorgeous (robot) girls set to explode on contact with selected NATO generals. Working with Peking, Goldfoot will then instigate atomic war between America and Russia, leaving the Chinese to control the aftermath.

While in London in mid-December 1965, AIP announced two new coproductions with Anglo-Amalgamated—the proposed sequel to *Dr. Goldfoot and the Bikini Machine*, called at the time *Dr. Goldfoot and the S Bomb*, and *2267—The Sleeper Awakes*, which was never realized. The concept for the *Goldfoot* sequel came from producer Fulvio Lucisano, who knew that costars Ciccio and Franco, the Abbott and Costello of Italy, would guarantee a European hit with the picture. To complete financing, Lucisano brought in good friend Sam Arkoff

Dr. Goldfoot and the Girl Bombs Dr. G and his beautiful bombs

on the American end; Robert Kaufman and Louis M. Heyward, together and separately, tried to provide sensible rewrites on the screenplay. Receiving a copy of the *Goldfoot* screenplay from Arkoff in early March 1966, Price drafted back a note: "Thanks for the script which I like and hope doesn't get ruined in rewrite—hate bothering you but getting ready to go to Europe requires preparation and must make plane/hotel reservations. Could I know today when I'm needed there."

By March 25 production was under way in Rome on what was then being called *Dr. Goldfoot and the Love Bomb*. Director Mario Bava (who had a highly creative eye) may have been money in the bank in Italy, but he was the wrong director for the project and at the time of filming was preoccupied with marital problems.

In one scene, Price plays a dual role as the last surviving NATO commander, General Willis, with an eye patch and a pronounced stutter. After "st-t-t-t-udying" his "speech p-p-p-p-patterns," Dr. Goldfoot has a robot blow up the general ("But only give him half a charge—remember, we're indoors") and then impersonates him in order to take over control of NATO and the world. (Price once commented that director Bava made up much of the film as he went along and that he [Price] had to play the second part because another English-speaking actor couldn't be found on short notice!) Addressing a great deal of his dialogue directly to the camera, accompanied by sly glances and much smirking, Price is even called upon to wear a habit and pose as the mother superior of a girls' school, pitching his voice in a falsetto and draping a black veil coyly over his bearded face.

The Italian release titles were *Le Spie Vengono Dal Semifreddo* and *I Due Mafiosi Dell'F.B.I.*

REVIEWS

Los Angeles Herald Examiner, December 2, 1966

"*Girl Bombs* is so bad it taints the theatre popcorn."

Los Angeles Times, December 2, 1966 Kevin Thomas

"Each week brings a new James Bond takeoff that is even worse than the last. So it's meaningless to say that *Dr. Goldfoot and the Girl Bombs* hits rock bottom—though how a science fiction spy spoof could be lousier staggers the imagination. . . . In the title role, as before, Vincent Price seems to be having lots of fun—it's a pity he can't share it with us, but the bad dubbing and the stupid script make sure there's no chance of this."

SAMUEL Z. ARKOFF

"As for *Dr. Goldfoot and the Girl Bombs*, we fed several pictures to Vincent that, if times had been different, if horror pictures had been doing well, we probably wouldn't have made. Since we had him under contract, we had to use him.... AIP had Vincent for close to twenty-five years, and after a time, according to his contract, he could only do horror or sci-fi pictures exclusively for us. He couldn't do anything in that line for anyone else. He could do other pictures, but not horror pictures. And I had a big definition for horror pictures. If he slapped someone's face, that was a horror picture. It was a very complete definition! I don't know if Vincent enjoyed doing all those films; he certainly enjoyed doing some more than others. I don't remember his ever protesting, however. Even *House of a Thousand Dolls*. No, I really don't recall that. Vincent was a man who recognized obligations. I'm not saying he liked every one; I think there were a couple of times when we had some minor differences. But basically I never had any problems with Vincent, which is more than you can say about the bulk of actors and of course actresses today. He not only had talent, but he was a professional, which is also more than I can say for a lot of actors. And those are the qualities that make you appreciate a man like that. I mean, Vincent was the only actor who ever picked up a check!"

73. THE JACKALS

20th CENTURY-FOX

Released 1967

CREDITS

A Killarney Film Studios Production; *Executive Producer*, Hyman Kirstein; *Producer/Director*, Robert D. Webb; *Screenplay*, Lamar Trotti, Harold Medford; *From a story by* W. R. Burnett; *Cinematography*, David Millin; *Art Director*, Bert Aurik; *Music*, Bob Adams, Joe Kentridge; *Editor*, Peter Grossett; *Wardrobe*, Ruth St. Moritz; *Makeup*, William Bell; *Running time*, 105 minutes; color and Widescreen.

CAST

Vincent Price (*Oupa*); Diana Ivarson (*Willie*); Robert Gunner (*Roger "Stretch" Hawkins*); Bob Courtney (*Bandy*); Patrick Mynhardt (*Gotz*); Bill Brewer (*Stoffel*); John Whiteley (*Marico*); Gert Van Den Bergh (*the Drunk*); James White (*the Teller*).

THE FILM

The Jackals is a standard Western story reset in South Africa. It was a remake of 1948's *Yellow Sky* (set in an Arizona ghost town, with James Barton as the grandfa-

ther); in fact, the screenplay for both pictures was adapted by Lamar Trotti from a story by W. R. Burnett.

Five outlaws terrorize a grizzled miner (Vincent Price) and his scrappy, tomboy granddaughter, Willie (Diana Iverson), into surrendering the gold from their strike. When the girl and her "Oupa," her grandfather, are forced to split fifty-fifty with the bandits, the leader, Stretch (Robert Gunner), starts to go soft in the face of the old man's honor. Instead of revealing their predicament to the friendly native warriors whose suspicions have been raised, Oupa convinces them that the bullet in his leg was an accident and the five strangers are working the mine at his request. Eventually, Stretch turns against his former cronies when they plot a double-cross to take everything, and in the end, the good guys ride off into the sunset together.

The picture was announced as *The Scavengers*. The first-draft screenplay, titled *Yellow Sky* and written solely by Harold Medford, was dated July 1966. Filming began during the third week in September under American director Robert Webb; on the first page of his script, Price penned in "finished Oct 10th 1966."

The Jackals

205

The Jackals With Diana Ivarson and native warriors

Despite the setting—the Transvaal gold strike—this turn-of-the-century story has an inescapably contemporary feel, compounded by an appalling sound track which attempts to combine sixties cocktail piano music with native African instruments. Apart from the standard "leader with a heart of gold," none of the four outlaws manifests a separate character until so far into the movie that we've lost interest.

Vincent Price received sole star credit. Surprisingly, the quirky prospector is one of his nicest performances, certainly one of his most unusual. As portrayed by Price, Oupa sometimes seems a trifle demented; the script describes him as "a little touched in the head," and he resorts to a fair amount of "Gabby Hayes chuckling," which, after a while, begins to sound natural. Hair dyed white-blond, Price employs a drawling, southernesque accent and an uneducated dialect he would use again in *More Dead Than Alive*. But there is an honesty, a warmth and depth, about the crazy old man who drinks straight out of the bottle and keeps on his battered hat even when he goes to bed. Price has a lengthy speech explaining how he and his granddaughter came to discover their strike; it is delivered with a naturalness, a casual charm completely unlike the mannered affectations the Gothic/horror pictures required him to utilize.

Price did double duty on location in South Africa. Fox's director of publicity in Johannesburg wrote Price on the actor's return to Los Angeles that he was "more than grateful for your ambassadorial activities" and for "creating so much goodwill towards our industry and Fox in particular." Price also spent time looking at local art; some of the articles he wrote for his *New York Daily News/Chicago Tribune* syndicated column included material on African art and artists. He was quoted eloquently on the language of art which "transcends any barriers of color or race."

74. HOUSE OF A THOUSAND DOLLS

AMERICAN INTERNATIONAL PICTURES

Released November 8, 1967

CREDITS

Constantin Film/Hispamer Films; A Harry Alan Towers Production; *Executive Producer*, Louis M. Heyward; *Producer*, Harry Alan Towers; *Director*, Jeremy Summers; *Screenplay English version*, Peter Welbeck [*pseudonym*

Harry Alan Towers], *Screenplay Foreign version*, Carmen M. Roman; *Cinematography*, Manuel Merino; *Art Director*, Santiago Ontanon; *Music composed and conducted by* Charles Camilleri; *Title song by* Don Black, Mark London; *Performed by* Cliff Bennett and the Rebel Rousers; *Editor*, Allan Morrison; *Wardrobe*, Augustin Jiminez; *Makeup*, Mariano Garcia; *Hairdresser*, Pepita Rubio; *Running time*, 78 minutes; color and Techniscope.

CAST

Vincent Price (*Felix Manderville*); Martha Hyer (*Rebecca*); George Nader (*Stephen Armstrong*); Ann Smyrner (*Marie Armstrong*); Wolfgang Kieling (*Inspector Emil*); Sancho Gracia (*Fernando*); Maria Rohm (*Diane*); Luis Rivera (*Paul*); José Jaspe (*Ahmed*); Juan Olaguivel (*Salim*); Herbert Fuchs (*Abdu*); Yelena Samarina (*Madame Viera*); Diane Bond (*Liza*); Andrea Lascelles, Jill Echols, Kitty Swan, Ursula Janis, Loli Muñoz, Karin Skarreso, Monique Aime, Lara Lenti, Caroline Coon, Marisol, Sandra Petrelli, Françoise Fontages (*The Dolls*); Milo Quesada, Fernando Cebrián, Irene G. Caba.

THE FILM

Vincent Price reviewed the screenplay for *House of a Thousand Dolls* while in Johannesburg filming *The Jackals*. Afterward, he drafted a telegram to producer Harry

House of a Thousand Dolls With Martha Hyer

House of a Thousand Dolls As Felix Manderville

Alan Towers: "Script interesting—would prefer witholding final decision until return home early next week—will contact you immediately then—thanks and regards." The self-consciously titillating story of white slavery in modern Tangiers gave Price another opportunity to play a magician, abducting young women in his famous disappearing act on behalf of the mysterious King of Hearts for the exotic "House of Dolls."

AIP announced *House of a Thousand Dolls* on its current production program in November 1966. Hammer Films veteran Terence Fisher was slated to direct the film in Dublin and actually scouted locations there. (Price preserved a script called *Sax Rohmer's House of Dolls*, set in Victorian London and marked for production in Ireland, with the words "Vincent Price?" penciled in after the character name James Manderville. Other cast possibilities indicated in attached character breakdowns are Klaus Kinski and Rupert Davies.) The project was postponed until the spring of 1967 due to Fisher's illness. When at last filming got under way in March, it was in another country (Spain), with another director (Jeremy Summers), in a West German/Spanish coproduction which dubbed most of the cast. Vincent's script, a third revision titled *House of a Thousand Dolls*, is dated April 3, 1967, and has the actor's notations and comments throughout. Producer Towers had in fact written the screenplay under his customary pseudonym.

Price's role is really a supporting one, since most of the action involves the detective (George Nader) who is trying to track down the missing girls. Vincent displays suave affability in disarming audiences with casual patter while his blindfolded female accomplice "reads" their minds. However, *House of a Thousand Dolls* was a surprisingly exploitative picture, with several deaths and the bloody flogging of a manacled, bikini-clad woman. Price dies in this one, too, in a rather showy, several-story fall down an open staircase, his white-satin-lined cape billowing about him. But it turns out he isn't the King of Hearts, after all. The real villain is girlfriend Martha Hyer. (Did I spoil it for you?) Hyer also had an interest in art and owned a collection of French Impressionist paintings. Off the set, she and Price spent time together in the Prado. According to the actor: "What she and I didn't know was that they were making a dirty version of the film at the same time. Every day we'd have off, they'd make a dirty version. We went visiting on the set one day and there was everyone naked!"

The film was released in West Germany in December 1967 as *Das Haus Der Tausend Freuden*, with a ninety-minute running time; in Madrid in June 1968 as *La Casa de las Mil Muñecas*.

REVIEWS

Motion Picture Herald, November 15, 1967

"That mischievous team of Vincent Price and AIP have this time around given us a contemporary drama about white slavery.... For the most part, it is fun to watch the magnificently caped Price, cane in hand, carry on once more in his inimitable tongue-in-cheek style. With Price as its main selling point, and with proper exploitation, this could do nicely...."

Box Office, November 20, 1967

"AIP's latest acquisition from the international film market. This exploitation entry ... has an intriguing title which capitalizes on that best-seller which is soon to be a 20th Century-Fox release, *Valley of the Dolls*...."

Los Angeles Times, December 22, 1967, Kevin Thomas

"This tawdry tale benefits from the ... durably elegant presence of Price...."

75. WITCHFINDER GENERAL
(U.S. Title: Conqueror Worm)

AMERICAN INTERNATIONAL PICTURES
Released May 15, 1968

CREDITS

A Tigon British Film production; *Executive Producer*, Tony Tenser; *Producers*, Louis M. Heyward, Philip Waddilove, Arnold Miller; *Director*, Michael Reeves; *Screenplay*, Michael Reeves, Tom Baker; *Additional Scenes*, Louis M. Heyward; *Based on the book* Witchfinder General *by* Ronald Bassett; *Cinematography*, John Coquillon; *Art Director*, Jim Morahan; *Set Dressers*, Jimmy James, Andrew Low; *Music*, Paul Ferris; *Editor*, Howard Lanning; *Wardrobe*, Jill Thomson; *Makeup*, Dore Hamilton; *Hairdresser*, Henry Montsash; *Dubbing Editor*, Dennis Lanning; *Location Manager*, Ewan Pearson; *Special Effects*, Roger Dicken; *Running time*, 87 minutes; color.

CAST

Vincent Price (*Matthew Hopkins*); Ian Ogilvy (*Richard Marshall*); Rupert Davies (*John Lowes*); Hilary Dwyer (*Sara*); Robert Russell (*John Stearne*); Patrick Wymark (*Oliver Cromwell*); Wilfred Brambell (*Master Loach*); Nicky Henson (*Trooper Swallow*); Tony Selby (*Salter*); Bernard Kay (*Fisherman*); Godfrey James (*Webb*); Michael Beint (*Captain Gordon*); John Trenaman (*Trooper Harcourt*); Bill Maxwell (*Trooper Gifford*); Morris Jar [Paul Ferris] (*Paul*); Maggie Kimberley (*Elizabeth Clark*); Peter Haigh (*Lavenham Magistrate*); John Kidd (*Magistrate*); Hira Talfrey (*Hanged Woman*); Ann Tirard (*Old Woman*); Peter Thomas (*Farrier*); Edward Palmer (*Shepherd*); David Webb (*Jailer*); Paul Dawkins (*Farmer*); Lee Peters (*Infantry Sergeant*); David Lyell (*Foot Soldier*); Alf Joint (*Sentry*); Jack Lynn (*Brandeston Innkeeper*); Beaufoy Milton (*Priest*); Gillian Aldham, Margaret Nolan, Sally Douglas, Donna Reading, Tasma Brereton, Sandy Seager, Philip Waddilove, Derek Ware, Susi Field.

THE FILM

Devotees have tried to create in horror-film chronicles a "Michael Reeves Cult" of near mythic significance. The River Phoenix of the late sixties, Reeves died young

after directing only three feature films; *Witchfinder General* alone, as violent and grim as it is, merits analysis, and Vincent Price's contained performance remains a favorite of many fans. During England's *interregnum* (1649–60), Matthew Hopkins (Price) and his brutal assistant, Stearne (Robert Russell), roam the English countryside "doing God's work," putting a sadistic end to "witches" tortured into confession. When their efforts result in the hanging of a village priest (Rupert Davies) and the rape of his niece (Hilary Dwyer), the girl's soldier

Witchfinder General As the Witchfinder, Matthew Hopkins

Witchfinder General With Hilary Dwyer

Witchfinder General: The death of Matthew Hopkins

fiancé (Ian Ogilvy) vows revenge, eventually hacking the Witchfinder apart with an ax.

Tigon Productions owned the rights to Ronald Bassett's novel *Witchfinder General*, loosely based on an historical figure appointed by Parliament during the English Civil War to root out sorcery and witchcraft. They offered the project to the twenty-three-year-old Reeves, who had just wrapped *The Sorcerers*, one of Boris Karloff's last films. Reeves and collaborator Tom Baker (not the actor who was television's longest-lived "Dr. Who") wrote a screenplay which Reeves conceived as a vehicle for actor Donald Pleasence. When *Witchfinder* became a coproduction with AIP (in order to secure the balance of the financing), that company not surprisingly insisted on its contract star Vincent Price. In August 1967, AIP's "man in London," Louis M. Heyward, was selling Price on the project in an enthusiastic letter outlining the virtues of the project: location shooting ("up to your navel in antiques"), a well-constructed script, and Reeves, whom he believed Price would find "one of the most inspiring things that's happened to you as an actor in a long time. He is not only bright, imaginative, and well-organized, but he has the *cujones* to force a crew through to doing things the way he wants to. . . . He wafted off in a faerylike cloud of ecstasy when he heard we were casting you in the lead."

That's not exactly true. Reeves hadn't wanted Vincent in the picture; he was unhappy working with the actor and made no secret of his displeasure. He declined to extend Price the courtesy of meeting the plane when the American arrived in London. Shooting began on September 17, 1967. On his very first day of filming, Price took a fall from his horse and spent the afternoon in bed, bruised but unhurt. Reeves refused to visit the fifty-six-year-old actor, sending producer Philip Waddilove to ensure compliance with production insurance requirements. Apparently, Reeves felt that ignoring his star, or goading him into anger would result in a fiercer, stronger characterization. Price didn't complain; convincingly bewigged, imposing in heavy boots and white-satin-lined cape, he gave a performance which is generally described as "restrained." In the end, Price was apparently happy with what he did, but there is a fine line between "restraint" and "constraint."

Price always got on terrifically well with the crews on his pictures. "Deke" Heyward remembers one day on location at Bury St. Edmonds when the catering truck didn't arrive. Vincent had his driver take him into town. At his own expense, he bought fresh vegetables, pasta, and shrimp and took it all back to the kitchen of the hotel, where he whipped up lunch for sixty.

The original draft of the *Witchfinder* screenplay called for Price to experience yet another screen death by fire.

Witchfinder General With Robert Russell

After Hopkins's assistant, Stearne, has been killed with a large pike, the hero, who was then called Margery, rips the lance from the body and flings it at Hopkins, imbedding it in the Witchfinder's chest. Staggering back, he knocks over a flaming vat of coals, which sets fire to the dungeon. Margery rescues fiancée Sara as Hopkins is engulfed by the flames. However, production in the dungeon location, Orford Castle, was permitted only from 6:00 P.M. to midnight, and the final scene was scheduled for Price's very last night on the picture. Pyrotechnics were impossible under all circumstances, and the bludgeoning of Hopkins with an ax was substituted. Over thirty setups were shot in that single night.

Composer Paul Ferris, whose lyrical and atmospheric score for *Witchfinder* remains a favorite with fans, has a small role as the husband of the blond woman who is burned to death. His pseudonym, "Morris Jar," was an homage to colleague and Oscar winner Maurice Jarre. Because actor Robert Russell's speaking voice was deemed unsuitable to the bulk and rough character of Stearne, it was rerecorded by Jack Lynn, who played the Brandeston innkeeper in the film.

Witchfinder wrapped on November 13, 1967; Reeves's final cut was turned over to AIP in the spring of 1968.

The British press kit to U.K. exhibitors suggested they organize a "Local Witch Hunt in Your Town"(!). AIP elected to market the film in the United States as an entry in its Poe series and got Vincent Price to record a voice-over, inserted during the credits, of Poe's poem "The Conqueror Worm." The original title card, which read *Matthew Hopkins Witchfinder General*, was only partially changed, however, and American prints read *Matthew Hopkins Conqueror Worm*. For American video release, an image track was culled from the Continental version of the film, which included two scenes shot twice to include female nudity. Contractual or copyright problems resulted in the substitution of Ferris's evocative music with a synthesizer track by Kendall Schmidt. The British version of the video has an intact score but a highly censored print and of course the original title and no voice-over poem.

Chronically gracious, Vincent wrote Reeves a letter after he saw the film, calling it "a very impressive, moving and exciting picture. Congratulations! The contrasts of the superb scenery and the brutality, the action of the hero forces against the inexorable almost pedantic inaction of the forces of evil, make for a suspense I've rarely experienced. I'm sure you have a big success and a long feather in your cap. . . . So, my dear Michael, in spite of the fact that we didn't get along too well—mostly my fault, as I was physically and mentally indisposed at that particular moment of my life (public and private)—I do think you have made a very fine picture, and what's more, I liked what you gave me to do!"

Despite their antagonism, of which everyone must have been aware, Michael Reeves was set to direct Vincent Price in his next AIP assignment, *The Oblong Box*, but he withdrew from the project and was replaced by producer Gordon Hessler. And on February 11, 1969, Reeves was dead at age twenty-five. Always mercurial, he had become wildly volatile and was under doctors' care for anxiety and depression. Previously, for weeks, he had sat silently on the floor in a corner of Deke Heyward's office, cloaked in "an air of sweet desperation." The coroner's determination was death from a combination of medication and alcohol. It was an open verdict.

REVIEWS

London *Times Saturday Review*, May 11, 1968, John Russell Taylor

". . . [*Witchfinder General*] is quite happily and deliberately a horror film: that is to say, it has no particular pretensions to being anything else. . . . There is much in [it] which would win Michael Reeves an important reputation if he were dealing with some more pretentious, but fundamentally no more serious, subject. . . .

In particular, the unexpectedly downbeat ending of the film . . . has an all-out passion and intensity. . . . Mr. Reeves is no longer merely promising. He already has real achievements behind him: not merely good horror films, but good films, period."

London *Sunday Times*, May 12, 1968, Dilys Powell

". . . 17th century hanging, burning, raping, screaming, and Vincent Price as England's prize torture-overseer. Peculiarly nauseating."

Hollywood Citizen News, May 17, 1968

"A disgrace to the producers and scriptors, and a sad commentary on the art of filmmaking. . . . A film with such bestial brutality and orgiastic sadism, one wonders how it ever passed customs to be released in this country."

Box Office, May 27, 1968

"Fans of the horror film will be glad to know that Vincent Price is back to add another portrait to his gallery of arch-fiends . . . bathed in the most stomach-turning gore imaginable. . . . As an added attraction, there's a healthy dose of sex, a rarity in this kind of story, and even an artsy-craftsy intercourse bit lifted heavy-handedly from films of the *Hiroshima Mon Amour* variety."

Films and Filming, July 1968

". . . *Witchfinder General* has no explicit 'message,' but it does say something about the springs of despair, and it says it forcefully. It is a very frightening film. . . . Roles are reversed. . . . It is [Price as the Witchfinder] who wears the ruffled shirt and finely-stitched clothes. He rides on a white horse. And he wears white gloves, which he delicately adjusts, as his victims are given a trial by ducking. . . . Matthew Hopkins is the best of Price's recent performances. *Witchfinder General* is emphatically not a horror film; it is, however, a very horrifying one. . . ."

VINCENT PRICE

(*Classic Images*, June 1992)

"[Working with Michael Reeves] was a very sad experience. He was a boy who had a lot of problems, terrible problems which nobody seemed to know about. He was very unstable . . . difficult but brilliant. He was about twenty-seven when he committed suicide. He was very difficult to work with because he didn't know how to tell an actor what he wanted. It was sad. . . . All I can tell you is that he communicated the wrong way, and he rubbed everyone the wrong way. But we all knew he had a tremendous talent, so we tried to overlook it. We tried to do it our way and yet do what he wanted us to do. It's hard to explain, but he was a very difficult man to work with. . . . I remember he came up to me one time and said, 'Don't shake your head.' I said, 'I'm not shaking my head.' He responded, 'Well, your body is moving so that means you're shaking your head.' I mean, what can you say?"

76. MORE DEAD THAN ALIVE

UNITED ARTISTS
Released December 1968

CREDITS

Executive Producer, Aubrey Schenck; *Producer*, Hal Klein; *Director*, Robert Sparr; *Screenplay*, George Schenck; *Cinematography*, Jack Marquette; *Art Director*, J. Arthur Loel; *Set Decorator*, William L. Kuehl; *Music*, Philip Springer; *Editor*, John Schreyer; *Wardrobe*, Tye Oswald, Joyce Rogers; *Makeup*, Gary Liddiard; *Hairstyles*, Jean Burt Reilly; *Running time*, 101 minutes; color.

CAST

Clint Walker (*"Killer" Cain*); Vincent Price (*Dan Ruffalo*); Anne Francis (*Monica Alton*); Paul Hampton (*Billy Eager*); Mike Henry (*Luke Santee*); Craig Littler (*Karma*); Beverly Powers (*Sheree*); Clarke Gordon (*Carson*); William Woodson (*Warden*).

THE FILM

In November 1967 the trade papers reported that TV leading man Clint Walker had been signed to a two-picture, nonexclusive movie contract by producer Aubrey Schenck for which the first assignment would be *More Dead Than Alive*. Originally scheduled for January 1968, filming began in June.

More Dead Than Alive is a morality tale about the psychology of killing, the passing of the gun and the gunslinger from the Wild West. Despite a "twist" ending and R-rated violence, the merely workmanlike direction, the stolid Walker, and a ghastly music track reminiscent of Western series of the sixties combine to give the feature film more the feel of a made-for-TV movie.

"Killer" Cain's debt to society is paid after eighteen years in the Arizona Territory penitentiary (the same fortress set from the 1939 *Beau Geste*). Predictably, the only job the ex-con (Clint Walker) can find is as a trick shooter in a traveling "Shooting Show and Death Dis-

play" operated by Dan Ruffalo (Vincent Price). Cain displaces former star Billy Eager (Paul Hampton), a young man whose resentment of the notorious gunslinger borders on the psychopathic. Eventually, Billy cracks up; he brutally murders Ruffalo and steals the proceeds of the show before he is gunned down by an outlaw with a grudge against Cain. And, ironically, the reformed "Killer," who tries to settle down on a ranch with his artist-girlfriend (Anne Francis), is himself dispatched by a relative of one of his own victims of twenty years earlier.

Price is second-billed above the title as the silver-tongued frontier showman. He delivers his dialogue in a colloquial Western dialect interspersed with salty expressions: "Dammit all," "I'll bark what I damn well please!" and "Yer a *big* sonovabitch!" The wannabe sharpshooter Billy is dismissed with "You ain't *nuthin'*—just a little pissant." (*Bloodbath at the House of Death*, however, gets the award for most unamusing and gratuitous use of vulgarities.) Price's "Rufe" is a likable scalawag, a straightforward, canny man of business who convinces Cain to accept his past rather than fight it. That glib barker patter (including the traditional, "*Step* r-r-r-right up, ladies and gentlemen! *Hur*-ry, *hur*-ry, *hur*-ry!") rolls richly and persuasively from Price's lips. With infectious glee, he dresses up his new star: "Ev'rything's gonna be black! Hee-hee! Everything black but the silver! Look at that buscadero belt—ain't that snazzy, huh? It's just what a killer's supposed ta wear, ain't it?"

More Dead Than Alive has the distinction of affording Vincent Price his most spectacular death scene—far showier than any in his horror movies (yes, even gorier than *Witchfinder General*). Alone in his trailer, Rufe is pouring a whiskey when in stalks the jealous Billy, whom the showman replaced with the legendary "Killer." Goaded into creating a reputation of his own, Billy proceeds to pump Ruffalo full of lead, firing six bullets at close range. Price's demise—as he staggers back against the wall, jerking with each shot and slumping to the floor, wide-eyed and staring—is photographed with relish in slow motion. Special-effect "squib" explosions splatter blood several inches in the air, all the more impressive against the white of Price's loose shirt. A stupefyingly inappropriate music track makes the spectacle somehow even more macabre. (Sneaky VCR playback will detect that the sound-effects track was inaccurately laid in, and therefore Price seems to react to the first bullet just a second *before* it is fired.)

REVIEWS

Variety, December 18, 1968

"Good Western actioner. . . . Though burdened with several story loopholes and some confusing action se-

More Dead Than Alive As Dan Ruffalo

quences, the attempt to produce a programmer western with a number of offbeat elements has succeeded. . . . Vincent Price [is] surprisingly good in a change of pace part of an essentially kindhearted impresario. . . . There may be spectator reluctance at first in accepting Price as an uncouth Southern showman who speaks ungrammatically, but the vet horror star overcomes this. . . . No question but that film could do with less than its generous dose of blood and violence — except that there seems to be no other way for U.S. oatermakers to compete with their Italian counterparts. . . ."

Hollywood Citizen News, January 16, 1968

"Vincent Price has one of his scene-chewing specials as the carnival man and relishes it as much as you probably will."

Film TV Daily, May 14, 1969

"Vincent Price does a professional job. . . . A death scene with its use of slow motion is extremely vivid."

More Dead Than Alive With Clint Walker

77. THE TROUBLE WITH GIRLS

METRO-GOLDWYN-MAYER

Released May 1969

CREDITS

Producer, Lester Welch; *Associate Producer*, Wilson Mc-Carthy; *Director*, Peter Tewksbury; *Screenplay*, Arnold Peyser, Lois Peyser; *Story*, Mauri Grashin; *From the novel The Chautauqua by* Day Keene and Dwight Babcock; *Cinematography*, Jacques Marquette; *Art Directors*, George W. Davis, Edward Carfagno; *Set Decorators*, Henry Grace, Jack Mills; *Music*, Billy Strange; *Song "Clean Up Your Own Back Yard,"* Scott David, Billy Strange; *Editor*, George W. Brooks; *Costume Design*, Bill Thomas; *Makeup*, William Tuttle; *Hairstyles*, Mary Keats; *Choreography*, Jonathan Lucas; *Running time*, 104 minutes; color and Panavision.

CAST

Elvis Presley (*Walter Hale*); Marlyn Mason (*Charlene*); Nicole Jaffe (*Betty*); Sheree North (*Nita Bix*); Edward Andrews (*Johnny*); John Carradine (*Mr. Drewcolt*); Anissa Jones (*Carol*); Vincent Price (*Mr. Morality*); Joyce Van Patten (*Maude*); Pepe Brown (*Willy*); Dabney Coleman (*Harrison Wilby*); Bill Zuckert (*Mayor Gilchrist*); Pitt Herbert (*Mr. Perper*); Anthony Teague (*Clarence*); Med Flory (*Constable*); Robert Nichols (*Smith*); Helene Winston (*Olga Prchlik*); Kevin O'Neal (*Yale*); Frank Welker (*Rutgers*); John Rubinstein (*Princeton*); Chuck Briles (*Amherst*); Patsy Garrett (*Mrs. Gilchrist*); Linda Sue Risk (*Lily-Jeanne*); Charles P. Thompson (*Cabbie*); Hal James Pederson (*Soda Jerk*); Mike Wagner (*Chowderhead*); Brett Parker (*Iceman*); Duke Snider (*the Cranker*); Pacific Palisades High School Madrigals (*Choral Group*).

THE FILM

Price and Presley may seem an unlikely combination. Probably not many Vincent Price fans know he made a picture with the King—not King Karloff but Elvis the Pelvis. While not one of Presley's most memorable films, *The Trouble With Girls* does a fine job in re-creating a period and showcasing a bit of Americana—the medicine show.

Presley is the manager of the Chautauqua, a traveling tent exhibition of "silver-tongued orators and dazzling entertainers" which invades Radford Center, Iowa, for a week in 1927. Young and old are treated to lectures ("From Cannibalism to Culture"), demonstrations (French cooking), entertainment (stars of the Met), carnival rides, snow cones, and cotton candy. When the lead singer of the Bible Group comes down with laryngitis, Elvis gets a chance to do what he does best. (He also has a country solo at the denouement of the picture.) The plot becomes less frivolous when Sheree North is sincerely affected by a lecture on immorality by Mr. Morality (Vincent Price) and repudiates her married lover, Dabney Coleman. Coleman turns up dead, and a young Chautauqua employee is arrested, but Elvis persuades North to admit that she killed Coleman in self-defense.

Chautauqua was announced as a project in June 1959; at one time, Glenn Ford was slated to star. It was first associated with Elvis in 1961 and then, three years later, was reported to be a vehicle for Dick Van Dyke under another producer. In April 1968 it was back at M-G-M for Elvis, and filming began in the fall. Elvis and Col. Tom Parker sent Vincent Price a telegram care of M-G-M with "congratulations and best wishes on the start of *Chautauqua*." Sometime before release the title was changed to *The Trouble With Girls*, which had little to do with the plot but was easier to pronounce.

Actually, Price and the singer have no scenes together. Larger than life, in a dark pin-striped suit, wide-brimmed hat, and red-lined cape, Mr. Morality is a walking Bartlett's, finding a quotation for every occasion. Vincent Price's many years of experience on the lecture circuit gave him a real credibility at the lectern; his encouraging, optimistic speech is delivered straight and is quite stirring.

A lengthy memorandum to director Peter Tewksbury from producer Lester Welch, dated September 13, 1968, gives a great deal of insight into what they wanted from Price in his role and just how important they considered his contribution:

"Subject: Mr. Morality/*Chautauqua*—Mr. Morality in our film represents more than any character the dedication and high purpose of the outstanding and authentic Chautauqua lecturer as they actually were at the height of the Chautauqua movement in this country. For this reason, although there are moments of gentle, erudite humor for him to play, it is my feeling that he should be played with the greatest dignity, honesty and belief. Also because what he says during his lecture is solely responsible for causing the most important turn of our plot (i.e., by inspiring and converting Nita [Sheree North's character] to a new, fresh way of life) he must never be considered as or treated as a comedy character

The Trouble With Girls As Mr. Morality, with Nicole Jaffe and players

or buffoon. Also, more than any other performer in our unit, his lecture has great relevance to today's confused world, and it is quite exciting to be able to hear his words voiced to a contemporary film audience in the context of entertainment. They can well influence more than just Nita."

Wow! And you thought it was just a cameo.

REVIEWS

Variety, May 8, 1969

"Elvis Presley is lost in this one. . . . Title suggests a gay comedy but it's a mass of contrived melodramatics and uninteresting performances that do not jell into anything but program fare. . . ."

New York Times, December 11, 1969, Roger Greenspan

". . . a film that succeeds so amiably in its parts that the relative weakness of the whole doesn't matter too desperately."

Monthly Film Bulletin, January 1970

"Vincent Price makes an odd and quite appealing guest appearance.

78.   THE OBLONG BOX

AMERICAN INTERNATIONAL PICTURES

Released June 11, 1969

CREDITS

Executive Producer, Louis M. Heyward; *Producer/Director*, Gordon Hessler; *Associate Producer*, Pat Green; *Screenplay*, Lawrence Huntington; *Based on the story by* Edgar Allan Poe; *Additional Dialogue*, Christopher Wicking; *Cinematography*, John Coquillon; *Art Director*, George Provis; *Music*, Harry Robinson; *Music Conducted by* Philip Martell; *Editor*, Max Benedict; *Wardrobe*, Kay Gilbert; *Makeup*, Jimmy Evans; *Hairstyles*, Bobbie Smith; *Running title*, 91 minutes; color.

CAST

Vincent Price (*Julian Markham*); Christopher Lee (*Dr. Newhartt*); Rupert Davies (*Joshua Kemp*); Uta Levka (*Heidi*); Sally Geeson (*Sally Baxter*); Alister Williamson (*Sir Edward Markham*); Peter Arne (*Samuel Trench*); Hilary Dwyer (*Elizabeth*); Maxwell Shaw (*Tom Hackett*); Carl Rigg (*Mark Norton*); Harry Baird (*N'Galo*); Godfrey James (*Weller*); James Mellor (*Holt*); John Barrie (*Franklin*); Ivor Dean (*Hawthorne*); Danny Daniels (*Witch Doc-*

The Oblong Box With Hilary Dwyer

tor); Michael Balfour (*Ruddock*); Hira Talfrey (*Martha*); John Wentworth (*Parson*); Betty Woolfe (*Mrs. Hopkins*); Martin Terry (*Sailor*); Anne Clune, Jackie Noble, Ann Barrass, Jan Rossini (*Prostitutes*); Zeph Gladstone (*Trench's Girl*); Tara Fernando (*Gypsy Dancer*); Tony Thawnton (*Man in Tavern*); Anthony Bailey (*Talbot*); Richard Cornish (*Groom*); Colin Jeavons (*Doctor*); Andreas Melandrinos (*Baron*); Hedger Wallace (*Major*); Martin Wyldeck (*Constable*); Oh! Ogunde Dancers (*Africans*).

THE FILM

The Oblong Box is set in England in 1860. After Sir Edward Markham (Alister Williamson) is hideously mutilated by an African voodoo ritual, he is kept under lock and key back at the family estate by his brother Julian (Vincent Price), his unspeakable face hidden by a crimson hood. When Sir Edward finally escapes, he seeks revenge on those he feels betrayed him, especially his brother, for whom the hideous torture was actually intended as retribution for the horseback hit-and-run of a native child. Edward is eventually killed, but not before he passes the curse on to Julian, who will henceforth bear the same disfigurement. An early version of the script called for Price to play both Markham brothers.

On October 16, 1968, Vincent received a letter about *The Oblong Box* from producer "Deke" Heyward addressed "Dear Mother." It stated that the scriptwriter, Lawrence Huntington, was scheduled to direct: "I am certain you will get along with [him] quite well. He is bald. All of us are looking forward to the light and joy that accompanies your visits and hope we have another *Conqueror Worm* on our hands. I am keeping brandy warm and the birds cold until your arrival."

When Vincent arrived in London on November 12, the picture was slated to be directed by Michael Reeves, the *enfant terrible* behind *Witchfinder General*. Price's notes for activities on that day include "Costumes. Mike Reeves." (In fact, the unit list for the picture, which Vincent must have utilized, since the back of it is covered in notes and doodles, lists Reeves at the helm.) The next week was spent in costume fittings, a meal with friend Sam Jaffe (the highly regarded agent who would copro-

216

duce *Theater of Blood*), and visiting the British Museum and the National Gallery. The picture began filming on November 20. Apparently, however, Reeves was unhappy with the script and already "terribly sick," according to Gordon Hessler, who picked up the reins when Reeves bowed out before shooting any footage. Born in Germany of a Danish father and English mother, Hessler had worked in American TV on *Alfred Hitchcock Presents*. Once on board, Hessler hired friend Chris Wicking to contribute additional dialogue for Price, to give the exasperated star some kind of character to work with, and to create scenes in locations (like the busy tavern) which would increase production values. Although billed as another Edgar Allan Poe picture, the plot of *The Oblong*

Box was none of Poe's doing; the title only was borrowed from a story by the much-maligned author.

Hilary Dwyer, whom Vincent had raped in *Witchfinder General*, plays his attractive fiancée in this film. A year later, she would be cast as his daughter in another Hessler picture, *Cry of the Banshee*. Despite a young love interest, Vincent looks somewhat drawn in *The Oblong Box* (as he did in *War-Gods of the Deep*.) If it was a makeup problem, Christopher Lee, outfitted with an appalling silver Beatle wig, didn't fare much better. At any rate, no makeup artist (of the time) could have matched audience expectations of the horror behind Sir Edward's mask.

The Oblong Box is one of the few movies in which

The Oblong Box On the set with Christopher Lee

Vincent Price received sole billing over the title, and probably not one for which he appreciated the distinction.

REVIEWS

New York Times, July 24, 1969, A. H. Weiler

"All things considered, however, *The Oblong Box* (the coffin in this cheerless charade) might have been better left unopen."

Monthly Film Bulletin, July 1970

"[It] is firmly stamped with the vigour and assurance that one is coming to associate with the horror films of Gordon Hessler. . . . Vincent Price manages to suggest unnameable horrors as [the] tormented brother."

VINCENT PRICE

(*Films and Filming*, August 1969)

"I think I prefer the control of the studio [as opposed to location shooting]. Certainly for any kind of intimate scene. And besides you can usually work much faster, and so it's easier to preserve a continuity of emotion. The main trouble with location work, particularly in England, is that nobody is equipped for it; I mean, for example, they can't screen out the noise of airplanes. [Working on *The Oblong Box*] we had to complete a location fairly near Shepperton. Well, we must have only been ten feet from the end of Heathrow runway. At one point Gordon Hessler came up and said, 'Vincent, I don't want you to raise your voice in this scene.'. . . What could I say. 'But I can't hear a thing, and the poor man can't hear me.' And that's just dreadful because it means you have to dub, and to me dubbing is a disaster. But Gordon did a very good job with it, because he only took on the film a couple of days before we started shooting. . . . It's strange, but I think that when you're trying to make people believe, then it's terribly important for these films to have an element of 'make-believe' about them, and you can only get that inside the studio."

GORDON HESSLER

"We made it as imaginative as we could, given the material we had, given the three weeks we had to shoot it in. Because of its financial success, AIP gave me a contract for four pictures." [During filming, Hessler asked Price as a favor to take a meal with a Nigerian prince who was affiliated with the dance company taking part in the film and wanted to meet him.] "Instead of pouring out about all the films he'd done, like many actors, Vincent never talked once about himself. He only talked about African art and parts of Africa he'd been to. Amazing; it was a

revelation. I was staggered. That's the kind of person he was."

CHRISTOPHER LEE

"I remember very clearly when I first met Vincent. It was at Shepperton Studios. I was walking toward the restaurant to have lunch; obviously I'd been doing something on the film before he arrived. A car drew up, Vincent got out. He was probably staying at the Cadogan Hotel. He came over with a *great* big smile on his face, and we shook hands, and he said, 'Oh, I'm so happy that we're doing this picture together.' It wasn't until years and years later that I heard that Vincent had been told that I was very remote and very reserved and very difficult to talk to and had no sense of humor, all that sort of thing. So Vincent was obviously prepared for the *worst*, and I *like* to *think* he was agreeably surprised. . . . We only had one scene. I was lying on the floor, expiring in a welter of blood, gurgling away with my throat cut, trying to speak. And Vincent came in wearing a colossal cape which came right down to the floor, and he knelt down beside me for one of those ridiculous lines like 'Who did this to you?' or 'Where did they go?' He had to roll me over, and I remember after he delivered the line, this *sotto voce* remark: 'You're lying on my train.' [Asked if he was able to keep a straight face or if it broke him up:] I *think* it did the latter. And no *doubt* it was *intended* to!"

79. SPIRITS OF THE DEAD

LES FILMS MARCEAU-COCINOR AND PRODUZIONI EUROPÉE ASSOCIATE

*Distributed by American International Pictures
Released July 23, 1969*

CREDITS

Based on stories by Edgar Allan Poe; *Song:* "Ruby" *sung by* Ray Charles; *Narration,* Vincent Price; *Running time,* 117 minutes; color.

Metzengerstein

CREDITS

Director, Roger Vadim; *Screenplay,* Roger Vadim, Pascal Cousin, Clement Biddlewood; *Cinematography,* Claude Renoir; *Set Decorator,* Jean Andre; *Music,* Jean Prodrom-

Spirits of the Dead

ides; *Editor*, Helene Plemiannikov; *Costumes*, Jacques Fonteray.

CAST

Jane Fonda (*Countess Frederica*); Peter Fonda (*Baron Wilhelm*); Carla Marlier (*Claude*); Françoise Prevost (*Friend of Countess*); James Robertson-Justice (*Countess's Adviser*); Anny Duperey, Andreas Voutsinas (*Guests*); Philippe Lemaire (*Philippe*); Serge Marquand (*Hughes*); Audoin de Bardot (*Page*).

William Wilson

CREDITS

Director, Louis Malle; *Screenplay*, Louis Malle, Clement Biddlewood; *Dialogue*, Daniel Boulanger; *Cinematography*, Tonino Delli Colli; *Set Director*, Ghislain Uhry; *Art Director*, Carlo Leva; *Music*, Diego Masson; *Editors*, Franco Arcalli, Suzanne Baron; *Costumes*, Ghislain Uhry, Carlo Leva.

CAST

Brigitte Bardot (*Giuseppina*); Alain Christina (*Wilson*); Katia Christiana (*Young Girl*); Umberto D'Orsi (*Hans*); Daniele Vargas (*Professor*); Renzo Palmer (*Priest*).

Toby Dammit

CREDITS

Director, Federico Fellini; *Screenplay*, Federico Fellini, Bernardino Zapponi; *Cinematography*, Giuseppe Rotunno; *Set Director*, Piero Tosi; *Editor*, Ruggiero Mastroianni; *Music*, Nino Rota; *Costumes*, Piero Tosi; *Special Effects*, Joseph Natanson.

CAST

Terence Stamp (*Toby Dammit*); Salvo Randone (*Priest*); Fabrizio Angeli (*First Director*); Ernesto Colli (*Second Director*); Marina Yaru (*Child*); Anne Tonietti (*Television Commentator*); Alvardo Ward, Paul Cooper (*Interviewers*).

THE FILM

This anthology by several of the great European directors succeeded as neither an art film nor a horror film. Orson Welles was originally scheduled to contribute a segment as well, but even his input probably wouldn't have impressed critics, who generally panned the picture. Vincent Price's contribution consisted solely of the recitation of the first and last verses of the Poe poem "Spirits of the Dead," a voice-over lasting a total of twenty-seven seconds, which was added by AIP to the finished foreign film. *Spirits of the Dead* opened in Paris in June 1968 as *Histoires Extraordinaires* with a running time of 123 minutes. In Italy, it was called *Tre Passi nel Delirio*. English alternatives included *Tales of Mystery* and *Three Steps in Delirium*.

REVIEWS

Motion Picture Herald, July 23, 1969

"*Spirits of the Dead* is an ambitious attempt by three of Europe's most capable and respected directors . . . to wed the approach and techniques of art film to the horror-fantasy material of Edgar Allan Poe. Their success in this enterprise is difficult to estimate, since AIP, in picking up the American distribution rights, has apparently tried to tailor it to a less sophisticated shocker-exploitation audience. The three-part film, billed by AIP as "Edgar Allan Poe's ultimate orgy of evil and unbearable horror," is poorly dubbed into English, is interspersed with gloomy offscreen recitations by Vincent Price, and features a simpleminded voice-over narration for viewers who don't quite understand what's going on."

Hollywood Reporter, August 26, 1969, John Mahoney

". . . lacks the budget, polish, style, and solid terror of the best Roger Corman contributions to the Edgar Allan Poe series. . . ."

80. SCREAM AND SCREAM AGAIN

AMERICAN INTERNATIONAL PICTURES

Released February 11, 1970

CREDITS

Executive Producer, Louis M. Heyward; *Producers*, Max J. Rosenberg, Milton Subotsky; *Director*, Gordon Hessler; *Screenplay*, Christopher Wicking; *Based on the novel* **The Disorientated Man** *by* Peter Saxon; *Cinematography*, John Conquillon; *Art Director*, Don Mingaye; *Production Design*, Bill Constable; *Music*, David Whitaker; *Title Song by* Dominic King and Tim Hayes; *Song "When We Make Love" by* Dominic King; *Editor*, Peter Elliott; *Wardrobe Supervisor*, Evelyn Gibbs; *Makeup*, Jimmie Evans; *Hairstyles*, Betty Sherriff; *Running time*, 94 minutes; color.

Scream and Scream Again Cover of the movie tie-in paperback

Scream and Scream Again With Alfred Marks

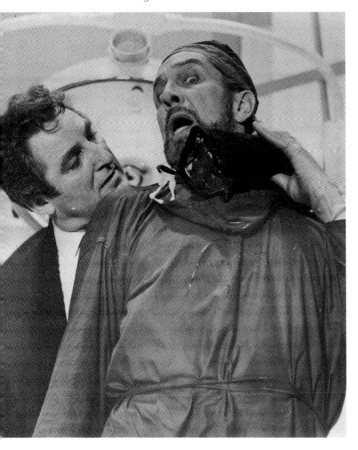

60c PAPERBACK LIBRARY 63-273

ONE DAY YOU'LL OPEN YOUR NEWSPAPER AND CHILL TO
THIS STORY OF MODERN WITCHCRAFT

SCREAM
AND
SCREAM
AGAIN

(Original title: The Disorientated Man)

The mutilated body of
a beautiful girl
begins a blood
orgy of supernatural horror.

PETER SAXON

SOON TO
BE AN
AMERICAN
INTERNATIONAL
MOTION
PICTURE

CAST

Vincent Price (*Dr. Browning*); Christopher Lee (*Fremont*); Peter Cushing (*Benedek*); Judy Huxtable (*Sylvia*); Alfred Marks (*Supt. Bellaver*); Michael Gothard (*Keith*); Anthony Newlands (*Ludwig*); Peter Sallis (*Schweitz*); David Lodge (*Detective Inspector Strickland*); Uta Levka (*Jane*); Christopher Matthews (*Dr. David Sorel*); Judi Bloom (*Helen Bradford*); Clifford Earl (*Det. Sgt. Jimmy Joyce*); Kenneth Benda (*Professor Kingsmill*); Marshall Jones (*Konratz*); Julian Holloway (*Griffin*); Edgar D. Davies (*Rogers*); Yutte Stensgaard (*Erika*); Lincoln Webb (*Wrestler*); Nigel Lambert (*Ken Sparten*); Steve Preston (*Fryer*); Lee Hudson (*Matron*); Leslie Ewin (*Tramp*); Kay Adrian (*Nurse*); Rosalind Elliot (*Valerie*); The Amen Corner.

THE FILM

Scream and Scream Again is a creepy contemporary science-fiction story, one of the few present-day horror pictures Vincent Price made. The story unfolds in a series of seemingly unrelated events—intrigue in a Fascist foreign government, bizarre serial killings in London, the medical experiments of a respected doctor—which are eventually linked to the machinations of a race of "composites," superbeings aiming at ultimate power.

Max Rosenberg and Milton Subotsky had the rights to the Peter Saxon novel for their Amicus Productions and brought the project to AIP, which announced "*Screamer,* a super-suspense horror mystery feature" for its 1969 production schedule. Gordon Hessler was signed to direct, and filming began in London in May. According to Hessler, the original script was written by producer Subotsky and was unplayable. Hessler was allowed to bring in Chris Wicking, who built up the political angle and gave the picture its perturbing vision of the future. The film is disturbing for that very reason;

221

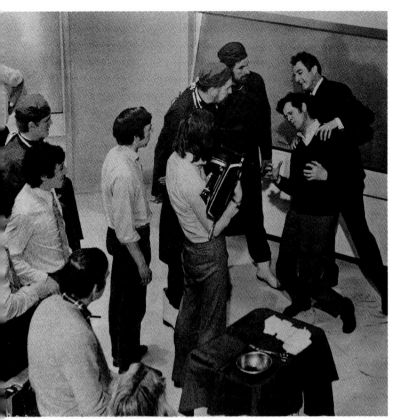

Scream and Scream Again Rehearsal: Christopher Matthews (*surgical gown, far left*) Price (*center*), VP's double, director Gordon Hessler (*victim*), Alfred Marks

its "realistic" violence, which includes rape, murder, political terrorism, and torture, has an uncomfortable air of credibility about it. Additionally, the plot is convoluted right up until (and after?) the end, when the unconnected events are tied together.

Audiences then and now can only feel cheated at the highly publicized teaming of Price with British horror stars Christopher Lee and Peter Cushing. Cushing's cameo consists of a single three-minute scene, and then he is murdered. In a larger role, Lee gives one of his more unaffected performances; like Price, after nearly an hour into the film he has made only one appearance. Ultimately, Price and Lee are together on-screen for exactly fifty seconds. Price, too, delivers a straightforward performance as a doctor/scientist, restrained but considerably more animated than he was in *Witchfinder General*, an indication of how natural he could be when literate dialogue gave him the opportunity. At the climax, Price's character, Dr. Browning, becomes a sympathetic figure, genuinely dedicated to "the good of humanity," horrified when he understands how thoroughly power can corrupt. He meets his end, dissolved in his own acidic "disposal tank"; the long-suffering Price actually

submerged himself in a horrible, bubbly yellow concoction which was so horrible that director Hessler can't even remember what it actually was.

REVIEWS

Hollywood Reporter, February 10, 1970

"AIP's *Scream and Scream Again* seems destined to a fairly profitable run.... It has the successful touch of the vampire, the scientist perfecting the perfect race of beings, dismemberings, some lovely nude bodies, and a continuous guessing game as to what's going on throughout its 94 minutes.... Though Cushing appears only in a single scene and Lee in slightly more, leaving Price to fully uphold the reputation of the three, the initial work will be done out front with the beckoning talons of the three pulling their fans to the box office...."

Variety, February 5, 1970

"... Price is once again effective as the rock generation's Boris Karloff, not a bad guy really but a misunderstood mad scientist a little ahead of his time.... Look for *Scream and Scream Again and Again*."

Los Angeles Times, February 21, 1970

"... a superb piece of contemporary horror, a science fiction tale possessed of a credibility infinitely more terrifying than any of the Gothic witchery of *Rosemary's Baby*.... Above all, it is a minor masterwork of style and suspense so unusual and so all-of-a-piece that it really can't be reviewed at length without spoiling its impact."

Films and Filming, April 1970

"This is one of those stories which begin as a series of unrelated incidents, and the audience has to wait patiently for the connecting link to become apparent. I forget at what point the sense of anticlimax first began—was it when Peter Cushing is polished off after only one short scene?—but by the end of the second half hour, it had gripped me mercilessly. The primary feeling about this enterprise is that no-one connected with it had any real idea in which direction it should go. Despite the presence of the three top names in the field of horror/SF, they are all grievously wasted...."

Motion Picture Herald, August 4, 1970

"... offers surprisingly more sophistication and style than its title would have you expect.... Vincent Price lends his familiar dignity and class to the production...."

GORDON HESSLER

"I don't think Vincent really liked the films I made. He didn't understand *Scream and Scream Again*. He didn't know what he was doing in the picture; he thought it was all weird and strange. Nobody understood it. Deke Heyward didn't understand it. But it took off with the young people; it was an enormous success. . . . Vincent liked the more traditional horror film, Gothic, classical. [But it never] affected his performance; he was *into* it, whatever he was doing. He was wonderful to work with. . . . The shame is that Vincent wasn't put in the right parts; that's the thing. If he hadn't been in horror pictures, he'd be a *fantastic* actor; playing big character parts, where he could really get into the depth of the role. . . ."

CHRISTOPHER LEE

"Dreadful title. Of course we both had a good laugh over that. Vincent and I wondered, 'Do you think this is going to be the audience's reaction?' We spent our entire *lives* laughing—laughing, laughing, laughing, laughing. . . . We were all aliens if I remember rightly. I couldn't work it out at all. I suddenly appear in that operating theater and force Vincent backwards into this *noisome* vat—which certainly wasn't anything to do with bodily fluids, I can tell you *that*. And Vincent slowly walked back and, with immense dignity, stepped into it and lowered himself *right* under the surface. I thought at the time, My *God*, that must have been a *horrible* thing to have to do; I'm glad it wasn't *me*! But he did it, of course, being the great professional that he was. One of us certainly said—it was inevitable, I don't remember which of us said it—'God, it looks as if someone's had an *accident*!' "

81. CRY OF THE BANSHEE

AMERICAN INTERNATIONAL PICTURES
Released July 22, 1970

CREDITS

Executive Producer, Louis M. Heyward; *Producer/Director*, Gordon Hessler; *Associate Producer*, Clifford Parkes; *Screenplay*, Tim Kelly, Christopher Wicking; *Story*, Tim Kelly; *Cinematography*, John Coquillon; *Art Director*, George Provis; *Set Dresser*, Scott Simon; *Music*, Les Baxter; *Editor*, Oswald Hafenrichter; *Wardrobe*, Dora Lloyd; *Makeup*, Tom Smith, Betty Blattner; *Hairstyles*, Ivy Emmerton; *Running time*, 87 minutes; color.

CAST

THE ESTABLISHMENT: Vincent Price (*Lord Edward Whitman*); Essy Persson (*Lady Patricia*); Hilary Dwyer (*Maureen*); Carl Rigg (*Harry Whitman*); Stephen Chase (*Sean*); Marshall Jones (*Father Tom*); Andrew McCullock (*Bully Boy*); Michael Elphick (*Burke*); Pamela Moiseiwitsch (*Maid*); Joyce Mandre, Robert Hutton, Peter Forest, Guy Deghy (*Party Guests*). WITCHES: Elisabeth Bergner (*Oona*); Patrick Mower (*Roderick*); Pamela Farbrother (*Margaret*); Quinn O'Hara (*Maggie*); Jane Deady (*Naked Girl*). VILLAGERS: Hugh Griffith (*Mickey*); Janet Rossini (*Bess*); Sally Geeson (*Sarah*); Godfrey James (*Head Villager*); Gertan Klauber (*Tavern Keeper*); Peter Benson (*Brander*); Terry Martin (*Rider*); Richard Everett (*Timothy*); Louis Selwyn (*Apprentice*); Mickey Baker (*Rider*); Carol Desmond (*Girl*); Ann Barrass, Nancy Meckler, Hugh Portnow, Stephen Rea, Maurice Colbourne, Dinah Stabb, Tony Sibbald, Neil Johnston, Rowan Wylie, Tim Thomas, Ron Sahwek, Maya Roth, Philly Howell, Guy Pierce.

THE FILM

Cry of the Banshee was the last of Vincent Price's period horrors. Price plays a sixteenth-century magistrate dedicated to rooting out witches (having had plenty of experience in *Witchfinder General*). When the local commune is attacked by nonbelievers, Oona, the witch priestess, curses Lord Edward Whitman—"his flesh, his blood, his wife, his children and his house"—which about covers it. She conjures Satan to send an avenger who arrives in the guise of a disheveled groom by day, a throat-slashing evil spirit by night, and dispatches the family one by one.

AIP acquired the rights to Tim Kelly's screenplay in January 1969, but filming didn't begin until around the first week in October. Director Hessler again brought in Chris Wicking to clean up the script; their idea to shoot in Scotland was prevented by budgetary restrictions. Instead, *Banshee* was shot largely on location in England, at Grim's Dyke House at Old Reading, once the home of Sir Arthur Sullivan's lyricist, Sir W. S. Gilbert. The costumes had originally been made up for the lush historical drama *Anne of the Thousand Days*. Acclaimed Austrian actress Elisabeth Bergner, who had played Shakespeare on-screen opposite Laurence Olivier, came out of retirement to play the witch/priestess. Her name was misspelled "Elizabeth" in the credits.

Vincent Price has few moments in which to explore the character of the hedonistic patriarch Lord Edward.

Cry of the Banshee As Lord Edward Whitman

Cry of the Banshee With Andrew McCullock (*left rear*), Carl Rigg (*foreground*), Marshall Jones, and Hilary Dwyer

Despite director Hessler's penchant for pushing limits, the film is somehow coy. There's an air of incest throughout the Whitman family, but it's not very sexy; the satanic cult worship isn't spooky at all. The usually reliable Les Baxter contributed a modernized score which was completely incongruous. (Music written for the first cut in England by Wilfred Joseph was replaced by AIP execs when the film came back to the States for final approval.)

For publicity purposes, *Cry of the Banshee* was promoted as Vincent Price's 100th film. The wrap party was a costume affair to celebrate; the two-hundred attendees included cast members from *Scream and Scream Again*.

REVIEWS

Variety, July 30, 1970

"... Vincent Price is again the medieval evil ... [and] it is a measure of Price's image that he can enjoin a banquet room full of guests, 'Drink, dance, be merry!' and the line comes out ominous. ... [The production creates] a very believable look of the Middle Ages, with ... outdoor scenes particularly having the rich earthy red and brown hues of early Dutch paintings ...."

Hollywood Reporter, July 31, 1970

"... [*Banshee*] is probably the weakest of the AIP horror features. ..."

Box Office, August 10, 1970

"One of the better in the long, long line of Price-Poe-AIP British horror films . . . ."

Los Angeles Times, September 18, 1970

"It is a tale of remorseless terror, worthy of Edgar Allan Poe himself. A doggedly resourceful film company (AIP) relentlessly flogs a generic workhorse, deploying weary actors to skitter through the castles and meadows of the British Isles, baring breasts and flogging one another with brushes dipped in panchromatic blood. . . . A phrase, a verse, is cribbed from Poe, tacked on the film's main title and sprinkled into the ads. The tormented poet takes the rap again. Insidious . . ."

82. THE ABOMINABLE DR. PHIBES

AMERICAN INTERNATIONAL PICTURES

Released May 18, 1971

CREDITS

Executive Producers, James H. Nicholson, Samuel Z. Arkoff; *Producers*, Louis M. Heyward, Ronald S. Dunas; *Director*, Robert Fuest; *Screenplay*, James Whiton, Wil-

The Abominable Dr. Phibes As Dr. Anton Phibes

The Abominable Dr. Phibes With Joseph Cotten

liam Goldstein; *Cinematography*, Norman Warwick; *Production Designer*, Brian Eatwell; *Art Director*, Bernard Reeves; *Music*, Basil Kirchin *in association with* Jack Nathan; *Editor*, Tristram Cones; *Wardrobe Supervisor*, Elsa Fennell; *Makeup*, Trevor Crole-Rees; *Hairdresser*, Bernadette Ibbetson; *Special Effects*, George Blackwell; *Running time*, 93 minutes; color.

CAST

THE PROTAGONISTS: Vincent Price (*Dr. Anton Phibes*); Joseph Cotten (*Dr. Vesalius*). THE GIRL: Virginia North (*Vulnavia*). THE VICTIMS: Terry-Thomas (*Dr. Longstreet*); Sean Bury (*Lem Vesalius*); Susan Travers (*Nurse Allen*); David Hutcheson (*Dr. Hedgepath*); Edward Burnham (*Dr. Dunwoody*); Alex Scott (*Dr. Hargreaves*); Peter Gilmore (*Dr. Kitaj*); Maurice Kaufmann (*Dr. Whitcombe*). THE LAW: Peter Jeffrey (*Detective Inspector Trout*); Derek Godfrey (*Crow*); Norman Jones (*Sergeant Schenley*); John Cater (*Waverley*); Alan Zipson (*1st Police Official*); Dallas Adams (*2nd Police Official*); James Grout (*Sergeant*); Alister Williamson (*1st Policeman*); Thomas Heathcote (*2nd Policeman*); Ian Marter (*3rd Policeman*); Julian Grant (*4th Policeman*). INTER-

The Abominable Dr. Phibes With Virginia North

226

The Abominable Dr. Phibes Dance rehearsal: Price (*left, arm raised, in dark greasepaint to black out face*), choreographer Suzanne France and Virginia North

ESTED PARTIES: Hugh Griffith (*Rabbi*); Aubrey Woods (*Goldsmith*); John Laurie (*Darrow*); Barbara Keogh (*Mrs. Frawley*); Charles Farrell (*Chauffeur*); Graveyard Attendant (*John Franklyn*); Walter Horsbrugh (*Ross, the Butler*). Singer of "Dark Town Strutters Ball," Paul Frees; Singer of "One for My Baby," Scott Peters.

THE FILM

"Anton Phibes is a self-made man. He lusts synthetically, drinks hydraulically and plans nine diabolical murders for your entertainment."

The Abominable Dr. Phibes is one of those films in which it all came together—an ingenious script, witty production design, perfectly complementary musical score, snappy editing and pace, and, above all, a lead character who is clever, loyal, tragic, and dead.

Anton Phibes is horribly mutilated in a car crash when he races to the side of his critically ill wife. The burned body of the chauffeur is mistaken for Phibes's own; over

The Abominable Dr. Phibes "Because, when the acid reaches him, he will have a face—like *mine!*

the next few years the doctor of theology and musicology secretly reconstructs his shattered body and devises a suitable revenge. He dispatches the London surgical team he holds responsible for his wife's death according to the biblical plagues visited upon the pharaoh: the curses of boils, bats, frogs, blood, rats, hail, the beast, locusts, the death of the first born, and finally, darkness. Set in 1929, the basic premise of the story would be resurrected for Price's contemporary seventies picture *Theater of Blood*—a misunderstood artist, presumed dead, enacts revenge on a group of people whom he holds responsible for a great wrong. With the aid of a trusted female companion, he murders them ritualistically. The law is always one step behind him, and only the head of the group survives. And at the end our hero goes on to his just reward.

There is truly nobility in Dr. Phibes's single-minded devotion to vengeance. For all the humor in his pantomime, Price brings out the drama in a title character who is somehow majestic and elegant despite his fate. Required to deliver all his lines in a recording studio, Price creates a brilliant vocal effect for a man who used his "knowledge of music and acoustics to re-create" his voice, even to occasionally having trouble pronouncing more difficult words, such as "anesthetized" and "attributed." "[Playing in the Corman films] had to be larger than life. Baroque—not just Gothic but baroque. It's tremendous fun to play, it's so wild. Now Phibes is an entirely different thing. Phibes is all inside, seething and boiling, and you can't do too much of that because movies are too facial, so it all has to be sublimated. I have to do a lot with my eyes and hands."

As Phibes's nemesis, Vesalius, the head of the surgical team, Joseph Cotten is just as classy a figure as Price. (The two had met in 1938 as tousle-haired young stage stars with Orson Welles's Mercury Theatre.) The enigma of Phibes's mute assistant, Vulnavia, is an unspoiled vision; her communication with Phibes transcends speech. In the quirkiness of the smaller roles, there's the same uniquely English fruitiness found in James Whale's *Bride of Frankenstein*. Even the credits are clever—under an instrumental version of "Over the Rainbow" (not written in 1929!), the characters are divided up into the Girl, the Protagonists, the Victims, the Law, and Interested Parties. And at the end, after the final bell of the music score has tolled, there's that inimitable Vincent Price chuckle.

Preliminary crew announcements for *The Curse of Dr. Pibe* appeared in the spring of 1970; Robert Fuest, fresh from AIP's remake of *Wuthering Heights*, was signed to direct. "Bob Fuest was one of the best directors I ever worked with," Price commented later, "because he was making *mad* films and he was a *mad* man!" By September, Vincent Price had been cast in the title role of what was now called *Dr. Phibes*, set to roll in London in late October. Goldstein and Whiton's original script varied from the final filmed version; while essentially the same story, important plot elements and character names are quite different. One scene was described as taking place in the prestigious Victoria and Albert Museum, in which was to be displayed "a very realistic replica of an extremely fiendish man, à la Jack the Ripper." Vincent penciled a note into the script margin: "Tussaud's surely?"

Another change involved the moving scene in which Phibes recites poetry seated at his wife's dressing table while black-and-white slides of her are projected above him. (Actress Caroline Munro (*The Golden Voyage of Sinbad*) is uncredited as Victoria, appearing in the pictures and Phibes's final "tomb for two.") Instead of slides, the original script called for the display of framed photographs including shots of Phibes himself, "obviously several years younger, with Victoria, gaily holding champagne glasses in a toast to a third man in the photograph, F. Scott Fitzgerald . . . Victoria doing a charleston on a table at some wild party, while Phibes applauds with the then Prince of Wales . . . Phibes and Victoria dressed for a masquerade ball as Napoleon and Josephine." Presenting the audience with even a representation of a preaccident Phibes would have been as unsettling as having Vulnavia speak.

Price's final working script was titled *The Curse of Doctor Phibes* and dated October 30, 1970. The picture began shooting on November 9 with an eight-week schedule. AIP concocted an even bigger publicity campaign than the one for *Cry of the Banshee* to promote *Dr. Phibes* as Vincent's 100th feature film. It wasn't, either—no matter how you count 'em. But it made for good copy, and Price, ever amenable, went along with the story. The world premiere was held at the Pacific Pantages Theatre on Hollywood Boulevard—a black-tie event in the style of a 1930s Hollywood gala, with a classic-car cavalcade and over a hundred stars in attendance to honor Price. The evening, which benefited Variety Clubs International's Boys Clubs in East Los Angeles, was broadcast live on Steve Allen's TV show. Mayor Samuel Yorty declared "Hollywood Salutes Vincent Price Week." Virginia North flew in from London and was escorted by Paul Frees. Jim Nicholson was also there, but partner Sam Arkoff was in London preparing for the production of *The Return of Dr. Phibes*.

The original ad art spoofed the current popular film *Love Story* and its campaign: "Love means never having to say you're sorry." Unfortunately, confused audiences didn't know what kind of a picture to expect from "Love means never having to say you're ugly," so the promotion had to be redesigned with a serious "horror-style" tag line: "He came back from the dead for revenge! An open coffin, an empty grave, and nine doomed men!" The picture was both reviewed and released under two titles: *Dr. Phibes* and *The Abominable Dr. Phibes*.

REVIEWS

Los Angeles Free Press, May 1971

"If the Phantom of the Opera had a dead wife whom he loved with the passion of *Love Story* and made up a shopping list like Adrian Messenger . . . he'd be Vincent Price as Dr. Phibes and he'd be in a better movie than any of the above. . . ."

Chicago Today, May 1971

"It's scary, stylish, wildly funny and a menace to nail biters in the suspense department . . . Price has never been better. His performance is actually touching at times. I can hardly wait to see it again."

VINCENT PRICE

(*The Guardian* [London], August 18, 1973)

"*Phibes* was something I had to take very seriously when I was doing it so that it would come out funny. All the same, it was just agony for me because my face was covered with plastic, and I giggle and laugh the whole time, day and night, and the makeup man and I were practically married because the makeup kept dissolving and he had to patch me up every five minutes."

WILLIAM GOLDSTEIN

"The idea came to me in a dream. I began a collaboration with Mr. Whiton, a high school chum from New York, on *The Fingers of Dr. Phibes*. It caught on very quickly at AIP, and within six months after they had the first look, they were in preproduction. They picked it up with the idea that there would be a series—we were told in the beginning perhaps five pictures. . . . *Phibes* is a love story. That's its great strength. Orpheus—love beyond the grave, that purest of loves. Phibes is not a common murderer. He considers himself the Death Geometer to the Universe. He wishes only to return to the Eden that he knew with his wife. When that's thwarted, there is a price to pay, a price which is commensurate [with the enormity of the crime], but always in his inimitable style. . . . We were hired to do the sequel, but the AIP story editor [Robert Blees] was working on a parallel script [with director Robert Fuest], and that was the script that they used. It was bad luck."

83. DR. PHIBES RISES AGAIN

AMERICAN INTERNATIONAL PICTURES
Released July 1972

CREDITS

Executive Producers, James H. Nicholson, Samuel Z. Arkoff; *Producer*, Louis M. Heyward; *Director*, Robert Fuest; *Screenplay*, Robert Blees, Robert Fuest; *Based on characters created by* James Whiton and William Goldstein; *Cinematography*, Alex Thomson; *Production Design*, Brian Eatwell; *Music*, John Gale; *Editor*, Tristram Cones; *Wardrobe*, Ivy Baker; *Makeup*, Trevor Crole-Rees; *Running time*, 89 minutes; color.

CAST

Vincent Price (*Dr. Anton Phibes*); Robert Quarry (*Darius Biederbeck*); Valli Kemp (*Vulnavia*); Fiona Lewis (*Diana Biederbeck*); Peter Cushing (*Captain*); Beryl Reid (*Mrs. Ambrose*); Terry-Thomas (*Lombardo*); Hugh Griffith (*Ambrose*); Peter Jeffrey (*Inspector Trout*); John Cater (*Waverly*); Gerald Sim (*Hackett*); John Thaw (*Shavers*); Keith Buckley (*Stuart*); Lewis Flander (*Baker*); Milton Reid (*Manservant*).

THE FILM

"The coffin hasn't been built that can hold him!" boasted the ad campaign for *Dr. Phibes Rises Again*. Most fans felt Dr. Phibes shoulda stayed put, since this confusing, effete sequel was an unworthy vehicle for him.

With the reversal of the embalming process which brought on the final curse of darkness at the end of *The Abominable Dr. Phibes*, Anton Phibes journeys to Egypt to search for the ancient River of Life, which will enable him to restore his beloved Victoria. Robert Quarry is called upon to be rude and generally unlikable as Phibes's 150-year-old nemesis, Biederbeck, who seeks the same secret in order to prolong his own existence. Members of Biederbeck's archaeological team meet considerably less elegant demises than those devised for the first picture; at the end, Biederbeck loses his bid for eternity and dies watching Phibes and Victoria punt down the river to the truly immortal strains of "Over the Rainbow."

Dr. Phibes Rises Again was filmed in London and on

Dr. Phibes Rises Again With Valli Kemp

location in a desert in Spain in December 1971 through January 1972. The original Vulnavia, Virginia North, reportedly was pregnant and was replaced by Miss Australia of 1970, model Valli Kemp. Describing the scene in which Phibes extols "If music be the food of love, play on!" and stuffs grapes into her mouth, she relates: "[Vincent] then gets another grape and shoves that in my mouth, so I have two grapes in my mouth and I daren't swallow them because if I did, I'd burst out laughing. Then he picks up a pineapple and goes to put that in my mouth as well, but then he shakes his head when he realizes it's too big, the pineapple that is, and he puts it down. That is all in the film, and it's hysterical, as it is complete improvisation."

In April, while the film negative was being cut, Price received dupe segments and a guide track, together with the text of new lines, for postsynching. Some dubbing was necessary due to the usual vagaries in filmmaking; however, additional changes were required in order to clarify story points muddled in the script. There were numerous pages of revisions, and Price's text has question marks beside many lines. Instructed to keep as close as possible to the guide track, the actor recorded the material at Ryder Sound Studios in Hollywood.

Rises Again apparently was makeup artist Trevor Crole-Rees's swan song; after thirty-eight years in the industry, he left the business to run an English country pub. In a March 1972 letter to Vincent, he talked about the film after Price had wrapped his scenes: "The last few weeks of the Phibes dragged. . . . Quarry took the old age makeup very well and it stopped him talking for a while—however he was very pleased with the rough cut he saw and I think he learnt a lot from the film." In a personal appearance at a fantasy film festival in England, Robert Fuest remembered: "In makeup, [Robert Quarry] used to sing Gershwin . . . and Vincent Price looked around the corner and Quarry said, 'Didn't know I was a singer, did you, Vincent?' And Vincent said, 'Well, I knew you weren't a f——ing actor!'"

Unfortunately, Vincent's vocal rendition of "Over the Rainbow," which was specified in the script to run under the credits in the feature film, was excised from the video version. There are also discrepancies about the title of the picture—some one-sheet posters placed an exclamation mark after the word *Again!*

REVIEWS

Hollywood Reporter, July 19, 1972, Ron Pennington

"Overall this sequel is even better than the original and should meet with good reception. . . . Vincent Price again brings life to Doctor Phibes in what is one of his

Dr. Phibes Rises Again With Robert Quarry (*left*) and "Clockwork Wizard"

231

most perfect horror villains in his long list of evil-doers. . . ."

Los Angeles Herald Examiner, August 12, 1972

"The sequel is not as neat as the original, but it still rates high in the squirm and chuckle market. . . . [Phibes is] played by Vincent Price with perfectly timed relish. . . ."

SAMUEL Z. ARKOFF

"We looked the field over [for a star for AIP's horror series], and frankly, the people we felt could do it didn't have the stature. Vincent was really the only one we felt had the strength, the breadth. First place, physically he was a dominating man. He also had a dominating voice. He also played all kinds of roles. Vincent really had everything; he could play anything. He could play Shakespeare. He'd been in some big pictures. There was a magic to Vincent's name. Of all the horror kings, if you call them that, he was the grandest. He played it that way; Vincent liked playing it bigger than life. That bigger-than-life quality, that's the one quality a real horror star—any star—needs to have. When you were with Vincent Price, you knew you were with someone who was *important*."

Dr. Phibes Rises Again Dr. Phibes and Vulnavia amid the rubble of his mansion in Maldine Square

232

84. THEATER OF BLOOD

UNITED ARTISTS

Released April 1973

CREDITS

Executive Producers, Gustave Berne, Sam Jaffe; *Producers*, John Kohn, Stanley Mann; *Director*, Douglas Hickox; *Screenplay*, Anthony Greville-Bell; *Based on an original idea by* Stanley Mann, John Kohn; *Cinematography*, Wolfgang Suschitsky; *Production Designer*, Michael Seymour; *Set Decorator*, Ann Molo; *Music*, Michael J. Lewis; *Editor*, Malcolm Cooke; *Costume Designer*, Michael Baldwin; *Makeup*, George Blackler; *Hairdresser*, Pearl Tipaldi; *Stunts* arranged by Terry York; *Special Effects*, John Stears; *Choreographer of Meths Drinkers*, Tutte Lemkow; *Running time*, 104 minutes; color.

Theater of Blood As Edward Kendal Sheridan Lionheart

CAST

Vincent Price (*Edward Lionheart*); Diana Rigg (*Edwina Lionheart*); Ian Hendry (*Peregrine Devlin*); Harry Andrews (*Trevor Dickman*); Coral Browne (*Miss Chloe Moon*); Robert Coote (*Oliver Larding*); Jack Hawkins (*Solomon Psaltery*); Michael Hordern (*George Maxwell*); Arthur Lowe (*Horace Sprout*); Robert Morley (*Meredith Merridew*); Dennis Price (*Hector Snipe*); Milo O'Shea (*Inspector Boot*); Eric Sykes (*Sergeant Dogge*); Madeline Smith (*Rosemary*); Diana Dors (*Maisie Psaltery*); Joan Hickson (*Mrs. Sprout*); Renee Asherson (*Mrs. Maxwell*); Bunny Reed, Peter Thornton (*Policemen*); Charles Sinnickson (*Vicar*); Brigid Erin Bates (*Agnes the Maid*); Tony Calvin (*Police Photographer*); Tutte Lemkow, Stan-

Theater of Blood The Critics (*from left*): Renee Asherson, Charles Sinnickson, Jack Hawkins, Robert Morley, Ian Hendry, Madeline Smith, Harry Andrews, Coral Browne, Robert Coote, Arthur Lowe

Theater of Blood With Diana Rigg

ley Bates, Eric Francis, Sally Gilmore, John Gilpin, Joyce Graeme, Jack Maguire, Declan Mulholland (*Meths Drinkers*).

THE FILM

Theater of Blood is not merely a horror movie; it's a stylish, handsome, witty black comedy and a tour-de-force for Vincent Price. It boasts an irresistible premise, one of the all-time inspired ensemble casts, first-rate production values, and can be argued as the *magnum opus* of Price's film career.

One by one, London's most critical theater critics are being murdered: stabbed by a maniacal mob, removed of a pound of flesh (the heart), skewered by a spear, dragged by a horse, etc. The methods of death are straight out of Shakespeare; in fact, they're directly related to the final season of the Bard presented by the renowned Edward Lionheart, who committed suicide when he was denied the 1970 Critics Circle Award for Best Actor. But "Lionheart is immortal! He can never be slain! Never, *never!*" And with the aid of his dutiful, equally demented daughter (Diana Rigg), the great tragedian carries out the revenge every thespian who has ever trod the boards has been *dying* to exact.

Principal filming for *Theater of Blood* began on July 10, 1972, and wrapped on August 17. It was the tenth film Vincent Price made in Britain since 1964 and marked the

234

horror debut of director Douglas Hickox, who cut his teeth with black comedy on *Entertaining Mr. Sloane* (1970). An amazing group of some of Britain's top character actors was assembled; Hickox insisted, "The cast of our film is so good that all I had to do as the director was open the dressing-room doors and let the camera roll!"

Among that cast was the highly talented and unique Coral Browne, who, ironically, had turned down the film twice. " 'No, *no*, I can't be doing that, one of those *scary* pictures with Vincent *Price*—don't be *ridiculous*,' " she recalled was her initial reaction. "And then Bob Morley phoned up and said, 'We haven't been together since *The Man Who Came to Dinner* [onstage in 1941]. *I'll* do the *Theater of Blood* if you'll be in the *Theater of Blood*.' And then Jack Hawkins phoned up and said, 'If you and Bob are going to be in it, I'll be in it, too.' Then Michael Hordern did exactly the same thing, and before you knew it, we had a cast—a very, very, very, very, very good cast." In deference to Vincent's image, he and Coral always insisted that they first met in a graveyard, when the critics gather to bury the first of their comrades dispatched by the vengeful Lionheart. (According to the shooting schedule, this may actually have been true.) As the gravedigger, Price was kitted up in muddy Wellies, sleeves rolled up, a battered hat on his head, face smeared

Theater of Blood "Meredith Merridew, this is your dish!"

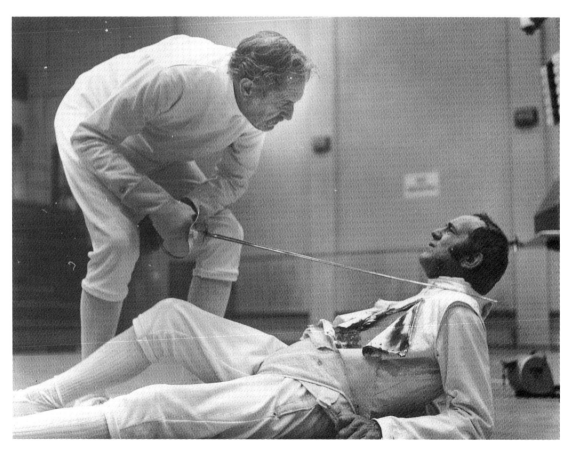

Theater of Blood
With Ian Hendry

235

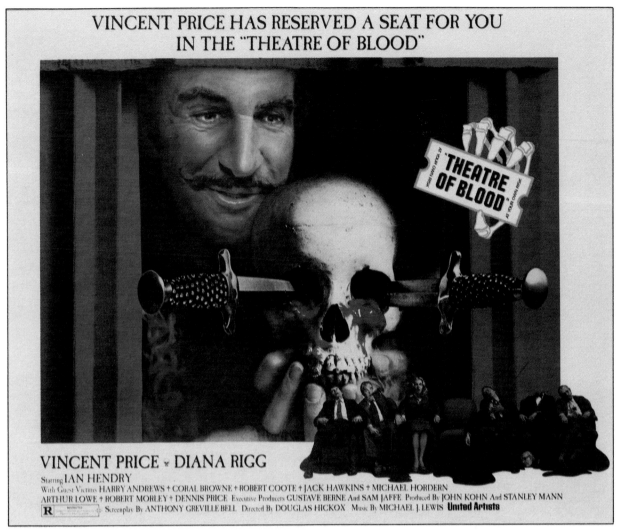

Theater of Blood Half-sheet poster

with grime. The elegant Miss Browne eyed him askance: "And I thought, 'Oh, this *man*, oh, this dirty-looking old creature,' and took absolutely no notice a'tol." But coexecutive producer and longtime friend Sam Jaffe remembers that the two artists were quickly "*very* friendly."

Theater of Blood exploited some fabulous locations. Empty for fourteen years, the Putney Hippodrome in southwest London, built in 1906, was transformed into Lionheart's Burbage Theatre. The awesome fencing sequence between Price and Ian Hendry was shot in the gymnasium of the American School in London. Coral Browne scheduled her final shampoo, set, pedicure in the basement of the trendy salon of Robert Fielding in Knightsbridge's Brompton Road. (The camp hairdresser, Butch, surely one of Vincent Price's most memorable characters, was unimaginatively named Fernando in the original script.) For Lionheart's suicide attempt the production had to obtain permission from the Port of Lon-

don Authority to drop a weighted dummy, wearing full evening dress and red-lined cape, over the side of the balcony of Alembic House. (Interestingly, the original script called for Lionheart to have a visibly twisted neck, maimed in the fall.) And for the flamboyant actor's actual demise in the burning theater, stuntman Peter Brace made the rooftop leap under the direction of stunt adviser Terry York.

Makeup artist George Blackler had worked on *Tomb of Ligeia* and later would create the face of Dr. Death for *Madhouse*; he and director Hickox wanted Lionheart's disguises to look as if they had been applied by the actor himself from an old theatrical kit. The picture's superb, Oscar-caliber score by young Welsh composer Michael J. Lewis was hauntingly passionate and ghoulishly cheeky, as the scintillating screenplay required. Even Lionheart's admiring public, the Meths drinkers, were played by several well-known British names from the world of international ballet. These coconspirators were led by Norwegian-born composer, dancer, and choreographer Tutte Lemkow (the choreographer of *Casino Royale* and the title character in the film version of *Fiddler on the Roof*).

Cast as Lionheart's devoted daughter, Diana Rigg has always spoken of the *Theater of Blood* assignment with fondness. "I did it for fun, because it appealed to my sense of humor; I had no idea it was going to be so enormously enjoyable, which it was, mainly because of Vincent, who is heaven. . . . Vincent was often in costume appropriate for delivering a lot of very famous Shakespeare soliloquies. He would always find out if the next shot was a long shot, medium, or close-up. If it was a medium or close-up, he'd clamber into the oldest pair of slippers I have ever seen. My problem was to keep a straight face looking at Vincent delivering these soliloquies sublimely in costume with his feet in those carpet slippers."

Theater of Blood gave Vincent Price one of the choicest roles of his career, horror or otherwise, and he excelled in every nuance. The script allowed for considerable depth; he is outrageously over the top (the hairdresser alone is worth the price of admission), ironically menac-

ing when taunting his victims, and poignantly tragic as he gently cradles his dying daughter, tenderly twisting a lock of her hair in his fingers. Actually, in the Shakespeare excerpts Lionheart performs, he seems like a pretty good actor; certainly not the narcissist Price portrayed in *His Kind of Woman* or the vaudevillian martinet in *Curtain Call at Cactus Creek*. (Sharp eyes will notice that throughout the picture Vincent wears different types of tape on his right ring finger, which he had broken lifting rolled carpeting at home and wanted to protect during filming.)

This picture shares a title discrepancy similar to Price's 1940 film *Brigham Young*. Although advertising and publicity material spell the first word the British way, *Theatre*, release prints (even in the United Kingdom) are titled *Theater of Blood*.

When pressed, Vincent would usually designate *Theater of Blood* as his favorite of his movies: "I think that was the best feeling of achievement and satisfaction that I ever had from a film." He obviously respected *The Eve of St. Mark*, *Laura*, and *Dragonwyck*, among others; possibly he never had a better time making a picture, and *Theater of Blood* did introduce him to the great love of his mature years. (It was also the response most fans

Theater of Blood Robert Morley, VP, Dennis Price, Robert Coote, Ian Hendry

Theater of Blood "Thou art a soul in bliss; but I am bound upon a wheel of fire, that mine own tears do scald like molten lead . . . Howl, howl, howl, howl, O, you are men of stones . . . She's dead as earth . . ."

expected, and Vincent never, ever disappointed a fan.) He summed up the experience succinctly: "My favorite funny film. . . . Endless possibilities. A splendid cast. I fell in love with one of them, Coral Browne, married her, and lived happily ever after."

REVIEWS

Chicago Sun Times, April 20, 1973 Roger Ebert

". . . a superior film in every way . . . the script has genuine wit and malice; the production is handsome; and Vincent Price, whose horror-movie roles don't often give him much latitude, gets a magnificent chance to ham it up this time. . . ."

Los Angeles Times, April 20, 1973

". . . A triumph of stylish, witty Grand Guignol, it allows Price to range richly between humor and pathos as a crazed Shakespearean actor, and his performance revitalizes that tired-out adjective, magnificent. Indeed, if horror pictures were taken seriously, he would surely be an Oscar contender next year. . . . [T]he premise . . . enables Price to make of it on one level an eloquent tragedy and a stinging comment on the often cruelly lethal power of drama critics. *Theater* . . . obviously offers a formidable challenge to Price, who not only does a superior job of portraying an inferior actor but also assumes various disguises, and suggests that poor crazy old Lionheart never played Shakespeare so well sane. It's hard to think of any other star who could pull this off as stunningly as

Theater of Blood Critic Harry Andrews forfeits his pound of flesh to "Shylock" (Price) and "Portia" (Diana Rigg)

238

Price, because most actors who could do Shakespeare as well as he does probably couldn't resist condescending to the horror film context. Yet in the film's final moments, Lionheart becomes as tragic as any of the Shakespeare heroes he plays. . . ."

New York, May 14, 1973, Judith Crist

". . . a company of England's finest have joined Vincent Price . . . to participate with joyous gusto in a delicious concoction entitled *Theater of Blood*. . . . Vincent Price is king of the genre, with all his lush villainy beautifully supplanted by marvelously bombastic Shakespearean recitations. . . . To all involved, in fact, our gratitude for restoring that fine sense of fun to a genre more honored of late in its exploitation than by a creative exploration of its intelligent entertainment values."

San Francisco Chronicle, May 19, 1973, Anitra Earle

"If it's true you are what you do for a living, I can only wonder why anyone as rich, celebrated and allegedly distinguished as Vincent Price continues to fiddle around playing ghoulish lunatics in potboilers like *Theater of Blood*. . . . [It demonstrated a] lack of taste, a totally unrealistic approach to any and all life situations, combined with retchingly realistic deaths and tortures. . . . Also wasted are some classy special effects such as the burning down of a beautiful old theater—a trick that was probably both expensive and dangerous. . . ." [Get a life.]

85. MADHOUSE

AMERICAN INTERNATIONAL

Released March 1974

CREDITS

Amicus Productions; *Executive Producer*, Samuel Z. Arkoff; *Producers*, Max J. Rosenberg and Milton Subotsky; *Associate Producer*, John Dark; *Director*, Jim Clark; *Screenplay*, Greg Morrison, Ken Levison; *Based on the novel* Devilday *by* Angus Hall; *Cinematography*, Ray Parslow; *Art Director*, Tony Curtis; *Music*, Douglas Gamley; *Editor*, Clive Smith; *Wardrobe*, Dulcie Midwinter; *Makeup*, George Blackler; *Hairdresser*, Helen Lennox; *Running time*, 89 minutes; color.

CAST

Vincent Price (*Paul Toombes*); Peter Cushing (*Herbert Flay*); Robert Quarry (*Oliver Quayle*); Adrienne Corri (*Faye*); Natasha Pyne (*Julia*); Michael Parkinson (*Himself*); Linda Hayden (*Elizabeth Peters*); Barry Dennen

Madhouse As "Dr. Death"

(*Gerry Blount/TV Director*); Ellis Dale (*Alfred Peters*); Catherine Willmer (*Louise Peters*); John Garrie (*Harper*); Ian Thompson (*Bradshaw*); Jenny Lee Wright (*Carol*); Julie Crosthwaite (*Ellen*); Peter Halliday (*Psychiatrist*); Special participation, Boris Karloff, Basil Rathbone.

THE FILM

Madhouse was another missed opportunity, all the more frustrating for the handful of genuine moments between two gentle gentlemen. Faded horror-film actor Paul Toombes (probably not his real name—remember Boris Karloff a.k.a. William Henry Pratt) attempts to make a

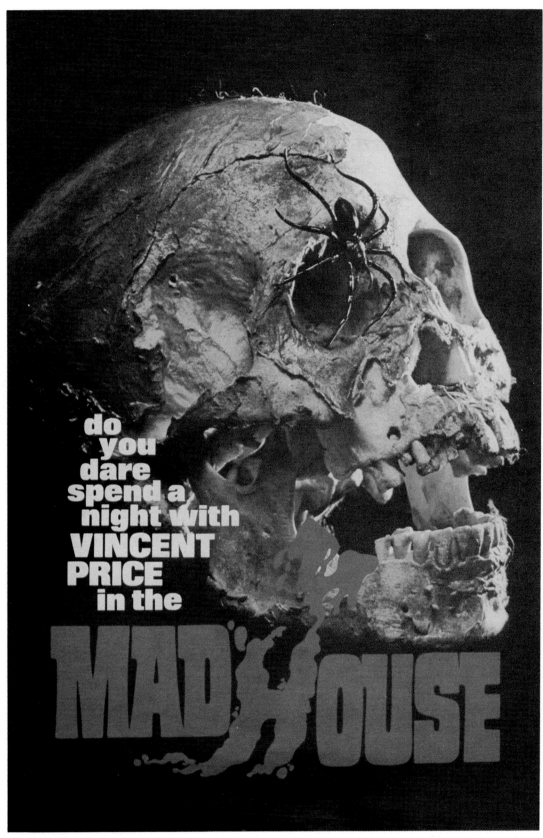

Madhouse Three-sheet poster

TV comeback several years after the brutal, unsolved murder of his fiancée and his own subsequent nervous breakdown. Once in production for the show, he finds himself implicated in a new series of murders connected with his famous screen character, the skull-faced Dr. Death. In the penultimate climax of the picture, Vincent Price again seemingly meets his end in the flames of yet another impressive (and dangerous) pyrotechnic wonder. But after all, Paul Toombes was an actor extremely skilled in character makeup and at pretending to be other people. We haven't seen the last of Dr. Death. . . .

Madhouse was the first film to team Vincent Price and Peter Cushing in equal roles, although Robert Quarry asserts that he was cast to play the "Cushing role;" that the picture was a kind of "horror *All About Eve*," with Quarry playing an actor being groomed as the successor to the older, established star. The project had a long history. AIP announced they had acquired the rights to the book *Devilday* in April 1970; at that time, Price was to star, and *Dr. Phibes* director Robert Fuest was to direct. By the end of November 1971, Nicholson and Arkoff were listed as coproducers of a screenplay by Murray Smith, and shooting was scheduled for mid-1972. The project surfaced again in April 1973, when Arkoff (following partner Nicholson's untimely death) concluded an agreement with Max Rosenberg and Milton Subotsky of Amicus Productions to produce *The Revenge of Dr. Death*, with a screenplay by former film publicist Greg Morrison. Production was slated to begin in May with one-time editor Jim Clark directing.

Madhouse With Robert Quarry (*left*) and Peter Cushing

Madhouse "Paul Toombes" signs an autograph for a fan

241

The picture, which was retitled along the way, was filmed at Twickenham Studios and on various London locations. Many of the scenes were shot at Pyrford Manor, a fifteenth-century residence often used by Queen Elizabeth I. Clips presented as early "Paul Toombes" pictures came from *Pit and the Pendulum, Tales of Terror, The Haunted Palace, Masque of the Red Death, House of Usher*, and *The Raven*.

The role of a popular horror star was hardly a stretch for Price. Whether signing autographs for fans, appearing on a London chat show, or reminiscing with reel and real-life friend and colleague Cushing, there is much of Vincent Price the man in Paul Toombes the character. On his dog-eared copy of the film's production unit list, Vincent checked off names of crew members for gifts of wine and liquor at the end of the shoot. The extensive register included over two dozen otherwise ignored "techies."

After Vincent had wrapped his scenes for *Madhouse* and returned to Los Angeles, he received a lengthy, anguished lament from Jim Clark, who was "in a miasma of impotent rage." The director was having terrible disagreements with Subotsky, "who has bulldozed his way into the cutting room and is at this very moment cutting a swath through the film. . . . I feel responsible towards you, and as a friend I shall defend our mutual interest just as long as I can—but I fear, in the end, that we shall both suffer at *their* hands, and it is your name that will sell the film, and mine that will receive the blame for making a poor picture. . . . They are retaining all the action of course—but every time anyone opens their mouth Milton tries to cut the line—for no other reason than 'it bores me' or 'we don't need it.' It is pure butchery and I don't really know why I'm surprised. . . . All love—we miss you—Jim."

With the video release of *Madhouse*, the voice of its star, the ex–Yale Glee Club member, was again the victim of rights permissions. End credits of the theatrical release ran under Vincent's tremulous rendition of a sentimental period-type ballad: "Although I miss / Your tender kiss / The whole night through, / I miss you most of all / When day is done." For both the U.K. and U.S. video versions, the vocal is replaced with an instrumental version lifted from elsewhere in the picture.

When the fabulous Elvira, Mistress of the Dark, broadcast *Madhouse* on her TV show *Movie Macabre*, she introduced it: "Vincent Price fans rejoice! Yes, Vinnie's back, and we've got him! Just watch how this one manages to recycle numerous, the lady said *numerous*, numerous other Vinnie the P classics! And remember the stock footage of a burning structure? Try and remember how many times you've seen this very same shot before!"

Madhouse Resurrected from a fiery end: Price with Adrienne Corri

REVIEWS

Variety, March 26, 1974

". . . Price is now at a point in his long career where his familiar flamboyance is used to evoke audience sympathy as much as fear. . . . Price and Cushing mellifluously outdo each other as uncharacteristic nice guys. . . ."

Hollywood Reporter, March 27, 1974

". . . a totally predictable, superbly entertaining horror film . . . efficiently controlled, adequately frightening and excellently acted throughout. . . . For once Price is not the villain and brings dignity and sympathy to his role. A number of clips from old AIP movies double for "Dr. Death" movies. . . . Thus, *Madhouse* becomes something of a *Sunset Boulevard*, horror-film style. . . . The music by Douglas Gamley includes a song . . . sung charmingly over the closing roll by none other than Mr. Price himself."

Los Angeles Times, December 6, 1974, Kevin Thomas

". . . The premise of *Madhouse* is too good to have been wasted on a film that is as ineptly developed as it is titled. Still, the film has some visual elegance: Vincent Price, leonine as ever, holds forth in great form, and his fans may be willing to overlook a plot that totally defies credibility. . . . Price and his director, Jim Clark, achieve some genuinely ambiguous moments, suggesting the blurring between fantasy and reality, art and life, that belong in a far-better-realized film. . . . With more care and thought, *Madhouse* could have been another *Targets*, the Peter Bogdanovich film that made such excellent use of the byplay between Boris Karloff the man and his menacing screen image."

VINCENT PRICE

(*Burney [England] Evening Star*, June 14, 1973, Frances Horsburgh)

" 'So you want to know what frightens me? The other night someone rang me up from the States at one o'clock in the morning. Now, I have to get up at six when I'm filming, so I wasn't very pleased.' 'Do you ever get nightmares after shooting one of those scenes?' he asked me. 'Yes, I do,' I said. 'I have these nightmares all the time that some silly son-of-a-bitch is going to phone me up in the middle of the night. That really frightens me!'" Mr. Price chortles into his coffee. 'I guess he hung up after that.' The tall, elegant sixty-two-year-old actor and I are lunching in his caravan. . . . He looks like a lean Rhett Butler—a man born to sport a slouch hat, a silk waistcoat and a brace of aces. Outside, a touch of Derby Day Fever has gripped the film crew, and the star has given them all a pound to place on the horse of their choice. 'Whoever wins I get ten percent,' he quips. . . . This soft-spoken sophisticate is an enthusiastic Anglophile . . . with an enviable reputation inside and outside the business for kindness, generosity and approachability. They were calling him back onto the set as Dr. Death. Mr. Price eyes himself in the mirror. 'Do I look human?' He looses a loud disquieting laugh. 'Well, vaguely anyway?' "

86. PERCY'S PROGRESS
(U.S. Title: It's Not the Size That Counts)

EMI FILMS

Released September 1974 in the United Kingdom

CREDITS

A Welbeck Production; *Executive Producer*, Larry Gordon; *Producer*, Betty E. Box; *Director*, Ralph Thomas;

Percy's Progress With Leigh Lawson and Denholm Elliott

Screenplay, Sid Colin; *Inspired by the novel* **Percy** *by* Raymond Hitchcock; *Additional Dialogue*, Ian La Frennais; *Cinematography*, Tony Imi; *Art Director*, Albert Witherick; *Set Decorator*, Fred Carter; *Music*, Tony Macaulay; *Editor*, Roy Watts; *Running time*, 101 minutes; color.

CAST

Leigh Lawson (*Percy*); Elke Sommer (*Clarissa*); Denholm Elliott (*Sir Emmanuel Whitbread*); Judy Geeson (*Dr. Fairweather*); Harry H. Corbett (*Prime Minister*); Vincent Price (*Stavros Mammonian*); Adrienne Posta (*PC 127*); Julie Ege (*Miss Hanson*); Barry Humphries (*Dr. Anderson*); Barry Humphries (*Australian TV Lady*); James Booth (*Jeffcott*); Milo O'Shea (*Dr. Klein*); Ronald Fraser (*Bleeker*); Anthony Andrews (*Catchpole*); Bernard Lee (*Barraclough*); Madeline Smith (*Miss Bristol*); Alan Lake (*Derry Hogan*); George Coulouris (*Godowski*); Jenny Hanley (*Miss Teenage Lust*); Diane Langton (*Maureen Sugden*); Carol Hawkins (*Maggie*); Marika Rivera (*Madame Lopez*); Penny Irving (*Chiquita*); Judy Matheson (*Maria*); Gertan Klauber (*Pablo*); Paul Maxwell (*UN Delegate*); Michael Barratt (*Himself*); Barnard Falk (*Himself*).

THE FILM

Percy's Progress was a redundant sequel to *Percy*, a 1971 comedy (of sorts) about the world's first penis transplant, by the producer/director team that had previously been responsible for some genuinely amusing English comedies, including several in the *Doctor . . .* series.

Determined to give up women, the cocksure Percy spends nearly a year at sea on a private sailboat, avoiding all human contact. He also avoids being exposed to PX 123, a virulent strain of chemical warfare which has contaminated the world's water supply and rendered all landlubbing and H_2O-drinking males impotent. Since Percy has subsisted solely on Bollinger '69 champagne,

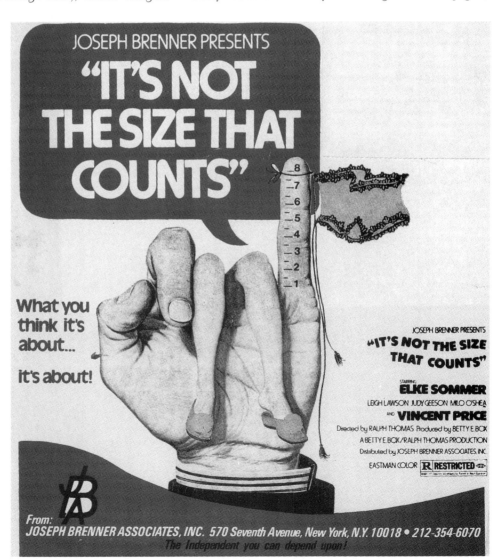

Percy's Progress
Ad for U.S. distribution

244

he now has not only the most famous one in the world; he has the only working one in the world. Subsequently, each nation of the world holds a "Miss Conception International" contest to select a representative who will do their patriotic duty with it, uh, him. Stavros Mammonian (Vincent Price), the world's richest man, even goes so far as to abduct Percy in the hopes of convincing him to beget a Mammonian heir. As the billionaire, Vincent Price is confined to a wheelchair on-screen for the first time since *House of Wax* in 1953. Ultimately, nature takes its course, and the drug's effects wear off. Australian writer/satirist Barry Humphries, best known as the "manager" of Dame Edna Everage, appears in two roles, as a scientist who helps discover the "cure" and as the "Australian TV Lady," an unabashed impersonation in face, form, and monologue of his brilliant alter ego, Mrs. Everage, prior to her self-elevated D.B.E.

Although *Percy's Progress* originally was purchased by financier Larry Gordon in 1974, it wasn't until March 1976 that Joseph Brenner Associates announced American distribution of the picture. Retitled *It's Not the Size That Counts* and cut to ninety minutes, the U.S. release was further delayed until November 1978. The ad copy ran: "What you think it's about—it's about!"

REVIEWS

London *Sunday Telegraph*, September 1, 1974, Tom Hutchinson

"... It could have been an occasion for some rasping satire on a blue theme, but the bludgeon of obviousness beats that possibility to squelchy pump.... There are occasional jokes that irritated a few laughs out of me.... Basically, though, the whole thing doesn't come off as the good unclean fun that was intended. The idea that every woman is a sexpot just craving for Percy has a masculine arrogance which, eventually, I found rather repellent.... [It will undoubtedly have] a very successful box office."

Hollywood Reporter, April 3, 1979

"... one raunchy comedy.... Elke Sommer and Vincent Price—more prominently billed than Lawson—have only minor footage and contribute little beyond recognizable names.... the rest of the cast [play] their comedy with a mock foolishness that's downright embarrassing to watch. But, let's face it, so's the entire movie."

87. JOURNEY INTO FEAR

A. STIRLING GOLD LTD. PRODUCTION

Released Fall 1975 in Canada

CREDITS

New World Productions, Ltd.; *Writer/Producer*, Trevor Wallace; *Director*, Daniel Mann; *Based on the novel by* Eric Ambler; *Cinematography*, Harry Waxman; *Production Designer*, Cameron Porteous; *Editorial Supervision*, Jack McSweeney; *Music*, Alex North; *Running time*, 95 minutes; color.

CAST

(IN ORDER OF APPEARANCE) Sam Waterston (*Graham*); Zero Mostel (*Kopeikin*); Yvette Mimieux (*Josette*); Scott Marlow (*José*); Ian McShane (*Banat*); Joseph Wiseman (*Colonel Haki*); Shelley Winters (*Mrs. Mathews*); Stanley Holloway (*Mr. Mathews*); Donald Pleasence (*Kuvetli*); Vincent Price (*Dervos*).

THE FILM

Journey Into Fear was the second screen version of a novel previously shot in 1942 for RKO coscripted and supervised by Orson Welles. In preproduction it was touted as "perhaps the biggest budget commercial feature to come out of Canada in years, with a cast known far beyond Canadian borders." Relying on glamorous locations in Istanbul, Athens, Genoa, and Vancouver, and West Vancouver's Panorama Studios, the picture was shot for around $3.5 million over seven weeks in July and August 1974. Most likely it merely presented another opportunity for Vincent Price to go museuming and to get away from less realistic screen horrors. The convoluted plot is dull and fragmented, with Sam Waterston as a research scientist in oil and natural resources caught up in a web of international intrigue. A number of many celebrated talents are wasted on both sides of the camera in this derivative, unthrilling "thriller." (Director Daniel Mann had an impressive list of credits, including Oscar-winning *Come Back, Little Sheba*, *The Rose Tattoo*, and *Butterfield 8*). During production the trades reported that "Actor Vincent Price, who has a wide reputation as a screen villain, found the tables turned in Genoa, Italy, when a thief made off with approximately $2,000 cash, his driver's license and all his credit cards — and Price was only out for a stroll with a lady friend. . . . [On set] a special effects scene didn't come off as planned and Vincent Price's shirt and pants were burned to shreds. . . ."

Without benefit of fez or makeup, the actor looks even less like an Arab in this picture than he did twenty-five years earlier in *Bagdad*. Presenting himself as a likable, book-toting scholar, he turns out to be the genial but coolly ruthless mercenary who employs incredibly inept hit man Ian McShane to bump off Sam Waterston (an assignment at which he fails nearly a dozen times). Price is convincing as the professor and suitably steely when it's revealed he's a bad guy, too — another of his mastermind villains, infrequently involved in anything lethal himself. "I've already said that I like you, Mr. Graham," he confesses amiably but seriously to his target. "Let me add that I *dislike* the prospect of violence as much as you do. *Hmmph* [with a little laugh]. I'm lily-livered — there, I admit it freely. No — a killing in this case would be . . . clumsy. I should be as happy as you if we could dispose of our business in a more reasonable and civilized manner. I really and sincerely mean that." The special effects that "didn't come off" in rehearsal involved Price's "flashy" demise — shot in the chest with a flare pistol.

Canadian journalist Michael Walsh said it all: "Journey Leads to Obscurity — At The Movies . . . What we were promised was an exciting and atmospheric thriller. What we've been given is just bland and confusing. . . . [Daniel] Mann's directorial coma left his actors pretty much on their own. Some, like Zero Mostel and Shelley Winters, overwork their hambones and flog overly familiar shticks. Others, like Donald Pleasence and Stanley Holloway, assessed what was required of them and give professional, if undistinguished, performances. The standouts, though, are Vincent Price and Yvette Mimieux. Price, as the chief villain, and Mimieux, as the brief love-interest, each took the care to develop their characters beyond the superficial and easily dominate the scenes in which they appear. [Sam] Waterston plays his starring role with all of the effectiveness of Barbie's friend, Ken, offering the kind of polyurethane performance that made me wish that Price's assassin, Ian McShane, was more efficient. . . ."

Contractual and legal complications held up the picture's Canadian release until the fall of 1975; it received little exposure. In the U.S., it premiered on HBO January 9, 1976.

REVIEW

Cleveland Plain Dealer, September 27, 1975

"While not a great movie, it can be watched throughout with interest and engagement. The plot is pure grade-A pot-boiler, [but] the picture has a nice feel to it."

88. SCAVENGER HUNT

20th CENTURY-FOX

Released December 25, 1979

CREDITS

A Melvin Simon Production; *Executive Producer*, Melvin Simon; *Producer*, Steven A. Vail; *Coproducer*, Paul Maslansky; *Associate Producers*, Craig S. Yace, Hana Cannon; *Director*, Michael Schultz; *Screenplay*, Steven A. Vail, Henry Harper; *Story*, Steven A. Vail; *Adaptation*, John Thompson, Gerry Woolery; *Cinematography*, Ken Lamkin; *Art Director*, Richard Berger; *Set Decorator*, Ed Baer; *Music*, Billy Goldenberg; *Original Songs*, Billy Goldenberg, Carol Connors; *Editor*, Christopher Holmes; *Costume Supervisor*, Bob Harris Jr.; *Makeup Supervision*, Paul Stanhope Jr.; *Hairstylist*, Marilyn P. Phillips; *Running time*, 116 minutes; color.

CAST

Richard Benjamin (*Stuart Selsome*); James Coco (*Henri*); Scatman Crothers (*Sam*); Ruth Gordon (*Arvilla Droll*); Cloris Leachman (*Mildred Carruthers*); Cleavon Little

(*Jackson*); Roddy McDowall (*Jenkins*); Robert Morley (*Mr. Bernstein*); Richard Mulligan (*Marvin Dummitz*); Tony Randall (*Henry Motley*); Dirk Benedict (*Jeff Stevens*); Willie Aames (*Kenny Stevens*); Stephanie Faracy (*Babbette*); Stephen Furst (*Merle*); Richard Masur (*Georgie Carruthers*); Meat Loaf (*Scum*); Pat McCormick (*Carnival Barker*); Vincent Price (*Milton Parker*); Avery Schreiber (*Zoo Keeper*); Arnold Schwarzenegger (*Lars*); Liz Torres (*Lady Zero*); Carol Wayne (*Mr. Parker's Nurse*); Stuart Pankin (*Duane*); Maureen Teefy (*Lisa*); Hal Landon Jr. (*Cornfeld*); Marji Martin (*Kay*); Jerado Decordovier (*Indian*); Emory Bass (*Hotel Manager*); Byron Webster (*Restroom Attendant*); Wally K. Berns (*Drunk*); Jerry Fujikawa (*Sakamoto*); Sid Gould (*Elevator Repair Man*); Art Koustik (*Zoo Director*).

THE FILM

Scavenger Hunt died a critical death, but there is much merit in this much-maligned slapstick comedy. The story line is absurdly simple, with the accent on the absurdity. Milton Parker, a board-games tycoon, rolls the dice by dying and leaving his $200 million estate to fifteen beneficiaries who must compete against each other to inherit in a winner-take-all scavenger hunt.

In his role as Parker, Vincent Price's contribution to the film consists of a single scene played behind the opening credits. With tousled hair and mustache brushed with white powder, he plays a kind of wall-mounted electronic leapfrog game with delectable nurse Carol Wayne, blowing her an eloquent raspberry as she appears to be winning. He doesn't speak a word. When his frog croaks, so does he. Later, a tape recorder plays back his instructions to his relatives to explain the rules of the scavenger hunt. (In 1976, Vincent guest starred in an episode of *The Bionic Woman* called "Black Magic" almost identical in premise. At the opening, he plays a deathbed scene with a trusted companion and then infuriates relatives with a videotaped will informing them that they must participate in a scavenger hunt for his fortune. At least Price fans got more for their money out of the TV appearance, since Vincent also played his own brother and hung around for the rest of the show.)

Much of *Scavenger Hunt*'s location work was shot in San Diego in April 1979. Originally scheduled for release during Easter 1980, the movie opened Christmas Day 1979 in more than five hundred theaters, and was "supported by a massive advertising promotion and publicity campaign" by Fox. Initial returns were disastrous, but apparently picked up in the New Year.

Many reviewers referred to *Scavenger Hunt* as "a poor man's *It's a Mad Mad Mad Mad World*." The basic ingredients are the same: a stellar cast, silly slapstick, visual gags, and a theme of greed. But the script was

Scavenger Hunt With Carol Wayne

regarded as uneven, and director Michael Schultz (*Car Wash*) came under almost unanimous criticism.

REVIEWS

Los Angeles Herald Examiner, December 25, 1979

"... *Hunt* has a terrific comic character-actor cast ... and its premise ... though slim, is certainly viable. But Michael Schultz ... simply places the camera in the actors' general vicinity and then encourages them to scream and leap about in senseless frenzy...."

Los Angeles Times, December 27, 1979, Kevin Thomas

"... For all its ripping off and destruction, *Scavenger Hunt* does contain a bit of a moral on the evil and folly of greed, which means it's probably okay to send the kids, who are those most likely to enjoy the picture anyway."

Box Office, January 21, 1980

"... good for a few laughs.... Some of the actors, such as Vincent Price, Roddy McDowall and Scatman Crothers, are virtually wasted."

89. DAYS OF FURY

PICTURMEDIA LIMITED
Released March 1980

CREDITS

Markwood Productions, Limited; *Producer/Writer*, Fred Warshofsky; *Narration*: Vincent Price; *Running time*, 91 minutes; color.

THE FILM

Filmmaker Fred Warshofsky wrote and produced this adaptation of his own book *Doomsday: The Science of Catastrophe*. The renowned science authority had previously been responsible for *21st Century*, the successful CBS series with Walter Cronkite, and had also helmed more popular specials, such as *In Search of Ancient Mysteries* and *The Outer Space Connection*. Vincent Price was approached in April 1979 to record the narration for the project, titled *Days of Fury*, by the distributor, Picturemedia. "The theme is most timely," they explained in their pitch letter, "and deals with subjects very dear to us—our survival. Our thinking is that Vincent Price, a man so long associated with the world of shock and terror, will be a perfect conduit to emphasize the natural shock and terror inherent in the context of *Days of Fury*."

The picture was an "up-to-the-minute account of disasters that have changed our world . . . and where they might strike next." It included footage of earthquakes, volcano eruptions, jet-plane collisions, and the collapse of a suspension bridge.

Price recorded his vocal track in July 1979.

90. THE MONSTER CLUB

ITC FILMS
Released May 19, 1981, in the United Kingdom

CREDITS

A Sword & Sorcery Production; *Executive Producer*, Bernard J. Kingham; *Producer*, Milton Subotsky; *Associate Producer*, Ron Fry; *Director*, Roy Ward Baker; *Screenplay*, Edward and Valerie Abraham; *Based on the novel by* Ronald Chetwynd-Hayes; *Cinematography*, Peter Jessop; *Production Designer*, Tony Curtis; *Music Coordinator*, Graham Walker; *Songs*, B. A. Robertson, Night, the Pretty Things, the Viewers; *Soundtrack Music*, John Williams, UB 40, Expressos, Alan Hawkshaw, John Georgiadis, Douglas Gamley; *Editor*, Peter Tanner; *Makeup*, Roy Ashton, Ernest Gasser; *Monster Masks*, Vic Door; *Running time*, 97 minutes; color.

Days of Fury

The Monster Club Eramus (Price) bites into R. Chetwynd-Hayes (John Carradine)

The Monster Club An explanation of monster genealogy

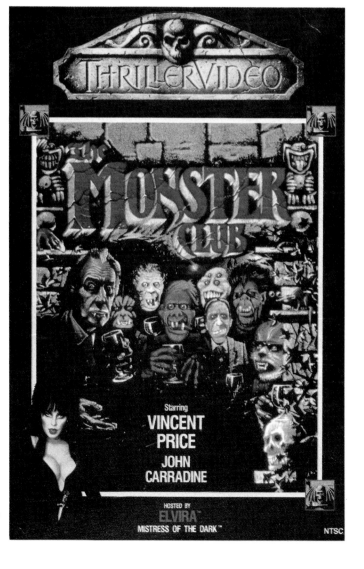

The Monster Club Cover of the laser disc release

CAST

Vincent Price (*Eramus*); Donald Pleasence (*Pickering*); John Carradine (*Ronald Chetwynd-Hayes*); Anthony Steel (*Lintom Busotsky*); Stuart Whitman (*Sam*); Richard Johnson (*Lintom's Father*); Barbara Kellermann (*Angela*); Britt Ekland (*Lintom's Mother*); Simon Ward (*George*); Anthony Valentine (*Mooney*); Patrick Magee (*Innkeeper*); Fran Fullenwider (*Buxom Beauty*); Roger Sloman (*Club Secretary*); James Laurenson (*Raven*); Geoffrey Bayldon (*Psychiatrist*); Warren Saire (*Young Lintom*); Neil McCarthy (*Watson*); Lesley Dunlop (*Luna*).

THE FILM

Price's first horror film since *Madhouse* (1974), *The Monster Club* was another miss, a combination of three intriguing segments tied together by a hokey framing story and self-conscious, pseudohip musical numbers.

Vincent plays a vampire (for the sole time on the big screen) who happens to bite into famed horror author John Carradine. By way of apology, Price takes his victim to an exclusive private haven, "the Monster Club." There the friendly bloodsucker acquaints the human with complicated monster genealogy and regales him with three tales of vampires, ghouls, and a creature called a shadmock. Afterward, Price proposes Carradine for membership, citing all of Man's obvious qualifications to be regarded as "the greatest monster of them all."

Vincent's connecting wraparounds with John Carradine demonstrate just how tricky it is to send up the genre, and one's self. Carradine is heavy-handed and humorless, while Price is smooth and confident, throwing aside double entendres with aplomb born of experience. *The Monster Club* was also Vincent's first lengthy motion-picture role since immersing himself in the life and character of Oscar Wilde for his one-man stage show. The delivery of his lines is different from much of his earlier film work; smoother, even more mellifluous.

Producer Milton Subotsky had commissioned the script of *The Monster Club* some years before he assigned Roy Ward Baker, who was famous for speed and economy, to direct. Baker hadn't helmed a picture in five years, not since *Legend of the 7 Golden Vampires* with Peter Cushing, having been working in television on *Danger: UXB*. Subotsky wanted a cast replete with horror greats, but Cushing passed, and Christopher Lee was living in California at the time. Since 1977, Vincent Price had essentially forsaken the screen for the stage and Oscar Wilde. But ever amiable, Vincent liked the script he received in January 1980 and wanted to do a so-called horror picture that would be suitable for younger viewers. Accordingly, *The Monster Club* began filming at EMI Elstree in April on a five-week shoot; Vincent's scenes were lensed in one week in early May.

In order to market at the 1980 Cannes Film Festival, a promotional comic was created to illustrate the layout and look of the movie; the result was a slick book in the style of the early *Eerie* and *Creepy* magazines. Published by Pioneer Press, written by *Starburst* magazine founder and ex-editor Dez Skinn and illustrated by John Bolton and David Lloyd, the limited run of one thousand copies quickly became collectors' items. It was artist Bolton who created the enormous four-foot-by-three-foot painting for the film which Price uses to explain monster genealogy to Carradine.

When the finished picture was presented to British censors, it received an "AA" certificate (no children under fourteen), thus denying it to the very audience for which it had been intended. After minor alterations, the film passed and was granted the all-important "A" (no children under five).

REVIEWS

Variety, May 29, 1981

"Not one you'd care to join. This club's a disco for Transylvanian freaks, and the link setting for an anthology of three gothic tales with a touch of levity and comic satire. The Milton Subotsky production, alas, has the aspirations of its budget—low. Strictly a program entry with limited prospects. Vincent Price seems to have an enjoyably hammy time as a jovial vampire who spins the three yarns. . . ."

Monthly Film Bulletin, May 1981

"With a cast topped by such veteran blood-curdlers as Vincent Price and John Carradine and a character list that includes two horror filmmakers (a producer and director), one might have hoped for a touch of sophistication. . . ."

VINCENT PRICE

London, (*Daily Mail*, May 20, 1981)

"He lit his seventh cigarette in as many minutes (he only takes a few puffs). . . . 'I see *Monster Club* as a sort of vampire disco, as a fun picture for children. It is scary but not frightening. My vampire for instance is quite kindly . . . and I have insisted on a line in the script to explain that I have retractable teeth. This had to be written in because I found I couldn't talk with the vampire fangs in my mouth.' " [This is apparently true. The lines "Where are your fangs?" and "They're retractable when not in use" are written into the script's margin in Vincent's handwriting.]

91. HOUSE OF THE LONG SHADOWS

CANNON FILMS

Released June 23, 1983, in the United Kingdom

CREDITS

Golan-Globus Productions; *Producers*, Menahem Golan, Yoram Globus; *Associate Producer*, Jenny Craven; *Director*, Pete Walker; *Screenplay*, Michael Armstrong; *Suggested by the novel* **Seven Keys to Baldpate** *by* Earl Derr Biggers *and the dramatization by* George M. Cohan; *Cinematography*, Norman Langley; *Art Director*, Mike Pickwoad; *Music*, Richard Harvey; *Editor*, Robert Dearberg; *Wardrobe*, Polly Hamilton, Alan Flyng; *Makeup*, George Partleton; *Running time*, 101 minutes; color.

CAST

Vincent Price (*Lionel Grisbane*); Christopher Lee (*Corrigan*); Peter Cushing (*Sebastian Grisbane*); John Carradine (*Lord Grisbane*); Desi Arnaz Jr. (*Kenneth Magee*); Sheila Keith (*Victoria Grisbane*); Julie Peasgood (*Mary Norton*); Richard Todd (*Sam Allyson*); Louise English (*Diana*); Richard Hunter (*Andrew*); Norman Rossington (*Stationmaster*).

THE FILM

For the first time in years, several greats of the Gothic/horror genre were brought together for a picture. The overly melodramatic script and weak direction resulted in equally over the top performances, and *House of the Long Shadows* failed to meet expectations of the highly publicized teaming.

The contrived contemporary plot has American author Desi Arnaz Jr. bet his English publisher he can write an old-fashioned spook story in twenty-four hours. A deserted manor house in Wales provides the perfect atmosphere; it starts to storm and one by one, the stars arrive. Scions of a doomed family, they reveal a terrible family secret they have kept for forty years: when the youngest brother was only fourteen years old, he slaughtered a village girl pregnant with his child. The family sentenced the boy to imprisonment in his bedroom; after four decades, they have come to free him but discover that he has escaped his confinement and roams unseen among them, dispatching the group one by one in his maniacal revenge. Sounds like the stuff novels written by clever American writers are made of, doesn't it?

The trades announced the teaming of the Big Four in June 1982; *Long Shadows* was shot on location in England during five weeks in August and September. The story was an updated version and the sixth screen adaptation of a spoof by George M. Cohan, which was itself based on a novel by Earl Derr Biggers titled *Seven Keys to Baldpate*. Screenwriter Michael Armstrong described the picture as a "Gothic suspense thriller, a pastiche of the thirties and forties. It's creepies and perpetual thunderstorms. We wanted to bring [the four of] them together for the first time, and the characters were written totally for each actor."

But half an hour into the film, we still can't tell if *Long Shadows* is meant to be funny or scary, and consequently it succeeds at neither. The seniors are excessively dotty, rather charming, and seemingly harmless, so when the mystery deepens and cast members are abruptly subjected to particularly gruesome deaths, the violence is incongruous. Unlike Bob Hope, who excelled as the straight man in the comedy thrillers *The Cat and the Canary* and *The Ghost Breakers*, Desi Arnaz Jr. is neither witty nor humorous; too glib, he's often simply rude.

The four leads don't disappoint. Cushing, still slim and athletic, affects an endearing lisp; as the indignant voice of reason, Lee is unusually natural; in a smaller part Carradine is fine, if an unlikely patriarch of men only a dozen years or so younger than he. Price's role calls upon him to do little more than personify the ultimate, popular "Vincent Price image": to be elegant, suave, theatrical, erudite. He has one or two lines of the type which worked in *Theater of Blood*—when his sister is found garroted with piano wire, he theorizes regretfully about the murderer, "He must have heard her singing"—but in this more serious context, the quips are not amusing.

House of the Long Shadows has a "twist ending" of the "it was all a dream" variety which makes much of the preceding action inexplicable—a suitable anticlimax for a picture which promised much and gave little.

REVIEWS

Screen International, June 25, 1983

"Audience rating: a fun film for middle of the roaders and all addicts of the vintage Gothic Horrors in which the four principals have so often starred. Business prediction: good to very good in mid-market popular cinemas. Critical comment: a very entertaining pastiche of those classic creepies, all cobwebs and creaking doors, which once had us cowering in the stalls but now seem fairy tale beguiling when compared with the much sicker and bloodier contemporary horrors that are coming at us from all directions ... the assembled Masters glide through with all the elegant menace at their command."

CHRISTOPHER LEE

"At the end of it all, I supposedly kill Vincent with an ax. The camera was tracking with him as he backed away; I was behind giving him the lines just before I attack him. And I completely dried; there was this terrible silence. And I said, 'God,' under my breath, 'I've forgotten the line, I've forgotten the line!' The camera was still turning over, and Vincent was standing in front of it. And I said, 'Somebody—what's the *line*?' And Vincent just stood there and started to smile and said, 'You're doing this on purpose.' And I said 'No, I'm *not*, I'm *not*, I'm *not*!' Vincent said, 'You are doing this on *purpose*. It's quite obvious to me and to everyone else.' I was very embarrassed and started to giggle, and he started to giggle, and they cut the camera. It was just wonderful to see it happen. Me, you know, whirling this ax above my head and smashing it down on him, and actually offscreen I was hitting a huge piece of rolled-up carpet.... We filmed in this house which had several floors, and our makeup and dressing rooms were right on top of the building, needless to say, with *four elderly* gentlemen. I remember Vincent telling me, 'My damn knees, my legs'—he was having problems going up stairs; well, we were all having them. One day, somebody said, 'Get Mr. Price down, we want to set up the scene,' and so we waited and we waited. 'Is Mr. Price coming down?' 'Yes he says he's on his way.' And he appeared, materialized, in front of everybody on the set, ready to do the setup—but he was *not* wearing his trousers. He was immaculately dressed, including his jockey shorts, but no trousers. Bow tie. No trousers. He said, 'Yes, I'm ready when you are. What's the hold up?' It happened! . . . It was a marvelous experience for the four of us, we had a wonderful time, but unfortunately. . . .

House of the Long Shadows Peter Cushing, Price, Christopher Lee, and John Carradine

House of the Long Shadows
With Desi Arnaz Jr.

on which, well, could have been a great deal better, to put it politely. All of us—Peter and John, Boris as well, and Bela, too. If you've got the best script, the best director, the best cast, the best of everything, you'd have to be a *terrible* actor to make a mess of it. We never had the *advantages*, in these films, of having the top script-writers, the top directors, the top budgets, the top locations. We really *did* have to create the proverbial silk purse out of the proverbial sow's ear. We *did* it because of the kind of *people* we were, as people—we were *proud* of our profession, we were dedicated and very, very, very determined. And in spite of all the setbacks and the problems and the difficulties, and there were many of them, for both of us, over the years, for all of us—we weren't going to let it get to us."

92. BLOODBATH AT THE HOUSE OF DEATH

GOLDFARB DISTRIBUTORS, INC.
Released March 30, 1984

CREDITS

Wildwood Productions; *Executive Producers*, Laurence Myers, Stuart D. Donaldson; *Producers*, Ray Cameron, John Downes; *Director*, Ray Cameron; *Screenplay*, Ray Cameron, Barry Cryer; *Cinematography*, Dusty Miller, Brian West; *Art Director*, John Sunderland; *Music*, Mike Moran, Mark London; *Editor*, Brian Tagg; *Wardrobe Master*, Paul Vachon; *Makeup*, Eric Allwright; *Hair-dresser*, Elaine Bowerbank; *Special Effects Supervisor*, Ian Rowley; *Running time*, 92 minutes; color.

CAST

Kenny Everett (*Dr. Lucas Manderville*); Pamela Stephenson (*Dr. Barbara Coyle*); Vincent Price (*Sinister Man*); Gareth Hunt (*Elliot Broome*); Don Warrington (*Stephen Wilson*); John Fortune (*John Harrison*); Sheila Steafel (*Sheila Finch*); John Stephen Hill (*Henry*); Cleo Rocos (*Deborah Redding*); Graham Stark (*Blind Man*).

THE FILM

Bloodbath at the House of Death contains in one movie every fault for which Vincent Price's films were sometimes criticized, fairly or unfairly. The witless script is a confusing, unsuccessful spoof of the genre; it is replete with tasteless violence and adolescent sexual innuendo; the supporting cast doesn't; and Price is lumbered with demeaning dialogue which can only be delivered in a

The story of our *lives* as actors, really. One spent so much of one's life dignifying material that was not worthy; giving our very best as professional actors of experience and knowledge and, if I may say so, a certain degree of talent, saying, 'Well, this *isn't* very good, but we'll make it the best we possibly can because that's the way we are.' I don't think we've ever done anything as actors of which we should have been *ashamed*. We've been in *films* which we shouldn't have been *in*. . . . I think as actors, Vincent and I were similar in many ways. We were proud of our profession, and we did the best we possibly *could*, trying to *transcend* the material with which we were—*bedeviled*—*cursed* you might almost say. Vincent already had a wonderful career behind him in which he'd played in a large number of very, very big pictures in *major* roles, before he got into this Gothic genre. I, virtually, made my *name* in it. We frequently found ourselves saddled with scripts, direction, and so

Bloodbath at the House of Death As the Sinister Man

completely unnatural, over-the-top performance.

The picture opens with hooded figures invading Headstone Manor and committing a jolly mass ritual slaying of the eighteen occupants—dismembering, axing, hanging, ad nauseam. A few years later, Kenny Everett and Pamela Stephenson head a team of scientists investigating paranormal activity traced to the house. Unbeknownst to them, the mansion is the headquarters of an extraterrestrial Satanic cult led by the Sinister Man (Vincent Price). Failing in attempts to frighten off the scientists, they summon their master to aid in cleansing his House of Death. "Yes, I know we screwed up the first time," apologizes Price. A great pyre is lit to facilitate Satan's appearance, and inadvertently Price's robes are ignited as well. "Oh, this is just great!" he fumes. "The Exalted One is about to arrive and I'm on fire! I'm gonna miss the whole goddamned thing!" Evil look-alikes for the investigative team materialize, destroy their human counterparts, and

then take off in a spaceship. The final title reads: "The End—or is it The Beginning?" Now *that's* a truly horrific thought.

Kenny Everett was a British radio disc jockey in the early 1980s who became a comedian, with popular programs on Thames Television and the BBC. *Bloodbath at the House of Death* was selected as the vehicle for his first film. An earlier equally hilarious choice, *Suicide: The Movie*, was never made, having foundered the year before. "That movie just wasn't there," explained director Ray Cameron, who was also making his feature debut. Cameron and partner Barry Cryer had written all of Everett's TV material. Optimistic publicity promised that *Bloodbath* would "do for the *Friday the 13th* slash/horror movie genre what *Airplane!* did for disaster films."

Filming began on June 6, 1983, on location in a rambling mansion near Potters Bar in Hertfordshire, England. Cameron was very happy to have Vincent Price

Bloodbath at the House of Death "Yes, I know we screwed up the first time."

255

making an appearance or two in the film, "which for a horror fanatic like me is really the icing on the cake." Notes jotted in his script indicate that Vincent tried to improve some of his dialogue—it didn't help. Although he still has the self-consciously mellifluous delivery he cultivated for his one-man Oscar Wilde show, half of his lines contain four-letter words. Perhaps it was meant to be novel to hear the urbane Price swearing, and in other circumstances it could have been, but the use of the vulgarities in *Bloodbath* is so self-conscious, it's only cringe-making.

Bloodbath was "aimed at as wide an audience as possible." The rep handling world sales asserted: "We're certainly not going to get ourselves out of the kids' market which makes up such a wide part of Kenny's audience." However, the sex and violence earned the picture an "X" rating, eliminating the under-eighteen crowd. Wherever the film was aimed, it totally missed the mark. There's something in *Bloodbath* to offend absolutely everyone—it's sexist and racist; degrades the handicapped; stereotypes Catholics, Germans, and gays; and worst of all, simply isn't funny.

REVIEWS

Screen International, April 7, 1984

"Audience rating: devoted addicts of Kenny Everett's television shows. Business prediction: average to good in down-market popular cinemas. Critical comment: Regrettably, and ironically, censorship for the cinema excludes the sub-teen and early teenage young audience that regularly watches Kenny Everett and could be expected to find this ratbag of overlong sketches hilariously funny...."

93.   THE GREAT MOUSE DETECTIVE

WALT DISNEY PICTURES

Released July 2, 1986

CREDITS

Producer, Burny Mattinson; *Directors*, John Musker, Dave Michener, Ron Clements, Burny Mattinson; *Story Adaptation*, Pete Young, Vance Gerry, Steve Hulett, Ron Clements, Bruce M. Morris, Matthew O'Callaghan, Burny Mattinson, Dave Michener, Melvin Shaw; *Based on the book series* **Basil of Baker Street** *by* Eve Titus; *Supervising Animators*, Mark Henn, Glen Keane, Robert Minkoff, Hendel Butoy; *Animation Consultant*, Eric Lar-

The Great Mouse Detective: Prof. Ratigan as the "Supreme Ruler of all Mousedom" (photo: Walt Disney Productions)

The Great Mouse Detective Prof. Ratigan and his henchmen (photo: Walt Disney Productions)

The Great Mouse Detective Producer/Director Burny Mattinson, Director John Musker, VP (photo: Walt Disney Productions)

son; *Character Animators*, Matthew O'Callaghan, Mike Gabriel, Ruben A. Aquino, Jay Jackson, Kathy Zielinski, Doug Krohn, Phil Nibbelink, Andreas Deja, Phil Young, Shawn Keller, Ron Husband, Joseph Lanzisero, Rick Farmiloe, David Pruiksma, Sandra Borgmeyer, Cyndee Whitney, Barry Temple, David Block, Ed Gombert, Steven E. Gordon; *Art Direction*, Guy Vasilovich; *Editors*, Roy M. Brewer Jr., and James Melton; *Music Supervisor*, Jay Lawton; *Ink & Paint Manager*, Becky Fallberg; *Songs:* "The World's Greatest Criminal Mind" "Goodbye, So Soon," *Music by* Henry Mancini, *Lyrics by* Larry Grossman, Ellen Fitzhugh; "Let Me Be Good To You," *written and performed by* Melissa Manchester; *Running time*, 74 minutes; color.

CAST

THE VOICE TALENTS OF: Vincent Price (*Professor Ratigan*); Barrie Ingham (*Basil*); Val Bettin (*Dr. Dawson*); Susanne Pollatschek (*Olivia Flaversham*); Candy Candido (*Fidget*); Alan Young (*Flaversham*); Diana Chesney (*Mrs. Judson*); Eve Brenner (*the Queen*); Basil Rathbone (*Sherlock Holmes*); Laurie Main (*Dr. Watson*); Shani Wallis (*Lady Mouse*); Ellen Fitzhugh (*Barmaid*); Walker Edmiston (*Citizen*); Barrie Ingham (*Bartholomew*); Wayne Allwine, Val Bettin, Tony Anselmo, Walker Edmiston (*Thug Guards*); Melissa Manchester (*Bar Singer*).

THE FILM

Disney's twenty-sixth full-length, animated motion picture, *The Great Mouse Detective*, is a delightful, exciting pastiche of a Sherlock Holmes adventure. Its hero is a brilliant rodent sleuth who also lives at 221B Baker Street and who must match wits with his own "Napoleon of Crime," the evil genius Professor Ratigan. Several times in his career Vincent Price had the opportunity to voice animated characters, but Ratigan remains a performance as delightful and memorable as the best of his live-action roles.

Price received two short initial scripts of *Basil of Baker Street* in December 1983. Production began in 1984, following a four-year period of story development under the four directors and story men. The mystery begins with the kidnapping of a (mouse) toy maker, whose daughter, Olivia, implores Basil and the detective's faithful friend Dr. Dawson to help her locate her father. Together they uncover the diabolical scheme of the evil Professor Ratigan, who intends to replace the Queen with a toy facsimile in order to become her consort and "the supreme ruler of all Mousedom!" The trade papers claimed that Price's contract called for him "to do his four day's work over a period of two years," and his own notes on the

back of correspondence from the producers indicate that he recorded at least some of his dialogue on June 11 and 12, 1984. However, following changes in both Disney management and production, he was back in the studio in March 1985.

Thirty-two-year-old Glen Keane was the supervising animator and designer responsible for developing the main characters, with the exception of Basil. He and Matthew O'Callaghan drew nearly all of Ratigan's scenes. Initially, the wicked "Prof. Moriarty-rat" was being depicted as thin and wiry, but it was decided that his form should instead be large and powerful in order to present a greater contrast to the slight build of Basil. For the crucial element of vocal characterizations, the filmmakers took their inspiration from classic Hollywood films and ironically stumbled on Vincent Price through one of his own movies. Because they had initially been considering Ronald Colman's voice as a model for Ratigan's, the animators screened *Champagne for Caesar*. Although he was asked to *audition* (for the first time "in about forty-eight years!"), according to Keane, as soon as Vincent Price came on, "we realized we had found the perfect actor for the role. Price's expressive voice and attitude inspired us to further redesign the character." Ratigan barks orders at minions, murmurs baby talk to his beloved pet cat, jubilantly croons a not-so-fond farewell song to his opponent, and snarls in bestial rage at the climax in which the elegant professor deteriorates into a demented animal. Vincent Price's unutterable *glee* is infectious, and he leads the audience on an auditory roller-coaster ride.

Tentatively slated for release in the summer of 1987, the film was ready in July 1986. The actual animation took just over one year, involving 125 artists. Prior to release, the powers that be at Disney were concerned about what they perceived as the "same problem" that "sank" Steven Spielberg's entertaining and imaginative live-action *Young Sherlock Holmes*: "too British." The studio marketing department invited the animation department to suggest new titles for *Basil of Baker Street*. Apparently the animators thought that *The Great Mouse Detective* was as imaginative as renaming *Snow White*, *Seven Little Men Help a Girl*. In fact, an in-studio memo was found tacked to the animation department bulletin board announcing that the studio had retitled all of its classic films. Management wasn't amused at such suggestions as *The Wooden Boy Who Became Real*, *The Little Deer Who Grew Up*, *Puppies Taken Away*, *The Amazing Flying Children*, and *Color and Music*.

Unbelievably, Disney had problems with the picture in Norway, where the State Film Censorship Board voted unanimously to bar children under age of 12. (Also nixed was a re-issue of *Fantasia*.) For the film's U.S. release,

Price took part in a June 30, 1986, media blitz for which he was scheduled for twenty-one ten-minute interviews between 8:00 am and noon. (He was permitted to "rest" between 9:20 and 9:30, and again from 10:50 to 11:00!)

The film underwent an additional name change when it was rereleased in February 1992 as *The Adventures of the Great Mouse Detective*. For the world television premiere on the Disney Channel on August 1, 1994, the title was back to *The Great Mouse Detective*. Only Basil could unravel that mystery!

REVIEWS

Los Angeles Times, July 2, 1986

". . . the most entertaining animated feature the Disney studio has produced since *Jungle Book* in 1967. It's the first one completed since Walt Disney's death in 1966 that the artists could show to him without apologies or explanations. This unpretentious film with its strong, well-told story could be the long-awaited hit to spark a renaissance in American animation. . . . As Prof. Ratigan, Vincent Price dominates the vocal cast in a wonderfully off-the-wall performance, far removed from his usual suavely evil villains."

Backstage, July 4, 1986

"Prof. Ratigan is truly evil and styled in a Barrymoreish persona . . ."

UCLA Daily Bruin, July 29, 1986, Jennifer Boynton

"Vincent Price, as the voice of Prof. Ratigan, is the type of villain I remember from the old *Batman* tv show; like the Joker or the Penguin, he is thrilled by his own evilness. It charms him. Basil's not-entirely-nice personality (his character seems inspired by Robert Stephens' portrayal of Holmes in Billy Wilder's underappreciated *The Private Life of Sherlock Holmes*) only makes him more endearing."

VINCENT PRICE

[At the time he was recording Ratigan's exultant song "Goodbye So Soon," Price explained:] "Ratigan is the *ultimate* villain. He's got a huge sense of humor about himself, but dead seriousness at the same time about crime. When the actor gets there and the voice begins to happen (and in playing it you exaggerate, because it's an exaggerated character), you suddenly begin to see the character—the animation—taking on *your* humanity, which of course is what they want. Because the more *human* the mouse or the rat is, the better it is for the picture."

94. THE OFFSPRING

CONQUEST ENTERTAINMENT

Distributed by The Movie Store Entertainment
Released September 1987

CREDITS

Conquest Entertainment; *Executive Producer*, Bubba Truckadaro; *Producers*, Darin Scott, William Burr; *Director*, Jeff Burr; *Screenplay*, C. Courtney Joyner, Darin Scott, Jeff Burr; *Cinematography*, Craig Greene; *Production Designer*, Cynthia K. Charette, C. Allen Posten; *Music*, Jim Manzie; *Editor*, W. O. Garrett; *Special Makeup and Effects*, Rob Burman; *Running time*, 101 minutes; color.

CAST

Vincent Price (*Julian White*); Susan Tyrrell (*Beth Chandler*); Clu Gulager (*Stanley Burnside*); Harry Caesar (*Felder Evans*); Terry Kiser (*Jesse Hardwick*); Rosalind Cash (*Snakewoman*); Cameron Mitchell (*Gallen*); Martine Beswicke (*Katherine White*); Lawrence Tierney (*Warden*); Megan McFarland (*Grace Scott*); Terry Knox (*Burt Horny*); Mirriam Byrd-Nethery (*Eileen Burnside*); Bob Hannah (*Harry Essex*); Katherine Kaden (*Mary Hardwick*); Gene Witham (*Jake McCoy*); Tommy Burcher (*Lester McCoy*); Didi Lanier (*Amarillis*); Angelo Rossitto (*Tinker*); Ron Brooks (*Steven Arden*); Gordon Padison (*Leonard*); Barney Burman (*No Face*); Tim Wingard (*Bullock*); Leon Edwards (*McBride*); C. J. Cox (*Pike*); Tommy Nowell (*Andrew*); Ashley Bare (*Amanda*); Sergio Aguire (*Ambrose*); Jajary Bennett (*Jake*).

THE FILM

The Offspring is an ultraexplicit horror anthology which attempted to evoke the grim spirit and crude unpleasantness manifested in the EC horror comics. It was the debut feature for several young ex–film school students with a fondness for the horror classics of the thirties, but a predilection for the nudity, violence, and graphic gore of the eighties.

As an enigmatic town historian, Vincent Price reveals the terrible secret of Oldfield to a reporter investigating how an executed murderess might have been affected by her mysterious birthplace. In the opening story, a nerd who is infatuated with a beautiful coworker kills her when she rejects him. Before the funeral he slips into the morgue and has sex with her dead body. Yes, that's right. Nine months later, the unholy result digs its way out of her grave and comes to Papa. The second segment features an ex-con who forces the secret of immortality from a voodoo priest, to his eternal regret. In the third, when a carnival glass eater abandons his sideshow-freak family for the love of a normal girl, he loses his ability to accomplish his trick safely, with heartrending consequences. The final story takes place at the end of the Civil War, when renegade soldiers are captured by a band of orphaned children who are very disrespectful to their elders.

Twenty-three-old director Jeff Burr assembled a fine cast of name performers and shot the four episodes in July and August 1985 on location in his hometown of Dalton, Georgia. Postproduction wasn't completed until February 1986. Burr was determined that his framing story be "fully integrated" with the rest of the picture. "The problem with most anthologies is that the connecting scene is usually lame and thought of after the fact," he explained.

Before the filming in Georgia in the summer of 1985, Burr and Scott got Vincent's address from a celebrity map and showed up on his doorstep, script in hand. The star invited them into his home and spent twenty minutes listening to their pitch, apologizing that the bread he was baking wasn't ready to share with them. Price had some nice things to say about the screenplay but felt that it was the kind of project he had been trying to get away from.

However, after the filmmakers screened the second story segment for him in February 1986, he accepted the part of the "narrator." Thrilled with a commitment from the famous actor, the writers revised the script to try to tailor it to his screen persona, to "do something really wild with it," in Burr's words. Rewrites were submitted to Price in March prior to his departure on a lecture cruise in the Caribbean. "Needless to say," wrote Burr in the cover letter, "this role is going to be a lot of fun for you!" Apparently not. Vincent drafted a telegram to his agent, decrying the new dialogue as "boringly repetitive and nothing to do with what I agreed. . . . Think you should ask them what it's all about. Not one word of the agreed-upon script which I learned is left . . . dialogue is endless and fatuous. . . . Why didn't they change it before I left—I would have turned it down."

Needless to say, the original material was reinstated. And when he arrived on set for rehearsal, Price was, in Burr's words, "nothing but a total, total professional; beyond professional. He treated me no differently than Otto Preminger." Later Price honestly explained why he pitched "a big sort of fit. . . . Because rewrites were turning my part into something totally fantastic and totally unacceptable to me. . . . I figure after all these years, I

have earned the right to throw my weight around. I know why people want me. I have the name and the reputation, so I figure I should have a say in the way my parts are written." Price's footage was shot in two days in April 1986, ironically at Roger Corman's studio in Venice, California. Despite line changes by Price himself and as sincere a delivery as the veteran could muster, the connecting segments remain an extremely weak link in what is a predominantly tasteless, uncomfortably graphic (and to that extent, thereby successful) low-budget horror picture. Price himself had doubts about the final product, confiding shortly after filming to columnist Marilyn Beck, "I'm frankly worried. I'm afraid they might have gone too far."

Lensed as *From a Whisper to a Scream*, the film retained that name in all territories but the United States, for which market the domestic distributor wanted a one-word title and christened it, for no particular reason, *The Offspring*.

REVIEWS

Los Angeles Times, December 8, 1987, Michael Wilmington

". . . an anthology horror movie in which four typically loathsome and creepy tales, mostly about bloody revenge, are related . . . by Vincent Price to a skeptical, shrewish outsider played by Susan Tyrrell. It's definitely no *Dead of Night*, and it suffers from the same blood-swilling excesses of most modern horror movies. But the anthology structure, occasionally inventive camera work and the performances of Price and others keep it a cut, or a slash, above its more obnoxious competitors."

VINCENT PRICE

(*Drama-Logue*, June 19–25, 1986, Katherine Braun)

". . . It seems [Price] is to eat lunch, visit with his guests and be interviewed all at the same time and all in a [trailer] space about four feet by six feet. . . . How does he like appearing in yet another horror-suspense film? 'That question is asked a million times,' he answers, his voice raised, all cordiality gone. 'I've made a very successful career out of doing them. I'm bored talking about it. I'm too old. And they aren't horror films. Edgar Allan Poe is the major short-story writer of America. He did not write horror stories. He wrote psychological Gothic tales. . . . In France, in England, in Italy, in Madrid, they're taken very seriously as a genre film. This is an obsession of the press. Do you ask Al Pacino how he likes doing gangster roles?' he thunders. 'I'm bored talking about it,' Price says with finality. . . . Twenty minutes later, Price is outside, talking very seriously. 'What can

Original poster art for *From a Whisper to a Scream* (released in the U.S. as *The Offspring*

I say about it?' he asks with intensity. 'So I've been identified with a certain genre, and luckily some of them turned out to be classic films. You're very lucky in this profession to be identified with anything. Half the people I meet talk to me about cooking. Then I host a show called *Mystery!* on PBS, and people talk to me about that. Young people talk to me about the Disney film I've just done; they don't talk to me about horror films. . . . I go mad not doing things, so I find myself sometimes in things I shouldn't be in or maybe didn't give enough thought to. I try to make them as good as I can. . . . I've been in this business fifty-one years. I've done an

The Offspring As Julian White, the historian of Oldfield

The Offspring With Susan Tyrrell

enormous amount of work. And not all of it good and not all of it bad. A lot of it very good. And a lot of it very bad. But it doesn't matter. I've worked. That is really my thing.' "

95. THE WHALES OF AUGUST

AN ALIVE FILMS PRODUCTION
WITH CIRCLE ASSOCIATES, LTD.

Released October 1987

CREDITS

Executive Producer, Shep Gordon; *Producers*, Carolyn Pfeiffer, Mike Kaplan; *Director*, Lindsay Anderson; *Screenplay*, David Berry, *based on his play*; *Cinematography*, Mike Fash; *Production Designer*, Jocelyn Herbert; *Art Directors*, K. C. Fox, Bob Fox; *Set Decorator*, Sosie Hublitz; *Music*, Alan Price; *Music Arranger and Conductor*, Derek Wadsworth; *Editor*, Nicholas Gaster; *Costume Designer*, Rudy Dillon; *Makeup*, Julie Hewett; *Hairstylist*, Peg Schierholz; *Island Facilities Coordinator*, Roger Berle; Made in association with Nelson Entertainment; *Running time*, 90 minutes; color.

CAST

Bette Davis (*Libby Strong*); Lillian Gish (*Sarah Webber*); Vincent Price (*Mr. Maranov*); Ann Sothern (*Tisha Doughty*); Harry Carey Jr. (*Joshy Brackett*); Frank Grimes (*Mr. Beckwith*); Frank Pitkin (*Old Randall*); Mike Bush (*Young Randall*); Margaret Ladd (*Young Libby*); Tisha Sterling (*Young Tisha*); Mary Steenburgen (*Young Sarah*).

THE FILM

This fragile watercolor is an evocative portrait of grace and tenacity; if it were only half the film it is, it would still be remarkable for its once-in-a-lifetime casting. *The Whales of August* gave Vincent Price his first purely straight dramatic role in decades, and distributors launched an Academy Award campaign to secure him a nomination for Best Supporting Actor. Unfortunately, Price's innate acting talent was overshadowed by his popular screen horror image; he received no such tribute.

Lillian Gish and Bette Davis play two sisters, one forbearing and and serene, the other troubled and contrary. After sixty summers together on an island off the coast of Maine, they contemplate giving up not only the family home but their independence as well. Ann

Sothern is their blowzy friend, and Vincent Price portrays a charming Russian gentleman caller who briefly passes through their lives.

Price considered the deferential, courtly Mr. Maranov "an interesting kind of man, charming and civilized, but having made a career of being a houseguest. I was impressed with the script and was very excited to work with the ladies. I was also attracted by the flamboyant language with which this Russian émigré speaks." Maranov makes his entrance carrying the catch of the day, and in spite of the old-fashioned plus fours and a battered hat on his head, we can well imagine real-life satisfied fisherman Vincent proudly returning from a morning's pleasure. He obviously relished the opportunity to discuss subjects other than madness, doom, and death and returned to the slightly formal speech which also characterized *Victoria Regina*'s Prince Albert onstage back in 1935.

In 1981, coproducer Mike Kaplan first saw David Berry's play at the Trinity Square Repertory Theatre in Providence, Rhode Island. He immediately envisioned it as a vehicle for Lillian Gish, (whom he had met eighteen years earlier as the publicist on *The Comedians*) and possibly for Bette Davis as well. He had the usual trouble getting funding for such a specialized film, one which lacked the obligatory surefire box-office star— presumably, Davis and Gish were only talented. *Whales* was announced as a comeback vehicle for Gish in April 1984, and at that time, John Gielgud was to costar as Maranov. Over two years later, in July 1986, the film was still in preproduction, with Davis, Gish, Sothern, "and for a final coup, Sir John Gielgud." But a scheduling conflict led to his replacement by Vincent Price. *American Cinematographer* called the casting "daring"; director Lindsay Anderson explained that he cast on "instinct" and that in Britain "we're not so completed blinkered about [Price] to see him only in [the horror] world."

The $3 million film was shot in the fall of 1986 in eight weeks on Casco Bay, a rugged island a rough forty-five minute boat ride from Portland, Maine. Media feature stories, especially after completion of the film, reported difficulties with the two female leads. In a draft of a note to the coproducer, Price wrote: "I'm happy to go along with all the hysteria on the set, but I feel I must ask that *my* problems, as they arise, be considered as serious as the others . . . no film is about one, two, three, etc. people—it's about all of us—and the story! I *know* the problems, and I feel I *can* HELP. . . . The sloppy cuts, rewrites, and revisions have given me a *hint* of *lack* of concern for Maranov—I'm happy to go along with what's *left* but need to know *that* at least is being PROTECTED!" There were good times, too, on what Price described as "a very dear story about nothing. . . . I really enjoyed the

The Whales of August Four Legends: Price, Ann Sothern (*standing*), Bette Davis (*seated left*), and Lillian Gish

filming. . . . It was so great to get away from the horror stuff." He and Davis shared a few laughs: "[Bette] smoked those eighteen million cigarettes and we giggled a lot. [She] kept calling it *The Whales of November* because it kept getting colder and colder. We were really very uncomfortable. . . . It wasn't the jolliest picture I've ever been on, but then the jolliest pictures are sometimes the ones that turn out worst."

The Whales of August won the 1988 National Media Owl Award, an honor sponsored by the Retirement Research Foundation for presenting a positive image of aging and the aged.

REVIEWS

Variety, Cannes Film Festival Reviews, May 13, 1987

"Price, in his first non-horror film in 25 years, brings a warm sophistication to his gentleman caller, even if his light Russian accent slips in and out."

Los Angeles Times, October 23, 1987, Kevin Thomas

"Vincent Price . . . has such elegance that it matters little that his Russian-flavored accent is not always persuasive. . . ."

Newsweek, October 26, 1987, Jack Kroll

"Price, with his ravaged handsomeness, gives his best performance in years. . . ."

London Evening Standard, May 26, 1988

"*The Whales of August* isn't about friendship alone. Mainly, it's about mortality. And it's acted by a quartet of players old enough and brave enough themselves to look death in the face and not flinch. They show us the marvellously moving result of what they see. . . . Vincent Price [plays] with all the nuances that his horror roles have left dormant for decades. . . ."

VINCENT PRICE

(*Orange County Register*, August 3, 1987)

"The film touches a number of points: a conflict of wills, the sense of family, the particular quality which makes people from Maine absolutely a breed apart. The structure and language are beautiful and simple. Coral and I were amazed at how it held our attention. The characters are like figures in a Greek tragedy in a minor way, and you have these amazing actresses playing them."

(*Parade*, "Are You Afraid of Vincent Price? Portrait of a Gentle Genius," May 1, 1988, Ellen Hawkes

"'I don't think I would have made so much of myself if it hadn't been for the Depression. When my brother, Mortimer, graduated [from Yale], the world was his oyster. He was an enchanting man, but he never took advantage of his opportunities.' With sadness, Price adds that his late brother was the basis of his portrayal of the winsome Russian aristocrat in *The Whales of August*. 'I

The Whales of August With Lillian Gish

used my memories of him to show a man who is very charming but in no way working toward anything. When *I* graduated, there were no jobs. The world was not our oyster, but a very small pebble you had to push around with your nose. So I realized you have to seize every opportunity that comes along.' Price not only seized opportunities, but also created them."

96. DEAD HEAT

NEW WORLD PICTURES
Released May 1988

CREDITS

A Helpern/Meltzer production; *Producers*, Michael Meltzer, David Helpern; *Associate Producer*, Allen Alsobrook; *Director*, Mark Goldblatt; *Screenplay*, Terry Black; *Cinematography*, Robert D. Yeoman; *Music*, Ernest Troost; *Editor*, Harvey Rosenstock; *Makeup Effects designed and created by* Steve Johnson; *Running time*, 86 minutes; color.

CAST

Treat Williams (*Roger Mortis*); Joe Piscopo (*Doug Bigelow*); Lindsay Frost (*Randi James*); Darren McGavin (*Dr. Ernest McNab*); Clare Kirkconnell (*Rebecca Smythers*); Vincent Price (*Arthur P. Loudermilk*); Keye Luke (*Mr. Thule*); Robert Picardo (*Lieutenant Herzog*); Mel Stewart (*Captain Mayberry*); Prof. Toru Tanaka (*Butcher*); Martha Quinn (*Newscaster*).

THE FILM

"You can't keep a good cop dead."

Vincent Price took a role in this gruesome action-comedy because he said he wanted to work with Treat Williams and Joe Piscopo: "I think they're very fine artists." However, most critics agreed that *Dead Heat* wasn't a very fine film.

Officers Mortis (Williams) and Bigelow (Piscopo) are assigned to investigate Dante Laboratories when the company's chemicals are linked to the bodies of dead criminals who don't stay dead. Once inside, the team discovers the "Resurrection Room," where the not-so-dear departed come back to life. Someone locks Officer Mortis in a decompression chamber and kills him; resurrected, he has twelve hours before total cell degeneration finishes him for good. All he wants to do is find the person who flipped the switch on him. It turns out that the "think tank" which developed the apparatus was bankrolled by dying millionaire Arthur P. Loudermilk (Vincent Price). Unfortunately, renegade coroner McNab (Darren McGavin) has also been relying on the machine for his own personal gain, restoring indestructible crooks who steal for him. Eventually, Officer Bigelow is zombiefied, too, and despite the pleas of a distraught Loudermilk, the miracle equipment is destroyed.

Dead Heat As Arthur P. Loudermilk after resurrection

The special effects created for *Dead Heat* (animal carcases in a butcher's shop are reanimated, body parts are blown off people and sewn back on, etc.) are extremely imaginative. For those with a peculiar sense of humor, many of the lines are so twisted they're funny. Someone explains that robbers killed by police have recent scars. "You mean they've had surgeries?" "I mean they've had autopsies."

The picture began shooting in August 1987 on a thirty-seven-day schedule with a budget of $5 million. Vincent Price's first appearance as the genius behind the incredible scheme is in the dying Loudermilk's videotape message to his daughter. Propped up on pillows in bed, frail and ill, his face is pale, his voice weak. (Price is wearing the same paisley dressing gown he sported in *Madhouse* in 1974 and in a *Love Boat* episode in 1978!) But when Loudermilk, too, is resurrected, he looks ma-h-h-hvelous. Resplendent in an expensive white suit, ice blue shirt, and tie, Price is so natty that his socks match his dress handkerchief. His voice is strong, his delivery forceful and humorous as he extolls the perks of life after death.

REVIEWS

Variety, May 11, 1988

". . . involvement by Treat Williams, Joe Piscopo, Darren McGavin and certainly Vincent Price must stand as a huge embarrassment . . ."

VINCENT PRICE

"[It's] a cameo part, which translated into English means a small part and small salary. . . . Like Loudermilk, I think we are all unwilling to leave our worldly goods behind us when we die. However, Loudermilk believes that if you can't take it with you, then you can at least stick around longer to enjoy it. It's always a challenge for me to take on a role like that, to see if I can succeed in making a character come to life in the relatively short time I'm on the screen."

MARK GOLDBLATT (Director)

"When Vincent drove himself to the studio for his first day of shooting, he was wearing blue jeans and the largest pair of bright red sneakers I had ever seen. With his genial smile and great good humor, he seemed very young at heart, quite pixieish, in fact. We only had Vincent for three days of shooting, often very long days. He was always prepared, knew his lines perfectly, and was always enthusiastic and in good spirits. . . . Vincent Price is not only an icon of the cinema; he's a charming, sweet, intelligent, incredibly cultured gentleman who was wonderful to work with. He would try anything in terms of his performance. He had great stories and experiences to tell. And he was sweet and considerate—just a marvelous man. The opportunity of working with a guy whom I have loved on the screen for so much of my life was a great honor, and his is a wonderful performance."

Dead Heat Price wearing the same dressing gown in a scene from *Madhouse* fourteen years earlier

Dead Heat Loudermilk on his deathbed

97. BACKTRACK

A DICK CLARK CINEMA
PRODUCTION

Premiered December 14, 1991, on Showtime

CREDITS

Executive Producers, Steve Reuther, Mitchell Cannold; *Producers*, Dick Clark, Dan Paulson; *Coproducer*, Lisa Demberg; *Director*, Dennis Hopper; *Screenplay*, Rachel Kronstadt Mann, Ann Louise Bardach; *Story*, Rachel Kronstadt Mann; *Cinematography*, Ed Lachman; *Production Designer*, Ron Foreman; *Music*, Michel Colombier; *Editor*, Wende Phifer Maye; *Costumes*, Nancy Cone; *Makeup*, Pat Gerhardt; *Hairstylist*, Leslie Anne Anderson; *Running time*, 115 minutes; color.

CAST

Dennis Hopper (*Milo*); Jodie Foster (*Anne Benton*); Dean Stockwell (*John Luponi*); Vincent Price (*Lino Avoca*); John Turturro (*Pinella*); Fred Ward (*Pauling*);

Charlie Sheen (*Bob*); C. Anthony Sirico (*Greek*); Julie Adams (*Martha*); Sy Richardson (*Captain Walker*); Frank Gio (*Frankie*); Helena Kallianiotes (*Grace Carelli*); Bob Dylan (*Artist*); Joe Pesci [unbilled] (*Leo Carelli*).

THE FILM

"When murder is your business, you'd better not fall in love with your work."

Backtrack, with its eclectic cast, received no theatrical play in the United States but was released in Europe in a version which filmmaker Dennis Hopper disowned. American audiences saw the picture on cable television and home video.

After an avant-garde conceptual artist (Jodie Foster) witnesses a mob rubout, she fears reprisal and flees across the Southwest. The hit man sent to silence her (Dennis Hopper) becomes increasingly infatuated; after he has captured her and they have spent some time together, she returns his interest. They turn the tables on their pursuers on both sides of the law and head off into the sunset together. . . . This story line calls for enormous suspension of disbelief and, amid the violence, seems

Backtrack U.K. one-sheet

271

particularly sexist. The language is unendingly vulgar, and Foster displays nearly full frontal nudity in a shower scene with Hopper watching.

Dennis Hopper had known Vincent Price since the actor/director was around sixteen; they shared a common passion for art and art collecting. The version of the script submitted to Vincent for consideration of the role of the Mafia don who sends Hopper out to bump off Foster was titled *Time to Die*; Price shot his handful of short scenes at the end of May 1988. He is elegant, soft-spoken, gently commanding, but seems a curious choice for such a part. At home amid the marble statues and antiques of his opulent mansion, Mr. Avoca is comfortably clad in the handsome sweaters Vincent Price himself favored offscreen. He leaves the scene of the film's final explosive debacle via private helicopter, the only time Price "flew" in an aircraft for a film.

The picture was retitled *Catchfire* in Europe; severely edited, Price's best scene was excised. It was alternately known as *Do It the Hard Way*. For U.S. home video release, the "director's cut" was restored.

REVIEWS

[London] *Film Review*, January, 1991

". . . I'm not sure that *any* cut [of *Catchfire*] would completely have salvaged a film that almost utterly wastes a good storyline and super-strong cast, and which boasts one of the most slapdash and least satisfying endings known to man."

London Observer, January 27, 1991

"It would have been more coherent, certainly more perverse and pretentious, in its original cut, but it would still have been pretty ridiculous."

New York Post, December 12, 1991

"Although the movie botches its character development midway through, there are more than enough good ideas, images and performances to justify Showtime's rescue mission."

DENNIS HOPPER

"When I was eighteen and under contract to Warner Bros., I spent a lot of time at Vincent and Mary's. I used their kiln, and I fired tiles there. . . . I saw my first abstract paintings at Vincent's house in 1954; my first Jackson Pollock, Richard Diebenkorn, Franz Kline. . . . At one point, Vincent gave me a painting and said, 'Keep this, because one day I think you'll probably collect art.' Vincent was the one who gave me the idea, the courage and the intensity, to be able to say, 'Yeah I *like* this stuff, and

Backtrack With Dennis Hopper

I'm gonna stand by this stuff,' and not to be disturbed by the fact that other people might not understand my preference. As far as art is concerned, my whole life would be enormously diminished without having met Vincent Price. . . .

I don't remember how I got the brilliant idea to have Vincent in *Backtrack* [laughs]! He was wonderful—he did it as a favor to me; he didn't need to do that part. . . . [For the final scene], rather than having a helicopter actually take off, I had a crane rigged to hoist it up about fifteen yards off the ground, and Vincent didn't want to get into it. He was concerned about it falling; he said, 'Oh, my God, you don't know how bad my legs are. I got injured in a picture, and I've never been right since.

98. EDWARD SCISSORHANDS

20th CENTURY-FOX

Released December 7, 1990

CREDITS

Executive Producer, Richard Hashimoto; *Producers*, Denise Di Novi, Tim Burton; *Associate Producer*, Caroline Thompson; *Director*, Tim Burton; *Screenplay*, Caroline Thompson; *Story*, Tim Burton, Caroline Thompson; *Cinematography*, Stefan Czapsky; *Production Designer*, Bo Welch; *Art Director*, Tom Duffield; *Set Decorator*, Cheryl Carasik; *Set Designers*, Rick Heinrichs, Paul Sonski, Ann Harris; *Music*, Danny Elfman; *Orchestrations*, Steve Bartek; *Conducted by* Shirley Walker; *Organ Music by* O-Lan Jones; *Editor*, Richard Halsey; *Special Makeup and Scissorhands Effects Produced by* Stan Winston; *Costume Designer*, Colleen Atwood; *Costume Supervisor*, Ray Summers; *Department Head Makeup*, Ve Neill; *Hair Designer*, Yolanda Toussieng; *Special Effects Supervisor*, Michael Wood; *Assistant to Tim Burton*, Diane Minter; *Running time*, 100 minutes; color and Panavision.

CAST

Johnny Depp (*Edward Scissorhands*); Winona Ryder (*Kim*); Dianne Wiest (*Peg*); Anthony Michael Hall (*Jim*); Kathy Baker (*Joyce*); Robert Oliveri (*Kevin*); Conchata Ferrell (*Helen*); Caroline Aaron (*Marge*); Dick Anthony Williams (*Officer Allen*); O-Lan Jones (*Esmeralda*); Vincent Price (*The Inventor*); Alan Arkin (*Bill*); Susan J. Blommaert (*Tinka*); Linda Perry (*Cissy*); John Davidson (*TV Host*); Bill Yeager (*George*); Marti Greenberg (*Suzanne*); Bryan Larkin (*Max*); John McMahon (*Denny*); Victoria Price (*TV Newswoman*); Stuart Lancaster (*Retired Man*); Gina Gallagher (*Granddaughter*); Aaron Lustig (*Psychologist*); Alan Fudge (*Loan Officer*); Steven Brill (*Dishwasher Man*); Peter Palmer (*Editor*); Marc Macaulay, Carmen J. Alexander, Brett Rice (*Reporters*).

THE FILM

In 1982, Vincent Price narrated *Vincent*, a six-minute, stop-motion animated film produced under the Disney banner about a boy who is "considerate and nice," but who "wants to be just like Vincent Price." In the next eight years, Tim Burton, the director of the imaginative black-and-white short, would make the features *Pee-wee's Big Adventure* and *Beetlejuice* and the megahit *Batman*. Burton's next project, *Edward Scissorhands*, was another

Something could go wrong.' I assured him that nothing would happen, but he was very scared of that. . . . You know, Vincent was responsible—he's the one who for *years* would tell me, 'You know, you're really gonna make it when you start playing villains. Forget this other stuff. You're a good enough actor to play villains.' . . . Vincent was the most gentle, wonderful man I've ever met, so for me to think of *him* as a villain is impossible [laughs]. He had an incredible voice, an incredible presence. I only have dear and admirable thoughts of him. He was the genuine article."

fantasy, a poignant, semiautobiographical allegory about an innocent boy-creature with scissors instead of hands who finds himself an outcast in the "normal" world. The Avon lady (Dianne Wiest) brings Edward (Johnny Depp) down from his castle-cocoon on the hill into a suburbia populated by cruel schoolboys, women with large hair, and the sister in his new family, played by Winona Ryder. The girl eventually sees beyond Edward's leather-and-steel exterior to the soul beneath. But events prove all too clearly there is no place for his simplicity amid the complications of society, and Edward returns alone to the isolation of his castle, taking with him the memory of the young girl's love.

It was hardly surprising that Burton offered the role of Edward's patriarch to his icon, Vincent Price. As described in the script, the Inventor "is an older man, wrinkled and getting frail. There is an unmistakable, sad aloneness about him." Burton saw Price's screen characters as misfits and outsiders, but the actor transcends melancholy in his portrayal—elegant as always in a frock coat and flowing cravat, his Inventor is full of joy and an innocence he invests in his "son" Edward. The role is small but pivotal, with three scenes, all flashbacks in Edward's mind as he recalls his genesis. The first begins with a panorama of an imaginative, Rube Goldberg–like assembly line in the Inventor's laboratory, which does nothing more insidious than bake cookies. The Inventor watches the various stages of the process with a child's happiness, picking up a completed cookie in the shape of a heart as a new idea occurs to him. In the second scene, when Edward is half complete, the Inventor reads him a book on etiquette and then teaches him how to laugh with a silly limerick. In the final, poignant moment, the old man suffers a fatal heart attack just as he is presenting Edward with his Christmas present—a pair of graceful human hands. He crumples to the floor, and Edward can only reach out impotently, cutting the pale, beloved cheek with shining scissors which now will never be replaced.

In the early days of preproduction (the last few months of 1989), the media touted both Tom Cruise and Tom Hanks for the title role in *Edward Scissorhands*. Johnny Depp's name was also mentioned, and eventually the role went to him, with shooting scheduled to begin on location in Texas in March 1990. Vincent Price received a copy of the script on February 22, 1990. On the page where the Inventor reads the limerick to Edward, the actor signed his name and wrote: "June 20th 1990 Shooting 3 days." Principal photography was completed on July 20.

The studio bet on a limited 70-mm release to generate "sufficient critical accolades for the unheralded film to put it on equal footing with the crowd of high-profile movies slated for Christmas." On December 7, 1990, Fox's *Edward Scissorhands* opened in nine cities in 70-mm, six-track Dolby sound.

Vincent Price's beautiful daughter Victoria, who at the time was twenty-eight, has a cameo in the picture as one of the reporters trying to elicit a comment from Edward after he is arrested. It's hard to miss the slim, leggy blonde with the full mouth and bright blue eyes.

REVIEWS

New York Times, December 5, 1990, Janet Maslin

"[Edward] amazes the neighbors with his rare feats of snippery. He's a wizard when it comes to poodles. In a sense, Mr. Burton is too. His *Edward Scissorhands* is as crazily single-minded as a majestic feat of dog-barbering, with much the same boldness, camp ebullience and fundamentally narrow wit. Like a great chef concocting an exquisite peanut-butter-and-jelly sandwich, Mr. Burton invests awe-inspiring ingenuity into the process of reinventing something very small. . . . That something is a tale of misunderstood gentleness and stifled creativity, of civilization's power to corrupt innocence, of a heedless beauty and a kindhearted beast. The film, if scratched with something much less sharp than Edward's fingers, reveals proudly adolescent lessons for us all."

New York Times, December 23, 1990, Caryn James

". . . a sweet fairy tale at heart, but this story of a modern Frankenstein monster works best when it is satiric."

Christian Science Monitor, January 16, 1991, David Sterritt

". . . there's a message it wants to send—about the need for understanding people who seem different, and about the way some folks really don't fit into the usual social and personal molds, and shouldn't be expected to. . . ."

JOHNNY DEPP

(*Movieline*, October 1994)

"I buy a lot of paintings and drawings and some photographs, s*** like that. It's good to have things around that feed you. One of the greatest things that Vincent Price—really a f***ing sweet man, very, very smart—ever told me was: 'Buy art.' That's a good piece of advice that I'll treasure forever. . . . He called me every year on my birthday—he was a Gemini, too—and left me these beautiful messages. One of the most incredible moments I've ever had was sitting in Vincent's trailer, and I was showing

Edward Scissorhands As the Inventor

Edward Scissorhands The Inventor teaches Edward (Johnny Depp) to laugh

him this first-edition book I have of the complete works of Poe with really amazing illustrations. Vincent was going nuts over the drawings, and he started talking about *The Tomb of Ligeia*; then he closed the book and began to recite it to me in this beautiful voice, filling the room with huge sounds. Such passion! I looked in the book later, and it was verbatim. Word perfect. It was a great moment. I'll never forget that."

TIM BURTON

"There was a connection, an emotional link for me, growing up and watching the Poe films. I was very quiet; somehow I always felt like I was eighty years old. Those kinds of feelings at that age are fairly abstract; you really don't know what to do with them. I think suburbia in California isn't that dissimilar from Poe. I mean, it was like the tremors in *Fall of the House of Usher*—earthquakes, and living near the airport, the houses would all shake when the planes took off. It had to have an effect.... Vincent's characters had a sensitivity, a heightened sensitivity, heightened awareness. There was an energy he had; it was evident in everything. The combination of his voice, the way he looked—there was always something going on under the surface.... It's hard to pick a favorite film. *House of Usher* is emblematic of a kind of feeling that I guess would be top for me. I always had trouble with a certain kind of mix of horror and comedy. *The Raven* wasn't one of my favorites. I liked *believing* Vincent; I *believed* him. Even though I know he was having a good time, I still believed him. What I see is someone who's enjoying acting, enjoying what he *does*, but not crossing the line, not making fun. He was very controlled. That kind of stuff [tongue-in-cheek] is talking down to the material, and he wasn't doing that in those movies.... Since I grew up pretty much exclusively a horror fan, I never really saw Vincent's other films until later. I don't know what I would have thought of them at that age, because I was so into the other thing; that's where it was for me. I think Vincent really *found* it with the horror stuff. And listen, I'm completely against categorization of people, you know—but I do think that that's where he truly shined. And I don't know if it's just because I loved him so much in it. He had that unique quality; other actors could do comedy, but only he could do what he did in the Poe films. Nobody wants to get pigeonholed, but you don't break through that by becoming bitter. Vincent broke through by embracing it—that's why I found him so inspirational."

99. THE HEART OF JUSTICE

TURNER PICTURES

Premiered February 20, 1993, on Turner Network Television

CREDITS

Brandman Productions, Inc., in association with Amblin Television; *Executive Producer*, Michael Brandman; *Coexecutive Producer*, Barbara Corday; *Producer*, Donald P. Borchers; *Associate Producer*, Sarah Bowman; *Director*, Bruno Barreto; *Screenplay*, Keith Reddin; *Cinematography*, Declan Quinn; *Production Designer*, Peter Paul Raubertas; *Music*, Jonathan Elias; *Editor*, Bruce Cannon; *Costume Designer*, Betty Madden; *Makeup Supervisor*, Belinda Bryant; *Running time*, 100 minutes; color.

CAST

Eric Stoltz (*David Leader*); Jennifer Connelly (*Emma Burgess*); Dermot Mulroney (*Elliot Burgess*); Dennis Hopper (*Austin Blair*); Vincent Price (*Reggie Shaw*); Keith Reddin (*Simon*); Paul Teschke (*Alex*); Arthur Eckdahl (*George*); Ross Leon (*Officer McCrane*); Harris Yulin (*Keneally*); John Capodice (*Harte*); Katherine Lanasa (*Hannah*); William H. Macy (*Booth*); Bradford Dillman (*Mr. Burgess*); Gail Neely (*Jean*); Felicity Huffman (*Annie*); Hawthorne James (*Harry*); Joanna Miles (*Mrs. Burgess*); Richard Minchenberg (*Ray*); Theresa Bell (*Interviewer*); James W. Adams (*Book Salesman*); Dorothy Dorian James (*Receptionist*); Isaac Clay (*Adamson*); Donald Craig (*Wilson*); Kurt Fuller (*Dr. Leonard*).

THE FILM

"Vengeance is the heart of justice."

Vincent Price made what became his final film appearance in this made-for-cable movie. Despite the fact his role in *The Heart of Justice* was a cameo, Price was once again lending his name to an artistic experiment—a series of made-for-cable projects planned as a showcase of new writing talent.

The film noir thriller follows an award-winning newsman (Eric Stoltz) investigating the grisly murder of a trash novelist (Dennis Hopper) by the scion of a prominent family. Through a series of audio recordings dic-

The Heart of Justice As Reggie Shaw (photo: Erik Heinila, Turner Pics.)

tated by the killer (Dermot Mulroney), the reporter uncovers the background of a psychotic young man who was obsessed with the author and the peculiar relationship he had with his sister (Jennifer Connelly). It's the sister who supplies Stoltz with the tapes, and predictably the two of them end up consummating their burning lust for each other in a dark alley. And after he's fallen for her, quit his job at the paper, and burned all the evidence against her brother, she dumps him.

The Heart of Justice was filmed in Los Angeles in the fall of 1991; Vincent's shooting script is dated October 4–17, 1991. The picture first aired over a year later, under TNT's "Screenworks" banner on February 20, 1993, and there were plans to distribute the movie to the international television market as well. The project was the fourth in an admirable series entitled "Writer's Cinema," produced by Brandman in association with Amblin Entertainment (Steven Spielberg's company) for Ted Turner. The first three had been David Mamet's

Water Engine, Horton Foote's *The Habitation of Dragons* and Lee Blessing's *Cooperstown*.

Director Bruno Barreto had been responsible for the award-winning Brazilian feature *Dona Flor and Her Two Husbands*. The performances in *Justice* are credible, but the action seems heavy-handed and slow-moving, although the music is highly reminiscent of the best of Bernard Herrmann's evocative scores for Hitchcock. The "trick" ending is a confusing anticlimax.

Vincent Price has two brief scenes as a wealthy, homosexual *bon vivant* named Reggie Shaw. Prior to the opening credits, he shares Dennis Hopper's last meal; according to Hopper, it was the opportunity to work with Vincent which "enticed" him into doing the picture. Over lunch, the erudite Shaw talks about his friendship with British poet W. H. Auden and, pondering the merits of the poached salmon, graciously signs the bill. Fifty-six years after his professional debut, Price's voice is mellifluous as ever, his timing understated, his smile as

The Heart of Justice With Dennis Hopper (photo: Erik Heinila, Turner Pics.)

warm. Later, when Eric Stoltz shows up unannounced at the exclusive private club, Shaw vouches for the younger man, and they discuss the murder. Afterward, he sips a martini, raising the glass in a toast to acknowledge that the reporter has been dining with "a charming old fart like me."

Charming, to the last . . .

REVIEW

Variety, February 18, 1993

". . . a TV movie that's all dressed up but essentially goes nowhere. . . . Even Vincent Price is seen in a cameo role, having lunch with the doomed novelist just before he is gunned down. . . . *The Heart of Justice* is too stiff and studied a genre piece to make an impact."

100. ARABIAN KNIGHT

MIRAMAX FILMS
August 25, 1995

CREDITS

An Allied Filmmakers Presentation; *Executive Producer,* Jake Eberts; *Created and Directed by* Richard Williams; *Screenplay,* Richard Williams, Margaret French; *Additional Story and Dialogue,* Parker Bennett, Terry Runte, Bette L. Smith, Tom Towler, Stephen Zito; *Based on the book* **Nasruddin** *by* Indries Shah; *London Production Producers,* Imogen Sutton, Richard Williams; *Los Angeles Production Director,* Fred Calvert; *Los Angeles Production Producers,* Bette L. Smith, Fred Calvert; *Art Director,* Roy Naisbitt; *Master Animator,* Ken Harris; *Cinematography,* John Leatherbarrow; *Songs,* Norman Gimbel, Robert Folk; *Editor,* Peter Bond; *Running time,* 81 minutes; color and Panavision.

CAST

VOICE TALENTS OF: Vincent Price (*Zigzag*); Jennifer Beals (*Princess Yum Yum*); Matthew Broderick (*Tack, the Cobbler*); Jonathan Winters (*Thief*); Clive Revill (*King Nod/Narrator*); Toni Collette (*Nurse/Witch*); Joan Sims (*Witch*); Kevin Dorsey (*Mighty One-Eye*); Eric Bogosian (*Phido*); Stanley Baxter (*Gofer/Slap*); Kenneth Williams (*Goblet/Tickle*); Clinton Sundberg (*Dying Soldier*); Windsor Davies (*Roofless*); Frederick Shaw (*Goolie*); Thick Wilson (*Sergeant Hook*); Eddie Byrne (*Hoof*); Peter Clayton, Geoff Golden, Derek Hinson, Declan Mulholland, Mike Nash, Tony Scannell, Dermot Walsh, Ramsay Williams (*Other Brigands*).

THE FILM

The last feature film in which Vincent Price participated was released more than twenty years after the great actor made it. While the released version has problems resulting from its cut-and-paste nature, *Arabian Knight* is nonetheless a fitting movie tribute to an acting career which gave so much pleasure to both young and old.

In 1968, Canadian animator Richard Williams, working in the United Kingdom, began an Arabian Nights animated feature film which was being called *Nasruddin.* When Vincent Price was in London in January 1973, a few months prior to filming his eighty-fifth movie, *Madhouse,* he recorded the voice for the picture's wicked grand vizier. Back in Los Angeles a few weeks later, Vincent annotated a letter from Williams with "Brilliant animator." The filmmaker was in the process of sorting through takes from two recording sessions, reporting "there is really *so* much good stuff and funny asides and bits of zany development that it is a major job to select. . . . I am very grateful to you for being so kind to us, and for working so hard on such a weird and 'unknown' project. . . . I'm sitting in a tiny room here surrounded by my many caricatures of Vincent Price, working from the photos and from memory. . . . Anyway, I cannot thank you too much for your efforts—anything you would have done certainly would have done the job for us, but one never expected such a *relentlessly* creative and wildly unique contribution. . . ."

For a variety of reasons, mostly involving funding, the remarkable animation, every frame of it hand drawn,

Arabian Knight: The Thief, the Cobbler, and Zig Zag, the Grand Vizier, fight over the Princess's slipper (photo: courtesy Majestic Films)

Arabian Knight Zigzag hatches a plan for power (photo courtesy Majestic Films)

281

bounced around for two decades. It was reannounced periodically (as *The Thief, The Thief Who Never Gave Up,* and even *Once . . .*) but never actually finished. In the meantime, Richard Williams created the imaginative credits sequences for *What's New, Pussycat?, The Return of the Pink Panther,* and *A Funny Thing Happened on the Way to the Forum* and contributed to the unique blend of live action and cartoon for Disney, *Who Framed Roger Rabbit.* Finally, the project was taken out of Williams's hands because of budget overruns and, as *The Thief and the Cobbler,* was completed by animators in Los Angeles. With the exception of Vincent Price's grand vizier, all characters were revoiced, including the shy Cobbler, who had been mute. Incongruous Disney-style songs were also added. Williams's extraordinary footage was pieced together with newly drawn scenes, and a voice-over narration was laid in to explain resulting continuity and story gaps. The final budget for the picture—the first animated film since *Sleeping Beauty* to be produced in widescreen—was $25 million. Only a few months prior to release, the title was again changed to *Arabian Knight.* Most unfortunately, the curious little Thief, who had also been delightfully silent in the best tradition of early classic comedy, was given a voice—that of Jonathan Winters.

The adventure begins in the Golden City, which is protected from evil by three Golden Balls placed high atop the city's tallest minaret. The Ancients have prophesied that if the Golden Balls are ever removed, the city will fall. They have also foretold that the city can be saved by the simplest of souls with the simplest of things. Lazy King Nod has a dream that his kingdom will be destroyed by a wicked race of One-Eyed Men, but his crafty grand vizier, Zigzag, assures him such a thing cannot happen while the Golden Balls are safely on the minaret. The clever Thief finally succeeds in stealing them, although he loses them immediately to Zigzag's henchmen. The vizier takes advantage of the opportunity to give the king an ultimatum—that he, Zigzag, will "magically" restore the protective Golden Balls if the king will grant him his beautiful daughter, Yum Yum, in marriage. When the king refuses, Zigzag leaves the city to turn over the Golden Balls to the One-Eyes. In desperation, the king sends Yum Yum and humble Tack the Cobbler, who are in love, on a perilous journey to seek advice from the Great Witch. They return just as Zigzag, at the head of the giant One-Eye war machine, is attacking the city. The Cobbler shoots a tack (the simplest of things) into the works, which causes the war machine to self-destruct in a Rube Goldberg chain reac-

tion. Zigzag flees but falls into a pit and is devoured by ravenous alligators and his own pet vulture, Phido. In the midst of the confusion, the Thief at last manages to get his hands on the irresistible Golden Balls and, in trying to escape with them, is acclaimed a hero. The city rejoices as Tack and Yum Yum celebrate their wedding, while the Thief promises never to steal again. Well, maybe . . .

Imaginative, daring, completely surrealistic in segments which rely on optical illusion, *Arabian Knight* is a unique vision, although there are unavoidable comparisons to *Yellow Submarine* and other "head" movies. Despite occasional style clashes, it is the type of film which truly appeals to both adults and children. Several astounding sequences are depicted in such precise, minute detail, it's boggling to realize they're not computer generated but hand drawn in "ones," meaning twenty-four drawings for each *second* of film. (Most high-quality animated features are drawn in "twos.") The final battle between the enormous One-Eye war machine and the little human Cobbler is frightening, and there are other scenes straight out of classic silent comedy which are thigh-slappingly funny. The Thief is clad in a ratty cloak and a single slipper. A tiny halo of buzzing flies accompanies him wherever he goes, even struggling through drainpipes in his dogged pursuit of the Golden Balls. His Herculean labors to purloin them are as tirelessly monomaniacal and hilarious as the attempts of the Warner Bros. Coyote to capture the Road Runner. The Thief exists only to steal, oblivious to consequence or peril; at one point he expressionlessly divests himself without a second thought of every treasure he's already filched in order to reach for a new bauble.

Clad in a black cloak with orange trim, Zigzag, the grand vizier, has bluish skin, green eyes, and a black goatee. His face is all glinting white teeth; three rings glisten on each of his ten fingers. He meets a fitting end for his treachery: dropped into a pitch-black pit, all we can see are his eyes—and then five more pairs, with jaws to match, of the alligators he has mistreated. They are joined by his pet vulture, whom he has also tormented. Amid snaps in his direction, Zigzag moans mournfully, "Oooh, my bottom! / Oh, my top! Greedies, don't you ever stop? / You *too*, Phido—man's best friend? / For Zigzag, then / It is . . . the end. . . ."

Happily, for fans of Vincent Price, it will never be . . . the end. And anyway, the Thief steals the letters of "T-H-E E-N-D," along with the sprocketed film itself, until the cinema screen goes white.

Arabian Knight Zigzag assures King Nod of the city's safety, while in the background the Thief makes off with the Three Golden Balls (photo courtesy Majestic Films)

Il Mostro di Sangue (Italian poster for *The Tingler*, courtesy Roger Fenton)

AUTHOR'S NOTE

The sheer size of Vincent Price's *oeuvre* makes a single, comprehensive resource nearly impossible. In profiling his motion-picture career, I was able to screen ninety-four of the one hundred movies covered. (That complete figure includes the long-awaited *Arabian Knight*, a made-for-cable film, and two documentaries whose lengths of over seventy minutes accord them feature status.) I wanted to incorporate appendixes on Vincent's television and radio work, his stage roles, the decades he spent on the lecture circuit, and his prolific writing (published and unpublished), but reluctantly eschewed them to make the film coverage as complete as possible. A 288-page book can't do justice to eighty-two years of life as productive as Vincent's—I hope something of his spirit has come through. Knowing Vincent Price was a joy and a privilege; he remains a personal and professional inspiration.

Film cast and credits (which had to be severely edited for space) are listed in a consistent order throughout, and the names are spelled according to the prints; for example, Charles Bronson was Charles Buchinsky in *House of Wax*, Curt Siodmak wrote *The Invisible Man Returns* as Kurt Siodmak, set decorator Russell Gausman worked at Universal as R.A. Gausman, and so on. The names of the actors' roles were expanded to facilitate identification. Contemporary film reviews quoted give prominence to Vincent Price's performance, and not generally to costars or the picture as a whole. The sources of Vincent's comments, if not specifically attributed, are personal conversations, television and public appearances, and miscellaneous print interviews.

Reader comments are encouraged. Please write to P.O. Box 461311, West Hollywood, California 90046.